SOCIALISM'S DILEMMAS

WALTER D. CONNOR

SOCIALISM'S DILEMMAS:
STATE AND SOCIETY IN THE SOVIET BLOC

Columbia University Press
New York 1988

306.0947
C75s

Columbia University Press
New York   Guildford, Surrey
Copyright © 1988 Columbia University Press
All rights reserved

Library of Congress
Library of Congress Cataloging-in-Publication Data

Connor, Walter D.
  Socialism's dilemmas : state and society in the Soviet bloc / Walter D. Connor.
    p.   cm.
  Bibliography: p.
  Includes index.
  ISBN 0-231-06606-6
  1. Soviet Union—Social conditions—1970– 2. Europe, Eastern—Social
conditions. 3. Dissenters—Soviet Union. 4. Dissenters—Europe, Eastern. 5. Soviet
Union—Politics and government—1945– 6. Europe, Eastern—Politics and
government—1945- I. Title.
HN523.5.C66 1988
306'.0947—dc19   88-4318
                                                                      CIP

Book design by Jennifer Dossin

Printed in the United States of America

CONTENTS

ACKNOWLEDGMENTS

Considerable help was extended to me over the process of writing, and later collecting and organizing, the contents. The individual scholarly debts over fifteen years are really too numerous to acknowledge; the institutional ones are, at least, manageable. Chronologically, the earliest essays were written at the University of Michigan: colleagues in its Department of Sociology and Center for Russian and East European Studies were, and remain, a source of intellectual stimulation. The U.S. Department of State's Foreign Service Institute, during my eight years there (1976–1984) provided a challenging context in which I was happily able to combine governmental and academic concerns. If the quality of this work has not been enhanced by what I drew from many Washington colleagues on both the analytical and policy sides, the fault is surely mine.

Boston University and the Russian Research Center at Harvard have provided an ideal combined home for my more recent work; their intellectual, organizational, and clerical support has been invaluable. At the center, Rose Di Benedetto and Helen Constantine did a great deal of the typing; Barbara Sindriglis completed the final version.

Acknowledgments

At home, Eileen, Christine, and Elizabeth Connor, each with her own concerns, provided the sort of noninterventionist support that merit my love and gratitude.

Whatever their value, these essays represent some of the work of nearly a decade and a half: work that, for me, has been at times frustrating, at times exciting, but always stimulating. I consider myself fortunate in many ways, and in none more, perhaps, than the career I have followed and the places, geographical, occupational, and intellectual, it has taken me. Elements of choice and chance contributed to my embarking on that career, but one critical element was the friendship, encouragement, and argumentative challenge of a contemporary whose own life and scholarly promise were cut tragically short. It is to Frank Dishaw that this book, then, is dedicated—without him, it is unlikely that its contents would ever have been written.

SOCIALISM'S DILEMMAS

INTRODUCTION

The essays which make up this book cover a time span from the early mid-1970s to the mid-1980s; a period within which much has happened in the Soviet bloc. States continued the quest for long-term political stabilization; in the realm of society, diverse social, economic, and political forces emerged in sharper and more pronounced fashion, threatening, or limiting the possibilities of, stabilization and, for some, raising the specter of crisis. If an apologia be needed for a volume composed of essays for the most part previously published, it might be found in the fact that the problems with which I deal herein are in no sense short-term, or susceptible, on the historical record, to decisive or cost-free resolution even by regimes as possessed of power, and the will to use it, as are those of the USSR and the East European states. They are dilemmas, indeed.

Mikhail Gorbachev will not escape the issues and questions that emerged in the eighteen-year reign of Leonid Brezhnev, discussed in the first section. Indeed, more than three years on, he is credited with addressing them with unprecedented frankness and vigor. The question, however, is whether a "Gorbachev era," whose outcome no one can predict at this point, will see success in the economic sphere; in managing in its turn a better accommodation of the political process to the succession of generations than did Brezhnev's costly "stability of cadres" policy; in coping with—whether by repression or accommodation—the challenges from dissident thinkers and activists it will surely face; and finally in managing the very complex social policy problems which will emerge as socialist economies are pushed into a new track.

Both in the USSR and in the other bloc countries, one of the most important components of social history has been the formation of large working classes—among populations which, with the exception of Czechoslovakia, boasted only small proletarian components in the pre-socialist period. To the degree that Lenin's Bolsheviks in 1917, and East European leaders almost thirty years later, took power in the *absence* of large working classes, they were, according to Marxist doctrine, "premature," ahead of the development of their presumed social base. To some degree, then, the regime-guided formation of large cadres of workers is a success. But it is not, as several of the essays to follow indicate, an unqualified one. There are ambiguities in the development and consciousness, structure and opinions, of blue-collar workers who show signs of dependence on, and expectations of, regime economic and social policies, but who also give evidence of disaffection, resistance, and perhaps the development of a "class consciousness" critical rather than supportive of the political leadership. Such developments can give little comfort—and in the last ten years *have* given little—to those who occupy the seats of power from East Berlin to Moscow. This will surely get worse before it gets better.

At the end of World War II, or at the latest after the 1948 defection of Tito's Yugoslavia from the Soviet bloc, the objectives of Stalin's control of Eastern Europe came to include a homogenization of the diverse East European states along Soviet lines: the imposition of the "Soviet model" via the exaltation of state over society. The process of forced transformation thus launched, more ambitious by far than the maintenance of a "sphere of influence" in the terms of traditional international politics, has seen twists and turnings. If it has left the USSR "in" Eastern Europe, and East Europeans on the whole unhappy with this fact, it has not in the last forty years yielded the results postwar Soviet optimists must have expected. Social and economic transformations, refracted through the lenses of differing national traditions and cultures, have generated disaffection as well as the perception of progress. Processes of generational succession show persisting national differences, rather than homogenization—East Europeans with no direct experience of their countries' independent existence in the interwar period manifest, nonetheless, a memory and history formed outside the narrow bounds of Soviet-imposed orthodoxy. The very ethical/ideological grounds on which East European dissidents criticize their regimes have come to draw increasingly on national traditions and the broad heritage of the Western cultural world, and less on revisionist versions of the Marxism imposed on them after World War II. These processes and forces—so persistent, so critical, it seems to me, in understanding the political and social dynamic of Eastern Europe now and for the remainder of the century—also concern us here.

The "plan" of the book is a simple one. The first chapter, written specifically for this collection, provides some discussion of analytic categories and perspectives: ones which I find useful and/or important in the "enterprise" of studying political and social developments in the Soviet bloc. Chapters 2–6 then address a set of topics in the strictly *Soviet* context, from a review and interpretation of the emergence and significance of domestic political dissent in the late 1960s—and early 1970s—to a view of the Gorbachev "agenda" and its implications for grass-roots Soviet life from the perspective of mid-1987.

Chapters 7 to 11 focus "westward," on the East European states of the bloc. Temporally more concentrated, they address a linked set of problems of social change, class formation, political culture, and the politics of dissent, from the later 1970s to the period immediately after the suppression of the Solidarity movement in Poland in 1981.

Though minor surgery has been performed to smooth the transitions from chapter to chapter, virtually all those previously published (chapters 2–4, 7–10) have been left largely as they were written; the exception is chapter 6, originally published in 1986, and the currency of whose topic (aspects of internal policy in Gorbachev's USSR) seemed both to permit and to demand an updating for this volume. This does not signify that I am overly enamored of either my prose or my predictions and interpretations. There are no doubt many shortfalls in both; an author is especially likely to become aware of them when assembling a volume of this sort. But either updating or "postscripting" each piece seems to me a poorer choice than leaving *readers* to judge the adequacy and utility of these pieces against their perceptions and against events that transpired after they were written.

Following this line has, no doubt, made for some (not excessive, I hope) amount of overlap between chapters, repetition or restatement of themes. Here, I can only plead that this is inescapable. My training and "practice" as sociologist and political scientist, and my own perspective on what are the most important points where socialist state and society interact create a focus on certain sorts of interaction, on certain classes, and certain issues. Whether they are as critical as they have seemed to me is a matter, again, for readers to decide—and future developments to tell.

"Future developments," indeed, are already upon us, and those may add interest to what is contained here. For Soviet and East European specialists, the object of their studies has come in the past few years to resemble a moving target. Portents of change, from Gorbachev's commitment to a thoroughgoing program of Soviet internal restructuring to the increasingly evident systemic ills in an Eastern Europe where Soviet-style regimes remain "imports" with little deep-rooted legitimacy, are many. Nor are there any guarantees, given how much is at stake and how much remains controversial, that Gorbachev and his *perestroika* will survive and succeed in the USSR, or that similar benign processes of change will take hold in Eastern Europe. Thus, the present remains a period of "grand alternatives": at least as grand as we are likely to see in the Soviet bloc for the remainder of the twentieth century. However socialism's dilemmas are resolved, the questions of class and inquality, social policy and popular demand, political culture and dissent dealt with in the chapters to follow should figure importantly in their resolution.

ONE

STATE, SOCIETY, AND THE SOVIET MODEL

The essays in this book address, for the most part, *concrete* phenomena and issues in the Soviet Union and Eastern Europe. They do not pretend to test hypotheses drawn from theories of purported general, or even "bloc-wide," applicability against the reality of "real existing socialism." Rather, they attempt to reveal and explain aspects of that reality; some of them are well explored by other authors, others much less so.

I recall once reading a reviewer's characterization of an author's approach as "lightheartedly empirical." It was not meant, I think, to be uncomplimentary. I would happily accept such a designation of these essays, with respect to their mode of approach to the subject matter, though the matter itself is not lighthearted at all.

To say this, however, is not to say that they are purposely devoid of theoretical perspective, but only that in many of them that perspective, and its derivation, are implicit. What is the socialist state? How has its relationship to society varied, in time and place, within the life of the USSR and the Soviet bloc? What relevance have categories such as "totalitarian," "industrial," "developing," society to their provenance and dynamics? Questions of these sorts, and the answers to them partially or full-formed in my mind, provide some of the context within which various topics are explored.

Some of those kind enough to encourage me to collect these essays in the present form have also suggested that I attempt to make the implicit more explicit, to explore some of the ideas and concepts which have influenced and continue to influence my own perspectives and approach to questions. This chapter attempts to do that, dealing in order with "state" and "society" as suggested in the title and then with some thoughts on the nature of these systems, as well as offering along the way some introduction to the topics addressed in the chapters which follow.

STATE

Theda Skocpol, in her stimulating and controversial *States and Social Revolutions*, reminds readers that the state, "properly conceived, is no mere arena in which socioeconomic struggles are fought out. It is, rather, a set of administrative, policing, and military organizations headed, and more or less well coordinated by, an executive authority."[1]

States, thus, are not to be treated as if they were simply "analytical aspects of abstractly conceived modes of production, or even political aspects of concrete class relations and struggles. Rather . . . states are actual organizations controlling (or attempting to control) territories and people."[2]

However Skocpol's strictures might strike Marxian theorists she is criticizing, or other partisans of views of "state as emanation," students of Soviet and East European politics (and society) seem to have little need of such reminders. The "state" imposes itself on their consciousness, as it does in varying ways on the consciousness and lives of the citizens/subjects of the socialist societies. It is hard to "escape," in more ways than one.

The state-society problem in the Soviet/East European context is multidimensional; in varying aspects, the chapters which follow confront or touch upon it. But some explicit explanation of those dimensions may be useful here.

First, the analyst and the subject confront in the Soviet-type state a remarkably powerful, solid object; examined in a value-neutral way, a remarkable work of *construction*. Given the difficulty revolutionaries have had in turning to the tasks of governance and administration, in the exceedingly shaky transition from conspiratorial group to ruling elite, those who forged the prototype Soviet state, who constructed and imposed similar political institutions in Eastern Europe, succeeded well beyond the measure usually vouchsafed to would-be nineteenth- or twentieth-century revolutionaries. "Not revolution and destruction of established institutions, but organization and the creation of new political institutions are the peculiar contributions of communist movements to modern politics."[3]

Thus, Samuel Huntington's verdict on the significance of Leninism, taken broadly, and as far afield as the triumph of Mao's communists in China in 1949. Marx, ultimately, was little of a guide on matters of "state" to his adherents—a "political primitive,"[4] who, when he did conceive of the state under post-revolutionary conditions, saw it as a "political aspect" of a working-class victory and little else. Lenin—the Lenin of *What Is To Be Done?*, the organizing, tactical Lenin—forged an instrument, ultimately the Soviet party-state, which was much more than could be subsumed as an "aspect" of class relations. "Marxism, as a theory of social evolution, was proved wrong by events; Leninism, as a theory of political action, was proved right."[5]

Lenin also introduced a heavy element of voluntarism into a Marxist movement, identifying and confronting the contingency for which the Marxist canon seemed to leave little room. If it is a bit oversimple and too summary to divide Menshevism and Lenin's Bolshevism by reference to the former's greater adherence to the writ, and consequent unwillingness to risk a socialist seizure of political power until the economic/structural preconditions of such existed (the successfully carried-out industrial revolution, the growth of a big working class under capitalism), and the latter's willingness to seize the opportunity and the power under the quite "premature" conditions of Russia in 1917, it is not basically inaccurate.

Lenin risked, Lenin succeeded. He might have failed. This sense of contingency certainly is part of the intellectual framework of most analysts of Communist affairs, the contrast between the "chance" elements of 1917 (if Kerensky had jailed Lenin? had him shot? had Lenin died?) and the endurance of the political institutions he established (however much Stalin added and concretized) beyond individual lives and leaders. For "an amorphous social class" (and, one might add, a very small one; urban proletarians did not bulk large in the demography of 1917 Russia), "Lenin thus substituted a consciously created, structured, and organized political institution."[6] That political institution was to "liberate" itself quite effectively from social class, to achieve a striking degree of autonomy which has made of the analysis of the Soviet-type state, or societies subordinate to it, or relations between the two, a rather special enterprise, somewhat removed from the standard exercise of the analytic tools (and research methods) of political science and sociology, and generating a fair degree of cyclic debate about the gap between the "disciplines" and "area studies."[7]

The general intellectual orientation among specialists, then, has hardly conduced to underestimating the autonomy of the state. The Soviet-type state (to somewhat varying degrees, but on the whole rather consistently, across its various national manifestations) has been among those which, in Huntington's distinction, can and do govern, which belong "in the category of effective rather than debile political systems,"[8] along with the United States—forms differ greatly, but both polities do govern. It is one where political "institutionalization" has remained far enough advanced beyond political "participation" (under any definition of the latter) to be able in the vast majority of cases to channel, shape, and control that participation.

"Strong states," then, have risen in the name of Marxism; a Marxism which spoke of states' "withering away." It is Marxist theory which has had the most difficulty in confronting the state strong-via-autonomy, especially in these concrete cases. Some Marxist theorists have denominated, accurately or not, the state in bourgeois society as something distinct from the ruling class, as its "higher intelligence," as Frank Parkin notes, which sometimes will act in the long-term rather than the currently perceived interests of the bourgeoisie.[9] Skocpol also sees the possibility of "fundamental conflicts" between a state and a "dominant class."[10] That power can be concentrated by a state independent of class of course raises, in addition to a general Marxian analytical difficulty,[11] that of describing/defining in whose interests, to whose benefit, class, group, or cabal, contemporary state-socialist regimes rule—not exclusively, to be sure, the working class. Marxian understanding, at the analytic rather than propagandistic level, of the class/interest base of the Tsarist Russian and presocialist East European states (a diverse lot) is also somewhat hampered by a tendency to see the bourgeoisie everywhere. Few would argue with what seems to me the quite illuminating characterization of interwar East European "administrative-military bureaucracies" offered by Andrew Janos:

> Very early in the process of political development the administrative bureaucracy, or in some cases (such as Yugoslavia and Poland) the military, had emerged as autonomous forces in the political arena.

Contrary to popular belief this administrative-military complex, for our purposes "bureaucracy," was not the handmaiden of established social classes or of the national community as a whole, but eventually became an interest group in its own right. Members of the public administration and the military had developed a particular social consciousness. Together with some camp followers, particularly members of professional groups, they became a genuine "political class."[12]

State "autonomy," then, is possible, and indeed has presocialist precedents in the geopolitical/historical bailiwick of Soviet and East European studies.

Soviet history, "Stalinism," the extension of Soviet control to Eastern Europe after World War II, and the experience of the "total state" before and in that war, gave birth to a "model," a perspective, whose intellectual influence was and is great in the field and on practitioners: the *totalitarian* model. Over it, many disputes combining analytic and political issues have raged in the past two decades or so.

Totalitarianism, from one viewpoint, can be read as the description of the syndrome associated with the *extreme* autonomy of the state from class, from society; a hyper-autonomy. The image is one of the omnicompetent state, seeking to control all processes in society, answerable to *no* elements of that society; the components, in the classic formulation of Friedrich and Brzezinski, were:

- an official ideology "covering all vital aspects of man's existence";

- a "single mass party led typically by one man, the 'dictator'";

- "a system of terroristic police control";

- near-complete monopoly control of mass communication;

- similar control of means of armed combat;

- bureaucratic centralized control of the economy.[13]

Drawn from a "reading" of the Nazi and Soviet experience, the totalitarian model as analytic tool was, for historical reasons, applied mainly to the case of the latter and its "satellite" regimes. As model, one can say retrospectively that it picked up some of what turned out to be the "contingent" elements of the Stalin era (though saying this does not render any less complex the question of the model's adequacy at the how/where/when "margins" where difficult analytical issues are found).

One of those elements was the seemingly permanent commitment to terror: not as a response to challenge, not as the final instrument in social change at a forced pace, but as a "method of governance for the foreseeable future," a central element in Stalin's conception of his USSR as "the only proper institutional embodiment of the idea of socialism."[14] Soviet Russia in January 1953 Stalin regarded as a mature system. Terror was part of its maturity; a reasonable component, then, in any model denominated totalitarian.

Rejection of limit, rejection of *routinization,* is also reflected in the totalitarian model, if implicitly. Here, we confront a "voluntarism" (among many) of the Stalin era. As Moshe Lewin puts it, Stalin had reached, by 1934, the point at which he could promulgate any laws he liked, create and impose his own legal order, and within it, dominate society.

> There certainly was a deep craving among the officials as well as in the population for the security that only a firm legal framework could provide. To regularize, to consolidate, to reinsure, to ensure a ruly and predictable working of the responsible institutions, some kind of "constitutionality" was needed. Such was probably the state of mind in the *apparaty* by 1934 and later. The interests of the ruling elite as well as of the system at large, in terms of gaining or regaining popular support and cohesion, and providing predictable working conditions for the functioning of the state machinery... were in the deepest interests of the system and of its most important agencies.[15]

Instead, Stalin launched the Great Purge.

Terror as "normality" probably had psychological roots in Stalin, but it had developed earlier as the critical coercive element in transforming Russia, under Lenin, then Stalin. Stalin's commitment to a certain kind of industrialization, at a certain pace, with a particular way of generating capital from the peasantry, are reflected in Skocpol's words. "There was no abstract, general 'imperative of industrialization' at work here... [rather] imperatives of state-propelled, heavy industrialization, undertaken by a regime with a narrow and precarious political basis in a predominantly agrarian society where the peasantry was... hostile to the regime."[16]

Raymond Aron, writing earlier, was more succinct: "The Soviet planned economy needed absolute power because in a great many sectors it was obviously doing what the governed did not want."[17]

En gros, the totalitarian model was not terribly abstract—its elements were *descriptive* of all-too-evident elements of Stalin's Russia—and in this lay the foundation of its general acceptance. Full-blown totalitarianism, however, did not long survive Stalin. In the USSR, and in the East European states, where totalitarian patterns were of lesser duration and had not cut so deep, two elements of the model were removed. Terror on the broad-spectrum, "prophylactic" scale was narrowed, channeled. Autocracy in the sense of one-man rule gave way to narrow oligarchy—collective rule—disposing of the "leashed" security establishment as its *collective* instrument. State dominance meant the continuation of the "mono-organizational society," in Rigby's terms, but it was no longer run by a tyrant; it was no longer "Stalinism."[18]

The "oligarchical consensus" which has marked the rulers of a still quite autonomous state through the Khrushchev and Brezhnev periods stood for broad institutional continuity, minus terror and autocracy; for the "defense of those features that constituted the mono-organizational system."[19] But distinguishing between institutions and their mode of operation under different leaders has left ample room for controversy in the interpretation of Soviet history and of the perceived continuities or discontinuities therein.

Was Khrushchev's rule "Stalinism without excesses," a period wherein a new leader carried on, in a more moderate manner, within roughly the same set of institutions? Not to Stephen Cohen, who argues that excesses were the "essence of historical Stalinism, and they are what really require explanation."[20] Was Stalin—as tyrant and institution builder, accounting in the latter role for as much or more of the enduring Soviet political architecture than Lenin—Lenin's "true heir"? Was Leninism naturally a prelude to Stalinism? At a further historical remove, but not a question in which the post-Stalin "decompression" or the issues of Soviet political development in the Gorbachev era lack relevance—how many Lenins were there? If there were *two* (the hard, doctrinaire, repressive Lenin of the revolution and War Communism, and the moderate, pragmatic Lenin of the NEP, from 1921 on) and two "Leninist" political cultures, then Stalinism is the heir of the former, and the latter (Lenin's "real" choice?) is the option rejected by Stalin in the late 1920s—but "available" perhaps as a base of legitimation for a new Soviet political course.[21]

Beyond these questions, the move of the Soviet state beyond totalitarianism (or Stalinism) raised two other issues, each important. The totalitarian *model* (or "totalitarianism" as a description of things) included no seeds of its own destruction. More like a *perpetuum mobile*, it could not account for how the USSR emerged from totalitarianism into something "less." The system "adapted": it did not founder. Explaining the Soviet Union's stability since the mid-1950s, the institutional continuity without the props of autocracy and broad terror, has been a major task of the student of Soviet domestic politics ever since.

Second, the "all-powerful, proactive state vs. inert, re-active society" encompassed in the totalitarian model told us nonetheless little *about* society; "society" might have disappeared. But some scholars were understandably curious. Emigré research in the early 1950s among Soviet displaced persons allowed some retrospective looks at grass-roots life under Stalin. What was found confirmed a strong state indeed, but also the existence under it of some social processes. The subtitle of Inkeles and Bauer's classic *The Soviet Citizen: Daily Life in a Totalitarian Society* expressed both realities.[22] Later, in the emergence of a new brand of social history, historians turned their attention to social processes in the Stalin era.[23] Some works stressed a "complexity" of state-society interaction in Stalin's time not previously perceived, or to be found in previous treatments. Others were taken by critical audiences to be "revisionist" in the sense of distorting and whitewashing the horrors of the time, or exculpating Stalin of the guilt most judged him to bear, by way of arguing that the social/human outcomes of Stalinist policies contained a large measure of collision between policy from above and reaction from below, or by assigning too much significance to social support, or initiative from below, in producing those outcomes.

Controversy could hardly fail to ensue. Many such social historians saw themselves as counteracting a "Cold War bias" which had in their view suffused the study of Russia since 1917—and many of its best-known students. Such controversy is not easily settled; it continues over analytical and moral-political perspectives today, and will likely extend into the future.[24] At the extreme, it might be said that some "revisionist" social history nears the point where the autonomy of the Soviet "state" is almost denied, where politics *is* seen as an emanation of social forces—the point of Skocpol's criticism which marked the beginning of this discussion. This, surely, flies against the facts. But a rejection of the *search* for limits on that autonomy risks the return of society, 1928–1953, to the analytic shadows; clearly undesirable as well. Though interesting from many angles, the debate and controversy surrounding these issues of state-society relations and an indubitably bloody period in Soviet history are beyond the proper scope of an introduction to a set of essays whose topics are more diverse. Hence we must leave them here.

What endures, through all the interaction of Soviet political change and the controversy over the totalitarian perspective, it seems to me, is a rough consensus on two points, simple but important. First, the Soviet state is "strong," is "autonomous," is not, in short, to be forgotten. It is a reality, not a reflection, not an emanation to be explained by reference to society or economy. Second, just as surely, and to a growing degree over the years since Stalin's death, "society" too is reality, *not* totally explicable in structure and process in terms of the state's "outputs." Defining the relation, then, of society to the state, is an important issue—to it we now turn.

SOCIETY

Discussing state-society relations in the Soviet bloc, especially in the USSR itself, involves us in a grammar of metaphor. A "dynamic" society "strains" against the "bonds" of the state; "forces" in society press against state "inertia," "pressures build up" in a changing society, posing the question of whether the state will "open the safety valves" or add another, strengthening layer to the boiler containing those pressures—and of whether either type of tactic will work.

Such imagery parts company with the picture of the active, all-powerful state and inert society that characterized the totalitarian reading of Soviet-model reality. Again not terribly specific, it emerged as a broadly shared orientation on Soviet polity-society relations as the Brezhnev regime made it clear that Khrushchev's reforms would not continue, and the grayness of the Brezhnevian "clerks" made it equally clear that they were not likely to return to terror to generate change in the society below.[25] By the late 1960s, some analysts were expressing more confident expectations of a collision between a dynamic, developing, more complex society and a stand-pat, uninnovative, if strong, state than future events were to bear out. If logic conduced to a reading of trends in the USSR which could be seen, in a quasi-Marxian vein, as (societal) "forces," productive and otherwise, threatening to overwhelm the "relations of production" characteristic of the Soviet-type system, it turned out that there was enough life left in those relations to blunt the "prerevolutionary" potential. As Alexander Dallin put it, "Of all political systems, the Soviet seems most likely and most able to override, ignore, or distort what might otherwise or elsewhere be identified as natural or secular trends."[26]

"Society," then, has not yet overwhelmed the state. It has generated crisis in Poland. It has exerted, arguably, more pressure on East European regimes (some of them, at least) than on the Soviet "prototype." But, except *post factum*, it has been difficult indeed to get the state-society equation "straight," to make any firm predictions. Those who predicted, over the past twenty years, that the state would "hold," over against whatever social forces emerged, have thus far been right; especially if one includes, in Eastern Europe, the Soviet factor (invasion, or the credible threat thereof) as the ultimate guarantor of regime irreversibility. However, this does not mean that states have not, with varying degrees of alacrity and sophistication, accommodated in less than transformational ways (in-system, rather than systemic, change), gradually, to processes in society which are themselves typically gradual in the way they operate. "Pressures" building to explosive force are thus not the only scenario in which a tracking of society's relation to the state becomes relevant and useful.

Space considerations, and the tying of this chapter to those ten others which follow, preclude even a cursory examination of all dimensions of the relationship in Soviet-type societies (actually, in societies subordinated to Soviet-type polities), but the questions of class formation, its "success" or prevention, and the autonomy of their solution from direct state control provide a good place to start, and allow us to take into account some related issues as well.

A commonly shared perspective is that the Soviet-type state "liberated" itself from dependence on, constraint by, *any* class—most important, by the working class in whose name it presumed to command. Revolutionary intellectuals dominated the scene, committed to Marxist-Leninist transformations, and, as Konrad and Szelenyi put it in their work on intellectuals and class power in state-socialist systems, "the actual working class, because of its relatively small size, could be replaced by a philosophical abstraction."[27] Bolshevism, in the USSR and later in Eastern Europe, "substituted for the interests of the real working class the historic mission of the working class—the achievement of the dictatorship of the proletariat."[28] (In the conditions of Stalin's autocracy, of course, one can extend this further, as (a) "party" substitutes for the working class; (b) Politburo/Secretariat/Central Committee for the party; and (c) one-man rule for the higher "collective" bodies.)

Whether the displacement of the working class (small at the outset in virtually all the socialist states save Czechoslovakia), however, meant the state's becoming the agent of other "class" interests is a question whose answer is somewhat in dispute. Formulations have ranged from Djilas' "new class" notion[29] through various Marxist formulations to Konrad and Szelenyi's subtle and complicated argument which raises the possibility that the logic of the Soviet-model polity and economy tends to raise the intellectuals, broadly defined, to "class power."[30] Thus arises a host of interesting possibilities: "false consciousness" on the part of intellectuals, specific "interests" they may share opposed to those of workers, the conditions under which intellectuals make common cause with workers (see chapter 8). While their analysis leaves many contingencies open, "class power" as the outcome toward which systemic logic seems to drive the intellectuals looks to me a bit strained. Frank Parkin's formulations of state versus class(es) seem to me a more accurate and useful summary of the situation over most of the history of Soviet-type systems.

> The socialist state could be seen as actively inhibiting the intelligentsia from transforming itself into a dominant class, while simultaneously underwriting such privileges as it enjoys. Conversely, the state might be said to acquiesce in the subordination of the proletariat while also creating the conditions that shield labour from the harsh economic climate of market rationality and commodity exchange.... The party-state strips away the capacity of social classes to organize in defense of their collective interests and replaces open distributive struggle by a centralized system of allocation. Under such an arrangement there may well exist a privileged class, but not an exploiting, dominant class.[31]

Both intelligentsia and working class are addressed here, providing a good take-off point for discussion of an aspect of the developmental "logic" of soviet-type systems. The political elites, narrowly conceived, surely sought to preserve their power in "autonomy" from any class. But the processes of industrialization and *étatization* they unleashed, first in the USSR, then later in Eastern Europe, augured consequences potentially complicated, in the sense of the changing social base of a class structure that might emerge. The drive for industrial development promised a diminution of the large peasant share of society, a growth in the industrial work force by millions of "workers-to-be." The *statist* essence implied a massive growth in bureaucracy, planners, managers, and controllers; the general "mobilization" of effort, a growth in the number involved in services benign (education, health) and not so benign. Marxian socialism "needed" a working class. So said the ideology. Such a class could be built after a premature taking of power by Marxist revolutionaries; so said Lenin. But did Soviet-type systems—which surely needed "workers" and "intellectuals"—produce these as *classes*, or only as groupings?

A controversial question, to be addressed most profitably at two phases of development. The first (from 1929 to the onset of World War II, for the USSR; the late 1940s through the mid-late 1950s for most of Eastern Europe) is marked by rapid economic development, massive peasant-to-worker mobility and the growth of administrative cadres drawn from those of worker and peasant origin, a high degree of political repression, and generalized poverty. A coercively mobilized society changes shape, but remains rather amorphous; "new" workers rapidly outnumber the old, a large share of the society is "relocated" in terms of socio-occupational position. High mobility, fluidity, and the inequality of reward which Stalin sanctioned after 1931 all made for what the renowned Polish theorist Stanislaw Ossowski called "non-egalitarian classlessness,"[32] a characteristic the USSR and the USA, for different overall reasons but in both cases related to high rates of social mobility, shared. Processes and politics did not allow classes to coalesce out of their potential social bases in the Soviet-type system; hence it was "classless."

This diagnosis was shared by Feldmesser's analysis of class formation (or lack thereof) in a review of the Russian/Soviet experience from 1861 through the Stalin and into the earlier Khrushchev eras.[33] Just as aspects of the state-dominant Tsarist experience had prevented the development of classes in any stable sense, even while the rationale of the old "estate system" was being eroded by late nineteenth- and early twentieth-century economic development,[34] so under Stalinism classes were blocked in any solid development. The state sat astride the whole society; its "seat" was not dependent on the support of particular social classes, on collectivities with conscious and shared proregime attitudes balanced against other classes of antiregime orientation. Such, simply, were not allowed; hierarchy within society was not allowed to constrain the state. One did not enjoy the option of supporting the state if one "did well" by it, opposing if one did not. Rather, one did well (or had a chance to do well) if one supported; the consequences of opposition were all too clear.[35]

The argument for this sort of "classlessness" can be made most strongly for the Soviet case, for reasons both historical (pre-Soviet) and systemic-situational (the ferocity and duration of the Stalinist phase). But in Eastern Europe, the impact of coercive change was large as well, as labor force and society changed shape under great pressures (see chapter 7), among them political ones which counteracted class formation. The Soviet-type system produced an elite, a privileged group or stratum, but not a secure one—"ruling serfs," in Moshe Lewin's characterization of Stalinism, exercising "absolutist and arbitrary rule" over those below them, but dependent "on the arbitrary rule from above" as well.[36] There was no "tenure" for the newly privileged, no security for *any*, save the statistical unlikelihood that comes, with large numbers, to make the rank-and-file worker or peasant less likely candidates for arrest and repression. The "state" had developed a "hyper-autonomy."

Tsarist autocratic heritage and varied Western traditions of absolute monarchy and French revolutionary thought refracted in Bolshevik lenses came together in what Reinhard Bendix has called a "plebiscitarian" ideology, dictating that no traditional/local authority "should intervene in the relations between the absolute monarch and his subjects or between the nation and its citizens."[37] Soviet-type totalitarianism implemented this ideology "by effectively suppressing the organization of interests arising from the differentiation of the social structure."[38] The state had to some degree promoted that differentiation; what it suppressed, in so dealing with its expression, was a critical element in the formation of classes. "State and society lose their distinction when the social is absorbed by the political rank-order"[39]— Bendix here is close to Feldmesser. State may rule over society, state may absorb it; the difference here is grammatical to a degree. But society does not "absorb" the state, does not, at this phase, give birth to *classes* whose claims on the state might reduce its autonomy.

Individuals, ranked high or low in this social order of inequality, classlessness, and risk, could not, typically, "opt out" of the game by emigration or effective resistance. Within such constraints, there *were* beneficiaries, their numbers considerable. Peasants-become-workers, workers-become-bosses, enjoyed new status, and a segment of the intelligentsia, "mesmerized by the phenomenon of total power in its application for purposes of social change,"[40] provided some positive support for regimes in this first, "dynamic" phase. Regime monopoly of power and readiness to coerce provided the disincentives for any action against the new socialist order.

If this phase be seen as "modernization" (and there are reasons pro and con here, as the final section of this chapter will explore), then it was necessarily a period of strain, of potential destabilization, if one accepts (as I do) Huntington's "paradox"—that "modernity produces stability and modernization instability."[41] Urbanization, shifts from farm to factory, increasing educational levels, were all "contained" in their possible destabilizing effects by political institutions capable of maintaining control, even though at times many more people must have counted themselves among the deprived than among the beneficiaries of the system, and were hardly likely to accord it legitimacy. (Skocpol appropriately reminds us of the home truth, relevant especially to students of Soviet-type systems, that "even after great loss of legitimacy"—or, one assumes, the in absence of much to begin with —"a state can remain quite stable ... if its coercive organizations remain coherent and effective."|[42]

The management of this modernization process has not been successful everywhere in the Soviet bloc, but the resolution of crises has thus far prevented a reversal of the socialist order, if not quite demonstrating *irreversibility*. The state-society transaction has been, at times, internationalized; Soviet troops saved, or restored from nonexistence, the Hungarian regime in 1956. Consciousness of Soviet pressure probably limited the Polish peaceful renewal of 1956; Soviet threat "forced" the "self-occupation" of Poland in 1981 under the rubric of martial law. Soviet invasion in 1968 prevented what might have been a peaceful reformist transformation of many aspects of Czechoslovakia's Soviet-type polity. Some of these crises might be seen as those of modernization, others—surely Czechoslovakia in 1968—as occurrences well within the period of modernity. (Whether Soviet-type systems are irreversible because of the nature and articulation of political institutions and control, state penetration and proprietorship of the economy—"intrinsic elements"—or because of *Soviet* guarantees, is a question only history will answer, but one which goes well beyond the bounds of the geographic "bloc" to entangle Cuba, Nicaragua, Angola, etc., as well in its future resolution.)

These crises came after the death of Stalin, in another phase, when the social base, and the style of state-society transactions and "class" issues, had changed sufficiently to pose new political and analytic questions. In the lead-in to this phase, the death of Stalin brought an end to broad-spectrum terror. Khrushchev's reformist politics evoked no political instability in the USSR, but did help destabilize the Polish and Hungarian situations, where elites no longer had reliable recourse to terror. Beyond these discrete facts, a widely accepted interpretation of state-society relations sees the emergence of an implicit "social contract," especially prompted by the crises of 1956, wherein regimes "traded" consumerism and growth, and continuing forbearance from terror for the population's political "realism," acquiescence in unalterable domestic and bloc realities, and commitment to work sufficient to provide a base for the promised consumerist policies. Some cases— Poland, Czechoslovakia, Hungary, most explicitly after 1961—are "clearer" in this contractual sense than others (Bulgaria, Romania, the

USSR itself, at least until the coming of Brezhnev), where indeed no such contract can be inferred without a good deal of "interpretation."

Simultaneously, the process of change in the socio-occupational structure reached a plateau; the agrarian-industrial transition over, the socialist societies for the most part took on a more definite shape. Large, mainly hereditary working strata made up of second-generation socialist workers replaced the large ones made up of first-generation, ex-peasant workers (which had in turn replaced the *small*, mainly hereditary proletariats of the presocialist periods). Elites and intelligentsias ceased to expand in size so rapidly, and became more "hereditized" as offspring inherited parental status on the basis of education and cultural and political/administrative advantage. Smaller peasantries remained, still large by Western standards, but necessary to provide the food in systems not noted for high productivity.

Were intelligentsia and workers emerging as "classes"? With what implications for the state and its autonomy? These were (and are) questions of some moment; they run through a number of the chapters to follow. The "hardening" of the vertical structure of society via the lessening of mobility opportunities, the consequent greater "inheritance" of (class?) membership, the likelihood that near-hereditary elites might value a regime that preserved their advantage, while larger working strata, no longer upwardly mobile from the peasantry, might find to their dismay their deprived status self-reproducing, all evoked some elements of classic understandings of how classes *an sich* develop, and how classes become such *für sich*, become conscious of interests distinguishing them from other classes and giving them, perhaps, specific claims to advance versus the socialist state.

There is an irony in this—not simply the one inherent in a "working class" potentially challenging the state of which it is the presumptive social base, but one in what the slowing of social mobility, the consequent "hereditization," may mean. Marx, in formulating his class theory, thought little about intergenerational mobility; what he *did* think adjudged it not good for the development of classes.

Except for a few comments upon the special case of the United States, where the fluidity of "interchange between the classes" retards the development of proletarian class consciousness, Marx gave little attention to the possible influence of mobility upon forms of class relationship and class consciousness in employing the received notions of "bourgeoisie" and "proletariat."[43]

Presumably, Marx could not have foreseen that it would be precisely the growth-driven mobility which retards class formation (if the line of analysis running through many of these essays is correct) that would help stabilize ostensibly class-*based* regimes of a "Marxist" designation; nor that the slowing of mobility and the maturation of the societies under those regimes, with its potential for class formation, might introduce strains working counter to stability.

"Strains" again. But classes? The question is analytic/definitional, and answers will thus vary. I impose no tight definitional criteria of my own. Nor am I in the position of some Western Marxist critics of "real existing socialism" Soviet-style, whose analyses, with all respect, predispose them to detect a working "class," formed or in formation, since it is *only* the working class they wish to see overthrow or transform these regimes. Two things, however, do seem clear. First, that regimes are very reluctant to think, or admit, that they are dealing with anything so ominous as "classes" in other than the propagandistic/ideological sense. Not that they do not, increasingly, take account of forces in society (the "social contract" indicates otherwise), but they are more comfortable and do seek to preserve the situation wherein they face only "quasi-groups" and their "latent interests"—which "become politically relevant only through the perceptions of decision-makers."[44] Some regimes—the Soviet among them—*have* surely faced no more than this. In a combination of repression, reliance on nationalism and a traditional political culture (see chapters 2–4), and *ouvrieriste* policies in wage and employment, the USSR has maintained a quiescent stratum of workers with little evidence thus far of real "class" action. Reversal of those policies in some areas, as Gorbachev seems intent upon (see chapter 6), could evoke more by way of class behavior, however, from workers who now possess more of the potential social characteristics *of* a class.[45]

Polish regimes have not been so "lucky." Workers played a major role in the 1956 crisis; in 1970 and 1976, the "running" was theirs—and in 1980, the rise of Solidarity demonstrated more by way of organized, working-class consciousness than analysts had for the most part thought possible. The degree to which the "linkage" of workers and intellectuals through the Workers' Defense Committee (KOR), founded by some of the latter in 1976, promoted this result is problematic; one runs the risk of overestimating the intelligentsia "input."[46] But "solidarity" across the social gap cannot but have enhanced society's potential against the state here (see chapter 7). Notable as well is that while working-class-rooted, Solidarity came rapidly to represent a *national* movement; not a claim of workers against other classes sharing Polish soil, but a claim of workers and others against the state. In the end, the state's power was greater, but the chronicle is not over.

Poland is, of course, "unique"—but so are each of the societies in the bloc. In some, economic, proto-"class"-based protest and tension may combine with nationalism and broad cultural-ethical endowment, in others not. In some, the "main action" may *not* be class- or stratum-based. But the processes of social change, whose uncertain outcome occupies so much space in these essays, *do* operate across most of those diverse societies, under state structures of roughly similar design. "Fine-tuning" the relationship grows more challenging for decision makers. Gorbachev's push toward reform is not guaranteed success in the USSR, much less in the East European "mix"—some regimes ahead of the USSR on reform, others reluctant foot draggers who see possibilities of crisis reminiscent of those which followed Khrushchev's liberalization of 1956. States which cannot fine-tune, or lack the economic resources to do so, must rely more on coercion. Coercion works best when self-confidently and decisively applied. These are not qualities East European regimes have exhibited much in dealing with strains emerging in their societies in recent years.

WHAT ARE SOVIET-TYPE SYSTEMS?

What kind of states, societies, or "systems" are those of the Soviet type? What sort of summary labels, if any, can adequately characterize them? Over twenty years ago, Alex Inkeles suggested that three models might have utility in analyzing the Soviet Union;[47] a good enough, if imperfect, "fit" to deepen our perceptions. One, of course, was the totalitarian model; another that of the USSR as a *developing* society; the third put the USSR among those fitting the designation of *mature industrial* society. None was suggested as having exclusive validity— but then utility, not "validity," is the rationale for analytic models in any case. Do they, or do they not, help us "see" further, deeper, better?

All three, indeed, seemed to make sense then, and to me still do, as (partial) descriptions of Soviet reality. To varying degrees, the three-model span also offers a broad enough spread to accommodate the East European states, which offer considerable diversity among themselves. Many *institutions* which date from the USSR's totalitarian/Stalinist period endure into the post-Stalin period—most of them, in fact. The grafting of a number of such institutions onto the East European states, as well, was "successful" and enduring. Institutions and practices associated with totalitarianism have persisted, of course, most of all in Albania—outside the Soviet "orbit"—and in Romania under Ceausescu to a greater degree, perhaps, than in the USSR. Poland and the GDR saw the weakest totalitarian "crescendos" in the critical late-Stalin period (1948–1953); Hungary, Czechoslovakia, and Bulgaria experienced much harsher times.

Today, for reasons quite different, Poland and Hungary are the states furthest from totalitarian rule; the others are more "middling" cases. All, save Albania and perhaps Romania, have in recent times (taken broadly as the last twenty five years or so) assumed a shape and style we might denominate "posttotalitarian." By this, I by no means argue that they have left the totalitarian heritage behind: rather, and simply, that the state's central problem has been a still-ambitious and interventionist program of social control pursued now in the absence of mass terror as an instrument, and in the face of the decline of whatever ideological fervor once existed to provide a doctrinal impetus to totalitarian domination. Until *these* facts change, the totalitarian model will not lose its relevance.

Do we gain in perception by treating these Marxist-Leninist systems as species of "developing" societies? If appreciation of diversity of outcome within the "Soviet-type" designation is our objective, certainly so, since the answers, country by country, are quite diverse.

Even limiting ourselves to fairly simple indices of what is generally meant by development (industrialization, urbanization, increased educational levels, etc.), the diversity of initial developmental levels (prior to the onset of development under Soviet-model auspices) is striking. Tsarist Russia in 1914, and Soviet Russia in 1928 on the eve of the Plan era, was an agrarian society, with about 80 percent of the labor force on the land; "underdevelopment" by European if not by Asiatic standards. Albania, Bulgaria, Romania, and the southern parts of Yugoslavia were similarly "peasant/agrarian" societies as they entered socialism. But Czechoslovakia was in no sense such—farmers were outnumbered by those in other sectors well before its entry into the Soviet orbit in 1948; the industrialization accomplished under Austro-Hungarian auspices and those of the 1918–1938 Republic had been considerable. Hungary, and to a lesser degree Poland, had reduced the peasant majorities to a degree well below that of "Russia 1928" prior to socialism, while the GDR remained a special case of "medium" development by East European standards, as a less developed area of the German Reich.

The shared experience has been the state-driven attempt at development, or *further* development, in selected priority areas dictated by the Soviet model (heavy and extractive industry, some elements of infrastructure, "defense" capacity, etc.), and the pains thereof—mishandling of agriculture, decline of services, high reinvestment rates for a prolonged period leading to widespread falls in living standard. But the goal of "development," surely, *was* advanced. If at no time could it have been said that socialist Czechoslovakia was in the "developing" category, today the GDR, Hungary, Poland, and perhaps the USSR and Bulgaria are too far along, on the average, to fit here. *Regional* backwardness is still marked, of course, in the USSR and Yugoslavia, and Romania's chaotic economic policies have created more problems than have, in the net balance, been solved over forty years. (There are issues of definition and perception here, and not all readers will agree with the way I have resolved them. The imbalances so striking in the USSR—between GNP and living standard, between defense industry and light industry, between relative military strength and global economic power which cause some to call it a "semi"-superpower—argue that it may not yet have outgrown the "developing" designation. There is appeal, indeed, in the frequently encountered image of the USSR as either laggard among leaders or leader among laggards: the least developed of the "modern industrial" societies, or the best developed of those which fall short of this.)

All in all, it seems to me, we may appropriately conceive of most of these states as beyond the developing stage, but with severe problems which persist in the current phase of development, linked to the *way* development was achieved, and the continued dominance of state over economy and society. Are they examples of something we might then call "partial modernization," or some such term? Posing this question, on the assumption that modernity means something *beyond* development in the rather mechanical sense we have used here, allows us to look a bit deeper at outcomes and their meaning.

Rigby's distinction between "traditional, market, and organizational" societies—where, respectively, custom, contact, and command are the main modes of coordinating social activity and effort—offered, in a classic and much-cited 1964 article, a context in which to view Soviet development against the experience of other societies.[48] Though concrete societies mixed elements of all three kinds of coordination, past a certain level of complexity no society could rely solely or mainly on custom, or thus remain wholly or mainly traditional. The path onward toward modernity (that is, away from tradition) was a divergent one: "contract" and "market" obviously shaped a society marked by a measure of social and individual autonomy, of limits on state power, etc., not provided by the "organizational" path, where command radically restricted autonomy, and a quite autonomous state attempted to control broad ranges of behavior and succeeded. History, culture, and other variables would "push" a given society in one direction or the other as it moved beyond traditional organization. Allowing that these are "types," it is clear that the United States was a mainly market, the USSR a mainly organizational, society.

The particular shape of the "organizational" institutions of the USSR emerged, of course, not from any fully elaborated model in the minds of Lenin and other Bolsheviks pre-1917; it was, rather, the "product of concrete historical conditions,"[49] of a *process* extending from 1917 to 1939 (or 1928 to 1939), conditioned by the weight of Russian history (so heavily tilted in a nondemocratic direction), by the Leninist ideology, and by the selection of rapid economic development as a prime objective.

But those same institutions came to Eastern Europe as the result of the postwar imposition of Stalinism as a *model*; neither via a drawn-out process nor as a result of Eastern Europe's "historical" conditions, but, in Wlodzimierz Brus' words, "in a concentrated form, almost as a single stroke, and with all its basic properties appearing simultaneously."[50] The result amounted, it seems fair to say, to a reversal of direction for the Czechoslovak market society, and an intensification of elements of "organizational" rule where they existed to a lesser (Poland, Hungary) or greater (Albania, Bulgaria, Romania) degree among these nondemocracies, for a mix of historical and cultural reasons. If this was "modernity," it was one of a very specific sort.

But, even in the Russian/Soviet context, there is an alternative (and rather compelling) interpretation of the nature and meaning of the political process whereby the Soviet model was formed. Robert C. Tucker makes precisely the point, writing of "the strong element of 'archaization' in Stalinism, its resurrection of the historic tsarist pattern of building a powerful military-national state by revolutionary means involving the extension of direct coercive controls over the population and the growth of state power in the process."[51]

That "history" did not encompass *all* Tsars, but the state-building, society-weakening patterns of Ivan the Terrible, of Peter the Great, the consequent "binding" of people to the state, was the relevant history for Stalin as builder of the Soviet state. Alexander II, who had in the nineteenth century partly promoted, partly presided over, a loosening of the state's bonds (ending serfdom in 1861, providing for a more independent judiciary and local government institutions), was hardly a forebear. That loosening continued through a good deal of the late nineteenth and early twentieth centuries despite "reaction" under Alexander III and Nicholas II, opening, even if uncertainly, the possibility of Russian peaceful evolution toward a modernity with more of the market, less of the organizational, about it.

However fragile the basis of the Duma as a legislative body, of the constitution granted reluctantly in 1905, the provisional government which took power on the heels of Tsarism's collapse in February/March 1917 was totalitarian neither in action nor ambition, had a constitutional-liberal thrust, and lacked the violence of its Bolshevik successors. Given the predominance of the tradition of "strong state-weak society" in the past, "on the level of politics, the Provisional Government, because of its democratic character, involved a sharper break with the past, a deeper discontinuity, than did Leninism," in Zbigniew Brzezinski's words.[52] Brzezinski makes a point similar to Tucker's, but highlights the contrast between Bolshevik rule and *late*-Tsarist patterns. In this view, the

Bolshevik revolution not only was not a break from the predominant political tradition, but was, in historical perspective, an act of revitalized restoration. The late Romanov period was a period of decay, of the gradual weakening of the hold of the state over society. This was produced by the combined influence of social change (urbanization and industrialization, which also prompted the appearance of a more assertive bourgeoisie and intelligentsia and finally working masses) and of internal loss of vitality within the top elite, not to speak of the autocrat's own personal weaknesses. The overthrow of that ruling elite brought to power a new group, much more vital, much more assertive, and imbued with a new sense of historical mission. The political result of the Bolshevik revolution was thus revitalized restoration of long dominant patterns.[53]

Social revolution, in contrast, was fostered; workers were made of peasants; village dwellers became urbanites; illiterates learned to read — all, probably, faster than would have happened had "late Tsarism" survived, or the provisional government. But a state whose relation to society aimed at total domination had use for, and made use of, the results of that revolution—as had the strong states and Tsars of the past. "Development"—in Russia and the parts of Eastern Europe where it applied—did *not* mean forward motion politically (there is, of course, a value judgment here). The stability which resulted accompanied a peculiar version of modernity; even in the posttotalitarian phase of their politics, the Soviet-type systems carry the scars of the political process whereby they were formed, one wherein the state rejected the *recent* past for patterns typically more primordial.

The "mature industrial society" model—Inkeles' third—at first indication offers some promise of getting us away from politics and toward structural/organizational similarities between Soviet-type systems and others produced by economic imperatives. To some degree, of course, this is true. Work organization, technological development, reward differentiation, and numerous other factors operate to produce certain similarities across political-system boundaries, and many of these are appropriate and useful objects of investigation for those concerned with society as well as state.

But the two decades since Inkeles wrote have revealed increasing evidence of economic dysfunction and its impact on political and social life, which gives a peculiar twist to the notion of Soviet-model systems as examples of "mature industrialism." In terms of technological level, relative efficiency, and international competitiveness, Soviet-bloc economies have, overall, established an underwhelming record. As Western market economies have moved beyond industrial "maturity"—for ultimate good or ill—to "postindustrial" or "service economy" status, as the "newly industrialized countries" (NICs) of East Asia have come to dominate some of the industries the earlier-developed West left off, Soviet-type economies are mired, to one degree or another, in a coal-and-steel, labor-intensive industrial pattern, with service sectors as remarkably deficient as their agriculture is still remarkably absorptive of manpower. If not senescence, this is at best a maturity alarming rather than comforting: Gorbachev's realization of at least some of the long-term implications of these facts is surely one of the factors motivating his calls for "restructuring" *(perestroika)* across the bloc.

The problems are not only economic—but economics is generally an inextricable component of those that arise. In the notion of "mature industrial society" there is, perhaps, the implication that "major" political issues no longer stand on the agenda, no longer need resolution; that, perhaps, the "end of ideology" has arrived. Whatever retrospective critique such a notion has received in the West since the late 1960s, in Eastern Europe at least, it has been—and remains—quite off the mark. Issues—from the ambit of individual political, social, and economic autonomy to national independence—have been suppressed, not resolved; blunted, perhaps, but only temporarily by the years of economic growth and to some degree consumerism, and all the more likely to reemerge in periods of economic stress, such as came with the end of the 1970s and beginning of the 1980s.

If elements of the dominant Russian/Soviet "political culture" (see chapters 2–4) have moderated any tendency for economic grievances to translate themselves into "politics from below" in the USSR (repression and the identification of so many with a state that is, after all, their "own" in language and ethnicity, help as well), such is not so in Eastern Europe. There, elements of tradition and native political culture, alone or in combination with economic stress, continue to make for near-constant malaise interspersed with crisis. Soviet-type political institutions endure, but not without the need for episodic repression and/or accommodation.

In the "Western" part of Eastern Europe, where national cultures draw on democratic (Czechoslovakia) or individualistic/aristocratic traditions (Poland, Hungary), where Renaissance, Reformation, Counter-Reformation, and Enlightenment are parts of the "deep" history, the Soviets have faced a different sort of "public opinion" passed through generations raised under socialism (see chapter 10) and challenges combining anti-Russian nationalism and democratic strivings. In that part of Eastern Europe (Romania and Bulgaria in the bloc) which shares with Russia the Byzantine-Orthodox heritage and a history of more despotic rule, challenges have been less problematic, the "fit" of the Soviet model not as bad. (Such did not prevent Ceausescu from "playing the card" of Romanian nationalism to undergird his move for partial de-alignment from Soviet tutelage, though this has hardly had a major impact on Soviet assessments of their own security in the region.)

Perhaps the greatest long-term threat emerging from within Eastern Europe to Soviet establishment of a tranquil, "mature" sort of domination is the slow, but steady, drawing together of critical intelligentsia (many of them ex-Marxists) and broader elements of the populations around now-shared valuations of national political, cultural, and religious heritage (see chapter 11), over which dissidents and rank and file had often parted ways in the past. These constitute the "core" of national identities the Soviet regime had sought to manipulate and weaken in the course of a forty-year assault on East European cultures. The persistence or "recovery" of this consciousness also suggests that, in the unlikely event the long-term problems of Soviet-type economies are "solved," other grounds for protest and resistance will not be lacking. "Mature industrialism" as a model seems useful in analyzing the Soviet bloc, but mainly in the unresolved problems it helps to pinpoint.

"Strong" states, then, all in all, face a diversity of societies with differing degrees of resilience and autonomy, from precious little to considerable—the latter achieved either by resistance and the persistence of critical independent institutions (Poland) or by a reasonably stable accommodation in the state's, but also society's, perceived interest (Hungary). Some are "more" posttotalitarian than others, some are closer, others further, from the characteristics of a developing society. Some more than others might be classed as "mature industrial" —but the benchmarks of socioeconomic progress are changing, and this status may not indicate as much success as once it did.

Gorbachev, in 1987, seemed to be seeking a way to force both the USSR and the East European states onto a track connecting them with some of the *benefits* of autonomy, modernity, and economic efficiency enjoyed by market systems, but without taking them so far down that track of reform that the continuance of state dominance of society was imperiled. The fruits were surely attractive. In their pursuit, Gorbachev signaled a readiness to reduce the state's attempted micromanagement of many areas of economic, social, and cultural-intellectual life; for some, this was the harbinger of a new NEP, a return to Lenin "the pragmatist." To some degree, his "reading" of the situation could be consistent with some of the analysis offered here. But, in at least part of his mind, and surely in those of more cautious Soviet and East European leaders, the pull of central planning, detailed guidance, and "administered" prices remains strong, as does the institutionally expressed conviction that the maintenance of "order" *(poriadok)* is as important as the prospect opened by *perestroika.*

Predicting any outcome in detail is beyond the scope of this introduction (and, for that matter, of the essays which follow). In a period of intense interest in political dynamics within the Soviet bloc, one can only say that there lie before Gorbachev more potential roads to failure than to success. The future, as the past, will be rich in obstacles to a Russian or Soviet "reformer." Whether, in the future, scholars and analysts are called to account for failure or success in this latest effort to preserve a system by changing some of its parts, some, at least, of the perspectives discussed here should be useful in that accounting.

TWO

SOVIET DISSENT AND
SOCIAL COMPLEXITY

In the years since the fall of Khrushchev, two undertakings have claimed a good deal of the energies of students of Soviet politics and society. The first has been the attempt to elaborate new and more penetrating models of the Soviet system as the fit of the totalitarian model has grown looser and a relatively stable pattern of "collective leadership" has emerged. The second has involved an effort to understand and assess the significance of the growing and increasingly open political dissent in the USSR, which—through the medium of *samizdat*—has revealed to Western eyes a whole range of critical viewpoints taken by Soviet citizens toward their own society and government. These two undertakings, it seems, have come together relatively rarely. While the phenomenon of dissent is a matter of continuing and even growing interest to scholars and explanations of its rise are not wanting, there has generally been little in the way of attempts to integrate it into more gen-

Originally published as "Dissent in a Complex Society: The Soviet Case," *Problems of Communism* (March–April 1973), 22(2): 40–52.

eralized, analytical views or models of the sociopolitical system as a whole.

The present chapter will be a tentative effort in this direction. The model of the Soviet system it presents is a loose and partial one drawing on the ideas of many scholars, and it is not intended as a freestanding alternative to other models. Within the general framework it provides, dissent is viewed as both product and symptom of the confrontation of two phenomena in the contemporary Soviet system: on the one hand, the structural complexity of a society at a rather high level of development; and on the other, the persistence of a centralist-command mode of integrating the increasingly differentiated segments of that society. In the view taken here, dissent assumes the character of a "normal" phenomenon and one whose significance for the system as a whole is *problematic*, but not necessarily *dramatic*, in terms of the Soviet future.

PROBLEMS OF A COMPLEX SOCIETY

The USSR today is a complex society manifesting, as do other modern societies, a relatively high degree of structural differentiation. While the modernity of the USSR relative to other modern societies is a matter of some debate (and is, in a sense, one of the issues involved in this discussion),[1] it is of a degree sufficient to place the Soviet Union squarely among those nations whose complexity creates serious problems of coordination or integration.

Integration in "traditional" or "primitive" societies presents fewer problems given the fact that these very designations signify that these societies are less differentiated and less complex. The distinct structural entities in such societies are relatively few and tend to be multifunctional: the family is the unit of production and consumption, of education and socialization; and the functions of priesthood and kingship are frequently fused in the same role.

The modernization of a relatively simple society—entailing the processes of industrialization, urbanization, etc.—involves a progressive structural differentiation, a diminution of the importance of multifunctional units and their replacement by units more functionally specific and better fitted to the performance of needed activities. Roles, as well as the structures in which they are nested, become more specialized, and as the dissimilarity of human activities increases, integrative problems also multiply. Modes of integration rooted in custom and tradition, which were fully adequate to meet the integrative needs of simpler systems, no longer suffice; new modes are needed if the adaptive capacity of the society is to increase. And as a nation moves along the path from traditionalism to modernity, the problems of integration become major foci of struggle in the political arena.[2] Integration, in short, is an eminently political matter.

The success potential of varying integrative strategies, and hence the choice between them, seems to depend in large part on three factors: the degree of differentiation (or modernity) of the society in question in the period prior to the choosing of a "strategy"; the content of the antecedent political culture and its relative vitality, or chances of persistence; and the objectives of modernization itself. The case that concerns us here—that of Soviet Russia—presents interesting divergences from the "average" modernizing nation in each of these regards.

The Russian society of 1917, though severely disrupted by war and governmental collapse, was substantially more modern than it had been thirty years before—and more modern, certainly, than the societies of Africa and Asia were thirty years later, when they finally embarked on modernization after World War II. Substantial industrialization and development of communications and transport systems, as well as a rate of GNP growth sufficient to qualify imperial Russia as a nation nearing the "takeoff" point, had been achieved between 1885 and 1918.[3] The Bolshevik "modernizing elite" consequently faced a society already fairly complex—which meant that the integrative task would be of commensurate complexity.

While war and revolution had brought the end of Tsarism, the political culture that had been both its product and its support survived. That culture was characterized by parochialism and passivity on the part of the masses, by a quasi-mystical mode of relating to the Tsar-autocrat, and—in the absence of any strongly developed entrepreneurial orientations or traditions—by an acceptance of the state as the "doer," promoter, and coordinator of a broad range of social and economic matters.[4] Given such a legacy, as Zbigniew Brzezinski has observed, "a democratic Russia—either liberal or socialist—does not seem to have been a real alternative."[5] A political formula, if it is to fit a society, must be consistent with that society's cultural peculiarities, with its level of civilization, and with the prevailing notions of its citizens about the bases of political obligation.[6] The Bolshevik formula was a fairly good fit— even allowing for the obvious differences between its dynamic totalitarian thrust and the inertia of Tsarist authoritarianism.

The Bolshevik modernization program was both transformational and defensive in its objectives. While the internal implications of the Marxist-Leninist value system clearly included the necessity of a transformation from tradition to modernity, national security concerns were of no less importance. Stalin's enumeration of the defeats Russia had suffered in the past as the price of backwardness and his formulation of the objective of "socialism in one country" echoed the concerns of Russian defensive modernizers stretching back to Peter the Great. Added to the centralism so dominant in the inherited political culture, this ingrained preoccupation with national security virtually guaranteed that the differentiation of structures which would come with modernization would be integrated in a centralistic, "command" fashion, and that *control* would become an obsessive concern of the bureaucracy that would emerge to rule the society.

Whether control eventually acquired the character of an end or remained a means is a moot question,[7] but there is no need to enter into it here. For present purposes, it suffices to note that control was so critical an element in the structuring of the Soviet system during its modernization that general agreement prevailed among Western analysts well into the late 1950s on the totalitarian nature of the system.[8] Totalitarian integration shaped the Soviet system and, given the historical circumstances, was relatively well suited to the task. Yet this mode of integration represents only one alternative, however natural its choice may have been at the outset, and an understanding of the issues raised by its maintenance under the conditions of a maturing Soviet society may be useful in clarifying some of the major problems the system faces—problems which are reflected, as we shall later argue, in the style and content of domestic political dissent.

THE SOVIET PATTERN OF INTEGRATION

With the declining vogue of the "totalitarian model" among Western analysts of Soviet affairs, new models, approaches, and terminologies have been put forward in an attempt to provide the conceptual apparatus necessary for a clearer understanding of the post-Stalin system. Among the many contributions, a few are striking in the degree to which their authors concern themselves directly—though in different terms—with the same problems of differentiation and integration.

T. H. Rigby has distinguished three main modes of integration or coordination of social effort: custom, contract, and command, characterizing the determination of objectives, roles, and methods in "traditional, market, and organizational" societies respectively.[9] In customary coordination, the parties—superordinate and subordinate—are both "passive," inasmuch as objectives, roles, and means in the "ideal type" of traditional society are themselves "given." Contractual (i.e., market) coordination involves shared determination of the matters in question: that is to say, each party agrees to "perform" in a certain way in return for some consideration. Finally, command involves an active party who determines and a passive party who obeys. The type of society, obviously, is a question determined by the *relative* domination of one or another mode of integration. Typically, modern societies manifest different mixes *mainly* of command and contractual elements, purely customary forms having given ever greater place to other types of coordination.

In these terms, the USSR is an organizational society, and the modernized states of the West are market societies. The Soviet polity—i.e., the state-party bureaucracy—is generally seen as commanding the other specialized sectors: economic, military, educational, and the like; it does not deal with them in a process of negotiated give and take. The evidence seems to suggest that both command and contract are *viable* modes of integration. Whether they are equally efficient in the management of systems of growing complexity is another question.

Along similar lines, Mark Field sees the increasing complexity and differentiation of modern societies as a phenomenon problematic in its outcome. The process of differentiation, in his words, "implies a fair amount of autonomy for the differentiated spheres and the development of criteria of action specific to these spheres; it also raises the important question of the integration of these different areas through a system of exchange of outputs."[10]

Autonomy, however, is only a *tendency*, and among the outcomes of differentiation is that of " 'constricted' development, a situation in which one of the differentiated spheres will attempt to dominate the others coercively by restricting and regimenting their tendencies toward autonomy."[11]

In Field's view, the outcome of the Soviet mode of integration has been just such a "constricted" development. Differentiated and specialized as its subsystems are, the Soviet system as a whole is dominated by the polity—the state-party bureaucracy. Subsystem autonomy would imply integration by exchange of outputs; domination is antithetical to both.

Frederick Fleron's typology of political systems—i.e., monocratic, adaptive-monocratic, co-optative, and pluralist—is based on differences in the way political elites obtain from other, "specialized" elites the skills necessary for managing a society.[12] At one end of the continuum, a monocratic elite either possesses all the necessary skills itself or can mobilize them from among the specialists by coercion and without any quid pro quo; at the other, a pluralist system contains no "professional-careerist" political elite, and all elites are in competition. Fleron leans toward a view of the Soviet system as co-optative—that is, one in which needed skills are obtained by co-opting appropriate specialists into the administrative structure—thus placing it somewhere between the two extremes, but rather far from pure monocracy. While this view may be open to question, what is relevant to the present discussion is the fact that Fleron sees such a system, with its inherent bias toward monocracy, as facing a difficult problem—namely, the risk that "these specialized elites might attempt to trade their skills for some degree of participation in the political policy-making process."[13]

The remarkable similarity with which Rigby, Field, and Fleron frame the issue of integration—i.e., in terms of command versus contract, little or much exchange of outputs, coercing needed specialized skills or "trading" for them—directs attention to a critical question. This is the question of the fitness of the Soviet polity, as presently constituted, to manage a larger social system in which structural differentiation has given rise to many competing interests and where there are, at least potentially, two types of power. With regard to the latter, Boris Meissner has observed that "the power of the top bureaucrats rests in the *positions* they hold, while that of the intelligentsia is rooted in the authority and prestige inherent in the *functions* it performs."[14]

For a long time, the USSR managed to suppress the organization of the different interests arising from differentiation under the cover of an ersatz "plebiscitarianism."[15] In the system-building phase, such a policy was probably rational, because reliance on contract as a means of co-ordinating effort was not a viable alternative, given the ambitious objectives of forced-draft industrialization and the shortage of politically reliable and technically competent specialized cadres. Had the autonomous interests arising from differentiation been given freer play, it is quite possible that the industrialization of the Stalin era could not have proceeded so swiftly and successfully (discounting human costs).

THE STRATEGY OF PENETRATION

With success achieved, however, the situation changes, and the critical question noted above presents itself. For success has brought with it a high level of differentiation, an increase in the number and complexity of differentiated spheres within which persons develop specific "criteria of action," specific viewpoints. Still, however, the polity penetrates these spheres, seeking to maintain control over them according to its *own* criteria of action. This situation, it will be argued, produces much of the political dissent facing the Soviet regime today, and in a general sense the continuing penetration of the polity into other specialized spheres provides at least some of the dissenters with "item number one" on their agenda.

Totalitarianism, even in the extreme form assumed by its Stalinist variant, did not completely obliterate the distinction between state and society. In reality, there existed neither the resources nor the knowledge necessary to control many "important areas of socially relevant activity," such as leisure-time activities, mating, and child rearing.[16] But society, if not totally dominated by the state, was *penetrated* to an unprecedented degree by the polity, and this penetration still persists, even though it lessened somewhat in the post-1953 period. The consequences of such penetration for an increasingly *mature* (i.e., complex and differentiated) Soviet system have been a matter of concern to Western analysts and Soviet dissenters alike.

A strong diagnostic consensus regarding the effects of this penetration was reached among a number of scholars who contributed to a symposium carried in the journal *Problems of Communism* 1966–68 and initiated by Zbigniew Brzezinski's essay "The Soviet Political System: Transformation or Degeneration?"[17] The "greater institutional maturity of Soviet society," Brzezinski argued, had been important in prompting the abandonment of violence in political competition, but pattern-breaking "moves" by the polity had also grown more difficult because the society was "far more developed and stable, far less *malleable* and atomized" than in the past.[18] In this situation, the party's function had become less clear, posing the whole question of its "relevance" to the USSR of the 1960s:

Soviet history in the last few years has been dominated by the spectacle of a party in search of a role. What is to be the function of an ideocratic-party in a relatively complex and industrialized society, in which the structure of social relationships generally reflects the party's ideological preference? To be sure, like any large socio-political system, the Soviet system needs an integrative organ. But the question is, What is the most socially desirable way of achieving such integration? Is a "strong" party one that dominates and interferes in everything, and is this interference conducive to continued Soviet economic political, and intellectual growth?[19]

In a similar vein, Robert Conquest viewed the USSR as a nation "where the political system is radically and dangerously inappropriate to its social and economic dynamics."[20] Frederick Barghoorn, though disagreeing with Brzezinski on the urgency of the "transformation-degeneration" dilemma, agreed that the "existing Soviet political structures and the ideology which serves as a major source of their legitimacy are increasingly; irrelevant to a more and more diversified society."[21]

The substantial measure of Soviet success in the system-building phase had, in fact, created a situation in which—as noted elsewhere by Alfred G. Meyer—the problems of system-management were complex beyond the coordinating capacities of a political structure clinging to a penetration strategy at a time when that structure was no longer "creative."[22] Effective coordination required a favorable balance of innovative over conservative tendencies in Soviet political institutions—a balance that seemed to be lacking.[23] Conquest even saw, in the confrontation of polity and society, the "conditions of a classical Marxist prerevolutionary situation."[24]

The problems which evoked such alarming diagnoses from Western observers, and which are reflected in the less systematic but perhaps "richer" content of *samizdat*, seem to be reducible to two, which are interrelated: first, the quality of bureaucratic management of the economy and the larger society; and second, the style of political recruitment in a differentiated system ruled by a "politicized bureaucracy."

A PARASITIC BUREAUCRACY

The party elite, in the view of Western observers and of some Soviet dissenters alike, lacks the expertise, flexibility, and perceptiveness necessary for the creative coordination of social and economic forces. It contributes little to the society and has few relevant "outputs" to exchange with other specialized sectors. In Meissner's words:

> The ruling power elite is increasingly regarded as parasitic, for two reasons. In the first place, it represents a foreign body in the fabric of the elite structure of an industrialized society, since it does not submit to an economic rationality that is characteristic of an industrial merit society. The goal of promoting the conditions for existence and growth

is only of secondary relevance to it. Its primary objective is the consolidation and expansion of its power base.

Second, the ruling elite is immensely exploitative of the other social
groups. Through its absolute monopoly of power and unrestricted
control over the means of production and property of the state, it is
in a position to divert a disproportionately large share of the social
product to the achievement of its political objectives, and at the same
time to secure a higher personal income for its members.[25]

The Soviet dissidents S. Zorin and N. Alekseev, in their *samizdat*
pamphlet "Time Will Not Wait," further develop the themes of exploitation and parasitism, focusing particularly on the *nomenklatura*
system, which in their view elevates Soviet "managers" to a position
that is virtually unassailable and remote from the masses. They see
nomenklatura as a form of property "as inalienable as capital in a bourgeois society. It serves as a legal basis for our system much in the manner
of the law of private property under capitalism."[26]

The new, nomenclatured "class" is vertically differentiated. Each
level takes orders from the one above and gives them to the one below,
with the subordinate level having no right of appeal. Career making is
the watchword of the system and induces the upward reporting of successes and the concealment of failure, thus maximizing misinformation
at the top. Although the top is where the real "power" is, its misin-
formed and isolated state guarantees that its power will be used in an
irresponsible manner, with the result that what eventuates can scarcely
be called "control" in any sense of coordination. While the party is
typically seen as "running" the system, Zorin and Alekseev see a different system in which "there is no proprietor, but there is an all-
powerful and voracious consumer—the party-state bureaucracy."[27]

In short, the political elite emerges as the main extractor of "surplus
value" in the Soviet system. Though its language is more emotional
than analytic, the Zorin-Alekseev diagnosis seems to be in general agreement with many Western critiques which see the Soviet bureaucracy
as forced to rule by command rather than by contract because, having
no outputs to exchange, it can scarcely enter into contractual
relationships.

The political elite, certainly, is aware of the manifold problems it
faces—i.e., the problem posed by lagging economic growth rates and
recurrent agricultural crises, the problem of reconciling the practical
need to grant greater autonomy to economic managers with the eternal
compulsion toward control, and the problem of comprehending the

sources of dissent and the "style" and the actions of the ever-more-publicized dissenters. Its response to this last problem has indicated relatively little change of perspective. That response has been an on-again, off-again campaign against dissent through the incarceration of dissenters in labor camps or mental hospitals, supplemented by the linking of dissenters with Western imperialism or "international Zionism" and other variations on familiar propaganda themes. The calls continue for reinforcing the "ideological vitality" of the party, for an even more tough-tempered, uncompromising stand against "alien" ideas. Yet at the present stage, as the requirements imposed by the need for continuing economic development and adaptation press harder, it is unclear that ideology itself is relevant as a base for continued party dominance.

ELITE RECRUITMENT

What of the patterns of recruitment into this troubled elite? We know rather little about this—less, certainly, than we should like. Given the closed nature of Soviet society, we are in some sense reduced to judging the efficiency of recruitment not "in process," but by the outcome— that is to say, by who is in office, how those in office respond to the problems they confront, and how successful they are. There is plenty of room for disagreement here. Few would deny, however, that what Meissner terms the "ability to get ahead"—in terms not so much of functional efficiency as of personality, adaptability to an often arcane set of game rules, personal "connections" and the efficient use of them—plays a large role in the Communist Party of the Soviet Union (CPSU), certainly a larger role than in bureaucracies less "politicized."[28] This ability to "play the game" well does not necessarily reflect creative talent or individual initiative, nor is it likely to be accompanied by a readiness to pay attention to interests and pressures which are of potentially great significance but are not yet represented institutionally at the high-level bargaining table. Brzezinski doubts that the CPSU can remain vital when its personnel policies render it, "almost unknowingly, inimical to talent and hostile to political innovation."[29]

But whatever the party's *tendencies*, has it been so hostile and inimical as to drive most of the society's talent to careers in other sectors, and if so, who are left? The Medvedevs, the Amalriks have been driven away, but what of others who may be sympathetic to some of their ideas? What *is* dissent? Who is a dissenter? How much, if at all, might such terms cover the hidden ideas of some of the nameless persons within the bureaucracy itself? This is a worthwhile question. And if the rank-and-file *apparatchiki* are generally lacking in talent and innovative qualities, what about those higher-level party members who simultaneously belong to the specialized functional elites and subelites upon which the *apparatchiki* must to some degree depend? Barghoorn discerns among these elements some "latent and increasingly vigorous but still rather amorphous tendencies":

> To some degree at least these party members, who are under pressure to give their primary loyalty to the party but who are also by training and occupation functional specialists in industrial management or military science, for example, develop perspectives which diverge from those of the full-time party functionaries and may lead to friction or even to policy disputes between them and the former.[30]

As yet, we cannot tell to what extent such persons are effectively "co-opted" and cease to represent any basis for change. The degree to which the specialists have the *desire*, or the resources, to innovate is a matter for speculation (of which there has been a great deal). What seems important here, however, is to try to comprehend how far such "insiders" may share, or may come to share, some of the attitudes and evaluative criteria of the clear-cut dissenters. The Soviet elite is not "accessible" to the nonelite in the sense of the latter having any real control over the selection of the former.[31] Thus, if the ruling bureaucracy is to adapt to change in any real sense, the adaptation must be from within, although the *idea* of change and the range of alternatives may come from "outside" sources. Typically, students of Soviet politics and society have viewed the embattled bureaucrats (a term whose scope is rather unclear) as the "insiders," the dissidents as "outsiders." Is this view correct?

SOURCES OF DISSENT

As noted at the outset, it is my belief that Soviet political dissent can be regarded as both product and symptom of those aspects of the Soviet system discussed earlier: that is, the increasing structural and role differentiation resulting from modernization; and the adoption of a response to the accompanying integrative problems that has differed radically from the type of response developed in most Western societies. Command, rather than contract, has been the predominant Soviet mode of integration, and this choice has produced a society that conforms to Field's earlier-mentioned concept of constricted development.

To a large degree, it is this constriction that motivates political dissent, and it does so on two levels. First, the denial of autonomy to many differentiated spheres that are functionally important causes frustration and dissatisfaction, especially among the elite in those spheres, and engenders demands by them for increased autonomy in the name of "rationality," efficiency, expertise, or other values—demands which the leadership thus far seems unwilling to accommodate. Second, the leadership's more general commitment to maintaining "uniformity" in attitudes, value, and behavior in the society as a whole (in order to facilitate control over the specialized sectors) evokes broader protests against the lack of individual freedom, violations of legality, and the persecution of religious "nationalists" such as the Crimean Tatars and other groups. These protests come from a wider opposition that has grown beyond the bounds of the specialized intelligentsia.

It is precisely the unproductive "domination" of other spheres by the polity that is attacked by the authors of "Time Will Not Wait," and it is also one of the targets of the dissident Soviet nuclear physicist Andrei D. Sakharov. For while the party was indeed a major force—perhaps *the* major force—in dragging Soviet society into modernity, the form that this modernity has taken is a peculiar one which Edward Shils has characterized as a "tyranically deformed manifestation of potentialities inherent in the process of modernization."[32] One of the evidences of this "deformity" is a peculiarity in the way that "interests" which have become divergent by virtue of differentiation are articulated. In the past, many analysts would have thought interest articulation itself incompatible with a Soviet-type system, but most today would probably agree with Francis Castles' observation that "totalitarian regimes are not so much antipathetic to the articulation of interests, as to the formation of groups."[33]

In liberal-democratic systems, "outside" dissenters would move toward the formation of *associational* interest groups; in the USSR, insofar as dissenters are "organized," they are beyond the law, while *institutional* interest groups—e.g., the armed forces, the police, and (some) industrial managers—have a monopoly on officially tolerated "groupism." Interests outside the latter umbrella can, for the most part, be articulated only in ways that may be dealt with by the authorities as criminal. Herein, precisely, may be seen the reflection of "deformed modernity" as it affects the articulation of political demands. Given the level of differentiation in Soviet society and the degree to which the existence of differentiated spheres of activity has produced "criteria of action specific to these spheres" among those who function within them,[34] the system provides an incommensurately small number of mechanisms for expressing demands dictated by such criteria.[35]

Recognition that interest articulation through institutional interest groups does exist at the top level of Soviet policy-making raises some interesting questions. Is it possible that, at the Central Committee level or above, the party itself is penetrated by "dissidents" who might at least be potential articulators of the interests of noninstitutional "groups"? Or, to put it differently, does dissidence "cover" some within the power structure, as well as those on the "outside"? On the possible existence of a concealed "democratic" opposition within the leadership, one student of Soviet affairs writes:

> Seen against the background of the ever-growing and increasing reprisals against all kinds and shades of dissidents in the USSR, this sounds like an unlikely paradox. However if, despite the persecutions and arrests, a process of democratization is in progress among the post-Khrushchev leadership, it has its own peculiar dialectical logic. The reactionary elements of the leadership (and it is they who are in power, or else there would be no persecutions) are made very uneasy by the hierarchical proximity of their more democratically inclined colleagues. In the absence of absolute autocracy, which would permit the supreme dictator to eliminate all such top-level "heretics" individually, Brezhnev, Suslov and company can only permit themselves to persecute low-level democratic and opposition circles at the present moment. Thereby they probably reckon on depriving their more democratically inclined colleagues of support among wide sections of the intelligentsia, after which it should not prove too difficult to remove these colleagues. This was exactly the method once used by Stalin against the Trotskyites and other intraparty oppositionals: first there was a purge of the low-level party opposition, then action was taken against Trotsky, Zinoviev, Bukharin, etc.[36]

Supporting evidence for this idea may be found in the boldness with which top-level Soviet scientists like Sakharov have dared to criticize the authoritarian character of the system. In (relatively) close contact with the leadership, they could possibly have reasons for believing that it contains "reasonable and moderate circles."[37] The survival of the *Khronika tekushchikh sobytii* (Chronicle of Current Events) has also caused some to wonder if the KGB may not be penetrated by persons sympathetic to the dissidents. Yet it seems dangerous to rely too heavily on such evidence. After all, Sakharov and the other dissident scientists may simply be *wrong*, and the KGB's failure thus far to suppress the chronicle is subject to other, less optimistic interpretations. In a matter so speculative, it seems to me that the burden of proof must, at least for the present, remain with those who claim that the top leadership *does* include "reformist" elements with links to, or support in, the population of dissidents "outside."

"INSIDERS" AND "OUTSIDERS"

The complexity of Soviet society today is mirrored quite clearly in the variety of dissent itself. Dissent varies not only in style but also in content; not all dissidents criticize the same aspects of the system, for the same reasons. Just as the sphere of the system in which a nondissident works and lives determines to a significant degree his "criteria" and the way he sees the world (for example, a senior scientist at Akademgorodok and a general in the Soviet army undoubtedly see things in differing lights), so the dissidents, being drawn from diverse spheres of a highly differentiated society, show similar differences.

Dissidents holding high positions in a specialized elite and having a certain "authority" rooted in the functions they perform (the paradigm here is Sakharov) are in a sense insiders. Their style and their "prescriptions" and programs for change differ markedly in many cases from those of outsiders—the Amalriks and the Marchenkos—who have no "lever" by which to influence the system and whom the Politburo might regard (quite correctly in its own terms) as not "needed" in any way by society. (If Sakharov can lay claim to some high-level regard as a renowned research physicist and one of the "parents" of Soviet nuclear weapons, there is little to induce the Politburo to view Amalrik as anything more than a "spoiled" historian who "flunked" the defense of his dissertation and has since held a variety of menial and unskilled jobs on the margins of Soviet life.)

If one is, like Sakharov, on the inside, one's protest, logically enough, takes the form of persuasion aimed at the political elite. Hence, Sakharov's manifesto, "Thoughts on Progress, Peaceful Co-existence, and Intellectual Freedom,"[38] radical as it may be in content, is an attempt to *convince* the leadership of the "error of their ways" and make them realize the counterproductiveness of continuing "to do business as usual." Needless to say, Amalrik's *Will the USSR Survive Until 1984?*

is a very different sort of document—part exposé, part gloomy "futurology."[39] It and other documents such as "Time Will Not Wait" reflect the style, the viewpoint, and the position of outsiders whose most frequent and, in many cases, *only* contact with the elite is through the KGB.

But the scope of dissent is even wider than a range of ideas extending from "reformist Leninism" to more radical calls for Western-style multiparty government, full civil liberties, etc. There are other kinds of protest from sources quite different, such as the neo-Slavophiles, the "nationalists," and other groups (some of whom might be lumped together as a "right wing"). Given the current state of Soviet internal policy, the neo-Slavophile *samizdat* journal *Veche* is in no sense reactionary, but manifestos such as "A Nation Speaks" display strong elements of aggressive nationalism, anti-Semitism, and racism, occupying a position in the spectrum of Soviet dissent perhaps somewhat similar to that of Moczar and the Partisan faction in Poland.[40]

Dissent along these lines seems to reflect disgust and disgruntlement at the sham "internationalism" of the CPSU, at the "foreign aid" extended to "brotherly socialist countries" (adherents of this line strongly supported the invasion of Czechoslovakia in 1968), and at any increase in the role played by minority nationalities even in the symbolic structures of government. These "Russites" are, of course, more easily tolerated by the regime than the other types of dissenters, as much of their "program" makes them supporters of the Politburo and Central Committee hardliners. It is also not difficult to surmise that they must be well represented in the military and the KGB—certainly the predominant "ideology" among the former, their rhetoric, and their "criteria of action" seem more nationalist than anything else.[41] It is indeed quite conceivable that such circles within the elite encourage this sort of opposition, partly as a counterweight to the democratic movement, and partly because they realize how weak a basis the current official ideology provides for any kind of emotional linkage with the regime.[42]

To whatever degree the Russites may be manipulated by the leadership (or by some elements within the leadership), however, theirs seems to be as authentic a reaction to the system as that of the "democratic opposition." The currents of aggressive nationalism, anti-Semitism, and xenophobia are strong, and the brand of Marxism-Leninism that has been communicated to the Soviet masses over the years has done little to discourage them. The sectors of the system where such feelings flourish are no less integral parts of Soviet society than are those which tend to produce liberal dissenters.

DISSENT AND THE SOVIET POLITY

In the preceding pages, dissent in the USSR has been portrayed as a "natural" phenomenon arising out of the interplay between the growing complexity, or differentiation, of a rapidly modernizing Soviet society, on the one hand, and the persistent reliance by the regime on what have been termed "command-centralist" modes of integrating the differentiated segments of society in the face of rising demands for autonomy on the part of these segments, on the other. This leads us to the much more difficult task of assessing the long-term impact that dissent is likely to have on the future evolution of the Soviet polity.

To begin with, it seems doubtful that the alternatives that the Soviet system faces can be so succinctly summarized as "transformation" or "degeneration," "adaptation" or "decay," etc. The USSR is, after all, an amazingly stable society.[43] The institutional framework that had crystallized under Stalin by the mid-1930s remains essentially unaltered, and it shows no signs of imminent alteration. Despite all that has been said about insecurity in office as one of the characteristics hampering the administration of public affairs in the USSR, the average *apparatchik* seems, rather, to have a tight grip on job security and a real stake in the system. In an era when most "revolutions" have turned out to be somewhat ephemeral, the Soviet state and party have successively survived bloody civil war, a coercive transformation of the countryside costing millions of lives, the Stalinist terror of 1936–38, and the trauma of World War II. Few systems can boast such staying power, and those that can would seem to be unlikely candidates for degeneration in a period of relatively greater tranquillity.[44]

The *apparatchiki*, then, would appear to be still firmly in control. Even if there *is* internal dissent within the top-level elite, the conservatives would seem to have the advantage over any reformist elements —and they can "turn on" more repression at will, or back off when they deem it expedient. Moreover, they are not likely to lose their advantage. There are at least three reasons why this is so—reasons that have to do with interest articulation, the political culture, and the balance of resources.

Interests *are* articulated in the Soviet polity—not all interests, but certainly those which seem critical for the survival of the system. The large institutional interest groups are, in one way or another, "taken care of." They are not ignored, for they are important mainstays of the system. But this is scarcely true of the dissenters, even those belonging to the scientific-technical intelligentsia. The regime has largely ignored their demands, without any apparent reduction of its stability. Once again, the burden of proof would seem to fall upon those who argue that failure to respond to these demands must have important consequences for the system—at least in the reasonably foreseeable future.

The political culture links the bureaucratic elite and the masses more closely than it links the dissidents to either. The institutional framework that emerged in the Stalin era fitted fairly well with the antecedent political culture of Tsarist Russia at the most critical points, and to all appearances the *contemporary* Soviet political culture still fits this relatively unchanged institutional pattern quite well also.

The current culture, as reflected in the attitudes, the demands, the perceived "issues," and the general mental "set" of the masses toward the polity, might be said to be in a state of arrested development. The masses as a whole do *not* demand "legality," representative institutions, "freedom," which to them are unfamiliar and exotic concepts. Their economic demands are modest and are being met—if slowly and with occasional setbacks—so far as housing, consumer goods, and food are concerned. Perhaps, sometime in the not so distant future, they can even look forward to owning a Zhiguli car. In their own terms, they "never had it so good." Many of them have not even heard of the dissenters whose names are now so well known in the West, and those who have generally react in ways ranging from hostility to incomprehension—reactions that would hardly seem to justify the relatively optimistic view of the "popular masses" which some (though by no means all) of the dissenters themselves apparently entertain.[45] While dissent and dissenters may indeed be a natural product of more than fifty years of Soviet rule—and indeed may be "symptomatic" of Soviet society in its current phase of development—equally natural is the failure of the dissenters to strike a responsive chord among the masses at large, whose mentality is similar in so many important ways to that of the *apparatchiki* who rule in their name.

Finally, there is the problem of resources, by which we mean the essential sinews of political power. No detailed examination of these resources need be attempted here; for our purposes it suffices simply to ask in whose hands command of these resources resides. Who controls finances, jobs, and the preponderance of information available to the masses? Who has "legitimacy"—insofar as this can be measured? Who presently commands enough specialized expertise to keep the system running? In each of these cases, the answer seems clear: the party-government elite, which—in spite of the absence of institutionalized arrangements for the transfer of power at the top—has nevertheless proven remarkably successful in "replenishing" itself and preserving the foundations of its power.

By comparison, what are the resources at the disposal of the dissidents? While it may be true, as Robert Dahl has observed, that advanced economies "automatically distribute political resources and political skills to a vast variety of individuals, groups, and organizations," it is also true, as Dahl acknowledges, that there is no close correspondence between levels of economic development and the character of political systems.[46] Admittedly, the dissidents are by no means without resources, but those resources and their "convertibility" into power (or, more accurately, influence) are difficult to measure. A good deal of scientific and technical expertise? Yes, but presumably there is an adequate supply of such expertise available from the *non*dissident intelligentsia. Idealism, as opposed to the regime's cynicism/realism? Certainly, but in political competition idealists have generally fared no better, and perhaps worse, than realists. Again, some dissident factions have shown a capacity for innovative challenges to authority—witness the relative success of the Jewish emigration movement—but can this long continue in the face of "legal" responses like the "education tax"? Most difficult to assess, probably, is the relevance of nonelite mass support, as in the cases of nationalist and religious dissidence; but in any case this would seem to be a resource that could be mobilized to full effectiveness only in the presence of some critical *external* challenge to the system. Certainly, so far as the institutional levers of power are concerned, the dissidents at present control *none*, and this is critical.

In sum, while resources and skills may now be more widely distributed in the USSR than ever before and quite possibly the maintenance of centralistic, "hegemonic" political control is becoming more costly and inefficient as the society itself becomes more advanced, nevertheless the balance of resources today still seems to favor the maintenance of a hegemonic system.

SHAPE OF THE FUTURE

If change should eventually come, one can conceive that it might arise from one of two potential causes that at present are quite unpredictable: the massive trauma of protracted war and the failure of the "center" to hold, as in Amalrik's picture of "1984"; or the natural process of recruitment into the party bureaucracy of a new generation of cadres who,

as products of the post-Stalin era, might be "different" from their predecessors and more responsive to the issues now being raised by the dissenters but ignored by the institutional interest groups that have places
at the bargaining table of power today.

What change born of the trauma of war would be like is uncertain in
the extreme. Amalrik himself is unclear on this.[47] However, the possibility of the emergence of a relatively "democratic" polity of the sort
many of the dissidents apparently desire seems very slight indeed. Soviet
soil seems no more hospitable to such an outcome today than it was
in 1917. Moreover, speculations based on the occurrence of some such
trauma seem rather futile at present.

What, then, of the possible emergence of a new generation of bureaucrats more responsive to the need for change, more willing to grant
autonomy to diverse interest groups and to accept, for the party, the
more modest role of interest broker/conciliator? Jonathan Harris describes this hope of some of the younger intelligentsia:

> The younger members of the intelligentsia, in particular the students,
> are most coherent about the nature of change and most optimistic
> about the future. In their view, it is not the Soviet system per se
> which fails to respond to people's needs, but the present aged and
> rigid leadership. They place their hopes in a new generation of CPSU
> leaders, totally untainted by Stalinism. In their view, those who joined
> the CPSU after Stalin's death cannot possibly share the authoritarian
> outlook of the present generation of leaders, all of whom built their
> careers over the bodies of their colleagues who perished in the purges
> of the 1930s. Although now obliged to repeat the slogans of their
> superiors in the party, this younger group, it is argued, will be more
> willing to dismantle the controls over intellectual life when it takes
> over the reigns of leadership in the 1970s and 1980s. As one student
> insisted, the coming generation of CPSU leaders will be as receptive
> to new ideas as to jazz and miniskirts.[48]

Given our limited access to Soviet society, the fact that such hopeful
optimism is entertained by some who are part of that society should of
course be taken seriously. Yet some pessimism seems in order. The
CPSU is, after all, very much a *minority* of Soviet society, and the
segment of it that occupies the seats of real power is even smaller. The
CPSU does its own recruiting, and it does so according to its own priorities, its own mental framework, its own political culture; it is *not* a
voluntary association that one simply "joins." Even if a gap does exist
in the USSR between the older and the younger *political* generations,

with most of the youth on the relatively liberal side (though this is itself still open to question), will there not be among the young a sufficient supply of potential new cadres whose outlook is closer to that of the current *apparat* than to that of their liberal-minded "peers" to assure the continuation of the current pattern of political rule well into the 1970s and 1980s? Who is getting "in" now, if not former Komsomol activists and others whose attitudes are "acceptable" to the party? Can we assume that their "repetition of slogans" is merely a means of self-protection, or is it evidence of the same complacent satisfaction with the status quo that marks their elders? Today, aging men in the Politburo and Central Committee adamantly oppose the movements of dissenters generally younger than themselves. Is it not possible that tomorrow the dissenters will still be opposed by succeeding leaders closer to their own ages?

The fact is that the style of party rule has been a relatively stable thing, and for the reasons just mentioned it seems likely to remain so. It is the style which those who will take command in the 1970s and 1980s have been learning during their years of apprenticeship, and which they will probably bring into office with them. And it is precisely this style that most of the young dissenters of today are protesting and seeking to change. On balance, there is little reason to expect that their party peers will be significantly more receptive to their aspirations than are the present party leaders.

What, then, does all this signify in terms of the Soviet future? The widely accepted image of the Soviet polity as one that is immobile and faces degeneration or decay because of its inability to cope with the problems involved in managing an increasingly complex economy and society is a striking one, although it has recently been subjected to challenge from various scholars, including Jerry Hough.[49] Whatever the merits or weaknesses of such an image, it seems clear that many Soviet dissidents see the system in this light. But immobility, even if that term accurately characterizes the present state of the system, does not necessarily signify weakness. The polity may or may not be increasingly "irrelevant" to the economy and society; yet can one conclude that it cannot "hang on," or that the swelling of dissidence since the mid-1960s points the way to a different future?

To acknowledge, as Paul Hollander does, that the Soviet bureaucracy "is at once a barrier to significant change and a major pillar of the frozen stability of Soviet society" is not to prove that the bureaucracy itself will eventually be *forced* to yield to change, whether in the direction the dissenters wish or in others; the acknowledgment is, rather, a testimonial to the strength of that bureaucracy and its potential for endurance.[50] The "democratic movement" has a great deal to overcome, and for now at least the balance of advantage appears to lie with the bureaucratic immobilism of the current collective leadership and its supporters. The costs of managing a complex, differentiated society by command techniques may indeed be mounting, but even if this is the case, one cannot predict with any certainty when the bill will come due.

THREE

GENERATIONS AND POLITICS IN THE USSR

The "collective leadership" which displaced Nikita Khrushchev in 1964, and which in its early phase evoked so much speculation about the viability of committee rule in the USSR, has endured a decade and more—an impressive record in a period of global political instability. But whether one is inclined to persist in calling it collective rule or chooses to refer to "Brezhnev's Politburo" (he, at least, restored its old name), the members of the ruling body of the Communist Party of the Soviet Union (CPSU), the watchdog of the Soviet state and society, have aged. Gradually but inevitably, they will leave the scene, making way for their successors.

This chapter is *not* a venture in "Kremlinology." I do not propose to wade in surnames or to assess the durability of a Kirilenko succession in the face of claims by a Kulakov or by others more junior. Nor is it my intention to explore the factors militating for the inclusion or exclusion, in an emergent new leadership, of particular personalities

Originally published in *Problems of Communism* (September- October 1975), 24(5): 20–31.

among those eligible.[1] What the following discussion will attempt to do is to clarify some important aspects of contemporary Soviet political reality—mainly the problem (or nonproblem) of "generations" and the properties of Soviet political culture—as they relate to the politics and consequences of succession. Consideration of these matters will not enable us to predict the main personalities in the succession (at least I do not see how it can). What it may yield are some reasoned judgments, grounded in historical experience, concerning the path any new Politburo, *whatever* its composition, can be expected to follow, and how it will probably cope with both inherited problems and new ones.

GENERATIONS AND CHANGE

One might as well, at the outset, surrender to the temptation to use the term "generation"—but not without a caveat. The temptation is especially strong for Western analysts because the tenure of the Brezhnev-Kosygin "regime," whose passing is now anticipated in the near future, coincides roughly with an epidemic of youthful alienation, student revolt, and other manifestations of generational cleavage in the industrial West—a once seemingly endless crisis that peaked in 1968 and has only recently shown signs of abatement.[2] The Soviet Union was *apparently* free of such tensions, although they did affect Poland, Yugoslavia, and Czechoslovakia. But were they, perhaps, smoldering beneath the tranquil surface? If generational chasms open wide everywhere else, why should the USSR, despite its impressive apparatus of internal control, remain untouched? And if "youth" versus "age" is not the critical confrontation there, is it not still reasonable to surmise that the convictions and expectations of the "middle-aged"—the educated, "industrial" generation—may differ greatly from those of the "gerontocracy" in the Politburo?

In trying to assess whether generational differences exist and, if so, what their political impact is, or is likely to be, we should beware of confusing our own hopes and expectations with reality, or with evidences of what we assume to be reality. This is an easy danger to succumb to, especially when we have the convenient peg of generations (for we know one generation *must* succeed another) on which to hang our expectations, and the danger should be recognized as such.[3] Perhaps, after all, it is not the seeming gap between generations, but rather the impregnable solidity of the Soviet system, the stability of the Soviet "way of life" as it involves masses, elite, and the political process, that is the datum—the reality rather than the appearance. At least, raising this possibility provides a starting point for posing questions about Soviet generations and their relevance to the prospects for political change in the USSR.

These generational questions involve two distinct groups. First, there is Soviet "youth," i.e., the under-thirty population. Does a broad gap divide it from the Brezhnev generation and if so, what is the gap *about*, and will it make a difference to the future of Soviet politics? Second, there is the generation of presumptive Politburo "successors," those no longer young but younger than the current leadership. Do its members view their current rulers across some sort of chasm, and if so, is the nature of the chasm such that their succession to power can be expected to make a difference?

The question of youth can be handled in relatively short order. Western journalists are still inclined, on occasion, to point to the dissatisfaction of Soviet young people with the lack of consumer goods, to their desire for more rock music, miniskirts, blue jeans, etc., as evidences of a generation gap, and—more important—they view this gap as the portent of a transformed political future. It is understandable enough that they should be impressed by such manifestations of youthful discontent. One must gather impressions from *someone*, and Soviet young people are much more ready than their elders to talk freely to Westerners. However, the political implications are open to question, for such a gap—between youth who yearn for a certain life-style and their parents and political leaders who often deplore it—has demonstrably little to do with politics. (To paraphrase Andrei Amalrik, socialism with bare knees does not equal socialism with a human face.)

The fact is that Soviet youth in the mass is less differentiated from its elders along critical political lines than is its counterpart in the West. The combined machinery of tightly controlled youth organizations and a traditional, nonpermissive educational system focused on the "adult" concern of preparation for the world of work, rather than on providing a hiatus between infancy and maturity in which one "explores" one's feelings, beliefs, and needs, has had its effect. The social space in which Soviet youth might develop its own group consciousness, its own set of political orientations, has been tightly circumscribed by that machinery. Also, material affluence and a modicum of privacy, which have been essential to the development of youth cultures in the West, are still lacking in the USSR. Whatever generation gap does exist there, it does not involve a politicized "youth culture."

Even if such a culture did exist, it could have no near-term political effect, since it is not from youth's ranks that the successors to today's "gerontocracy" will come. Unlike the U.S. Congress, the mechanisms of Soviet government have not yet reached the point of welcoming those in their late twenties and early thirties to a share of the seats in power. Thus, the relevance of the current political convictions of Soviet youth, whether they be oppositional (unlikely) or conformist-apolitical (more likely), lies only in the distant future, by which time those convictions may or may not have changed but will certainly no longer be the convictions of youth.

More relevant, surely, are questions about those who *will* succeed to power, and what we may expect from them as the iron law of the actuary works to change the composition of the Politburo in their favor. Here, if there is a "gap" which will have a marked effect on the conduct of Soviet politics, it must, in my view, be of a particular type. Certainly we may anticipate gaps—in styles of management, in readiness to rely on technical expertise, in propensity to employ Marxism-Leninism as a rationalization for actions—that arise from career differences. An older generation whose educational/professional credentials were often attained after their potential leadership ability was noted by the party and a younger one whose similar credentials were their "ticket" of admission into the lower ranks of the elite can doubtless be expected to behave differently in some cases. But these differences, however significant, are not the stuff of which political transformations are made. The gap must come in the realm of "political culture" itself—in that region where questions about the purposes and uses of politics are explicitly raised. This being the case, it is well now to turn to an examination of political culture in the contemporary USSR.

SOVIET POLITICAL CULTURE

Years ago, one of the pioneering students of political culture argued that it was the product of "both the collective history of a political system and the life histories of the individuals who currently make up the system."[4] Considering what those histories have been in the USSR, it is hardly surprising that an astute analyst of Soviet affairs quite recently characterized the political culture of the Soviet Union as "almost unbelievably aberrant and deviant."[5] The Soviet political culture is clearly rooted in the extraordinary history of Russia over the last sixty years, portions of which, greater or smaller, have shaped the consciousness of both the elites and the masses. Without attempting an exhaustive inventory, I would argue that three major historically rooted elements characterize the current political culture: apoliticality, the conviction of impotence, and expectancy.

Apoliticality

It might seem paradoxical to assert that in a society so evidently "politicized," where such a wide range of behavior is accorded political significance by the regime, the overwhelming mass of the population is apolitical. Yet the paradox is only apparent. It is all very well to emphasize the heavily politicized content of the educational processes and the mass media, to which all Soviet citizens are exposed. It is, however, a very different thing to assert that this exposure results in a politicized population. If anything, the major effects—and probably the main purposes—of official socialization and communications efforts have been and are, on the one hand, to assure the public that there *are* no more major domestic political issues (these having all been resolved correctly and immutably in the course of Soviet history) and, on the other, to depoliticize social and economic issues, such as housing, incomes policy, environmental preservation, and access to education, in order to prevent discussions of these matters from reaching the point where any kind of political change might be entertained, even hypothetically, as a necessary step toward their resolution. If indeed these *have* been the purposes of the regime's virtual monopoly of education, communications, and extra-familial socialization, they have been pursued with vigor—and effectiveness—for the more than forty years since Stalin initiated the "second revolution."

To say that most Soviet citizens are apolitical is not to say that they are "parochials," as were, no doubt, many of the inhabitants of the Russian Empire, to whom the state was little more than a tax gatherer. Today's citizens are quite aware that they have a central government (they could scarcely escape such awareness); they are oriented *toward* it; indeed, in some generalized sense, they are in large measure loyal to it. But the fact of that government as a political mechanism, as an arena in which conflicts at high levels are resolved, with consequences for those citizens, remains vague and blurred.

Nor do most Soviet citizens, at least to my knowledge, find this strange. To them, "politics," insofar as its existence is perceived, is the business of the leaders, not of the common folk. Enough for them to identify with the system and to focus their grumblings about the vicissitudes of everyday life on the middle- and low-level bureaucrats (whom they see excoriated with monotonous regularity anyway in the pages of *Pravda* and *Izvestiia*).[6] Notwithstanding all the complaints of *Agitprop* about inadequate ideological training, low levels of political consciousness, etc., on the part of the masses, the Soviet leadership is probably quite satisfied, on balance, that it has such a docile population to deal with, presenting little need at the moment for the regime to resort to coercion to keep it in line. Those who view the complaints of *Agitprop* and ideological specialists about "shortcomings" as the tip of an iceberg whose submerged mass contains widespread, smoldering resentment forget that, like any bureaucratic organization, *Agitprop* must justify its continued existence, expenditures, and personnel demands. The line that in spite of great progress to date, there is yet "more to be done" is a conventional way of doing this.

Of course, the threat of coercion also plays a role in encouraging apoliticality. If one were to paraphrase Anthony Downs and attempt to construct an "economic theory" of Soviet "posttotalitarianism," one element would be the costs of political participation going beyond the permissible limits prescribed by the system.[7] In a democracy, citizens may remain politically uninvolved because they feel the system works tolerably well; or, alternatively, because they may calculate that the costs of political action to remedy the defects that they perceive are too high—in terms of energy, time, money, and foregone opportunities for other, nonpolitical gratifications—when balanced against the potential benefits to be gained. For citizens in a polity of the Soviet type, the costs of engaging in unsponsored political activity are high, and they are clear—harassment, loss of job, imprisonment—while the potential benefits are few and doubtful. The cost-benefit calculus is thus much clearer in the East than in the West, and it is one that leads many citizens of Soviet-type polities to prefer a safe apoliticality to a risky political activism.

(It is precisely this calculus that Solzhenitsyn has in mind in his recent writings when he urges people to withdraw support from the "official lie." Addressing himself to the intelligentsia, he argues that one cannot fight for change without costs, on "weekends and in our spare time, without giving up our scientific research institutes." Moreover, he warns that each citizen *will* stand alone, "in chilling isolation," at least at the outset; yet he invites his countrymen to brave the punishment they will receive for even the nonviolent, "spiritual," but *open* resistance he encourages: "A society so vicious and polluted . . . can only be cured and purified by passing through a spiritual filter. And this filter is a terrible one, with holes as fine as the eye of a needle, each big enough for only one person. And people may pass . . . only one at a time, by squeezing through. By deliberate, voluntary sacrifice.'"[8] If not utopian, Solzhenitsyn's exhortation is certainly idealistic. It asks much, perhaps too much, of a people for whom the consequences of open opposition have been only too clear.)

These observations may throw the particular "heresy" of Soviet dissidents into sharper relief. It is rooted not so much in opposition as in laying claim to participation. To be a dissident is to enter politics without a license, to participate without official sponsorship. It is to attempt (as in the writings of the Solzhenitsyns, Medvedevs, and Sakharovs) to restore "politics" as a weighing of alternatives. This is the major crime of the dissenters; their break with the apoliticality of the mass political culture.

The Conviction of Impotence

A different matter from apoliticality is an individual's socially conditioned assessment of his own political *efficacy*. Concerned he may or may not be about politics—but if he *were* concerned, could he have any effect? Were he to translate generalized feelings of support or opposition into action, would his acts strengthen or weaken the system in any way, or are the levers of power so far removed from reach as to make such efforts pointless?

This is a broad question, but the answer, in my view, is fairly clear. The Soviet citizen, whether comfortable or not with the feeling, experiences a sense of his own powerlessness. Though writing in the different context of the "Sovietization" of Eastern Europe, the Polish émigré writer Juliusz Mieroszewski captures this point well when he notes that the "goal [of Sovietization] is acceptance—not of the system (the party does not depend on this) but of one's own impotence."[9] And indeed, the whole history and experience of the Soviet population could scarcely have had any other effect. The Soviet people have been "mobilized" for industrial and agricultural efforts, for defense and reconstruction—and always from the top, whence their revolution emanated. Though sometimes consultative in style (for example, when discussions on public issues are conducted in the press with "broad representation" of public views), Soviet politics has been manipulative and prescriptive in substance. The great political decisions of Soviet history—ranging from Stalin's commitment to the rigors of coercive and rapid modernization, through Khrushchev's denunciation of the Stalin cult, to the current leadership's decision to pursue détente—may have been received with pain or pleasure by the masses, but they did not emanate from any structured participation by the masses in determining the course of policy.

No less able than other peoples to distinguish reality from appearance, the Soviet people have drawn the proper conclusions from such historical examples as to their place in the system. If we accept the view of Valery Chalidze that the regime has in any case convinced the population at large that it is the only possible regime and that, whatever flaws it may possess, "any other conceivable regime would be frightful,"[10] then such conclusions may not be painful for the majority. For the minority who harbor the germs of a "participant" orientation, for the "middle class" which has much to gain from legality, predictability, and rationality, the conviction that they are powerless, that to protest is to beat one's head against a wall, is no doubt agonizing, but it is nonetheless a real conviction.[11]

What Soviet political culture *lacks*, in a sense, is a citizenry, in the normative sense of a collectivity of persons, with participant orientations toward politics adequate to support movement toward what Gabriel A. Almond and Sidney Verba have called the "civic culture"—i.e., toward democracy. As these authors noted, democracies do not rely on participants alone; they require subjects and parochials as well, in a viable mix.[12] But when participants are in such short supply as they are today in the USSR, the prospects for democracy seem bleak indeed— even if a liberalizing regime were to plant the appropriate seeds.[13] The contemporary mass political culture may not require the type of government the USSR now possesses. It could tolerate and support a wider range of authoritarian or totalitarian, looser or tighter political structures—but hardly stable democracy. The point is not only that the older Soviet generations have been trained to the garrison disciplines of totalitarianism, but also that *no* generation has been socialized into the disciplines of democratic participation.[14]

Although the general schema formulated by Almond and Verba provided a framework for examining specifically democratic polities, one element of their characterization of a "subject-participant" culture is suggestive in the Soviet case: "Because participant orientations have spread among only a part of the population, and because their legitimacy is challenged by the persisting subject subculture and suspended during authoritarian interludes, the participant-oriented stratum of the population cannot become a competent, self-confident, experienced body of citizens."[15]

Many of the Soviet dissidents have a full participant orientation, but they are a minuscule part of the population. Their demands meet resistance and incomprehension from the persisting "subject" culture, shared by rulers and ruled alike. And the "authoritarian interlude," I would argue, extends over the whole of Soviet history.

What is most interesting—and potentially relevant—here is the connection of Soviet elites, including the "successors," to the mass political culture. As children, young adults, and persons commencing their careers, they imbibed that mass culture with its reflections of official dogma—i.e., the "demonology" of the encircling capitalist world and the roseate picture of a remote Communist future—and with its clear indications of penalties awaiting those who might aspire to political participation on any but its own terms. Their entrance into the "elite" political culture involves further socialization—into the uses and pleasures, the problems and risks, of power. The power they now possess makes them anything *but* impotent. Yet their intermediate, pre-elite socialization—as wielders of derivative power on the lower levels of party and state bureaucracies—can scarcely have done other than impress upon them the endurance, the immutability of the Soviet polity and its game rules. From such material, one does not anticipate the emergence of personalities who will transform the political system in any fundamental way.

Expectancy

This term admittedly lacks precision; if anything, it is distinguished mainly by its crudity. Yet it connotes an important fact, namely, that Soviet citizens, despite their apoliticality and convictions of impotence, are strongly oriented toward their polity's "outputs." Subjects and *not* parochials, they expect things of the state. And herein lies one of the main sources of the stability of the system—but also a source of potential danger, for the edge of expectancy can cut both ways.

Delivery of expected output, or delivery of the unexpected but welcome good or service, *has* been as critical a part of the Soviet mass experience of governmental performance as the deprivations the regime has imposed. The high evaluations placed by Soviet citizens on the provision of socialized medical care and universal basic education, as well as on the career and upward mobility opportunities afforded by the expansion of higher education, were major stimuli of social support for the regime even in the Stalin years, as mass interviewing of the refugees of that era demonstrated.[16] Largesse is scarcely the rationale for governmental provision of such services and opportunities; an industrial-izing regime needs to provide them in order to develop, mobilize, and maintain a more "modern" population and labor force. But the Soviet population, with a *historically* low level of expectancy (or output ori-entation), may experience them as "goods" freely allocated, to be bal-anced against the rigors and deprivations of a totalitarian regime.

Chalidze spoke recently to this point, blaming the "ideologues" for not informing the population that "the payment of pensions or the allocation of new apartments is not something for which the govern-ment should be thanked, but rather something that should be viewed as an obligation of the government under the Soviet economic sys-tem."[17] His criticism is no doubt well warranted, but the critical point here is that the ideologues may and probably have succeeded quite well in convincing the population that the government *is* to be thanked for such benefits.

(The relative moderation of Soviet mass expectations despite lifelong exposure to utopian rhetoric also contributes to stability. Modest but steady improvements in housing, in the availability of consumer du-rables, in the provision of food, have apparently been sufficient to keep the rank and file from Minsk and Omsk satisfied with their lot until that day when "Communism achieved" will banish scarcity.[18] Al-though, by Western standards, Soviet life is still mean and shabby, one of the greatest accomplishments of the regime, as "manager" of its subjects' expectations, has been to insure that Western standards do not become a critical reference point.)

This, however, is only one side of the coin: expectancy may also prove a source of weakness. To the degree that I am correct in arguing here that public expectations are a stable and important part of the Soviet mass political culture, they can be potentially dangerous in the event that they are abruptly violated.

Recent Soviet history provides us with examples of these dangers. The violent civil disturbances in Novocherkassk in 1962, evoked by sudden rises in the cost of foodstuffs the population expected to continue receiving at relatively stable prices, is a well-known one—and I doubt that any serious student would believe this to have been the *only* such disturbance that has occurred for such reasons. Andrei Amalrik under-scored precisely these considerations in his "1984" essay. He argued that working-class irritations and discontent, though real, were neu-tralized to a considerable degree by material progress, but speculated that a break in that progress, "an abrupt slowdown in the growth of prosperity, a halt or a move backwards, would evoke such strong outbursts of dissatisfaction, combined with violence, as would previously have been impossible."[19]

Other evidence, of a different sort, points to the powerful effect of the socialization processes in developing a certain level of "expectancy" among Soviet citizens. Some Soviet émigré arrivals in Israel, it seems, find the adjustment to a life and economy with less structured and formalized allocative mechanisms difficult. Even professionals alienated from the Soviet system—artists, doctors, scientists, etc.—seem in retrospect to have been "well adjusted" in the sense that their expectations with regard to a guaranteed market for their canvases and services, guaranteed facilities for their work, etc., had been met in the USSR, so that they found the absence of these advantages in Israel a source of difficulty.

Today, as Western nations face severe economic problems and domestic turmoil, the Soviet Union, as usual, seems quite stable—no doubt owing, in part, to an acceptable performance in meeting the mass expectations of the Soviet people. Yet the USSR has no guarantee that it can manage to do so indefinitely. If circumstances should reduce its output capacity, the expectancies built into the political culture, which now *support* the regime, could well turn against it. The risks inherent in building stability on capacity to "deliver" reflect the fact that virtually *all* the socialist regimes in the Soviet orbit—albeit in varying degrees—have moved "from utopia to pragmatism" as a central legitimating principle. Their claim on mass loyalties is rooted, now more than ever before, in their ability to "deliver the goods" within a demand structure that they can seek to moderate but cannot transform substantially or suppress.[20]

The Soviet political culture has been fashioned by history—by the history of the system (the blueprint of which is still so much the product of Stalin), by the life histories of Soviet citizens, and indeed by the history of pre-Soviet Tsarist Russia as well. There is thus the force of *inertia* behind it, a tremendous inertia which must be taken into account in any attempt to anticipate political change in the USSR, and which should make us wary of speculations that rely too heavily on an inexorable "logic" of development of the Soviet system or on the "necessity" of change as a result of the difficulty of carrying out coordinating and integrative tasks in an increasingly complex USSR. The impact of history, as we see it in the political culture it has formed, should not be slighted in answering the questions raised at the start about generation gaps. Some of the answers that relate to the short-term prospects for change are implied in this section. Explicit answers may be deferred until after we have examined some forces which may militate for long-term change—in particular, the various currents of dissent that have emerged in the last ten years and seem to point toward a differentiation of the political culture.

DISSENT: ALTERNATIVE SUBCULTURES

When the history of the Soviet Union of the 1960s and 1970s is written, dissent will figure as a major phenomenon. On the other hand, the system's phenomenal stability, its failure to crack or to change in character under the assaults of the politically alienated, will provide an equal amount of grist for the historian's mill.

Despite the stability of the system, dissent has nonetheless demonstrated the rise of differentiated political "subcultures" in the USSR, or at least shown that the seeds of such subcultures do exist. If the concrete manifestations of dissent might have been unpredictable, the emergence of the underlying attitudes could have been foreseen. The manifold problems arising from a policy of coordinating the relations between the polity and the specialized functional sectors of an increasingly complex system—i.e., between *apparat* and "functional elites"—in accordance with predominantly command rather than exchange criteria (see chapter 2) have worked to alienate some of those elites and even to cause them to deny the legitimacy of the system. However, a complementary phenomenon, pinpointed by Rudolf Tökes in a recent essay,[21] complicates any projections one might make on the basis of this alienation: while the regime since the mid-1960s has lost legitimacy in the eyes of many members of functional elites, its legitimacy has probably *grown* for the masses as a whole. As suggested above, the main reason for this is very likely that the regime has delivered the goods in material terms, thereby responding to the "secularized" criteria of legitimacy by which the masses measure governmental performance.

Dissent, then, has been generally—though not totally—an enterprise of the elite. Occupational status, education, and the remnants of a critical tradition among the intelligentsia have made the elites—scientific, technical, and creative—the logical carriers of "pure" political dissent, that is, of dissent which challenges the system as a whole. This kind of dissent requires the ability to construct and manipulate abstract ideas, to conceptualize political alternatives, to ask basic questions about the goals of the policy as well as its methods, whether in a "moral absolutist" or an "instrumental-pragmatic" framework.[22] The dissenters' prescriptions for change are diverse—ranging from Sakharov's advocacy of liberal democracy, through Solzhenitsyn's appeal for a benevolent and depoliticized authoritarianism (the furthest he deems the current leadership capable of going), to Medvedev's return to "true" Leninism —but all represent alternative systems, not simply "adjustments" in the polity of today. This may even be the case with some of the neo-nationalist, "Russite" dissent, which supports new forms of authoritarian politics as desirable in themselves.

Two points are worth making with regard to the potential of this variety of dissent. First, it involves only a small minority of those who belong to functional elites. The majority are presumably willing to accept the microlevel "exchange" relationship which exists between themselves and their political superiors and which assures them of relative affluence and security in return for competent service and political quiescence, though it denies them a role in setting goals. Second, the issues raised by the minority of dissenters seem to have little root in, and little resonance with, the concerns of the masses. Indeed, the absence of a link between the elite and the masses is one of the weaknesses of the "democratic movement" that have enabled the regime to contain it and to be flexible in coping with it. The specter of dissident members of the elite helping to generate, and then articulating, active resentments among the masses is one which must at times haunt Soviet leaders, but at present the latter have little reason to worry about so improbable a development.[23]

Very different from "programmatic" political dissent, with its alternatives to the current system, are the national-ethnic and religious forms of dissent. The issues that these kinds of dissent raise *do* concern members of the Soviet masses. At the mass level, "rights" such as the right to worship, to speak a given language, to keep one's identification with a given group, to live in one's own home *within* Soviet borders, mean more than the right to choose between electoral candidates; they are more than abstractions that concern the intelligentsia alone. Here, there is a commonality of concern that links dissident elites and the masses in a common enterprise—the protection and advancement of national and religious identity. But such demands differ from those of the primarily "political" dissenters in that they *could* for the most part be accommodated without major change in Soviet political structures, although they *would* imply changes in the substance of politics. In the ethnic and religious spheres, what the dissenters are demanding, essentially, are *immunities*, not from Soviet law as it it written, but from the systematic violation of legal guarantees that has been an operative principle of the system in action.

It is an interesting irony that the rise of dissident political subcultures around issues of ethnicity and religion is, to a significant degree, the product of Soviet mobilizational successes over the past fifty years. Soviet modernization, as manifested particularly in economic development, in the extension of universal basic education and literacy, even in the development of the state administrative network itself, has moved the non-Russian nationalities far from their predominantly "parochial" political culture of Tsarist times. Among the ethnic masses, there has developed a subject culture in which they are concerned with government outputs, and at the same time at least the germs of a participant culture have been planted among the ethnic elites. Could peasant illiterates "mobilize" in the way the Crimean Tatars have done? Similarly, could traditional agrarian populations, Russian or non-Russian, organize the networks of communication and action in defense of religious identity that groups ranging from the Evangelical Baptists to the Lithuanian Catholics have? The answer is clearly negative. But the process of modernization has distributed to national and religious groups, elite and mass alike, a modicum of *resources* for initiating unconventional political action.

These resources, diffused and limited as they are, can hardly be compared with the centralized coercive resources at the disposal of the regime, but they are more than nothing. They have enabled mixed populations of elite and masses to develop a shared political language and consciousness around certain issues of joint interest; to break, at least partially, with the apoliticality and feelings of impotence of the dominant political culture; and to assert expectations not officially "legitimized." They, like the dissidents whose focus is on the broader issues of political structure, have contributed to the restoration of "politics" in the USSR.

PRESENT AND FUTURE

The past decade has witnessed change in the internal landscape of Soviet political life, change that has emerged not because of but despite the regime's preferences. Manifested in ways ranging from nonviolent demonstrations on Pushkin Square to the creation of the now rich literature of dissent, it amounts to an open assumption by a small but committed stratum of people of a participant orientation toward politics. In *no* sense, however, has this change been legitimized and incorporated into the system. The boundaries of the system have remained stable despite the change in the landscape; dissent has been contained, though not rooted out.[24]

Various analyses during the same decade have offered differing diagnoses of the Soviet system's health. These have ranged from prescriptions that the system must change its ways or die[25] to conclusions that, afflicted though it undoubtedly is by various maladies to which any complex system may be subject, it still "works" effectively enough to rule out any diagnosis of terminal illness.[26] Certainly there have been grounds for both kinds of diagnoses, but more, it seems, for the latter. On balance, the Soviet Union has weathered the past decade rather well. Economic reform has been *very* modest by East European standards, and economic problems persist; but the economy has survived, even with a much smaller influx of Western technology and investment than the regime has eagerly sought. The relationship between the polity and the specialized functional sectors of society has changed little, if at all, but no evidence of consequent instability has yet emerged. In the international arena, the USSR has been the beneficiary of a certain amount of luck, but it has also drawn on its own resources to maximize its advantages. Almost a decade has now passed since some Western analysts saw the alternatives the system faced as transformation or degeneration. The system *has* faced them and has done neither—and it has survived.

Thus, it would appear that those who expect striking changes from the inevitable succession process will be disappointed. Yet it is often hard to temper rhetoric and expectations with recognition of current realities: one analyst suggests that changes to come in the Politburo will be "sweeping and important," but several lines later, in discussing differences in the "formative political experiences" of the current leaders and their presumptive successors, he finds "no strong grounds for believing that they are of major significance."[27] In my own view, any likely newcomers to the Politburo in the next few years have already been sufficiently exposed to the mass and elite variants of the political culture to guarantee that they will resemble their seniors. It is, after all, the only political culture they *know*, and given their ages, they began learning it in the Stalin era, have witnessed its durability in the Khrushchev years, and have seen it support the regime since 1964.

The extreme centralization of *power* in the Soviet system—a fact inexplicably overlooked by many whose reading of "popular" moods leads them to expect change—provides an additional guarantee of continuity. Even if we had strong evidence of generational fissures in the mass political culture, there is no reason to assume that Politburo (and Central Committee) recruitment policies must reflect them. The regime does not engage in random sampling to seek its successors. Those successors are the survivors of a process spanning their prior party-state careers, during which those noted by their seniors for incompetence, failures, or manifestations of heterodox ideas and "instability" have gradually been sifted out. The survivors are consequently all the more likely to lack such "negative" characteristics and to be more like their superiors than not. Moreover, until those superiors themselves move on, they can still demote and remove their presumptive successors. They retain the power to do so, and they will use that power.

There is still a further reason for being chary of placing undue importance on generational differences in the context of the political succession. Leaders are by definition atypical, unrepresentative of the age groups from which they are drawn. This is so in the Soviet Union as well as elsewhere, and there is no reason to assume that it will change. (Many Western scholars have by now spent substantial periods in the USSR, especially in universities. Possibly one can read the Soviet future there, but it is not written on the faces of the "typical" students with whom one may have a good deal of contact, but rather on those of the Komsomol activists, with whom one has rather less contact overall.)

On balance, then, the Politburo of 1980 or thereabouts should resemble in its dynamics—both in the "united" face it presents to the world and in the bureaucratic logrolling, interest brokerage, and infighting it hides—the Politburo of 1975. This is not to say that a "1980 model" Politburo will not introduce important changes in various policies, but only to suggest that it will operate in much the same manner as its predecessor has, combining incrementalism and sudden changes in unequal proportions. "Liberalization" or "tightening" in domestic life are alternative possibilities, as are movements "backward" or "forward" on a number of economic issues; yet, whatever turn decisions on policy issues may take, there seems little warrant to expect that they will be reached more openly, or be based on broader "consultative" practices, than has been the case in the last few years.

A new Politburo will inherit the advantage of a mass political culture which has found regime demands tolerable and output satisfactory in the post-1953 period. Whoever the main "personalities" may be (a matter of speculation, which I leave to others), they will likely maintain a firm grip on the monopoly of power in the face of potential domestic challengers. If events on the global scale do not disturb military security and economic performance, the successors should manage to continue "delivering" in accord with mass expectancies as in the recent past, and their legitimacy, secularized as it may be, will remain secure. If, on the other hand, a military conflict with China should develop and be prolonged to the point of excessive strain on economic and human resources (despite the popular support such a "defensive" war would initially engender), or if a change in the Middle East situation should lead to a large-scale involvement of troops and matériel abroad, history is likely to reassert itself, posing critical questions about the viability of the system under stress.

Then, aspects of the political culture which have been sources of stability could work instead to weaken the system. A regime which rests on the apoliticality of the masses in good times cannot be sure of the continuing support of apolitical masses in bad times. A regime secure by virtue of convictions of political impotence on the part of the masses cannot be confident of security if its coercive resources, which in the final analysis insure that impotence, are overstretched to deal with foreign enemies. And, a regime which has, for all its ideological rhetoric, gained support largely through a thoroughly "secular" satisfaction of the everyday expectations of most of its subjects can lose such support should the expectations grow to the point where they could no longer be met.

FOUR

WORKERS, POLITICS, AND CLASS CONSCIOUSNESS

Any treatment of the Soviet worker's political views must be in large measure impressionistic and unsystematic. First, Soviet social science research, however informative for some purposes, has *not* touched on critical political questions. It has, for the most part, been confined to problems of administration and management—*technique* problems— rather than those of politics, where critical choices are involved.[1]

Second, such social science research has been constrained by the official assumption that political loyalty, support for the system "as is," and views on particular issues are not differentiated by social strata. This, of course, amounts to a denial of much of what Western political sociology—not to mention that of socialist Yugoslavia and Poland— has revealed, and thus preempts investigation of some questions of great interest.

Third, it is likely that the political views of Soviet workers would be

Originally published in Arcadius Kahan and Blair A. Ruble, eds., *Industrial Labor in the USSR* (New York: Pergamon Press, 1979), pp. 313–332.

rather hard to characterize, even if Western or Soviet researchers had free access to them. The political vocabulary of the working class is deficient in analytic and evaluative terms. This is in large measure a product of formal education and informal socialization. The political component of Soviet education, from elementary grades through the university, is an exercise in learning to speak and, to some degree, to think in narrow, conventionalized terms about the Russian and Soviet past and present. Soviet political education mystifies the realities of power, the process of government, and the narrow arena in which "politics" takes place. The same, of course, is true of the organized political socialization which proceeds from level to level in the Oktiabriata, the Pioneers, and the Young Communist League.

Informal socialization is also conducive to limited political perception. If an adult generation knows little of politics, thinks of its leaders as "they," and sees a gulf between "them" and the people as natural and eternal, little can be expected by way of heightened political sophistication among their children. This is not to say that families do not subtly teach children ways of accommodating to and manipulating the system at a "low," personalized level. The family is a major source of such tutoring; but for the Soviet majority and for the majority of the working class, political sophistication is not a legacy of family life.

These qualifiers stated, the dimensions and limits of what we can do become, perhaps, a bit clearer. This chapter will examine the degree to which general indications point to the possibility of a "class"-oriented view of Soviet politics on the worker's part; sources of working-class support for the system; sources of working-class disaffiliation and neutrality vis-à-vis the system.

CLASSNESS AND CLASSLESSNESS

Whether the Soviet "working class" has its own particular perceptions of the political sphere depends on whether the workers actually constitute a "class" as this is understood by political philosophers, political scientists, and sociologists. It is a thorny question. Certainly no official claims are made that the USSR is a classless society. The formula which divides it into two nonantagonistic classes, workers and peasants, and one stratum, the toiling intelligentsia, still holds, although for purposes of sociological investigation this distinction has been found to be too general even for Soviet sociologists.[2] Western commentators miss the point when they tax a supposedly classless Soviet society with its clear disparities in income, prestige, and power; these are evidence of inequality and stratification, but not of the existence or nonexistence of classes.

Do workers exhibit the set of characteristics which loosely add up to "class consciousness"? Do the workers view themselves as a collectivity with common interests opposed to those of other collectivities, and with modes of behavior and an ethos proper to itself alone? Historically, there is little evidence of the emergence of what Feldmesser called "an effective reference group based on its own collectively defined norms."[3] In the twilight of Tsarism, archaic elements militated against it, despite the birth of an urban-industrial proletariat in the 1880s. The estate system remained the sole legal registration of social diversity, reflecting the unwillingness of the autocracy to recognize new forces of differentiation. At the turn of the century, some 90 percent of urban workers were still legally classified as peasants.[4]

Still, the share of second-generation or "hereditary" workers grew, and the concentration of workers in the relatively large factories of industrializing Russia fostered a common, shared consciousness.[5] This was expressed in some measure in industrial unrest in the 1905 revolt and, later, in 1917. It was to this potential class-in-emergence that Bolshevik and other socialist propagandists directed their efforts.

Large classes can maintain themselves better in times of tumultuous change than can small ones. However convincing the evidence that the Russian urban proletariat, increasingly hereditary, came to think of itself as a working class, its small size compared with other social strata is incontrovertible. Civil war and war communism saw it disrupted; the collapse of city-countryside linkages forced workers in Moscow, Petrograd, and other cities to seek food and other minima of survival in the country.

The New Economic Policy—aimed at rebuilding the industrial economy to the level of 1914 in production and capacity—reassembled the industrial work force, but brought no appreciable growth. With Stalin's forced-draft industrialization, this proletarian core was inundated by the massive recruitment of peasants. Just as a generation later the more class-conscious proletarians of Warsaw and Budapest would be dissolved in a massive peasant migration, so were the workers of the Russian cities.[6] The political and literary image of the manager of the 1930s breaking a mass of peasants into "industrial discipline" and "driving them into world production records" is an apt one.[7] However, to do this is to make industrial *workers*, not to forge a working *class* in the political sense. The political focus was to turn these recruits into loyal and supportive Soviet citizens, not to create a working class with its own criteria for judging whether this or that policy of state responded to their needs and desires.

The suppression of the Worker's Opposition and of trade-unionist tendencies within the party and the trade union bureaucracy amplified the effect. No organized force existed to promote working-class consciousness or to aggregate and articulate workers' peculiar interests. The regime did not want to contend with the spontaneous development of different class viewpoints. Where a person would get in Soviet society—from a bureaucrat's desk to a place on the assembly line, a field on a *kolkhoz*, or a space on the boards of a barrack in the *gulag*— would depend on his loyalty and his positive viewpoint. Everyone was expected to manifest loyalty equally, to march to the same drummer —independent of social class or stratum. As Feldmesser puts it, "Loyalty to a political leader and his ideology is...the cause, not the consequence, of one's hierarchical position."[8]

Economic development not only brought peasants into the worker stratum, but took many proletarians out. Upward mobility in these years of the early Five-Year Plans was a phenomenon that has not been recorded adequately, but it cannot have been other than profoundly consequential.[9] It was not so much a matter of co-optation, of the new Soviet regime promoting from the bench to the office the most "conscious," educated, ideologically committed workers. Often those who rose in the *vydvizhenie* were not terribly valued in the factory.[10] Rather, the opportunities to advance oneself through all forms of *rabfaks* by way of extramural and evening education appealed greatly to workers, who could then expect a job in rapidly expanding state bureaucracies. No longer was one tied to one's working-class birth; no longer need one be content in a status not of one's own choosing. Opportunities for mobility operate against class consciousness: they argue the impermanence of membership in a class and offer individual striving as an alternative to the struggle for collective advancement. The Soviet working class was open at both ends; a large aperture at the bottom, through which flowed peasant recruits to arduous and predominantly unskilled work, was complemented by a small but no less significant aperture at the top, through which many would escape the proletariat.

Thus developed the working class in a society which combined substantial stratification with a lack of firmly established hierarchical groups, and a significant "fluidity." Thus it was not dissimilar in some respects to another society whose lack of class orientation and consciousness so struck Europeans—the United States. Both manifested what the Polish sociologist Ossowski called "non-egalitarian classlessness."[11]

Under such conditions, it is difficult to talk about a Soviet working class. The concerns and political perceptions of Soviet workers are not theirs alone. Overlap with the peasantry and with the non-manual strata can be expected, and interstratum differences will often be ones of degree, not kind. There is little evidence in the USSR today of the increasingly assertive class consciousness of some other socialist proletariats. Therefore, it is more appropriate to talk about Soviet workers and the workers' stratum than about the working class.

SUPPORT AND CONFORMITY

It is illuminating and profitable today to read Inkeles and Bauer's *The Soviet Citizen*, a book based on the views of Soviet émigrés during World War II. Two brief quotes are indicative. The first follows the observation that Soviet citizens approved of the welfare state in principle, although they deplored its inadequate practices during the Stalinist era: "It must be recognized that if the regime is able to deliver such welfare benefits as the people expect they will trap a strong reservoir of favorable public sentiment."[12]

The second is also future-oriented in the perspective of the 1950s, but less speculative: "The younger people react more affirmatively to the "positive" aspects and less violently to the negative aspects [of the regime]. . . . younger people [are] more inclined to favor the institutional structure of Soviet society—state ownership, control, and planning and welfare institutions."[13]

Today is that future; the "younger people" are now well into middle age, and the system has delivered. Thirty years of peace have permitted the Soviet system to provide a decent diet, an adequate—if not spectacular—health system, and free public education. Scarcities have abated, and Soviet workers now enjoy many more of life's good things than they did in the past.

There is every reason to argue that the basic political perceptions of the workers' stratum are generally positive and prosystem. In the sphere of material expectations, wants have been met. The Stalin era émigrés heavily favored the retention of public education, socialized medicine, and other welfare-state items.[14] Their condemnation of the regime in no way reduced the attraction of a welfare state; few, even after exposure to the affluence of the United States and Western Europe, were convinced that free enterprise could deliver on their expectations. Given these trends among émigrés, contemporary Soviet workers' lack of exposure to capitalist affluence and their familiarity, through the media, with capitalist inflation and unemployment make them even less likely to perceive a need for basic change in their economy.

Support for socialism is, however, based less on principle than on what it can deliver. Government ownership of the means of production per se was not as salient to émigrés as what they presumably received under such a system. Some evidence indicated that workers were less inclined to risk change in the scope of state ownership than those in higher strata. While intelligentsia, lower white-collar employees, and skilled and ordinary workers overwhelmingly agreed that state ownership and control of transport and heavy industry was worth retaining, their opinions on state control of the light-industry sector were divergent; only about 23 percent of intelligentsia, 24 percent of white-collar employees, and 37 percent of workers favored continued state ownership in this sector.[15] According to Inkeles and Bauer, the greater readiness to have light industry uncontrolled reflects the intelligentsia's somewhat more pronounced ability to project themselves in the role of owners of light industry.[16] Workers, they argue, are likely to take a more dependent stance toward the state as material supplier, although this does not mean that they, any more than other strata, are completely satisfied. It does mean that, so long as they are provided for, they object less to regulated economic life than some elements of the intelligentsia.

The fact that workers are protected from unemployment is no small source of satisfaction. They are also the beneficiaries of a style of industrial organization with a fairly high tolerance for slacking and absenteeism. Trade unions, indeed, are not combative articulators of workers' interests, but managerial concerns about morale and a growing labor shortage soften the demands the system imposes. In one region, workers were estimated to have taken an average of seventeen extra days off, in addition to holidays, during six months in 1971.[17] Official figures, high as they are, probably underestimate illegitimate absenteeism, but its endemic quality is, in a sense, an index of its toleration.[18] Labor productivity figures indicate that Soviet workers do not work as efficiently as their West European counterparts. Part of this can be attributed to the fact that automation and mechanization are comparatively low; but part is probably a result of the fact that Soviet workers do not work as constantly, or as hard.[19]

This looseness of organization in the workplace cuts two ways. If the tolerance of absenteeism and loose enforcement of the rules "against" the worker as well as those "for" him indicates a "soft" aspect of the system which workers perceive positively, is not their absenteeism itself evidence of alienation and disaffection with the hours spent at work? I would answer this affirmatively, but the point to be made here is that the relative toleration of such irresponsible behavior is a concession on which workers depend. What, after all, would be the consequences for workers' perceptions of the regime's policy toward them were there a real tightening of workplace administration?

Delivering on material expectations is not the only reason why the workers generally support the Soviet system. Another, surely, is "Soviet patriotism," a much-abused phrase but one with considerable reality behind it. To the degree that one can derive satisfaction from being part of one of the global units that "counts," the Soviet worker can; he shares the status of citizen of a superpower only with his American and, perhaps, Chinese counterpart. This is no minor matter; knowing less and caring less to know of other systems than the intelligentsia, the workers are all the more readily convinced that their system is the best and that it is worth defending. Whatever the occasional grumblings, the Russian, along with the broader Slavic component of the working class, shows every sign of identifying with the Soviet system; he is receptive to the regime's calls for vigilance against foreign powers with designs on the USSR.[20]

Do workers in general regard the restrictions on movement, speech, and assembly under which they live as a necessary sacrifice in a country still facing the possibility of internal subversion as well as external aggression? Do they see these restrictions as "abnormal"? The evidence, impressionistic as it is, would seem to indicate that they find the restrictions quite bearable. Emigrés of the early postwar period showed, even after exposure to the freedoms of the West, a rather authoritarian turn in their thinking; they tended to respect a government that did not oppress or victimize its citizens, yet did control them for "good" purposes. This was manifested most clearly in the émigrés' evident enjoyment of the freedom the West allowed them as individuals, and in their concern over principles that allowed groups critical of the government to operate openly.[21]

Little seems to have changed in this respect. The twenty years and more of uncertain, up-and-down liberalization since Stalin's death has whetted the appetites of some of the intelligentsia for more autonomy.

However, that relative liberalization has removed much of what earlier alienated the workers; in their eyes, the system is probably more legitimate than ever.[22] It was terror, not control, that the workers feared; they dreaded arbitrary punishment, not the stern paternalism of a strong state. The gulf is wide indeed between the Western libertarian notion "That government is best which governs least" and the contrasting Soviet belief which might be rendered "That government which governs least is no government at all."

The recent reportage of Moscow correspondents, reflecting the USSR of the early 1970s, seems to bear out the observation made by Henry V. Dicks over twenty years ago:[23] Russians see themselves as needing a "strong moral corset."[24] Fearful of anarchy, they are willing to wear it. Such empirical research as has been done on the Soviet émigrés of the 1970s again seems to indicate concerns that the Western societies in which they now live are too loosely governed, too ready to countenance antigovernment activities in the conservation of individual liberty. This may reflect fears that such activities, if uncontrolled, could lead to a regime not unlike the one the émigrés left; the Bolsheviks, after all, were once a small fringe group with little mass support. Nevertheless, many of the émigrés expect any society to impose order, some *poriadok* appropriate to its central values, against those who would attack them. They find the seemingly unnatural tolerance of Western democracies such as Israel and the United States difficult to understand.[25]

One of the most striking indications of this readiness to perceive a political order, repressive and interventionist by Western standards, as proper and fitting is the tendency of many workers to reminisce on Stalin's time as a "good" one; it was a time when strong order *(strogii poriadok)* prevailed, and its demise has brought new and troubling phenomena to Soviet life.[26] This is not retrospective political hallucination, or not completely. What seems to concern such workers, discounting that segment of persons in any society who are authoritarian by natural inclination, is the change, cultural and social, that has come with the partial decompression of Soviet life. Change of that sort that is meant here—everything from the onrush of rock, "chic" display, and consumption to forces which continue to loosen the bonds of family life — inexorably moves a Russia, still parochial and traditional in many of its moods, toward a new society. It is not a comfortable process for many. Despite the social cataclysms of revolution, civil war, collectivization, and industrialization, Stalin's regime protected people from change; or at least that is the way it appears in hindsight.[27] From time to time, some yearn for the certainties, the toughness, the "no nonsense" of the pre-1953 world they remember; children were not rude, music was not raucous, disorder *(besporiadok)* was not so evident, and the future was more certain. On the whole, Soviet citizens do not crave change in some broad sense, but more of the same: improvements and increased facilities for living in the life they understand. Workers, surely, fit this picture.

Thus far, we have scarcely dealt in subtlety; the Soviet working class has been characterized as oriented toward a welfare state, expecting paternalistic concern and willing to yield autonomy for it; patriotic in the generally understood sense, and socially conservative in the sense that the expectation of social change as a "constant" has not been internalized. This describes a class well matched to a society which is the virtual opposite of the America Jean-François Revel has seen as the truly "revolutionary" one.[28] None of this is applicable to the workers alone; peasants, white-collar functionaries, and a majority of the intelligentsia share, at some level, much the same orientation. Interclass differences in sources of support for the regime under Stalin were not terribly marked, to judge from the Harvard Project's émigrés. There is little warrant to conclude that much has changed in this respect today.

In an earlier essay, I argued that the general Soviet political culture could be characterized as apolitical, suffused with the individual convictions of impotence to change or have significant impact on the system, and expectancy that benefits would be conferred by the state.[29] This is the mass political culture. The various dissident subcultures deviate from it in different ways.[30] If mass political culture can be so characterized, then the working class, as the major component of the mass, must also exemplify those characteristics. Its political consciousness is conventionalized and conformist; it is essentially apolitical and of a "subject" variety, a mass characteristic on which, as the regime must understand, much of the stability of the Soviet polity is based. Workers are convinced of their impotence, but this is not necessarily salient to a social stratum with few alternative images of a polity. Andrei Amalrik may well have been correct in citing the pains of impotence for those elements of the professional strata which have a stake in change; but for the workers, impotence is nothing but the natural balance of relations between subjects and regime.[31] Expectant the workers are; for them, welfarism is strongly ingrained. Their symbolic place in the system entitles them to the benefits the developed socialist society offers. For what it has conferred, they seem grateful—if quiescence be, in this context, the appropriate coin of tribute.

DISAFFILIATION AND NONSUPPORT

Despite the numerous material and emotional ties which bind workers to the polity, there are particular points at which workers are likely to perceive the political system as *not* working on their behalf, or at least as doing poorly on their behalf.

Consumer shortages in both the food and durables areas are important considerations. The urban social context of workers' lives, probably even more than that of the peasants, provides reasons for them to view themselves as permanently on the wrong end. In the larger cities, workers are not unaware of the special stores, the closed distribution networks where goods unattainable to them are in good supply. While their feelings may be moderated by the perception that these are, after all, "special" goods for "special" people, they cannot help but raise questions about fair shares. In food stores and other shops, workers are confronted with surliness, inattention, and the eternal negatives of service personnel whom they suspect of cheating, lying, and reserving for themselves or special customers the best in quality and the scarcest in quantity.

It is not only that workers are excluded from the special stores; neither their money nor contacts can assure them of very satisfactory treatment in regular retail outlets. Moreover, while in calm reflection most urban workers will acknowledge that their lot is better than that of the peasant, contact between the two often takes place in the pure cash, supply and demand, charge-what-the-traffic-will-bear arena of the collective farm market. Workers may acquire food the state stores cannot deliver, and pay the price with minimal immediate grumbling, yet later they reflect on what peasants do with "all that money." They may question why a half century of state and collective agriculture has not yet satisfied the demands of domestic consumers.

On the whole, such experiences do not seem to lead to reasoned and articulate critiques of the system. Rather, they find reflection in the eternal grumbling over shortages and the intermittent outbursts of localized food riots, anomic responses, unorchestrated and unstructured. Evidence of development beyond these manifestations seems minimal.

The threat of a decline in career opportunities represents a second source of potential dissatisfaction. Both rhetoric and past reality have generated in the working class aspirations going beyond prices, supplies, or housing conditions. Over the short run, job changing in a labor-short economy is evidence of this; over the longer haul, problems of greater magnitude arise.

The long-haul aspirations, of course, are those connected with social mobility across the generations. It is somewhat paradoxical, but understandable, that the Soviet regime, and those which have followed it in Eastern Europe, have exalted the working class, and at the same time have legitimated desires to rise from it. Communism, for all its collectivist emphases, has legitimated individual striving. Working-class parents desire to see their children rise to a white-collar job via education, and those children desire to leave the world of their parents behind. As the economy expanded and as the managerial apparatus grew, opportunities were created which could only be filled by the upwardly mobile. Until fairly recent times, these opportunities could match aspirations.

This is no longer the case. The shape of the labor force has stabilized; the share of the peasantry declines, but slowly; the nonmanual cadres no longer swell year by year; the large workers' stratum remains large yet, given the needs of the economy, appears, in prospect, too small. The son of a worker cannot assume that down the line an engineer's job waits for him. Mobility aspirations, once generated, develop an independence of the real state of the economy, but the real supply of "destinations" signaling an elevation of status is linked to growth and a changing distribution of labor.

The social dynamics of contemporary Soviet life seem to indicate a strong trend toward greater inheritance of social-occupational position. The Soviet intelligentsia seeks, generally successfully, to place its children in an institution of higher education to insure their inheritance of status. The working class, in a less competitive position vis-à-vis higher education, tends to retain its offspring; for many of them, a worker's job that is even more skilled, comfortable, and better paid than that of their fathers is a violation of hopes, just as the specialized secondary education into which official policy aims to direct them is seen as no substitute for the university.[32]

More broadly, the issue is one of welfare or egalitarianism versus performance or merit, a major problem in socialist social policy. Here, as the Polish sociologist Wlodzimierz Wesolowski recognizes, interstratum interest conflict develops.[33] For the educated and well placed, an emphasis on qualification, on merit, is desirable. A readiness to reward those who possess complex knowledge, as well as those who are prepared for higher education, redounds to the intelligentsia's benefit. Such policies, defensible in universalistic terms, tend to confer advantage on those already "advantaged."

They do not, however, serve the workers well. Their "interest" lies in policies which limit income differentials, and maintain the "social profile" of higher educational institutions by establishing a "floor" below which the share of students from worker and peasant origins cannot fall.

Reconciling these interests is a political matter. Soviet policy has been one of compromise: it is against extremes of income differentiation, while continuing to offer various sorts of significant material rewards outside normal wages and salary to the incumbents of valued occupations;[34] it stresses the search for talent wherever it rises on the one hand, while on the other it rejects quotas in higher education.[35]

Are Soviet workers' emotions exercised by all this? Do they consciously feel that theirs is a "raw deal"? Various observers have stressed the acceptance of "privilege" by the masses, the deferential attitude of the worker and common man toward the special status of his superiors.[36] For various reasons, I am unpersuaded that the term "deferential" is really applicable here; certainly it is less so in the USSR than in socialist societies with elements of a more traditional European social structure, such as Poland and Hungary.[37] However, there is a seemingly mute acceptance of the inequalities that exist. The question of equality is not yet politicized, but that is not the only index of the workers' discontent. There are other symptoms.

First, the abuse of alcohol, a phenomenon needing no extensive documentation here, is both an operating principle and an operating expense of Soviet industry. Industrial accidents, and lost days and hours, are linked to epidemic alcohol abuse that is rooted not only in a traditional Russian "drinking culture" of proven pathological potential, but in the monotony of working-class life on and off the job.

Similarly, the educational, cultural, economic, and familial characteristics of the workers' stratum produces, as elsewhere, an overrepresentation of workers and their children in criminal and delinquent activities. Perhaps law enforcement agencies have a tendency to concentrate attention on the groups from which they anticipate trouble; nonetheless, the involvement of this stratum in public offenses, crimes against the person, and property crimes indicates limits in its degree of "moral integration" in the social system.

Nowhere, probably, is the strain between the system's enunciated rules and the behavior of the worker more evident than in the attitude toward "socialist property." The multitude of articles in the general press and in legal journals attest to the epidemic nature of employee theft. Goods—finished or in process, for home use or consumption, for resale, for use in "moonlighting" repair work—disappear from factories at a substantial rate, with little evidence of concern on the part of those workers who do not steal.[38]

Underlying the phenomenon are two factors: one is structural and a characteristic of Soviet economic organization; the other is sociopsychological and perhaps characteristic of "underdog" psychology everywhere. American research indicates that persons generally opposed to theft would, if material circumstances forced them to steal, more readily victimize "large business" or "the government" than small business or, presumably, individuals.[39]

Consider, then, the USSR, where government and large business are united, where state administration, production, and retail distribution are all part of the same organizational colossus. If the logic of large organizations' ability to sustain individuals' depredations held in the Soviet Union as in the USA, little could be expected other than a high rate of victimization of the state by those whose rewards it controls and who cannot know why their occasional thefts "hurt" anyone. As Otto Ulc appropriately observed of Czechoslovakia, in a passage equally applicable to the USSR, the state, through the nationalization of the economy, became "the owner of more property than it could possibly protect."[40]

Are such thefts an inchoate form of political protest by their perpetrators? Certainly they indicate that the official line—that each worker is a co-proprietor of the national wealth held in "trust" for him by the state, and therefore by theft steals from himself—has failed to convince the common man. He understands only that control of the use and most of the distribution of that property has been removed from his hands. Beyond this, however, it is a matter of some interpretation.

The familiar sayings referring to theft and "slacking" in general— "We pretend to work, and they pretend to pay us"; "They cannot pay us so little that we cannot work even less"; and, more ominously, "He who does not steal from the state steals from his family"—are perhaps political in implication. Yet these are, whatever their factual basis, also opportunistic rationalizations. This is deviance, not dissidence; the worker who steals does not advertise the fact, does not make an open moral statement.

A useful way to put these actions in context, without denying them some political relevance, is to borrow from the sociology of deviance. David Matza's concept of "techniques of neutralization" argues that delinquents rationalize their acts by extending beyond legal limits those excuses, such as self-defense and insanity, that are recognized in law;[41]

so they can "neutralize" the guilt they would otherwise feel in violating the rules of a culture whose validity they still recognize, although their affiliation with it might be weak. Thus various techniques such as "denial of injury" (the illegal act caused no harm), "denial of the victim" (the victim deserved it, was himself at fault), and the "appeal to higher loyalties" (the situation was covered by a moral rule more authoritative than that of the law) are utilized by the delinquent.

Soviet workers seem to be no strangers to these techniques. To take an item, or several, home at the end of the work day, saying to oneself that "the plant won't miss it"—and find that one's co-workers agree— is not necessarily to elevate theft from an employer to a principle; it is simply to deny the injury. To say that one "pretends" to work in exchange for one's so-called wages is not to advocate wholesale defrauding of employers, but to deny that they are victims. To steal "from the state" when the alternative is theft from one's family is to appeal to higher loyalties, not to deny the state any legitimate rights. Subscribers though they may be to "official" values, Soviet workers show evidence of a "value stretch," wherein economic and social pressures bring about behavior adaptations that go beyond the rules; the values to which lip service is still given are stretched to the point where they are effectively negated. If this is a correct reading of the meaning of drunkenness, poor labor discipline, and economic and noneconomic crime among Soviet workers, then, given what has already been argued about the manner in which workers support the system, there may be reasons to expect a weakening of the ties that bind them to the system if future events impair the system's ability to deliver.

Soviet ideology still, as it has in the past, credits the working class with a leading role in society. This is an element in what Amitai Etzioni calls the "symbolic-normative system."[42] Why does the working class not conform to its own image? Etzioni argues that conformity requires that societal assets be so distributed as to make conformity possible. Such assets are both material and psychological. "The less the patterns of the distributive structure and the political organization parallel the patterns prescribed by the symbolic-normative system," the more deviance may be expected.[43] The problem is that the Soviet working class, while not a debased proletariat at the margins of human survival, is not the recipient of the assets the symbolic-normative system defines as its due. Nourished on a rhetoric of equality or preeminence that they cannot completely ignore, however cynically they may regard poster art and sloganeering, the workers have accommodated to their real situation in a realistic way: their deviations from the behavior expected of a "leading class" reflect their awareness of the gap between reality and the symbolic-normative sphere.

PRESENT BALANCE AND FUTURE PROSPECTS

We have reviewed the two sides of workers' presumed perceptions of the political order. Surely it is not going too far to say that characteristically working-class political perceptions are elusive, if they exist at all. It is not that workers' social location—their place in the hierarchies of power, income, and prestige—cannot be characterized, but that no clear consciousness linked to that location seems to have emerged.

The Western analyst, understandably enough, concerns himself with such things as the relative place of the worker in the system, the degree to which increases in his welfare have matched proportionately, the improving fortunes of other groups. Researchers know more about this than does the worker himself; it is the analysts who attempt to plumb the depths, to interpolate the needed information from the statistical handbook *Narodnoe Khoziaistvo SSSR*, not he. As long as things go reasonably well in his daily life, the worker finds his preferred reading in *Sovetskii Sport*. This is scarcely indicative of a high degree of political consciousness, either of a critical nature or of the sort the propaganda *(agitprop)* enterprise is avowedly committed to creating: but it is comfortable for the worker, and comforting to a regime with a significant stake in maintaining apoliticism.

Soviet workers are not the heirs of an industrial revolution of the Western type, marked by an interplay of individual entrepreneurial activity and state sponsorship, of market and planning, of gradual transition from a localized, low-demand economy to a large national economy with a complex division of labor. Their heritage is that of an absolutist state whose roots predate any industrial revolution and are traceable back to the Tatar yoke and the subsequent rise of Muscovite absolutism. Little wonder that Russia's workers do not behave according to the model of a "class."

Does the future promise any significance alterations? At the core of the question is the issue of the potential politicization of the working class. Such might result from two distinct sources, or a combination thereof: the dissident intelligentsia might join with the workers and mobilize them; or the economic problems of the workers might intensify severely. With respect to the former, the prospects seem bleak. Exile and repression have placed the dissidents on the defensive: retrenchment, rather than an extension and broadening of appeals, has been the order of the last few years, and remains so. In any case, few attempts have been made to forge intelligentsia-worker links on issues of specific concern to workers. Those that have been made, as far as we can tell, have fallen rather short of the mark: instances of stuffing mailboxes with appeals to workers to realize the nature of their economic and political conditions have prompted "loyal" and, probably, puzzled citizens, many of them workers, to turn such heterodox material over to the police.[44]

What of the workers' world itself, the everyday material conditions which determine satisfactions and complaints? Here, present and future may contrast with the recent past. The 1960s and earlier 1970s saw impressive growth in the absolute standard of living for workers. In this period, many were rehoused in new apartments, and the quality of their diet and stock of durables grew markedly. This generated substantial political capital for the regime; much of it came from the workers, despite the fact that they have not benefited, relatively, as much as other groups—notably the peasants—from the economic changes of the past several years.[45] The real increase in workers' living standards has been the stuff of their experience, not the comparative rates at which the welfare of various strata have grown. The future, however, portends a slower economic growth rate, and narrowed options for economic planners and political decision makers, who must ultimately choose between reinvestment and consumption.[46] The indications are that the rate of improvement in real living standards cannot be sustained at the pace to which workers and others have become accustomed. Is this critical?

Those accustomed to citing a "revolution of rising expectations" in the USSR may think so. For my own part, I consider the phrase itself a much-abused one in the Soviet context. What is most remarkable about Soviet mass expectations is their apparent continuing modesty. As Paul Hollander appropriately observed, the "key to the stability of the Soviet system lies in its management of expectations."[47] Indeed, the record of the regime in this area has been one of notable success. Signs of a revolutionary acceleration of expectations are not evident to me. To argue that the new, modest affluence of the major urban centers, and the traffic jams they have finally "achieved," portends even greater growth of mass expectations is to impose on the Soviet situation a kind of reasoning better fitted to the phenomena of the American experience. The Soviet situation stands in marked contrast to that of the better-developed states of Eastern Europe, where a shorter experience under socialism, a historically higher standard of living, and a much lesser degree of isolation from the West produce populations not only more affluent than the USSR, but also more dissatisfied. This is ironic in that the USSR, to foster social stability, bankrolls some of this gap in living standards through various types of economic aid to Eastern Europe.

Thus, working-class militancy or politicization turns mainly on the future ability of the regime to meet expectations of the current sort, modest but comulative increases in living standards. Thus far it has done rather well. While economic prospects are not rosy, projections of Soviet growth rates and consequent ability to meet demands do not support a prediction of impending catastrophe. In its large grain purchases from the West, the regime has shown clear sensitivity to the "bottom line"; Soviet citizens will put up with a great deal, but, having grown accustomed to substantial dietary improvements in the post-Stalin years, they cannot be relied upon to tolerate literal belt tightening. Localized riots have occurred over food deficits in some nonpriority cities, but these have been relatively few. The regime remains, presumably, ready and financially able to moderate the effects of poor harvests by further foreign purchases, should these be the price of tranquillity. Soviet workers, barring economic catastrophe of the sort which by its very nature cannot be predicted, should remain quiescent. In any case, there is no strong evidence to suggest that they will confront the economic problems of the future with a working-class orientation that clearly distinguishes their response from that of other strata.

In the end, their relative place in the stratification hierarchy seems to mean less to workers than the concrete improvements they have experienced. The issue of equality has not been politicized in working-class terms; workers have yet to show major concern over their treatment as workers, or over socialist modes of exploitation, or over contradictions in the social order that demand redress in furtherance of their interests as a class apart from the others. That class consciousness has not come to Soviet workers is a clear plus for the stability of the regime, however Marxist its rhetoric.

The politicization of inequality seems, as yet, far off for Soviet workers. In a society of comparatively low living standards, this parallels the situation which Christopher Jencks and his collaborators, all of an egalitarian bent, complained of in American society: the common man simply wants more in the concrete, and does not hanker after an abstract justice of equal distribution.[48] As long as so few issues agitate the Soviet worker, it will be difficult indeed to isolate political perceptions unique to him and, at the same time, charged with meaning for the system as a whole.

FIVE

CHANGING TIMES AND THE SOVIET WORKER

This chapter provides a rather different perspective on the Soviet worker and the working class than did the one preceding. Over six years—and the deaths of Brezhnev, Andropov, and Chernenko—separate them. With these events, and the lapse of time, comes a change of perspective and emphasis as well. The previous chapter, written in what turns out to have been the beginning of the Brezhnevian "twilight," addressed questions of workers' moods, attitudes, convictions, on which reliable data were scarce indeed, and moved from there to a rather negative appraisal of the potential for class consciousness and a politicization of economic issues among workers.

This chapter—written in the first eight months of Gorbachev's rule, and confined to the indications of his policies and directions evident

Originally written as "The Soviet Working Class: Change and Its Political Impact," on contract for the Bureau of Intelligence and Research, Department of State, in 1985. A shorter version was published under the original title in Michael P. Sacks and Jerry G. Pankhurst, eds., *Understanding Soviet Society* (Boston: Allen and Unwin, 1988). Minor revisions and two new introductory paragraphs have been added in this version.

only that far—focuses, unlike the previous one, on *structural* issues in the formation of the Soviet working class, and some of the (rather different) implications these seemed to bear for working-class consciousness by the mid-1980s. Those implications, seen in the light of the unfolding of Gorbachev's domestic policies in 1986 and 1987, grew all the more interesting, as chapter 6 indicates, for the potential of change and the Soviet consensus on "social justice."

The internal political agenda of the new regime is heavy with economic concerns. One of the most critical of these is dealing with the "human factor" in the Soviet economy. Whether—as it seems—the line to be taken is a technocratic one, demanding greater quantity and quality of work effort *within* a continuation of a highly centralized system of virtually total state ownership (outside agriculture), or a more "market" form which could include the attractiveness and risks of private-sector work for more of the labor force, the attitudes/reactions of the Soviet *working class* will be important in determining the results.

That working class is in a process of constant, if marginal, internal change. Cumulatively, however, it today reflects critical transformations since the Stalin, Khrushchev, or even the earlier Brezhnev period. This chapter examines three aspects of that transformation: the "hereditization" of the working class—the process whereby yesterday's ex-peasant class has given way to one recruited from the offspring of workers; the confrontation of a working class growing in general education completed and a job structure less prone to rapid change; and the developing potential tensions in the area of perceived *social justice*, as understood by this new working class, and as it may be affected by policies to be adopted.

HEREDITIZATION: THE PROCESS

Critical to an understanding of the impact of hereditization on the working class is an appreciation of how (relatively) late in Soviet history it occurred. Soviet statistics, and treatments of the topic, tend to be fragmentary—indeed, there is no reason to assume that data characterizing the picture for the whole USSR labor force exist.

In the main, hereditization has meant a shift *away* from a working class heavily weighted in the direction of ex-peasants: either males (and females) who spent part of their adult working life in agriculture, or who were born in rural/farm households, and spent the period through adolescence in that environment. G. Bliakhman, reporting a long-term

(1965–1979) study of workers born since 1950 in various enterprises in the Russian, Ukrainian, Byelorussian, Moldavian, Latvian, Tadzhik, and Georgian republics, noted the rapid decline of the "peasant" element over the years.[1] By 1979, in "old" industrial cities (presumably ones with a large recruiting pool of workers' children), no more than 15 percent of the factory work force born in 1950 and after were of peasant origin; only in newer cities did the share rise to 40 percent. Over half of Bliakhman's respondents were second- or *third*-generation workers.[2]

The situation Bliakhman outlined, based on a sampling of a broad range of geographical areas, took a long time for the Soviet economy and society to achieve. The great social transformations of the post-1928 period of the first two Five-Year Plans—indeed the whole period up to World War II—lie outside the scope of this chapter, so it need only be noted that in this period, as the USSR moved from an economy with 80 percent to less than 60 percent of the labor force in agriculture, the growth of the working class occurred virtually totally through the addition of recruits from the countryside, to the point that in most branches a solid ex-peasant majority characterized the makeup of the working "class."[3]

Wartime losses and the still-huge rural reserves meant that, well into the postwar and post-Stalin periods, significant inflows of peasants, upwardly mobile from village and *kolkhoz*, continued to dilute whatever hereditary elements were developing in the working class. As one 1977 source puts it, from the 1920s until "well after" World War II, the peasantry remained the large source of working-class recruitment.[4] This was pronounced in areas of low industrial development, where in the first postwar decade, the peasantry represented a large "pool,"[5] but nationwide figures also attest to the magnitude of the process. As one source puts it, from 1951 to 1953, an annual average of 660,000 collective farmers became industrial workers; from 1954 to 1958, this process continued at the rate of 140,000 per year (figures which do *not* include the mobility of collective farm "peasants" who became state farm "workers"). This represents a total of about 2.68 million such instances of mobility over an eight-year period. In the seven-year plan period, from 1959 through the mid-1960s, about 340,000–350,000 collective farmers left annually for industry, adding another "draft" well above a million to the blue-collar work force. From 1966 to 1970, about 220,000 collective farmers left annually for nonagricultural employment, a good deal of it in blue-collar industrial work.[6]

Large-scale gross movement of nonhereditary workers thus continued well into the post-Khrushchev period, as Soviet economic growth rates still created "demand" sufficient to drive the process of upward mobility from peasant to worker. Large *absolute* numbers meant, of course, problems of absorption, "adaptation" to urban-industrial life, demands on housing/services, etc. But as the receiving base of the industrial work force grew year by year, these impressive numbers represented more moderate proportional additions to the working class. Writing at the beginning of the 1980s, three scholars observed that the contribution of migrants from rural to urban areas *and* from agriculture to industry (roughly, the same people) to industrial labor resources amounted to about 17 percent of the total growth in 1961–65, about 12 percent from 1967 to 1970, and only about 9 percent in the 1970s.[7] At the same time, the proportional contribution of "school leavers and those discharged from the armed forces" grew from 30 percent (1961–65) to 57 percent (1966–1970) to approximately 92 percent in the 1970s—though these categories do not, of course, exclude peasant/rural *origin* people.[8]

Thus, over the years, and in a "natural" way that reflected (a) a gradual slowing of the economic processes that generated a demand for more and more new additions to the industrial labor force, (b) the maturation of a larger industrial labor force such that its numbers began to produce children who *could* contribute, by entering that same world of work, to the working class—a first generation of "mobiles" from the peasantry creating a second generation, nonmobile but "inheriting" worker status, and (c) the relative and absolute decline of the peasant recruiting pool in Soviet labor demographics, forces promoting the "self-reproduction" of the working class gained, for the first time, the upper hand. This happened at no precise, specifiable time, but it is history. It may be that a Soviet writer of 1964, asserting that the "internal reserves and the urban population have become the preponderant source of working-class replenishment,"[9] was early in making the claim. But the structural change he specified *has* come, and with it a different profile of the industrial labor force.

Today's working class, then, is more a product of self-reproduction than ever before. Individual studies of the "origins," "sources," "composition," of the work force in various areas, industries, or enterprise complexes cannot be summed up into a comprehensive nationwide picture, but nonetheless offer solid confirmation of the phenomenon— especially when they present age-specific data reflecting the very different social/class origin pattern of younger versus older worker cadres. (The next few pages present a part of the picture: readers interested more in the consequences of hereditization may prefer to skip them and move on to the the next section.)

The pattern of the wood industry in the Sverdlovsk region in the late 1960s, for instance, indicates striking differences in the share of the worker origin among current workers by age category.[10]

to 20 yrs	20–25	26–35	36–45	46+
69.7%	60.7	53.6	50.5	36.5

Similar forces, expanding the share of hereditary workers as age declines, work in the case of the Cheliabinsk tractor works, in data reflecting the early 1970s.[11]

16–20 yrs	31–34	50+
58.1%	56.0	36.5

Another "single-site" study, of the Kirov mine complex in the Kuzbass region in the late 1960s–early 1970s, yielded a similar picture of the worker-origin share among "new cadres" (which *may* refer to new "hires" in the period or may simply reflect the origin at *time* of hire of a work force in the period noted).[12]

18–25 yrs	26–35	36–45	46–55
80.0%	71.9	50.0	25.0

Maddeningly, a study of Taganrog—the Soviet city chosen for its reproduction of "typical" Soviet urban patterns by many Soviet researchers, somewhat similar to Muncie, Indiana's role as America's "Middletown"—reports age groups of workers as "young, middle, oldest," with very general indications of the hereditary share.[13]

Young	*Middle*	*Oldest*
66%	60	45–50

Another reference to what is evidently the same data set indicates, however, that the "young" group ranges up to age twenty-five, and includes 20 percent peasant origin in its composition.[14]

The most detailed data set available concerns the city of Sterlitamak, one of a number of cities in the Bashkir ASSR and nearby regions studied by N. A. Aitov. Sterlitamak's *total* worker population includes an only moderate 51.8 percent hereditary component independent of age, but in the presumably mid-late 1970s context of a study published in 1981, the age groups differ widely.[15]

16–17 yrs	18–20	21–25	26–30	31–39	40–49	50–60	60+
71.4%	71.2	63.0	52.3	43.9	41.7	43.1	27.8

The various localities/enterprises vary greatly in the "age" of industry, in the nature of surrounding areas, etc. The data, however they vary between high to quite low shares of "hereditary" workers among the older groups, show that the tendency to hereditization is stronger as one reaches the young worker groups—those which have the great bulk of their career as workers ahead of them, and who are distinct in many other ways as well from their older counterparts.

A summary picture of the degrees of hereditization is in a technical sense impossible, but the data arrayed in table 5.1—essentially as comprehensive a "list" of hereditary origin as I was able to assemble from a myriad of Soviet studies and references to studies—may provide some broad indications of the still-dim general picture, as well as an indication of variations over time and place, in the USSR from the mid-1960s to the present.

This statistical mélange could be subjected to extensive commentary, at least of a speculative sort. The 1975–76 figure for Elista, the capital of the Kalmyk ASSR—not a highly developed "historical" industrial region—seems high. Yet if Elista's blue-collar work force is *small*, it may very well be one whose relatively stable size reflects self-recruitment over a *long* period. (Rates of "hereditization" in the small USSR

TABLE 5.1. Workers of Working-Class Origin as Percent
of All Workers

Ufa-Orenburg	(1966)	38.0%
Ufa-Orenburg	(1970)	44.6%
Kazan	(1967)	49.0%
Sverdlovsk (wood industry)	(1967)	54.0%
Leningrad (machine building)	(1970)	54.7%
Bashkir ASSR	(early 1970s)	55.8%
Moscow *oblast'*	(1973)	55.8%
Cheliabinsk	(1973–74)	56.2%
Elista (Kalmyk ASSR)	(1975–76)	69.4%
Magnitogorsk	(late 1970s)	70.3%
Naberezhnye Chelni	(late 1970s)	69.1%
Sterlitamak	(late 1970s)	51.8%

SOURCES: various Soviet studies, available upon request from author.

proletariat on the eve of the Plan era were quite high as opposed to later years.) The Moscow *oblast'* figure for 1973 appears low—but then the *oblast'* is *not* the city, and Moscow's role as the national administrative center also may provide mobility opportunities of various sorts to the hereditary Muscovite which dilute the hereditary component of its blue-collar work force more than would be the case in more exclusively "industrial" cities.

The 54.7 percent hereditary component among Leningrad machine-building workers in 1970—a quintessential complex of all that the "working class" means, it would seem, in Soviet rhetoric—also seems low. Yet a later (unreported above) tabulation for a study in 1976–77 of the same sector lists only 38.8 percent as of worker origin, 17.0 percent as of farm *(kolkhoz* or *sovkhoz)* origin, and 16.8 percent as originating in white-collar families—for a total of 72.6 percent, with no reference to the absent 27.4 percent.[16] Perhaps the rest were demobilized soldiers at the time of entering the industry—but this is inconsistent with what the author seems clearly to treat as a set of *social origins*, rather than previous-job categories.

In any case, from these Leningrad data, it appears that the herediti-zation figure is not "inflated" by treating workers whose social origin is from *sovkhoz (state* farm) families as hereditary workers and by treat-ing those of *kolkhoz (collective* farm) origin as upwardly mobile from the peasantry. From other indications, this seems to be true as well of the other studies cited here.

Against these figures, it is perhaps useful to note the hereditization figure for the sample surveyed in the post–World War II Harvard Project on the Soviet Social System: 46.1 percent of the workers reported worker fathers, in what was regarded as a group rather successful by Soviet standards.[17] This was probably a *high* figure. Research on the early Plan era shows the force of the peasant "draft" at its beginnings.[18] In 1929, a figure of 52.2 percent is given for the "hereditary" share among workers in *all* branches of industry. This figure, we may be sure, fell, and fell rapidly. For example, of those who *started* work in 1926–27 in the Leningrad engineering and metalworking industry, 55.6 percent were from worker families; a figure down to 38.8% for 1930 entrants. Figures for the same industry in the Ukrainian republic are 60.1 percent and 48.0 percent respectively. In the metallurgy industry in the Urals area, the 1926–27 "draft" was 43.7 percent hereditary workers—this share had fallen, as the first FYP hit its stride, to only 29.0 percent in 1930.[19] The process of "peasantization" as the working class grew was under way—it would be decades before the trends of industrial maturation and slowing social change would once again create a mainly hereditary stratum of industrial workers.

The documents of the April 1923 (Twelfth) Party Congress, when the young USSR was in the process of drawing its at that point mainly hereditary proletariat back to the factories after the civil war disruptions, include the following words: "In the last analysis, the working class can preserve and strengthen its leading position not through the state apparatus, not through the army, but through industry, which reproduces *(vosproizvodit)* the proletariat itself."[20]

The factual status of the working-class "leading position" is best left uncommented-upon for now—prospects for the formation of the Soviet system we know today were not so clear in the early year of 1923. It was, indeed, through industry and its growth that a large blue-collar work force was *produced*. Whether the process should have been called *reproduction*, since the growth constantly diluted the hereditary element of the working class, is questionable. It would be, as we observed earlier, some time before the situation would justify the words of a 1967 Soviet study, that the "working class, having become the largest class in society, began to replenish itself mainly in its own account."[21] Having arrived at that point, the Soviet working class presented, to the analyst of social change, and to the person primarily interested in the political *implications* of such change, some important questions.

HEREDITIZATION: CONTEXT AND IMPACT

These questions—not yet all capable of answer—turn on large-scale developments in the history of Soviet economy and society, which either underlie the hereditization process just summarized, or which derive, especially in the area of changes in aspirations, expectations, frameworks for evaluating the performance of the regime, from that process.

After the launching of the first Five-Year Plan, first, the USSR embarked on a process counter to hereditization, which filled a growing proletariat with first-generation workers. Economic growth—in the sense of a concentration on the rapid, labor- and capital-intensive development of industry—created "demand" for new workers. Pressures on the rural sector—collectivization in the early post-1928 years, low living standards, and the social/cultural stigmata of village life well into the post-Stalin years—provided a "push" to complement industry's "pull." The slowing of growth later applied a brake to structural change in the overall labor force, and thus to the mobility processes that that change evoked.

Second, the now-larger working class became, more and more, a "self-recruiting" segment of society, its sons (especially) retained, as they completed their educations, in the category of their fathers. In structural terms, three elements in this transition are worth noting.

1. Past a certain point, the *peasantry* could no longer be treated as a recruiting pool, a labor reserve. As it grew smaller, it included less "surplus" to feed industry; as a relatively inefficient agricultural economy, the USSR *needed* a fairly large peasantry, and could not afford to let all who might "escape" from the countryside. Thus, the significance of the upwardly mobile peasantry-son "input" to the working class declined. The agriculture-to-industry transition could not be endless. In fact, it has fallen far short of the point reached by the United States or the developed capitalist West.

2. The *intelligentsia* has continued to grow, proportionally more rapidly than the working class, but still remains small. Its base size and growth rate are insufficient to generate "demand" sufficiently in excess (over the inheritance of intelligentsia status by intelligentsia offspring) to take many aspirants out of the working class' younger ranges. In general, the broadly defined "service sector," weighted heavily toward white-collar nonmanual work (or work transitional between this and blue-collar work), has suffered severely arrested growth in the Soviet economy, and has not provided alternate opportunities for any large number of young offspring of workers, especially male offspring.

3. The working class still grows, although slowly. The "production" bias of Soviet economic calculation, the relatively low per capita productivity in most branches, the relatively high percentage of unassisted or minimally machine-assisted hand labor, all indicate the likelihood of its remaining large: hence, it "needs" its internal recruits.

Third, other state policies in the area of education have also tended to "lock" working-class youth into their origin categories, further promoting the hereditization of this class (as well as of the intelligentsia situated above it). The state has put no obstacles directly in the way of working-class aspirations to complete *secondary* education (indeed the opposite)—but it has not expanded and has no intention of expanding the supply of spaces in higher education to meet the demand generated by completion of secondary education by the majority—rather than, as in the past, a small minority—of Soviet seventeen-year-olds. This is a policy response to a potential problem successive leaders have wished to avoid: a "mix" of levels of education and specialties out of synchronization with the projected needs of the national economy (i.e., the job structure as foreseen/projected by planners at a future time). Less acknowledged—indeed not at all—is the decision that Soviet leaders will *not* face the difficulty of dealing with an overlarge, underemployed "intelligentsia," its appetite whetted for social, economic, and influence/power rewards the system cannot deliver.

Thus, the expansion of secondary education in the 1970s placed a diverse mix of seventeen-year-olds at the transition bottleneck to higher education. They are, as statistics on access to full-time higher education show, quite diverse in their success rates. Worker offspring pass the bottleneck at a less impressive rate than their intelligentsia peers, whose quest is to reproduce their parents' occupational status.[22]

A more hereditized working class presents the regime with questions of context and consciousness of a new sort, which may prove troublesome in the rest of the century. The context in question is the *evaluative* context: the bases of comparison the worker may use to judge the "performance" of the Soviet system in providing, however relevant, both a (broadly defined) living standard and the opportunity to improve it. It is generally accepted that the comparison standards of Soviet citizens are overwhelmingly *temporal* rather than international: that, lacking the exposure to superior Western living standards that so many East Europeans possess, they compare their todays with their own yesterdays. For the most part, such a comparison shows (at least until recently) that Soviet system in a good light. Older citizens, especially, who remember vividly the pre-1953 period have reason to be impressed with how far they have come. Such people, whose "base line" lies in a period of severe food shortages and rationing, a laughably poor selection of consumer durables, and the urban world of crowded communal apartments, have seen *cumulative* change that allows them to absorb a certain amount of stagnation in current living standards, or even fallbacks in certain areas (such as that of food), with equanimity.

But for young workers—the "self-recruits" from working-class families—the context is not so favorable. The share of the population whose context includes the years of Stalin and depressed consumption is ever declining. We are dealing, overall, with a Soviet population heavily tilted toward those who have grown in a peaceful period, one wherein living standards *have* increased—particularly the younger ranges of this group, for whom even the Khrushchev period is a blank (people born in the month *Brezhnev* took power turned twenty-one in October 1985), and whose conscious experience coincides with years of slowing economic growth and moderate, if even perceptible, rises in the living standard. Young workers, then, must share in some sense a general "cohort effect" that arguably has elevated the *context* of evaluation of living standards, elevated expectations about what the system must and should deliver as normal aspects of the Soviet welfare package, and elevated the definition of what can be regarded as notable improvements. *Not* a "revolution" of rising expectations," this is, nonetheless, a potential problem for a regime which has failed notably in producing growth in per capita GNP sufficient to undergird continuing significant increases in welfare.

Beyond this, young workers may share another grievance. As against expectations fed by the past performance of a rapidly growing economy and a labor force rapidly changing shape, the opportunities afforded them for upward mobility, for "exit" from the class of their fathers, have not been impressive. The slowing of structural change, the "deficit" of places in higher education versus the increased output of secondary school graduates, and the disadvantages working-class youth face in competing for those places have all reduced the supply of such opportunities.

WORK COMMITMENT: EDUCATION, PROBLEMS, "REFORM"

With a good deal of warrant, Soviet commentators take pride in the increase over time in average educational levels, as well as the increased output of persons with higher education. This, as much as the building of a large, predominantly industrial, economy, is "progress," another indication of the historical parting of company with the agrarian, marginally literate Russia of the past.

Yet as ten-year complete secondary education has become more and more the norm, the "returns," qualitative and quantitative, have been less than unambiguously positive. Indeed, there is an element of paradox in an emerging situation wherein the increased educational levels of young recruits to the working class complicate, rather than ease, their fitting into the world of blue-collar work. From the world of the past, where young entrants to the factory possessed only marginal education and found the unfamiliar rhythms and skill requirements difficult to master, Soviet society has come to a present wherein both objective and subjective indicators point to a lack of fit between heightened levels of general education and an occupational structure less "upscale" than the schooling, pretentions, and expectations of those who must staff it in the present and the future. Soviet society remains *industrial,* rather than postindustrial. "At present almost 76% of all workers are occupied in the sphere of material production, and in the future no essential changes are foreseen."[23]

Within this industrial sphere, the share of simple, unmechanized, repetitive—and often dirty and arduous—labor is comparatively large. The forces which have contributed to this situation are obviously not subject to rapid reversal—hence the words of three Soviet authors who, while affirming that the Soviet economy needed workers of high skills and quality, allowed that it also required "workers of average and even low skills."[24] Soviet figures show progress in reducing the share of purely manual *(ruchnyi)* labor, but also indicate how *large* that share still is: from 1965 to 1979, in industry the share fell from 40.4 to 32.8 percent; in construction, from 60 to 49 percent.[25] Considering the pace of technological innovation and reshaping of employment patterns in the industrial West in this period, it is the "backwardness" of the Soviet mix that impresses here.

This structure of blue-collar work opportunities is increasingly out of line with the aspirations and expectations of those now entering the labor force; nor is the tension completely resolvable by raising economic rewards in compensation.

> In a socialist society, a fully normal general dissatisfaction is developing with those job positions where the work has little content, is heavy and unprestigious. Growth of general education normally strengthens this phenomenon. Raising the pay for heavy, manual, low skill and low prestige work only compensates to a small degree for its social inferiority, its unattractiveness.[26]

Education, then, is a "property" which renders adjustment to the nature and quality of much of the available work more difficult. The average *job* no longer presents challenges, interests, or conditions adequate for the average *person,* with average *education.* As the then director of the USSR Academy of Sciences' Institute of Sociological Research put it in 1980, the "structure of work places, where there is a high proportion of unskilled work, today does not objectively correspond to the more developed skill structure of the workers themselves, holds back and limits their development."[27] In fact, the supply of unskilled jobs *was* rising through the 1960s, and may indeed continue, even if at a moderated rate, to the present time. From 1959 to 1969, according to one set of calculations, the number of workers in *industry* increased by 39 percent; among them, those who engaged in monitoring automated machines increased by 142 percent, those using "helping mechanisms and machines" by 72 percent, and those engaged in (almost exclusively) manual work in auxiliary shops, etc., by 18 percent. Keeping in mind that Soviet economy in 1959, and the tiny number then monitoring automated equipment, 18 percent is no small number of additional hand workers.[28]

Trends such as these are unlikely to provide a supply of jobs young workers consider attractive. In a study of over ten thousand workers at the lower Kama industrial complex, researchers found that in 1982 two-thirds of the younger (evidently under forty) workers "felt that their educational level was higher than that required by their work. Among workers older than forty, the picture was the reverse; two-thirds felt that their education was lower than that required by production."[29] As early as 1975, the labor economist Iu. P. Sosin estimated in the authoritative Novosibirsk journal *EKO* that "industry is able to provide only 30 to 35% of young workers with work on a par with their knowledge."[30]

Two matters are involved here, and are especially important in the case of *young* entrants to the working class who are contributing so heavily to its hereditization; academic education per se and training in *work* skills. The first, certainly, has risen. The dimensions of its change over time require some notice. A large study in Gorky *oblast'* traced changes between 1965 and 1979, showing that in 1965 the industrial work force in the area was in its vast majority (86.8 percent) "short" of complete secondary education (fully 48.1 percent had only seven or eight years). By 1979, only 52 percent lacked secondary education, and of workers up to thirty years of age, only 20 percent were in this category.[31] In the Sverdlovsk area in 1969, only 23.2 percent of those starting work had a ten-year education; by 1975, almost 80 percent of those beginning had education to this level.[32] Figures from the ZIL automotive plant in Moscow contrast two levels of education (primary only and complete secondary) over three time periods, for the plant's labor force as a whole and (in parentheses) for the portion under thirty years of age in the given year.[33]

	primary	complete secondary
1959	53.5 (43.6)	8.4 (11.3)
1970	31.4 (10.0)	23.1 (38.7)
1979	15.2 (00.1)	50.7 (77.8)

Obviously, both the rise in educational level with declining age *and* the replacement of older, ill-schooled age cohorts by the younger are changing the face of the factory labor force—faster, from the foregoing comments, than the occupational structure is changing. Industry and the working class have in fact come to the end of the time when new recruits *can* be found in large numbers among the really ill-educated or rural and "undemanding." In the prewar and early postwar years the working class was "fed" by the redistribution of people from agriculture to industry, from rural to urban areas; by 1961–65, such shifts accounted for only 17 percent of the growth in labor resources, and this fell to 12 percent in 1967–70 and to 9 percent through the 1970s. Meanwhile, the share of growth attributable to school leavers and those discharged from the armed forces increased across the three periods from 30 to 57 to 92 percent.[34] As an author put it in 1984, "Practically the single mass source of replenishing cadres has become youth with a high, as a rule, educational and cultural level."[35]

Further evidence of the difficulty of the job-education match is found in factory administrations' seeking out of *rural* recruits, presumably at a lower educational and cultural level, to fill their ranks, because they are less demanding and present less of a problem of retention. As a *Pravda* correspondent writing from the Ukraine observed in 1983:

> Many enterprises in Sevastopol go on stubbornly filling their ranks with rural people instead of city dwellers, even though they have to "pay" for this by building dormitories, paying for private apartments, etc. But the plant managers contend that they get something for their money: the rural workers work harder, more of them stay at the plant and they're less apt to change jobs.[36]

In all this, then, there arises the specter of an overeducated blue-collar work force. Over the longer run, the utility of ten years of schooling on the factory floor may increase somewhat, taking into account problems and patterns of skill acquisition and advancement, of labor mobility and job changing (a phenomenon especially marked among young workers). But in the shorter run, a young labor force educated beyond their jobs will remain a major problem.

"Education" is mathematics, science, language, history—and in the

Soviet variant, a heavy dose of various ideological topics as well. It is *not* work skills, and despite the rhetorical emphasis through so much of the past on the "polytechnic" in Soviet education, the results of a near universalization of secondary education have not been reflected in any major acquisition of skills on the part of the seventeen- and eighteen-year-olds who go, in increasing numbers, from the classroom to the factory. As a study in the RSFSR in 1975–76 concluded: "Over 44 percent of all young industrial workers are secondary-school graduates. ...These educated youth are more demanding with regard to the nature of their jobs, the working conditions and the pay they receive. *But 80 percent of them have had no vocational training, and they are often used in unskilled jobs or those calling for heavy labor*" (emphasis added).[37]

The phenomenon of the production of educated seventeen-year-olds without job skills, and the matching of these with the economy's presumed needs, is a complex one, developed over time. In January 1977, the USSR Minister of Education, M. Prokofiev, noted that about 14 million people would complete secondary education in the 1976–1980 period. Of these, 6.5 million would continue their education either in higher education, the specialized secondary track *(tekhnikum)* or lower-level trade schools *(tekhuchilishche)*. But 7.5 million would go to work.[38] Later, in June of the same year, Prokofiev's deputy for labor training and vocational guidance cited the same figures, and wrote optimistically about the "interschool production training combines" *(mezhshkol'nye uchebno-proizvodstvennye kombinaty)*, organizations which evidently provided academic secondary schools with vocational training. These had grown from 250 nationwide in 1975 to about 500 by 1976–77, each serving an average of ten schools and offering instruction in "tens" of specialties. Summer work training was growing as well: in 1974, about 7 million ninth and tenth graders had participated in such programs; in 1976, 10 million.[39]

Some few years down the line, the optimism seemed misplaced. A 1977–79 study under Komsomol auspices, reported in 1981, found that vocational training (presumably of the MUPK variety) in secondary schools was generally useless. Over three thousand students questioned reported "work" on the order of classroom cleaning, light repairs to school equipment (81.7 percent), picking up scrap metal (65.0 percent), and the like. Only 27 percent had had work training in the summer.[40]

Research among tenth graders in Moscow secondary schools, in which students were asked about their career plans in 1981 and recontacted in 1982 to see how these had worked out, provided more reason to doubt the relevance of vocational training in academic secondary schools. The certificates of training issued by the MUPKs "had no force" in factories and plants, which generally found it necessary to retrain the newly hired in the same specialties acquired in schools. Of the tenth graders questioned as to whether they wanted to work or study further the vocation they were learning via the MUPK, only 14.2 percent answered yes, 50.9 percent answered no, and 34.9 percent had no response. In 1982's assessment of actual outcomes (presumably among the percentage of all graduates who had entered the labor force), 23.9 percent were working in the area of their training, 13.1 percent partly so, and fully 63 percent reported no relation between their jobs and the MUPK training.[41]

Thus, in the early 1980s, the arrangements to equip secondary school graduates (in large numbers destined, willy-nilly, to enter the work force in the same year as they earn their diplomas) with useful skills hardly resembled a well-oiled machine. M. N. Rutkevich explained, in a *Sovetskaia Rossiia* article in 1983, something of how the problem had come about.[42]

By the mid-late 1950s, higher educational institutions (VUZy) could not absorb all the graduates (then 40 percent of the 17-year-olds) of ten-year secondary schools. Khrushchev's 1958 educational reform aimed at correcting the problem of the "misplaced" (in the sense that complete secondary education was preparation for higher education, pure and simple), by tracking the fifteen-year-old finishers of *eighth* grade ("incomplete secondary education") to vocational-technical trade schools *(proftekhuchilishche).* But the latter, poorly developed and of low quality, could not do the job. Many fifteen-year-olds thus went to work unskilled and of little use to the economy (in 1965, about 42 percent of all eighth graders, while 40 percent went into ninth grade, and only about 17–18 percent went to some kind of trade school or *tekhnikum* training).

The drift into complete secondary education continued, and the realization that fewer, relatively, of this increasing population (high school graduates) could find places in higher education prompted a recognition that more labor training was needed in ninth and tenth grades. But such training was not developed and organized to the necessary degree. Hence, by 1980, while virtually no eighth-grade graduates were going directly to work, 60 percent were continuing into ninth-tenth grades, and nearly 40 percent were directing their steps toward one or another kind of vocation-technical training. But whereas in 1965 only 16.2 percent of tenth-grade graduates had gone to work without further training, by 1980, 41.2 percent of the larger-by-then graduate population were doing so, while only 16.3 percent were continuing in full-time VUZy (versus 41.4 percent in 1965). Of the remainder, 26.9 percent of 1980 tenth-grade graduates were in vocational-technical training, and 15.6 percent were in *tekhnikums* of the "secondary specialized" variety— both of these categories (as well as the 41.2 percent already working) representing, presumably, a "wastage" of effort in ninth and tenth grades, in that vocational tracks *could* have been entered after the eighth grade, and better preparation thus gained for the working life that awaited these young people after graduation.

Problems like these must underlie, to a large degree, the agenda of the 1984 Soviet educational reform. Some of them were part of the process of its discussion, justification, and introduction. The "center-piece" of the reform, with respect to the formation of the working class of the future, is to be found in the "secondary vocational-technical school" (*srednee proftekhuchilishche*, or SPTU). To these will eventually be sent, in the words of the reform document, double the number of young people (eighth-grade leavers) who currently attend them.[43] What does this imply?

A first implication is the continued growth of a species of combined education and skill training which derived originally from many of the problems discussed earlier in this work. The secondary PTU (SPTU) was essentially a creation of the late 1960s, made of the "addition" to PTUs of divisions or departments of general education, to allow them to confer the diploma indicating a ten-year academic education. This process of building "up" from the low-prestige PTU base accelerated, at least formally, in the 1970s. In the 1979–80 academic year, Soviet ninth and tenth graders were distributed, roughly, through the general academic secondary schools (5.5 million), SPTUs (2.07 million), and general PTUs (1.87 million)[44]—some in this sixteen-eighteen-year-old age group were, of course, already at work and do not appear in these figures. A decade earlier, in 1970–71, there had been only *180,000* students in the SPTU "track"—an increase of 1,000+ percent, with a 655 percent increase (from 615 to 4,026) in the number of SPTUs themselves. The "network" continued to grow in the early 1980s and, along the way, gave some indication that the SPTU had "worked" to reduce the *share* of age-eligible youth in the academic track and hence the "demand" for entry to higher education. As one Western observer put it in 1981:

Measures taken to redirect the educational and career orientations of Soviet school children proved surprisingly successful. The prestige of the PTU (*professional' no-tekhnicheskoe uchilishche*—trade school) and the *tekhnikum* (technical college) was raised by enriching their vocational programmes with a much larger element of general education, and by powerful campaigns of vocational guidance in the media. Some local authorities transformed many of their PTUs into "secondary PTUs", which provide a full secondary general education as well as trade training, and set quotas for the number of eighth-grade leavers who would have to enter them. This, combined with a greater realism amongst pupils about the prospects of obtaining a VUZ place led to a sweeping change in their educational aspirations. Pupils completing the eighth and tenth grades were atracted to the new secondary PTUs and post-secondary courses in tekhnikums. After decades in which it had enjoyed unrivalled prestige among Soviet youth higher education began to lose some of its attraction.[45]

If this seems a relatively benign assessment of a form of social engineering, the same author's noting that the redirection of so many young people (males, especially)[46] into the SPTU track meant that some higher educational institutions, *especially* those in the applied technology area, faced a student "deficit" led him to go further, and more critically, into the process.

It might indeed be claimed that Soviet boys have been "cooled out" to excess. Once they have taken up PTU or tekhnikum courses they seem to abandon higher education ambitions, even though the new general-education component of the curricula supposedly keeps open the chance of eventual VUZ entry. Perhaps this is not so surprising, as several Soviet commentators have pointed out, when skilled manual workers are as much in demand as graduate engineers and can command wages as high as, or even higher, than the latter. Moreover, the standard of teaching and attainment in the general-education part of PTU programmes is acknowledged to be much inferior to that in regular secondary schools and hardly constitutes an adequate preparation for entry to higher education. Because of these considerations, not to mention the obligation on PTU and tekhnikum graduates to complete a compulsory work assignment after training or to be subject to military call-up, the vocational track effectively rules out or considerably reduces the chances of acquiring higher education after it.[47]

This is indeed a formidable list of what the SPTU does, and how it serves some of the needs of the economy discussed previously. But it is well to pause on a few of these points.

Educationally, the "much inferior" academic training taken as expressed means that the SPTU gives a diploma, but *not* an education. It is not a better organized equivalent of ten-year academic secondary school with, somehow, a more serious vocational training than the earlier-mentioned *kombinaty* provided for academic students. It is not, and cannot be, "all things to all." Building on the old PTU, the SPTU begins with a questionable pedigree—the PTU has been legendary as a "dumping ground" for undisciplined, unbright youth. *Literaturnaia gazeta* in 1984 criticized the image of the "incorrigible [PTU students]: they openly smoke, use foul language, and skip classes."[48] The newspaper's implication that this is an undeserved image is not so important as how widespread it is and, presumably, the observable facts that confirm the image. An economics journal criticized the many "general education schools [which] direct young people into higher education and use the vocational-technical school as a threat to people who do poorly—and this against a background of inspirational speeches about 'the majesty of the working class.' "[49] During the 1984 discussion of the educational reform, an engineer argued that it was "high time to abandon, once and for all, the view of the vocational-technical school as a second-rate educational institution where the [academic] schools send their below-average pupils."[50]

But, one might observe, this *is* what they have done, and it is, in a sense, this that the state intends to do more of, via the educational reform. In a way, the issue is not "damage" to the structure of education as it has developed in the USSR thus far—after all, the relative universalization of "full secondary education" (i.e., the ten-year diploma) during the 1970s owed a good deal, statistically, to the SPTU. As a Western writer put it, labeling the aim of the 1984 reform "schools for a totalitarian-technocratic utopia," the "level of general secondary education in the vocational-technical schools has always been shockingly low, but the number of people officially credited with possessing a full secondary education grew enormously as a result of this measure [the "addition" of academic training to PTU's in the 1970s]."[51] The numbers make the point: a rise from 1,340,000 in 1965 to 4,030,000 in 1979 in the number of citizens credited with full secondary education.[52]

(Of course, it was not only the SPTU expansion that may have debased the coinage of the secondary school diploma. A writer in the Novosibirsk economics journal *EKO* noted that teachers' perceptions indicated large-scale grade inflation since secondary education had become socially near universal. Of [academic] school heads interviewed in 1982–83 in Tomsk and Novosibirsk, 75 percent thought the quality of graduating students had declined, and 95 percent felt their teachers were under pressure to award good grades. About half of those who had taken the standardized VUZ entry examinations had gotten grades of 2 in a scale where 5 is highest, and many of these in the same subjects where their secondary school grades were in the 4–5 range.)[53]

What, in the prereform period, drove so many young men into SPTUs? Given the still-considerable ambiguities in the data on the aspirations toward higher education of the tenth graders in academic schools, independent of social origin, it is hard to assume that it simply involved a "change of heart," an increasing appreciation of "workers' professions," even of the fact that young skilled workers *can* outearn young degree holders; this, after all, has been the case for some time. Some, surely, entered them because they found "trade school with diploma" more attractive than trade school without—although many had gone to PTUs in any case, indicating that not all eighth graders, certainly not all males, aspired to a diploma and admission to higher education. Some, perhaps, just "found" themselves in SPTUs—"converted" to such as they entered or during their period of enrollment.

Some may have seen the prospect of gaining the diploma via the SPTU as a track still leading to higher education, with less academic effort along the way. Soviet commentators, certainly, have been and are less than unanimous in their view of what one is likely to "do with" the education-training mix of the SPTU experience. Some laud the prospect of literate and *well-trained* young workers assuming their place in the factory, and by implication leave it at that. Others, however, focus on the relative advantage of ten-year academic-track graduates in the VUZ competition, and note that both SPTU and *tekhnikum* (specialized secondary education) graduates "have few chances to successfully handle the examination for higher educational institutions, and, getting there, have to study a whole program, calculated for graduates of the [ten-year academic] school." They have suggested shorter VUZ courses, conditioned on the type of secondary education or "special" VUZ programs for graduates of nonacademic schools, their nature to be expressed in the degree earned.[54] But all in all, the prospect of many SPTU graduates building on their *school* diploma toward higher education seems low.

This, also, would seem to be the state's intent in the 1984 reform. The draft guidelines for the reform speak of the various types of vocational-technical training still existing being reorganized into *one* type —the "secondary vocational-technical school"—to be set up under the auspices of "production association, enterprises, construction projects and organizations and, in rural localities, under the auspices of district agro-industrial associations, state farms, collective farms and interfarm enterprises."[55] There seems little reason, in this enumeration of sponsoring organizations, to think that the concentration on academic subjects will be weighted equally to that of the vocational, or that an SPTU diploma will carry the weight of one from the academic school.

Teachers—as in the responses to Khrushchev's educational reform of the late 1950s, "done in" by the mid-1960s—see problems in the ostensible "cramming" of a real secondary *education* into the SPTU. A report of a 1984 study of public opinion on the reform noted: "Every fifth teacher in secondary schools was opposed to the fact that the majority of youth would receive its vocational education in the PTU. They were concerned that the mass orientation of pupils toward the continuation of education in the PTU might create a lack of interest in studies in [an eight-year] school."[56] Thus, some teachers saw the prospect of ninth-tenth grade in the new "track" as a demotivating factor likely to affect student performance in the earlier years. They are not alone in this: an engineer, contributing to the *Izvestiia* discussion of the reform, argued that the "recruits" to the SPTU—overwhelmingly *boys*,[57] aged fourteen-fifteen—were not psychologically ready to be serious about choosing or learning a trade.

Thus, the SPTU "tracking" would not yield the results desired, while, were the "cut" between academic school and SPTU made on the basis of grades, it would be boys who would be tracked out of general education—an undesirable result.[58] To the contrary, another engineer (previously cited as arguing for a more sympathetic public understanding of the vocational-technical schools) asserted in a down-to-business manner that making an early career choice was a good thing.[59]

Parents, indeed, must be among those who tend to feel this way. A 1984 study indicated that while parents' "opinion" was *generally* in favor of the SPTU as the main mode of education, parents were more reserved in attitude when asked about their feelings about their *own* children going to an SPTU, as opposed to an ordinary academic school.[60]

Nor is it necessarily clear that the most affected population—eighth graders themselves—are likely to view the SPTU as a preferable route. In a 1973–74 study (when the SPTU was newer and fewer in supply) among about eleven thousand eighth graders, differences were marked among social-origin categories in the intent to go on in the ninth grade of academic school, but enthusiasm was moderate for the SPTU, even among workers' children.[61] Though the SPTU was more popular with working-class and peasant children than with white-collar offspring, almost three times as many opted for academic school, with a larger share also choosing secondary specialized *(tekhnikum)* training. Strikingly enough, even the eighth graders, of whatever social origin, who stated an intention to become skilled workers opted marginally in favor of ninth grade in an academic school over an SPTU (28.5 versus 27.1 percent). That the "diploma" side of the SPTU was not seen as conferring the same claim on access to higher education is evident: the eighth graders who confessed to desiring careers as specialists with higher education opted 70.5 percent for ninth grade, and only 2.7 percent for the SPTU.[62]

INTENT		ORIGIN	
	Worker	*Farmer*	*White Collar*
ninth grade	35.2%	33.7%	60.6%
secondary specialized	20.3	23.2	17.6
SPTU	13.6	13.8	3.5
PTU, evening school work	23.9	21.8	13.0
no decision	7.0	7.5	5.3

Whatever the impact of the new, reform-linked SPTU in adding skills, or in socializing the adolescent for entry into worker status, it will, if fully implemented—and this, of course, will remain a question for some time—affect the class *destinations* of large numbers of the young, and in a manner far from random. Directing more youth toward the SPTU and away from "pure" academic secondary education is not meant to multiply the career options of adolescents by providing academic diplomas to those who would not otherwise earn them, but to aim them toward entry into the working class. Who will "escape" this? Presumably, those whose academic qualifications, tutoring, etc., as manifested in the eighth grade (soon to be ninth, as programmed education will stretch from ten to eleven years) allow them to pass through the narrow gate into the academic track for the final two years (under the reform eventually tenth and eleventh) of secondary education. These students are likely to be disproportionately the "favored" by social origin, the educational and occupational levels of their parents, the per capita income within the household, and the readiness to *spend* on supplementary training, to encourage academic effort, even to use influence.

In this competitive context, the children of *workers* will be—as they are now—disadvantaged. This will remain especially true of *sons*; young males who, as we have seen, are in general more likely than females to "opt" at the end of eighth grade for the PTU/SPTU route. This process should intensify, and with it create an even *more* hereditized working class than otherwise.

Judging by the reform principles, the aim is to increase by "approximately two times" the share and number of eighth (ninth) graders who will enter the SPTUs. If we assume that the *base* is those who enter *both* SPTUs and PTUs (since the latter will be upgraded into the new "unified" SPTU), then the percentages below, synthesized from a number of sources on the *numbers* in various types of education in the 1979–80 academic year, and refined by some data on percentage shares, provide a "best estimate" of the rough pattern of eighth-grader "deployment" *prior* to the reform.[63]

Constructing on this basis a postreform pattern is simple. If we assume that the flow to the *tekhnikum* remains stable, and, according to the reform, assume the conversion of all PTUs into SPTUs, the following pattern, based on these 1979–80 figures, emerges.

to academic secondary (ninth grade)	52.0%
to SPTU	19.6
to PTU	17.7
to specialized secondary *tekhnikums*	10.7

The doubling of the SPTU's share is matched by a *near halving* of academic enrollments: quite a difference in the tracking of Soviet adolescents.

to academic secondary (tenth grade)	28.6%
to SPTU	50.7
to specialized secondary *tekhnikums*	10.7

Hope is reposed in the SPTU as the way of producing youth "fit" for the labor force, happy—or at least willing to stay—in their work. A study in three factories in the industrial city of Nizhnyi Tagil in the mid-1970s argued that while "better-educated" young workers made the best adjustment to factory life, it was not a matter of years alone —SPTU graduates did better than ten-year academic graduates or the products of the "regular" PTU. SPTU graduates were more satisfied with being workers (57 percent) than were their academic peers (38 percent). Prospects for changing one's status via part-time study clearly reflected this—of the tenth-grade academic graduates, 18.2 percent were studying part-time or by correspondence in VUZy, but only 5.6 percent of the SPTU products were (22.9 percent of these were studying in "secondary specialized" institutions while working, while only 19.17 percent of the "academics" were).[64]

Research in Leningrad on the friendship patterns of youth in various educational tracks reported, with approval, the "diversity" of the social contacts of SPTU students. Of such, 35.27 percent reported friendships with SPTU peers, 19.3 percent with children in other secondary schools; their contacts with "young workers" were cited as twice the latter (presumably 38.6 percent). If this is accurate, the sum of contacts with workers and the SPTU peers (whose future is also the workers' world) adds up to 73.8 percent—not surprising, surely, but an indication, if anything, of the degree of closure and homogeneity, rather than diversity, in the social world of SPTU trainees.[65]

From the viewpoint of the 1984 reform's designers, this is probably not a problem. Certainly, some of the writing which admits the tendency toward self-reproduction in the working class simultaneously denies that there is any implication here of inequality, of a slow dynamic, of a decline in opportunity to change one's life from that characterizing one's social origin. As one observer wrote in 1984:

> Continuity [preemstvennost'] of profession in the conditions of developed socialism does not signify a stabilization of the social structure of society, the inheritance [nasledovanie] of children of the "business," trade, profession of their fathers, but is a conscious resolution of youth to choose the same area of activity as that of their parents.[66]

The same author noted, disapprovingly, that in some circumstances parents' aspirations are less "realistic," more oriented toward achieving intelligentsia status, than either the children want, or the economy needs: in one study reported in 1979, while 5.4 percent of a set of tenth graders were willing to become workers, only 2.9 percent of their parents approved; 41.27 percent of the same group aimed at a VUZ, while 59.4 percent of parents desired this.[67]

The picture is not altogether clear. But it still seems unlikely that the social processes of the last fifteen years have moderated expectations among working-class youth to the point where frustration with failure to cross the line between working class and intelligentsia is no longer widespread, nor important. In this context, the hereditization already produced by forces discussed above, and the likely impact of the new selection process under the reform, may well exacerbate these frustrations. (Even if, as critical comments by education officials in the fall of 1987 suggested, the notion that academic and vocational education could be effectively combined for double the number of students in the new SPTU were to be abandoned,[68] this and other alterations in the original direction of the reform would be unlikely to moderate many of the frustrations inherent in *current* levels of working-class hereditization.)

CLASS CONSCIOUSNESS AND SOCIAL JUSTICE

It is in this connection that the question of consciousness—*class* consciousness, in a broad sense—arises. Looking at this from the perspective of what S. M. Lipset calls "the logic implicit in an apolitical sociological Marxism,"[69] we can argue several points. First, a "class" whose human content is rapidly changing, whose components are diverse, is not likely to develop a common *view* of the world around it. The "early" Soviet working class—that of the Plan era—was one growing rapidly "from the bottom" by the massive inflow of the peasantry, while at the same time losing, from the "top," both workers already in the plant, and young people of the working class, through a combination of educational and political promotion into professional-managerial strata. The newcomers from the countryside, as we saw earlier, became the majority in many sectors and branches, "swamping" the core proletariat of the pre-1929 period. Meanwhile, whether one considers it as the obvious *economic* consequence of growth, or as a conscious regime attempt to "co-opt" the young, ambitious, and talented of proletarian origin and thus deprive a working class of its potential natural leaders (probably both), the upward mobility of some workers/working-class youth subtracted from the core proletarian element. Such a mix as resulted was, in a sense, not a "class" at all, but a mix too diverse to share any of the similarity of perspective built over time in the same socioeconomic "space" that marks a class.

Second, as long as economic growth was sustained at a high rate, and with it structural change in the labor force, working and peasant youth *could* anticipate opportunities to "solve," via upward mobility, whatever problems they found in their present status (typically in this case also the status of their parents). Birth into the working class or peasantry was *not*, evidently, a life sentence. Some would be content, as everywhere, in following the previous generation's footsteps. Those who were not could anticipate exit via education (urban working-class youth) to the intelligentsia, providing they qualified mentally and had the combination of discipline and ambition necessary, or via the demand for new hands in a growing industrial sector, sometimes mediated by the military service which distanced young peasants from the *kolkhoz* and the countryside.

There is a paradox here. Regime propagandists and leaders, from Lenin on, saw a "guarantee" of the stability of the socialist order in the creation of a conscious working *class*—a large phalanx of blue-collar supporters of a regime come to power before such a proletariat existed in Russia, and thus in a sense prematurely. But in Stalin's and Khrushchev's time, and in the early Brezhnev period as well, the regime was arguably a beneficiary of something quite different: a social dynamism, a flow between social strata which helped *prevent* class formation.

At the turn of the century, Werner Sombart's classic book posed the question *Why Is There No Socialism in the United States?*[70] Sombart found his answer both in American ideology (a belief in opportunity and the ability to better oneself) and in American reality (empty space, dynamic economic growth, a lack of some ancien régime cultural, legal, and traditional barriers), and concluded that the American workers did not need socialism. The rules of the capitalist economy worked well enough for the ambitious—they did not require the change of the rules that socialism, as political and economic program, meant.

In a very different context—wherein the regime had already declared that it was building "socialism"—the opportunity to advance, to solve one's problems of living standard and status by individual mobility in a growing Soviet economy, was surely one key to the survival of the Soviet social order. Mobility opportunities are, in a sense, "de-solidarizing." All people in a category whose status and rewards are limited —the peasantry, the manual workers—are not "in the same boat" if the most discontented see a way of leaving the boat. Allowing for the vast differences in context, socialist organizers in early twentieth-century America found this a fact limiting their success (as well as anti-union legislation and company police); Soviet leaders from the 1930s through the 1960s could, and perhaps did, understand that the same phenomenon made their tasks of control easier, and lessened, in any period, the necessity to use coercive measures to insure support, or at least lack of opposition.

Thus, the third point. At long last, the USSR, *has* created a working "class" whose composition differs from what the regime has been used to, one possessed of many of the properties considered necessary to the formation of class consciousness, and with it the potential for becoming a political factor more to be reckoned with than in the past. The hereditized working class of today is "tapped" neither at bottom nor top to the degree of previous times: neither "inflow" from the peasantry below nor outflow toward the intelligentsia above radically alters its composition. It is self-recruiting, and within the limits its internal diversity imposes, it is more homogeneous than in the past.[71] It is not growing rapidly—but it is the largest category by far in the labor force. Slowing growth in an economic system still institutionally quite similar to what Stalin wrought guarantees, over the medium term, that the working class will remain large, will not be reduced by any overnight shift to an expanded service sector, and will pursue its fate in an economy whose total output will not increase rapidly. The "pie" is not growing noticeably larger.

Such a working class—large, hereditized, relatively homogeneous—is one in which a common consciousness of common interests may develop; in which the blocked opportunities for exit, which contribute mightily to the hereditization, can conduce to the conclusion that workers must pursue their goals *as* workers, via collective rather than individual action. This, if not the whole, is a critical component of *class* consciousness; more critical, perhaps, than that workers see their "class interests" as directly opposed to those of other groups (classes) in Soviet society. They constitute, in any case, the largest class by far—the effective majority of Soviet society.

None of this argument, of course, aims to equate the future political potential of the Soviet worker with his East European counterparts. Though an argument can be made that similar hereditization in East European working classes, and similar advances in workers' educational levels, contributed to militancy, discontent, and in the Polish case to a near revolution (see chapters 7 and 8), the Soviet context is different in several important respects. Though these factors are generally part of the "conventional wisdom" among students of Soviet domestic politics, it is a conventional wisdom that has been generally accurate.

1. a political docility on the part of Soviet workers facing a strong, entrenched political culture which contains few if any elements of a "civic" sort

2. patriotic attitudes widely diffused among the Soviet (especially Russian) working class, signaling a general acceptance of the system as legitimate and domestically rooted (versus the flawed legitimacy of externally imposed socialist political order in, e.g., Poland, Czechoslovakia, Hungary)

3. the perception and reality of the Soviet state (versus the Polish regime) as decisive, confident, ready to turn to coercion to the degree

needed to resist/crush "illegitimate" demands from semi-organized or organized social forces

4. the lack, thus far, of an obviously impending broad-scale economic crisis in the USSR which immediately threatens the living standards to which workers have grown accustomed

Thus, the impact of processes discussed here is not likely to manifest itself "tomorrow," or in a manner similar to that which marked the political and economic decomposition of Gierek's Poland and the rise of Solidarity. But the tension-producing effects are not necessarily relegated to the far future. If one is to take Gorbachev's rhetoric seriously, the general thrust of his objectives is likely to confront working-class desires/preferences/habits in several areas:

■ *work discipline:* the heavy reliance on the rhetoric of "discipline" in Gorbachev's statements, the emphasis on achieving so much of the twelfth FYP's goals via increased labor productivity, promise a pressure on workers surely beyond that felt in recent time, and this without the prior "carrot" in the form of a perceptible increase in the rate of improvement in living standards;

■ *labor mobility/unemployment:* though Gorbachev's plans do not threaten structural unemployment, the expressed need to concentrate resources on efficient industries and take a harder line toward the inefficient may imply an involuntary reallocation of blue-collar workers, and a break with the "job-tenure-in-place" pattern to which they have become accustomed;

■ *wage inequality:* the increase in inequality that *must* come if rewards are tied more tightly to some measure of the quality/quantity of work's results will create more self-described "losers" than winners, and, whether seen as truly linked to the individual's work or to the fortunes of his enterprise, will generate elements of tension and feelings of violated expectations;

■ *price increases:* decisive, or seemingly so, beyond his predecessors, Gorbachev may impose these. While "economically" justified, increases in prices for goods (or, possibly, services, such as some elements of medical care)[72] in the absence of better supply/higher quality would, again, be an "antipopulist" policy, exacerbating for many the effects of greater wage/income differentials.

All these policy developments would be consistent with Gorbachev's plans, outlined only roughly thus far, for a "technocratic" refurbishment of the economy. Should he move toward a more decentralized/ market/private-enterprise reform, the social tensions of rising prices/perceived economic inequality will be all the greater, and in a more unfamiliar environment, wherein the favored workers in heavy industry may find themselves at unaccustomed disadvantage, as did their Hungarian counterparts in the early days of the New Economic Mechanism (NEM).

However badly the Soviet economy works, Soviet citizens—among them the majority working class—have learned to work *it.* This working class is not as easily manipulated, for the reasons of greater educational attainment a id the "sophistication" attendant upon hereditization, as its predecessors. Its potential for reaction in ways undermining and disruptive, if not militant, to an economic package it finds unpleasant and, by its standards, unfair, is significant.[73] Nor does it seem likely that the demagogic side of Andropov's (and Gorbachev's continuing) war against "shirkers, idlers, drifters," etc., will galvanize worker opinion against a putative minority and satisfy some long-felt "thirst" for discipline and justice. This working class surely realizes that many of the practices workers engage in in the majority are the targets of such rhetoric.

The years to come will test, if the priorities of a new economic rhetoric take shape in policy, the linkage between regime and working class which has been forged out of political culture, patriotism, and economic/welfare measures which, while hardly making of workers the "leading class," paid a good deal of attention to their maintenance, especially in the Brezhnev era. Should Gorbachev's program prove little more than paper—as did the "Kosygin reform" of 1965—then Soviet workers will confront the consequences of life in an economy more familiar in style and content, but whose ever-slowing growth will impose on them problems perhaps no less severe.

SIX

SOCIAL POLICY IN THE GORBACHEV ERA

At mid-1987, two years and some months along as General Secretary of the CPSU, Mikhail Gorbachev—and his policies of "restructuring" and "radical reform"—represents something akin to a moving target, and one which seems, if anything, in a state of acceleration. After a start in 1985 more impressive in rhetoric and mood than in policy detail, by the latter part of 1986 and into 1987, in which this chapter takes on its current form, Gorbachev had "fleshed out" and presided over the elaboration of a program of economic and organizational change "radical" by any Soviet standard since Stalin's time. In a number of areas, Gorbachev's policies both promise to affect grass-roots Soviet life in profound ways and are potentially at risk—as is his leadership—by virtue of some of the resistance they may evoke at those grass roots, and the political issue which could be made of this by his opponents at the "center." This chapter, then, addresses some aspects of social policy as

The original version of this chapter was published as "Social Policy Under Gorbachev," *Problems of Communism* (July-August 1986), 35(4): 31–46. This version is substantially revised and updated to mid-1987.

they emerged on the Gorbachev agenda as of 1987—aspects closely intermingled with the economic policies he has adopted to counteract the long-term inefficiency and slowing growth of the Soviet economy. Social discipline in the service of predictability and productivity, work tenure and organization, wage and remuneration policy, all demand attention, as do the controversial implications in each of these areas for widely diffused and shared conceptions of "social justice," equity and equality, among the Soviet citizenry. We begin with a critical contextual element for all these—the present performance and mid-term prospects for consumption by the 270 million who constitute that citizenry.

CONSUMERISM AND CONSTRAINT

Soviet consumers could find little of encouragement in the public communications emanating from the Kremlin from the autumn of 1985, and—if they read improbably closely—there are some clearly discouraging indications. The lengthy "Consumer Goods and Services Program" published on October 9, 1985, set goals for the period to 1990— that of the twelfth Five-Year Plan—and to the year 2000, the current endpoint of so many Gorbachev projections.[1] Near-term goals, if not revolutionary in their promise, seemed beyond the reach of the modest-to-minimal growth record of recent years. The program promised to increase production of nonfood commodities by 30 percent above 1985 levels by the year 1990 and 80 to 90 percent by 2000, to achieve better siting of retail outlets, and to arrange for more convenient store hours. Beyond predictable references to clothing and footwear, furniture, and refrigerators, the document revealed the continuing "overload" on a central planning apparatus that apparently found it necessary to refer to the production of new types of automatic potato peelers, to promise a 100 percent increase in the production of quartz wristwatches by 1990, and to raise production of videocassette recorders to 60,000 a year by 1990 and 120,000 by 2000.

The program predicted that "payments and benefits provided to the population from public consumption funds will receive further development," but it also set the goal of creating "an extensive and efficiently operating system" of paid services, the volume of which is to rise 30–40 percent by 1990 and 110–130 percent by 2000. The commitment to an expansion of paid services was accompanied by comments on improving the quality of services to urban and rural populations and on making services available to all population groups and to people "with different income levels."[2]

Moreover, the economy seemed unlikely to fulfill *these* promises. There is a perplexing lack of correspondence between targeted 1986–1990 investment in the "nonproductive" sector and the promised delivery from this sector, suggesting that consumption is likely to be an "orphan" in the second half of the present decade. Investment bulks large in the targets of the twelfth Five-Year Plan, including investment in the energy and agriculture sectors—indeed, Gorbachev apparently had to compromise on his public position of mid-1985, which foresaw no significant rises in investment for these sectors.[3] Total investment was targeted to increase by 18–21 percent over the 1986–1990 period, but productive investment is to grow by fully 25 percent.[4] The adverse implications of this for investment in "nonproductive" sectors (health, education, housing, culture), which normally only account for about one-quarter of all investment anyway, were clear. This was not a "social budget."

Nor were resources moving toward the production of mass consumer goods in sufficient numbers to reduce the bottlenecks and pressures that have produced a spectacularly bribe-ridden Soviet economy. Both the Gorbachev rhetoric emphasizing technological investment in leading sectors of the economy (notably machine building) and the discrepancy between the overall investment growth target of some 20 percent and promises of growth in nonfood commodity production of 30 percent by 1990 seemed to tip the scales against any emerging abundance of consumer durables.

The somewhat bleak picture "one year along" under Gorbachev was, by and large, a fair guide to the situation which obtained for the consumer by mid-1987, and for much of the economy in general. The year 1986, indeed, started off with a bang—rising over 7 percent in the January-February 1986 industrial output over the same months in 1985. But the output in the early part of 1985, just prior to Chernenko's death and Gorbachev's succession, had been very low indeed, complicated by a severe winter; from the late winter on, the pace of improvement slowed throughout 1986.[5] Fewer-than-planned new production facilities came "on line," and the final reported figures on economic performance in 1986—though clearly better than 1985[6]—contained sufficient ambiguities and improbabilities to generate a complicated debate among Western analysts.[7]

By May of 1987, Aleksandra Biriukova, the Central Committee secretary whose "portfolio" includes consumer-related industry and services, was excoriating economic performance in some areas critical to a goods-hungry population. The traditionally favored "group A" industries, the heavy, "producer goods" specialists, had been tasked with using some of their capacity for producing consumer goods, and emphasizing the production of the more "sophisticated" rather than simpler items (with many of the latter, the Soviet consumer is already well equipped); their performance was underwhelming. Over 1985, they had in 1986 produced 4 percent more of the sophisticated range, but 8 percent of the simple items; but over the first three to four months of 1987, the rate of growth over 1986 was running at 7 percent for the sophisticated goods, and 26 percent for the simple "cake pans, casseroles, and soap dishes."[8]

New Year's Day 1987 ushered in more very cold weather and with it the strong likelihood that production would be off to a bad start. It also marked the commencement of the work of the new "state acceptance commission" system *(gospriemka)* in 1,500 large plants: announced in July 1986,[9] much heralded in the press from then on,[10] this involved a new mode of quality control via an end-of-line inspection service answering not to plant management but to the State Committee on Standards *(Gosstandart)*, with the mandate and the "teeth" to reject the shoddy goods previously passed. This, in turn, had its effects on (statistical) plan-fulfillment figures. According to a first deputy chairman of *Gosstandart*, only 83.9 percent of relevant enterprise output "passed" in January 1987.[11] Other figures indicated significant shortfalls as well (60 percent of the 1,500 plants under *gospriemka* failed to meet their January output targets),[12] although an April 30 report indicated that (only) 1 percent of industrial output had been rejected by *gospriemka* in the first quarter of 1987.[13] Whatever the case, two things were clear: first, enterprise managers and local party officials (whose own performance "ratings" depend heavily on the economic performance of plants on their turf) found the new situation confusing. In Karaganda *oblast'*, the local party secretary accused the *gospriemka* head at a large machinery plant of not being "concerned" with "plan fulfillment."[14] Second, *workers* in factories under *gospriemka* found unwelcome pay-packet consequences from the new rejection rates (see below).

That "objective circumstances" did not favor the Soviet consumer over the next five to ten years, then, seemed obvious. This raised for Gorbachev the necessity to mobilize energies, while disciplining expectations—to deliver the stick, or its functional equivalent, in the absence of a credible and motivating promise of carrots in the near term. The prospective belt tightening (on the basis, let it be noted, of the anything but dramatic growth of consumer welfare in the first half of the 1980s)[15] is not simply a matter of policy choice in a slow-growth Soviet economy. For various reasons; neither Eastern Europe nor the West is a likely source of the goods whose import might improve the consumer picture.

Eastern Europe is itself economically strapped, and so long as the Soviets understand that social peace there is maintained partially at the price of guaranteeing a living standard that, however threadbare, exceeds the Soviet norm, they should not be tempted to an over-reliance on the region as an interim source of goods to buttress Soviet living standards. Beyond social peace, a modicum of consumerism is necessary to keep East European citizens motivated as producers, at a time when Soviet policies on integration within the Council for Economic Mutual Assistance (CEMA) lean harder on East European economies than hitherto. In a paper prepared for the U.N. Economic Commission on Europe, Soviet economist Oleg Bogomolov predicted that the CEMA market as a whole "will continue to suffer (at least for the next 5–10 years) from an excess of demand (principally from the USSR) for food and consumer goods. There is, however, relatively little potential for expanding exports of such products."[16]

Western sources will doubtless continue to supply an important component of Soviet consumption, making good shortfalls in grain production. But even in this area relating directly to diet (at the base of "living standards"), developments look anything but promising. Falling Soviet oil-export revenues reduce available hard currency, intensifying the dilemmas of what to import from the West: technology and capital, grain, or other consumer goods?

On the agricultural front, it is not clear that the USSR is "due" some good luck with weather; without it, grain shortfalls will be worse, and the claims on diminishing energy-export revenues greater. The yet-to-be clarified agricultural consequences of the Chernobyl' nuclear reactor disaster raise further questions about the quantity and utility of output from farming in the generally marginal producing areas near the plant and, more important, in the Ukrainian bread-basket lands to the south and southeast.

At the Twenty-seventh Party Congress, Premier Nikolai Ryzhkov spoke of pay raises amounting to 25–30 percent for those in material production, plus allocations for raises for many in nonproduction branches, to be financed by "increased production and efficiency" of labor collectives. These, plus increases in public consumption funds, he predicted, would "lead to really appreciable changes in the living conditions and living standards of very broad strata of society" over the period 1986–90.[17] In the perspective of 1985 and early 1986, it was already difficult to square this with Bogomolov's commentary on prospects for near-term rises in consumption in the CEMA states:

> It is not impossible that until the end of the 1980s resources will be insufficient for the achievement of socially perceptible growth in consumption. . . . In these circumstances, there is likely to be development and satisfaction of aspects of demand that do not relate to increase in the supply of material goods but are important for the promotion of social contentment, namely, the improvement of working conditions and the multiplication of training and leisure options. That will help to augment workers' capacity for highly productive labour and promote their more active involvement in production and management.[18]

To what degree progress has been made in satisfying these other "aspects of demand" is a matter of doubt—or interpretation. Clearly, nothing yet has developed which would contra-indicate Bogomolov's "not impossible" comment on the absence of perceptible growth in consumption; wage policy, as we shall see below, has followed the rough indications Ryzhkov gave in early 1986—but the details of how raises are to be financed, the "risks" to them, and the pattern of raises all contain elements anything but welcome to the largest potential "constituency" in Soviet welfare politics: the blue-collar industrial workers.

DISCIPLINE

The broad Gorbachev policy has stressed discipline: work, sobriety, order, and honesty. In this, it reproduces the style of the Andropov interregnum, but not quite the "campaign" quality of the early months of 1983, when hapless Soviet citizens, shopping during working hours, were dragooned from queues and asked to account for their involvement in what was, after all, a mass-behavior phenomenon. Although Western commentary at the time tended to perceive enthusiastic mass support for Andropov's attack on the slackness of behavior, the dishonesty, and the corner cutting that had become epidemic in the latter years of the Brezhnev period, one may doubt that such feelings went very deep. The Andropov campaign literally aimed at the "man in the street," long starved of goods and convenient hours in which to purchase them. The stick of discipline was felt immediately; the carrot of more convenient store hours and better supplies was more a matter of future hopes.

Gorbachev, in contrast, in his first year concentrated more on dismissing, retiring, and otherwise separating from ill-discharged functions party and state leaders at various levels—from national to regional and local. In so doing, he has given Soviet citizens so inclined something to cheer about, as the incompetent, but especially corrupt (who used elevated positions to enrich themselves), are laid low. The Soviet rank and file is, after all, used to taking orders, to waiting upon (or trying to subvert) cumbersome bureaucratic procedures to secure services and decisions. While in the latter half of the 1980s, citizens are surely sophisticated enough to expect no alteration of hierarchical structures out of this, it cannot be a matter of total indifference to them that many of the highly placed are finally getting a comeuppance. (On the "downside," however, Gorbachev's enthusiasm in the rooting out of networks of corruption combines uncomfortably with what might be called (at best?) an insensitivity to ethnic issues, especially as these are perceived in central Asia. In both Uzbekistan and Kazakhstan, to be sure, large networks of corruption do exist, strengthened by families' ties and by the ethnic indigenization of so many posts. Rooting them out can present "nationalist" overtones—Gorbachev's dismissal of Dinmukhamed Kunaev, the Kazakh secretary and longtime Brezhnev crony, and his replacement with the Russian Kolbin provoked riots in Alma-Ata.)

Less popular, one must assume, is the campaign Gorbachev has made his own: the one against alcohol and the Soviet population's massive and frequent recourse to it.[19] Barely had Konstantin Chernenko been buried and Gorbachev settled in the General Secretary's chair when *Pravda* and *Izvestiia* announced that the Politburo had discussed means of "combatting drunkenness and alcoholism,"[20] setting the stage for further rhetoric, if not action. The former followed, with Central Committee resolution and a Council of Ministers decree in mid-May.[21] Beyond familiar pieties about expanded programs of medical treatment, the encouragement of more "creative" (i.e., sober) use of leisure time, and improvement in the quality of anti-alcohol propaganda, the main substance was a set of restrictive police measures. Alcohol sales were barred to persons under twenty-one; there were to be no sales of wine and vodka before 2:00 P.M. on workdays; and the number of retail outlets was to be reduced.

In contrast to the past, the Gorbachev regime does seem intent on enforcing such restrictions. Muscovites and visitors report the novelty of "dry" lunches in restaurants and changes in the previously bibulous pattern of Soviet official entertaining, including events on the Moscow diplomatic rounds. Soviet reports cite a reduction in retail sales outlets (those selling wine and vodka) of 50 percent during 1985 and a fall in sales amounting to 25 percent for the same year.[22] Restrictions on hours of sale, surely aimed at reducing workplace drunkenness, may—combined with a crackdown on labor-discipline violations in plants—have had some positive impact. It was claimed, for example, that the rise in industrial production figures in the fourth quarter of 1985 was attributable in part to more "discipline"—part of which must surely be a lessening of drunkenness, absences, accidents, and general slackness related to alcohol.[23]

Over the long term, however, there is ample reason to doubt that a behavior pattern so deeply rooted can be extirpated, especially habits that have put money in the state's pocket via its monopoly on alcohol production (even as they have taken it away in productivity) and that have contributed, in some measure, to the relative political quiescence of a population deprived of liberties and consumer goods long common in the West. If the regime under Gorbachev continues to "mean business," it may cut the production of liquor further, but only to see some of its market ceded to the producers of *samogon* (privately brewed alcohol). Illegal distillers, mainly rural, are targeted in Gorbachev's campaign, but their numbers are large and rural law enforcement notoriously difficult. Without more goods and services to reward greater discipline and productivity, there will be fewer incentives for the Soviet masses to moderate their drinking.

All in all, taking on a "pandemic" behavior like Soviet alcohol abuse is an enormous task: one as likely to generate cynically dismissive attitudes as to evoke grudging admiration, even among the sober population. There are enough indications that the campaign had lost some steam by early 1987 to warrant caution in any rendering of a verdict on the success of this part of the Gorbachev prescription for Soviet ills.[24]

Discipline at the social level, ultimately, is a matter of motivation —moral as well as self-interested (whether for gain or avoidance of penalty)—to behave within prescribed patterns (the "letter of the law," or something close to it). Moral motivation must be strong indeed if the consequences for the individual are more negative in adhering to the rules than in learning to sidestep them. Here Gorbachev faces a dual burden. Under Brezhnev as never before, negative incentives to obey laws weakened, while positive incentives failed to grow apace with desires for goods and services. (A positive incentive against offering bribes to salespeople and their asking for same is the opportunity to acquire an adequate amount of the goods involved in the transaction.) Under these circumstances, the views of Soviet people about such issues of everyday morality drifted far from the prescriptions of the laws.

Interesting evidence of this emerges in a 1982 Soviet study of popular attitudes toward legal norms (see table 6.1), based on a study of 2,000 workers in Moscow industrial enterprises. Respondents were asked about their attitudes ("actively positive," "neutral," "negative") toward the negative norms declaring certain acts illegal. Nothing about these figures should surprise any student of Soviet affairs—or anyone familiar to any degree with the strictures and opportunities of grass-roots Soviet life. Worth noting, however, is not only the very weak support for prohibitions of behavior that betokens participation in the "secondary economy," but also the clarity of the separation between public and private

TABLE 6.1. Attitudes of a Sample of Moscow Industrial Workers Toward Legal Norms (in percent)

Act Punished by a Given Law	Attitude Toward the Given Law			
	Actively positive	Neutral	Negative	No opinion
Theft from an apartment	92.6	—	—	7.4
Petty theft from an enterprise	16.6	78.6	3.3	1.5
Radio repair: repairman avoids filling out work order and pockets the fee personally	4.7	49.3	40.7	5.3
Swindling customers (charging for false weight, etc.)	76.7	20.7	—	2.6
Money bribe to salesperson to obtain a scarce item	12.0	30.0	54.7	3.3
Influencing criminal investigation to help a friend escape responsibility	44.0	17.3	33.3	5.4

Source: adapted from A. S. Grechin, "Opyt sotsiologicheskogo izucheniia pravosoznaniia," *Sotsiologicheskie issledovaniia* (1983), no. 2, p. 124.

"spheres" of moral calculation. Stealing from the workplace is one thing; from an individual's apartment, something else. Bribing a salesperson is "normal"; being short-weighted by the same, reprehensible.

If it is Gorbachev's goal to upgrade public morality to the level of private morality, one can only say that at present the resources to do so, ranging from the coercive to the positively motivating, are in less than adequate supply. Changing such public attitudes will require more than a campaign. Attempting at the outset to change them mainly by negative and punitive policies could produce, in lowered morale and more sophisticated patterns of avoidance, the opposite of the regime's objectives.

THE WORLD OF WORK

For all the costs—political, psychological, economic, and other—that the Soviet state as collective employer and paymaster, as well as pedagogue and policeman, has imposed on its subjects, it has provided rank-and-file workers guarantees against Western-style unemployment and insured job security in current jobs at the workplace. Indeed, that issues of the quality of Soviet work life have come into sharper focus in recent years in the writings of Soviet economists and sociologists is a mark of a certain industrial maturity,[25] of having solved in the main the basic problems of providing work and sustenance. While not so critical to the ambitious or to the large number each year who do change jobs in the USSR, this security has been, for many, an essential component of a welfare package that links regime and society in a social compact of sorts. It is a benefit to be balanced against the monotonous, sometimes arduous, unmechanized jobs in an industrial economy well behind the West in its evolution toward "postindustrial" or "service economy" characteristics.

There are now signs, however, that the Gorbachev regime may take steps that will imperil this fundamental security without either enriching the nature of work or increasing the rewards for it. Should this prove to be the case, the adjustments required of society could be, collectively, quite remarkable. The reasons for this departure are a "labor shortage" reflecting both demographic realities (the low numbers of young entrants into the labor force and large numbers of workers reaching retirement age) and an abysmally low level of per capita labor productivity. The latter also reflects overmanning as enterprise policy and underemployment of this "stockpiled" labor.

Experiments of limited scope to deal with this problem are not new —for example, starting in 1967, the managers of the Shchekino chemical complex were allowed to dismiss redundant labor and reward those who remained with higher earnings from a retained part of wage-fund savings. But the rhetoric confronting inefficient labor utilization—and, implicitly, the underlying job security—has escalated to a new level over the last year and a half. Early calls by Gorbachev for harder work and greater efficiency were accompanied by action, which although not massive, was certainly more than symbolic. In his Twenty-seventh Party Congress speech Gorbachev cited the dismissal of 12,000 workers of the Byelorussian railway system and cuts in industry and construction personnel of Zaporozh'e *oblast'*, and he held out the prospect that new machinery in agricultural industry might save the labor of as many as 12 million workers by 1990.

The merger of five ministries and a state committee into a unified State Agro-Industrial Committee in November 1985 signaled, to much publicity, the release of several thousand bureaucrats from their jobs. Although it was noted that they would receive benefits equal to their old salaries for a maximum of three months while awaiting placement in (unspecified) new positions, there was no indication of an immediate transfer to other work.[26] Transition payments notwithstanding, they were, effectively, "unemployed."

While one can predict or imagine responses ranging all the way from mild concern to cheers that a set of ministerial bureaucracies had released a reported 47 percent of their *apparat*,[27] an article in *Sovetskaia kul'tura* by labor economist Vladimir Kostakov at the beginning of 1986 raised a more alarming specter; if growth targets for labor productivity for the year 2000 were met, he argued, this would allow a reduction by 13–19 million in jobs in manufacturing.[28] He predicted that the "sharpness" of this process would be "significantly moderated" by routine retirements and by the arrival on the labor scene of smaller cohorts to replace larger existing ones. More significantly, Kostakov wrote of a shift of employment to the service sector—long a low-pay, low-status, understaffed part of the economy—as manufacturing "de-stocked" especially in the area of a minimally or nonmechanized labor. Indeed, he admitted, in the mid-1980s, "imperfections in the service sphere are harming material production most of all."

Although the image of a more modern economy, somewhat along the lines of "postindustrialism" (without using the term), was a benign one in Kostakov's depiction, the transition from industrial to service employment was cast in terms rather different from those that Soviet audiences are accustomed to hearing:

> The need to look for a job, something that many people...will certainly face, may also be new and unaccustomed for us. After all, we are used to just the opposite—the job looking for the person.... Considerable psychological restructuring will also be required, apparently. We consider it natural and necessary that, if for objective reasons a job slot becomes unnecessary, the employee should immediately be given another job. Very often, that is precisely why staff reduction takes place more slowly than it could even now. The managers of enterprises and institutions...prefer not to burden themselves with concern for the job placement of people who have been let go—especially since their possibilities for doing so are very limited. Now we will have to accustom ourselves to the thought that finding employment is, to a considerable extent, the individual's own concern, and that this search may require a certain amount of time—a sufficient, but not unlimited, amount of time.[29]

It was, perhaps, the tone of the commentary, rather than the rough demographic projections, that engendered unease. Whatever the case, an interview with TASS later in the same month gave Kostakov the opportunity to deny that unemployment would result from technological progress and enhanced productivity,[30] and a later article by him in *Sovetskaia kul'tura* provided a general discussion of economic progress and its conditions that was less pointed than the earlier one.[31]

If early 1986 presented some "waffling" on the issue of employment security, the policy line since has clarified, in a reassertion of Kostakov's reasoning. Employment security of the old Soviet type—essentially "tenure"-in-place at the job holder's option—is now derided as inequitable (the laggard collecting his wages on the same basis as the good worker) and uneconomical/inefficient. To the various (but often uncertain) positive incentives in the "experiments" of the past to encourage managers to be more sparing of labor have been added new ones. One of the old disincentives has been removed: managers need no longer (a matter of law since 1984, now a matter of policy too) find jobs for released workers, unless one is to be had, for which the individual is qualified, within the plant.[32]

In practice, many released will be so "reabsorbed," as factories move to multishift systems; many of Kostakov's 13–19 million will retire and not be replaced. Some will really "lose" jobs, be retrained, and find others. Whether some others will fall into anything like "unemploy-ment" Western-style remains to be seen; it does not seem likely. But the predominant rhetoric of 1987 holds a rather consistent tune—that *individuals* must assume more responsibility, that neither economics nor "social justice" requires the regime to provide employment for the unsalvageable, that, finally, the iron link to the job must be broken.

The economist Tatiana Zaslavskaia, in one of the many interviews she has given as a contributor to the "new economics," spoke of "va-cant" jobs, and said, "The transition to a new system of economic management will unavoidably lead to the disappearance of the vacant job, and, subsequently, to laying people off."[33] Nor was this a statement simply of a more demanding "morality." Leonid Abalkin, director of the Soviet Academy of Sciences' Institute of Economics, returned in an interview with a *New York Times* correspondent to Kostakov-type fig-ures, asserting that 20 million workers in industry and agriculture could be dispensed with by the year 2000, via "layoffs, mergers and a program of intense retraining"[34]—this in a broad review of a number of contro-versial aspects of the Gorbachev economic plan. It was not the only prospective change to which Soviet citizens would have to adjust.

WAGES AND PRICES

There is, surely, a strong egalitarian bent among a significant segment of the Soviet population, and one may assume that the Brezhnev-era wage policy, which saw a "drift" toward minimization of the earning advantages of engineering and technical personnel over manual workers and continuing advantages of the latter over people in rank-and-file positions in medicine, education, culture, and other services,[35] re-sponded in some fashion to this bent. Gorbachev seemed to have some-thing different in mind—a "shake-up" in favor of those "underpaid" (from the incumbents' point of view) nonmanual and service-sector occupations, which are expected to increase as a percentage of the labor force when manufacturing de-stocks unneeded workers. In the words of Bogomolov in late 1985, "Fundamental changes may be expected in systems of wage rates and in the differentials between pay of particular categories of workers. For example, the Soviet Union . . . intend[s] to raise the salaries of engineers and technicians, scientists, designers, teachers, and medical staff."[36]

The early signals were more than borne out, as wage policy became clearer in 1986 and 1987. The Gorbachev program, echoing the calls of so many economists for *less* egalitarianism in rewards between different levels of skill in the working class, and less of egalitarian drift in the relationship of workers' and college-educated professionals' pay, represented a radical departure from the *ouvrieriste* policies of the long Brezhnev era. As one Western student put it, Gorbachev was risking conflict (as Brezhnev had not) via a policy of "squeezing the traditional working class,"[37] in pursuit of a social policy which implied "a markedly different set of prospective winners and losers than obtained under the rule of his predecessors."[38] (Zaslavskaia, in a January interview with the Hungarian daily *Nepszabadsag,* had been scarcely less pointed: "If we want... radical changes... there will be a relative change in the situation of classes, groups and strata of society," with "advantage for some ...disadvantage for others.")[39]

In the midst of a virtual chorus of voices criticizing mistaken concepts of "social justice," which had grown over the years to identify this with equality of distribution, with "leveling" *(uravnilovka),* with "padding" the pay of those with low wage rates to bring them up to some "satisfactory" level *(vyvodilovka),* November 1986 saw a strongly differentiated (by Soviet standards) set of pay increases: 20–25 percent, on the average, for *workers* in production; 30–35 percent for the various categories of "white-collar" engineering and technical personnel (ITR), and 40–50 percent for "leading categories of specialists," such as designers, technologists, and foremen.[40] Perennially underpaid professionals in education, medicine, and other nongoods-producing services were to receive raises of around 30 percent[41]—some corrective to that contrast, so typical of the Soviet system, between skilled steelworker and rank-and-file M.D., wherein *he* earns much more than *she.*

Inequality *within* blue-collar ranks was furthered by a proviso that, on the typical six-grade Soviet wage schedule for a given industry or branch, workers at level three and above—but not those less skilled below—would be eligible for 12–14 percent bonuses for high-quality output;[42] one of the aims, as L. A. Kostin, first deputy chairman of the State Committee on Labor and Social Questions, put it, was the move from a situation where the "spread" on a six-grade schedule had declined from 1:1.58 to a more differentiated 1:1.8.[43]

But such raises—for *workers* at least—are not to be "automatic," but tied to plant output/deliveries and therefore conditional on material *and* labor saving, and "results": linked, *inter alia,* to savings that might be made by de-stocking unneeded workers and financing the raises of those who remain via wage-fund "recapture." Whether the pay of white-collar personnel will be tied so tightly to results is another question—and a sensitive one.[44]

Worse yet, for some blue-collar workers at least, was to come in 1987, with the introduction of the new *gospriemka* form of quality control, since this, essentially, determines what is the magnitude of "output," of "result," to which pay is tied. By 1985, according to Evgenii Antosenkov, the director of the research institute of the State Committee on Labor and Social Questions, the familiar sort of "drift" had taken place in the proportions of average blue-collar earnings made up by *base* pay and (output-related) bonuses. Scales introduced in the mid–1970s and since untouched had initially allowed for 30–35 percent of total pay to be earned as bonus; by the mid 1980s, the proportion had "crept" up to 45–50 percent, with consequences for the wage bill, for excessive generation of consumer rubles, etc.[45] *Gospriemka* procedures, to which bonuses were especially sensitive, came as a rude shock. In the Tiumen' farm machine plant, average wages fell a reported one-third in January 1987;[46] similar outcomes were reported in other factories, including a brief "sit-down" over the strictures of *gospriemka* in the giant, high-tech Kama river truck plant[47] in a *gospriemka* experiment in late 1986.

However the first "adjustment" to heightened quality expectations proceeds, the early 1987 experience *had* to place many workers, whose concerns had never extended to the utility or marketability of their products, in a considerable quandary. One who clearly, and understandably, missed the point inquired of *Trud*, the labor union daily, as to whether, since *gospriemka* and its demands required more work, he was not entitled to extra pay—*Trud*'s answer was negative,[48] quite in line with Gorbachev's remark in July 1986 to some citizens in Vladivostok that the state had "paid" for years for "no work" as if it were, and that this was over.[49] It also offered confirmation of Zaslavskaia's remark, in another interview, that "psychological tensions" were inevitable under the new conditions as a result even of justified "punishments by means of the ruble."[50]

To a weakening of the old security of employment, then, has been added a hefty dose of a new *inequality* in economic reward for Soviet citizens—not as a matter of corruption, illegal dealings, or "chance," but as a direct matter of policy. Policy also threatens the world to which they have grown accustomed, in the area of prices.

Price "reform," clearly, is on the agenda. Economists who have advocated an abandonment of various subsidization practices in specialized journals over the years are now in full cry in the newspapers, on radio and TV, "educating the public" to new realities. Citizens are being informed (or reminded) that meat is sold (when available) in state stores at less than half its production price, and of the tens of billions of rubles expended on milk and bread subsidies as well;[51] that rental prices in state housing, stable since 1928, cover less than one-third of *mainte- nance* costs,[52] and that there is an element of "unearned" income in the facts that affluent families pay no more for the same apartment than poor ones, apartments with amenities rent just as cheaply as poor ones, better-located cost no more than ones in less desirable areas. Broad price increases—for that is what "reform" means—are evidently not to come until the 1990s.

Gorbachev in this area shows an understandable reluctance to "bite the bullet" before a number of the macroeconomic elements of *pere- stroika* are in place. Suggestions that the state food subsidies be dis- tributed as wage rises and/or income supplements to "ease" the move into higher prices have been made;[53] and Gorbachev's economics have included advocating more security for those who cannot work because of disability, single-parent status, etc.[54] But this is still a matter likely to be controversial among the Soviet rank and file. Short of an explosion of productivity-cum-affluence, people will be more likely to remember yesterday's low prices fondly than to appreciate new income supple- ments. Nor, of course, do Soviet citizens necessarily perceive subsidized prices as *low* prices relative to their incomes. Writing in *Komsomol'- skaia pravda*, a reform economist, attacking the inefficiencies and ineq- uities not only manifest in below-cost prices but also in prices far above the cost of production maintained on items ranging from blue jeans to automobiles, confronted the issue of food prices in an uncharacteristi- cally blunt way.

Now for low food prices. Low compared to what country—the United States, Britain, the FRG, Sweden? Yes, our prices are somewhat lower. But not very much lower, not as low as they are often depicted by representatives of the State Committee for Prices. But when talking about the low cost of food the defenders of such comparisons seem- ingly forget the average wage here and in the industrial capitalist countries. Expenditure on food amounts to 15—35 percent of the family budget in the latter. But let us ask *Komsomolskaya pravda's* readers how much they spend on food. I think it will be much more. The argument about low foodstuffs prices has thus long since ceased to be valid in our country. The same, moreover, applies to books, children's clothes, toys, and so forth.[55]

If large ranges of consumer prices are decontrolled, it will be a very new experience for today's Soviet citizens. But with the coming of Gorbachev, the public discussion itself, before any massive removal of subsidies, was a new item in the environment, with implications no doubt equally interesting to partisans of reform and those who are less optimistic about making the new economics work.

AN OPENING TO PRIVATE ENTERPRISE?

Beyond the matter of *state*-set price, wage, and salary policies, the onset of the Gorbachev era refocused attention on the potential role of *non*-state enterprise, cooperative or individual, in the long-term economics of *perestroika,* and the kinds of concerns which might emerge in a social/political context that, at one and the same time, gave incomparably less place to such "options" than Poland and Hungary, but "hosted" a large second economy which performed so many functions in the legal twilight. Into earlier 1986, at least, things did not look good for an opening to more economic diversity. In what seemed to be a salvo aimed both at predatory forms of corruption, and at those "conversions" of time and materials to the rendering of the sorts of services Soviet citizens must seek elsewhere than the state sector, a Politburo session on March 27, 1986, addressed the bugbear of "unearned income," and *Pravda*'s report of the meeting indicated that

> plans call for the implementation of legal and other measures aimed at eradicating unearned income from illegal operations, theft, bribery, speculation, and unauthorized use of state-owned transport, machines, and equipment for personal profit.[56]

Considering the broad range of behavior that the Soviet mind has been inclined to view as "speculation" and the ubiquity of the unauthorized use of state-owned automobiles and trucks, this meeting targeted a great deal of everyday behavior.

At the same time, Gorbachev's earlier congress report suggested some ambivalence—or perhaps balance—on this score. The General Secretary called for consideration of progressive inheritance taxes (one way of getting at "unjust enrichment"), but followed this proposal immediately with a defense of those who gain "additional earnings through honest labor." Could the latter comprise private-sector activity?

The Central Committee resolution on "Measures to Intensify the Struggle Against Unearned Income" and the decree of the USSR Su-

preme Soviet's Presidium on "Intensifying the Struggle Against the Deriving of Unearned Income"—both published on May 28, 1986—made
this seem unlikely. Though the documents specified that work in "hand-
icrafts" or "individual labor activity" must be of a specially "prohibited"
type to be subject to a catalogue of penalties, they failed to indicate
what was legal or what is to be encouraged in the area of private initiative.[57] Unauthorized use of state-owned means of transport was made
a matter of administrative penalties (and of criminal prosecution for
recidivists), but there was no reference to offering services as part-time
taxi drivers in off hours—a modest "privatization" suggested by many
economists in recent years.[58] USSR General Procurator A. Rekunkov
suggested in an *Izvestiia* interview five days after the new decree that
a law on individual labor activity currently being drafted was aimed not
at prohibiting but at developing such activity, and that state registration
and taxation (to keep charges from rising too high) would encourage
such work.[59] Some analysts, myself included,[60] were skeptical about
whether such a decree would be forthcoming on the scale of the first,
and what it would, if issued, contain—as, one surely imagines, were
many Soviet citizens, both producers and consumers of such goods and
services.

Not quite justly, however, since a decree on individual enterprise
(November 1986)[61] and a "model" law on cooperative enterprise (October 1986)[62] *did* emerge; and in their wake, controversies and problems
of implementation. The individual labor law legalized, essentially,
twenty-nine varieties of "moonlighting"—some of them quite
predictable—but did not empower those of preretirement age to *leave*
the state economy for the risks and rewards of work on their own
account. Co-operatives in services and catering are not new in Soviet
history—here, in a sense, the commitment is to *restoration* of a form
of enterprise likely to be less controversial than the enterprise of individuals. At least, various "experiments" in cooperation have received
good press.[63]

Old dogs learn new tricks only with difficulty; leopards show no
readiness to change their spots. At the grass-roots level, where so much
of whatever promises to be dramatic in Gorbachevian social policy will
be acted out, there were signs of resistance aplenty to some of the new
departures. While, in mid-1987, it is by far too early to render any final
judgment (and, given the dynamic if sometimes frenetic thrust of Gorbachev's rhetoric, hard to equate his agenda with previous designs such
as the 1965 Kosygin reforms), it is only reasonable to take into account
some of the most recent evidence.

The "backwash," first of all, of the May documents *against* unearned income may have gone, at local levels, well beyond what the new economics sees as a quite precise and fine but *justified* line between the deriving of income above the "earned," and the generating of hard-won and deserved rubles, even in large amounts, by citizens more sober and hardworking than the average, plying their energies and skills in areas the state may, finally, be ready to consign to them. Rekunkov, in an *Izvestiia* interview several days after the decree,[64] reminded would-be prosecutors (or persecutors) that "envy" was the social enemy of many legitimate high earners, and that since local authorities themselves might be set against such, the role of the *prokuratura* was to moderate such situations and defend citizens' legitimate activities.[65] On Radio Moscow early in July, Rekunkov reminded listeners of a "new economics" tenet—that pay received in state enterprises for substandard or effectively "undone" work was also "unearned" income, and that the state fully aimed to *encourage* legitimate private labor as well.[66]

August saw an official in Rekunkov's *prokuratura* "condemning" local authorities who barred people from other *oblast's* from selling their food products in their own local *kolkhoz* markets (long legal);[67] in *Izvestiia* in September, a collective farmer with a private plot complained that a neighbor accused him of being a receiver of unearned income—though presumably his activities were quite standard and legal.[68]

Since the May 1987 introduction of the new private-enterprise rules, there have been predictable "hitches." Various Soviet reports cite the response among citizens who must register and purchase a license to engage in individual labor as moderate. Reticence here, understandable given the many decades of official rhetoric *against* precisely the motivations and interests that might draw people toward privateering, is matched by foot-dragging on the part of local authorities. Even in Moscow, a May 1987 article[69] reported, bureaucrats were demanding forms from would-be licensees that the law did not require, and limiting the hours in which they would entertain applications. That this was *not* the intent of central authorities seemed clear from an interview in *Pravda* in December 1986 given by USSR Minister of Justice Kravtsov.[70] In it he observed that in the past many laws had unjustly prohibited types of private work, although the 1977 constitution guaranteed citizens' "rights" in his area—a situation that ended with the new law. Far from there being any conflict between this law and the one on unearned income, their respective limits were quite clear: the list of permitted forms of individual labor was not exhaustive; that of prohibited forms was. No one had the right to say nay to a license applicant seeking to engage in an activity not on the prohibited list.

In practice, things are unlikely to work out so simply. How much benefit the *economy* will derive under the new law (which still, effectively, bars people of working age from full-time private work—although perhaps a yet-unrevealed agenda may foresee the full-time privateering of some of those to be "released" from industrial jobs) is surely questionable. Beyond this, two other points of tension are clear. First, the contribution private enterprises may make to an increasing economic inequality is a sensitive matter—tax policy aims at a high marginal rate for those who may earn extraordinary incomes,[71] but clearly the state also seeks to keep taxes within bounds that will not deter potential privateers. Still, this new risk of more inequality, in a context of rising prices *and* more inequality of wages and salaries in the state sector, cannot but raise questions in the ongoing debate over social justice (see below).

Second, many Soviet discussions exhibit a near-obsessive concern with the distinction between "honest (individual) labor" and the derivation of unearned income, of a sort which bodes ill for a new economics that seeks to promote enterprise and its approval by society, and shows some real ambiguities in attitudes toward supply, demand, and market. Attitudes that approve growers' selling of private-plot produce, but see "middlemen" who buy the same, bring it to market, and sell it as "profiteers"; that see food-growing as legitimate, but show doubts about flower growing and selling by the same peasants (evidently because private plots are "for" food production, and the profit margin on flowers is large);[72] that express some moral-social-"aesthetic" resistance to the private purveyor of services who charges a stiff price for jobs the state sector cannot do, or does badly; that see high earnings from such work as unearned, because, one suspects, they *are* high. These will be formidable obstacles, and in this area it seems certain that there is divided counsel among local, and perhaps central, leadership.

HABITS, EXPECTATIONS, AND "SOCIAL JUSTICE"

The "way of life" and the expectations built into the majority of the Soviet population by long socialization and experience will not make Gorbachev's tasks easier: the "grass roots" can resist, albeit in a different way from the local *apparat* or other top leaders in Moscow. To have seen, as many observers did in 1985 at Gorbachev's accession, a combination of leader whose newness and vigor were welcome to the public and a public mood longing, or at least ready, for a housecleaning to sweep away laziness and corruption and to "get Russia moving again" was to miss another dimension. The Soviet public is habituated to its own sort of welfare state, and does expect much from its leaders. That their material expectations are not at Western levels is not the point; rather, it is the contradiction between those expectations, on the one hand, and the inability of the economy as well as the refusal of current policy to meet them, on the other hand, that may present a long-term problem. As Victor Zaslavsky puts it:

> Judged from the viewpoint of those within the system Soviet popular expectations are not modest at all. They are not modest by any standards when one considers what is taken for granted by every Soviet citizen: the stability of state-supported prices of food, basic consumer goods, and services. Thus the price of housing has remained at the level of 1928, which makes housing, heating, gas, telephone, and other utilities practically free. The burden of price subsidies is becoming heavier for the state budget every year.[73]

Further insight into the web of expectations and criteria of evaluation found in the Soviet citizenry is emerging from the results of the Soviet Interview Project—a large-scale survey research program conducted among nearly 2,800 Soviet émigrés of the 1970s and early 1980s. For a leadership that might for economic reasons contemplate price rises for a broad range of items, presumably including food, it must be sobering to ponder how those still in the USSR may resemble the émigrés who, in James Millar and Elizabeth Clayton's words, "saw little relationship between the low price of subsidized meat in state stores and supply shortages. They seemed to want [below-cost-of-production] prices and a perfectly elastic supply at those prices."[74]

Complicating matters for a General Secretary evidently committed to a tighter link between performance and (unequal) pay, and to what must be relative consumer austerity over the next few years, yet who seeks to appeal to younger adults presumably tired of the rule of old men, are émigré survey findings that suggest it is precisely the post-Stalin "generation," born in 1941–1960, that views the Brezhnev era as the "peak period" of inequality in Soviet history and is especially attuned to economic issues in judging the regime.[75] The perceptions of Soviet economists, indeed the policy premises of the Gorbachev leadership, are much to the contrary. This at least is the case with respect to equality and "leveling." To the degree that the respondents in the SIP survey read "privilege" as signifying not only inequality but *corruption*, their view is parallel with the thinking of Gorbachev's reformers. One of these, the economist/historian Evgenii Ambartsumov, spoke in an interview with an Italian newspaper of Brezhnev-era corruption being greater than that under Stalin.[76]

More workplace discipline, less job security, are remedies difficult to sell while simultaneously trying to maintain or improve morale. Soviet Interview Project findings indicate that shop-floor personnel do not see themselves as the beneficiaries of an easy work pace stemming from overmanning. Paul Gregory finds that "workers and employees performing the actual routine tasks of the economy felt that there was less slack than [did] their supervisors."[77] Redundancy and redeployment are hardly likely to be welcome, especially among blue-collar workers, who will be affected if such policies are pressed forward. In the émigré sample, 37 percent of former workers cited security as a major source of job satisfaction (compared with an average of 31.4 percent for the total sample, and only 21.1 percent for professional people).[78]

There, in some sense, may lie one of the keys to the controversy over Gorbachev's social policy at the grass roots. Gorbachev has been called the "yuppie" General Secretary, one whose ideas appeal especially to college-educated, white-collar professionals, especially perhaps to the intelligentsia whose desires for more *information* about domestic and foreign events, more diversity and freedom in the arts and literature, have been met to a surprising degree—but whose ideas carry much less appeal to the traditional blue-collar demographic bedrock of Soviet society.[79] This, it seems to me, is accurate enough: Gorbachev's appeal is not to the age group born in 1941–1960 (and thereafter) *in toto*, but to the better-educated and dissatisfied segment of it. That appeal stresses effort, just, and differentiated, reward for effort, and results in quantity and quality, and seeks obviously to "reeducate" Soviet society about new principles, the necessity and justice thereof—especially those segments of society who run a risk of being "losers" rather than "winners" under the new dispensation.

And here, once again, there exists fertile soil for the nurturing of grass-roots problems. The image of the Soviet masses as habituated to security, a rather large measure of material equality, a loose linkage between effort and reward which translates into rather low effort at work, and marked by an attitude of disapproval toward the "striver" who seeks, obviously, to grow rich through legal or illegal means, is one generally accepted by economists and sociologists and other participants in the discussion, *whether they deplore it or not.* Some economists argue strongly that the "lid be removed" on wage/salary-earnings inequality —that this is the cold shower the masses need. In this, they attack the notion that social justice means equality in distribution of material goods;[80] they view the abolition of wage ceilings as a struggle against "parasitical" attitudes associated with a "leveling" mentality.[81] (For many of these, the manifest inequality in earnings that would come is only just, even if it is "hurtful" to the psyches of "losers." The issue of final income inequalities, and the [accepted by most] necessity of moderating these is to be left to post-factum income taxes, which would play a much larger role in a "new" USSR than in the old—and might even allow superearners to donate part of their "take" to cultural foundations in lieu of part of the tax.)[82]

Others, however, show a fundamental discomfort with such notions, or a perplexity about the "justice" of any really large differences in material reward, however sober, honest, industrious, and efficient the winners may be. Many of Zaslavskaia's statements, while they advocate more wage/salary differentiation in furtherance of social justice, and price/rent "de-control" as well, also seem insistent on making sure the "rich" are taxed (presumably heavily), and express what seems to be the conviction that really high incomes are probably to some degree "unearned"—and therefore anathema.[83] In the debate over social justice that has emerged,[84] there are articulate advocates of both "meritocracy" and "egalitarianism"—all evidently seeing their positions as "fitting" within the authentic thrust of *perestroika* and radical reform.

G. Lisichkin and V. Z. Rogovin, crossing swords over "tolerable" inequalities in 1986, provide in capsule form some sense of the differing perspectives. Each, *inter alia*, looked upon the same fact: a study revealing that more than half of all funds in savings bank deposits in the Latvian SSR are held by only 3 percent of the depositors.[85] To Lisichkin, unless one knew differently, there was no reason to assume that these were *not* the result of hard work, sobriety, enterprise and thrift—anything but unearned funds.[86] People needed, in Lisichkin's view, to learn how to make money.

Rogovin, very much to the contrary, argued that even if illegal and nonlabor income was not involved, such a disparity was simply "not socialist," and should not be tolerated.[87] Too much inequality, even in the service of economic renewal, is too much. But reading Rogovin with a "Western" bias to which I freely admit, the most striking point is an example he gives of the leveling mentality: a modestly paid office worker, who says of a former schoolmate of more affluent life-style, "I don't want to live like her; I want her to live like me."[88] What might seem jealousy or envy Rogovin sees as a "correct" attitude.

The debate and Gorbachev's struggle, of course, are taking place in the Union of Soviet Socialist Republics; we would not expect to find many self-confessed disciples of Milton Friedman or P. T Bauer there. The issues Gorbachev has raised have a history in the particular kind of economy and society that have developed in the USSR; to tread carefully, to worry about getting taxes high enough yet "right", even in the context of trying to motivate effort for reward, does not mark one as a "dogmatist" as opposed to market-oriented "pragmatists." This, after all, is Soviet politics, not pure economics. Certainly one of the most interesting—and challenging—aspects of the environment, at both the heights and the grass roots, in which Gorbachev must work is the strong possibility that most people prefer the views of Rogovin the "leveler" to those of Lisichkin. Whether, and how, they may exercise that preference will determine a good deal of what happens in the Gorbachev era.

SEVEN

SOCIAL CHANGE AND STABILITY
IN EASTERN EUROPE

The eastern Europe of the hardy travelers and diarists of the nineteenth and early twentieth centuries, that continental "backwater" at which so many statesmen scoffed, has been gone for many years. Its successor, defined so evocatively in Churchill's "iron curtain" speech, has been with us now for three decades—time which has shown that the curtain, if still in place, is rather permeable, and that behind it much has taken and is taking place.

Observers have frequently wrapped postwar Eastern Europe in large terminological blankets. On some points complementary, on other points contradictory, such characterizations have differed widely, depicting at one extreme precariously dammed reservoirs of simmering discontent, or stressing at the other the masses' political apathy and materialistic privatism. Not surprisingly, events and trends of the past thirty years have lent, and continue to lend, support to both images.

Thus, the riots and other public disorders of the mid-1950s, which

Originally published in *Problems of Communism* (November-December 1977), 26(6): 16–32.

alternated with periods of apparent quiescence under conditions of repression and retrenchment, yielded a mix of indications on which one might reasonably have predicted an unstable and uncertain future for the Soviet-dominated regimes and the Soviet-model socialism imposed throughout Eastern Europe save in Yugoslavia. On the same evidence —but with less optimism—one might also have discerned in the regimes' quick resort to forcible suppression and arrest an effective determination to maintain these systems, whatever their human costs and lack of legitimacy.

Today, however, our analyses tend to be proportioned to less "grand" issues than those addressed earlier, for the socialist regimes now seem durable parts of Europe's political topography. Most of these regimes have outlived the personalities first connected with them, yet with some adjustments the social and political orders which those early leaders spawned and consolidated endure. Against the backdrop of the postwar world, marked by a proliferation of new states, growing territorial disparities of wealth and power, political instability in many areas, and a seemingly ever less predictable global situation, Eastern Europe has been and continues to be a relatively stable area, although with some serious qualifications. Why, then, have the Eastern European regimes— imposed from without, dominated by the USSR, and indeed often acting on behalf of it—survived? So clearly defective in initial political legitimacy, how have they, nonetheless, maintained themselves through years of strife, tension, and uneasy accommodation with popular discontent?

An easy but oversimple answer would be *coercion*, its actual use and no less effective threat. Both internal coercion, that which the regimes mounted against their subject populations, and external coercion, Soviet power inside and outside Eastern Europe, setting limits to what the USSR's client states in the area might do, played a clear role, certainly, in imposing and maintaining a status quo, in spite of the wishes and aspirations of Hungarians, Poles, Czechs, and other peoples. But to accept coercion alone as the answer is to narrow one's view of East European sociopolitical dynamics to an unwarranted degree, and to risk missing other factors important for explaining the past and for identifying possible lines of future development.[1]

This chapter offers a retrospective and prospective examination of some of the sources of stability and, perhaps, latent future instability in the East European states. My focus is directed, not at all those "other important factors" which a preoccupation with coercion might obscure, but rather at one, broad enough in itself: the social consequences of economic growth and development in the new socialist states and the mass social mobility that resulted. I thereby attempt to link major social forces to the stability and "staying power" of what are for the most part political "importations," for my underlying premise is that the "high politics" of the East European leaderships are connected inextricably with the broader problems of everyday life and the responses—real or imagined—of the East European masses.

Looked at from one angle, then, the history of the socialist regimes is the history of the mass movement of populations from old to new contexts of work and life. The impact of that history on the minds of the socialist masses has been critical, I shall argue, for the stability these regimes have achieved in the past thirty years. Nevertheless, there is evidence that the history of mass mobility is indeed now history, irretrievably in the past, and that a new era with respect to social mobility is upon Eastern Europe, suggesting in turn that a period of instability may be dawning. Whether this potential instability will in fact materialize and with what implications for the use of "stabilizing" coercion and the effects thereof are matters for speculation.

THE PROMISE OF REVOLUTION

Whether imposed from without or a product of domestic revolution as in Yugoslavia, the new socialist order promised something profoundly new to those who lived under it—social equality. In the Eastern Europe that emerged from World War II, nothing perhaps could have represented a greater break with the past than the promise that the mighty would be laid low, that those "who had been nothing would be all." Even in economically developed and democratic Czechoslovakia, this presaged a thrust toward greater egalitarianism; in Hungary and Poland, given their traditional elitist social orders and yawning gaps between gentry and mass, it meant no less than transformation of the very bases and premises of society. Although the Balkan "peasant states" for the most part lacked indigenous aristocracies, there too the promise of equality in the material sphere, under a regime devoted to the interests of "toiling" workers and peasants, found strong resonance.

Revolutionary promises rarely achieve fulfillment once they leave banners and posters for the real world. Such at least was the case with the promise of equality. To be sure, the former elites disappeared, new criteria of social value favored proletarians in the allocation of ration cards, etc. But socialism came to Eastern Europe in the context of war's destruction, economic backwardness, and scarcity—with respect to material goods there was precious little to distribute. As did the Soviet regime in the 1920s, the new East European socialist regimes in the early postwar years faced the need for and attendant problems of rapid and large-scale economic development in order to create the modern industrial economies which were the presumed social base for socialism. And, following the path of their Soviet predecessor, the East European regimes rapidly abandoned "revolutionary" egalitarian policies for ones offering markedly differentiated rewards, for managers, engineers, and highly skilled workers in critical industries were in short supply. These personnel now would be rewarded "according to their work," and as scarce commodities they commanded relatively high rewards. Equality gave way to a clearly "functionalist" pattern of differentiated income.[2] For many rank-and-file workers and peasants, their relative place in the material hierarchy remained much as before.

A commitment to rapid industrial growth, in the context of poverty and scarcity, meant stressing investment over consumption, future economic capacity over current demand. Thus, the new socialist societies, lacking in any case the prerequisites of affluence, were pushed by their planned economies into still relatively greater scarcity. The gray and grim years of shoddy goods and shortages of necessities, of overcrowding in aged and deteriorating housing, of grand promises for the future and deficient diets in the present, descended upon Eastern Europe.

A balance sheet drawn in the early 1950s would have looked bleak indeed. Parliamentary democracy had not flourished in the region except in Czechoslovakia, yet subordination to the Communist regimes left *less* personal or institutional freedom than even the authoritarian interwar governments had afforded. Political terror and purge trials, while not on the scale of the 1930s in the USSR, nonetheless prevailed. Living standards were low; goods, scarce. For broad strata of the population, real incomes had fallen to levels below those enjoyed, or endured, at the close of the prewar period, with restoration of the war's material ravages proceeding slowly.

The potential for latent social unrest under such conditions is, of course, immense, and it was manifested in riots and popular disturbances in East Berlin and elsewhere in the wake of Stalin's death. It may sharpen our appreciation of the situation if we consider the following "representatives" of whole East European social strata. A member of the Warsaw *inteligencja*, for example, lived worse in 1951 than he had in 1938. His salary bought less food, commanded a smaller range of choice and quality in clothing, and gave him less living space. It mattered little whether he was a member of the "old" or new "socialist" professional strata; a position in this social category no longer commanded the same rewards as before—in Poland or elsewhere in Eastern Europe.

At the same time, for a Budapest worker in 1951, a week's work at his plant bought him a smaller market basket than those same hours had in 1939 under a regime of capitalists closely tied to the economy of Nazi Germany. This worker's diet had worsened in quality and quantity, while the general scope of his material life had narrowed, rather than broadened, under the socialist regime.[3]

The peasant's position during these same years is less easily characterized. In Poland and Hungary, long-overdue reforms distributed land hitherto locked within the boundaries of the large estates, thereby improving the peasant's lot. Thus, for a time, socialism could claim the credit for a fundamental reform which previous regimes had avoided. In much of the rest of Eastern Europe, presocialist landholding patterns, while uneconomical and problematic, at least provided the base for an independent peasantry. Here collectivization came more quickly—accompanied by resistance, deprivation, unsown fields, and a declining quality of life.

In general, then, after nearly a decade of socialism, the circumstances of most social groups evidenced only the barest improvement.[4] Grim statistics charted the much greater number of hours it took an East European worker to "earn" a kilo of meat, a pair of shoes, or other items in comparison with his American (or West European) counterpart. From this perspective, the social stability of the East European states is all the more impressive. The remarkable thing is not that riots occurred, or that they were suppressed, but that so few took place. Coercion and the penetration of society by the secret police explain a lot, but not the whole, of this puzzle. There were also more "positive" factors, socialist policies which perhaps tapped and effectively responded to mass desires. But to explore these relationships we need to change our angle of vision.

THE IMPACT OF ECONOMIC GROWTH

Socialism might not deliver equality; however, through the economic development it fostered it did create (in addition to straitened circumstances for the population) opportunity—opportunity to change one's work and one's life on a hitherto undreamed-of-scale. In other words, economic development demanded and created socio-occupational mobility.

It would be hard to overestimate the impact of this development. Europe as a whole, in comparison with the United States, offered less fertile soil for the Horatio Alger myth and ideology.[5] West Europeans and Americans *both* believed that social mobility—the chance for a blue-collar worker's or peasant's son to cross the border into nonmanual work, to go beyond the world of his father—was greater in the United States than in Europe (although actual differences in mobility rates were not very great).[6] The notion that peasants might change their lives, that workers might become managers, that children of the humble might in large numbers occupy desks in university lecture halls, was even more alien in Eastern Europe, which was economically and socially backward compared with the Western part of the continent. There, one's social location at birth seemed that which one would keep for the rest of one's life. Great and apparently unbridgeable gaps yawned between urbanite and rustic, between the person who worked with his hands and one who worked with his head. The Great Depression, which closed with such a tight grip on Eastern Europe in the "twilight" 1930s,[7] widened these gaps still further, reducing especially the opportunities for even the most ambitious and adventuresome of the peasantry to make it to a job in Warsaw or Budapest.[8]

The economic development that followed the imposition of socialism changed these circumstances profoundly. The rates of both intergenerational (father to son) and intragenerational (career) mobility increased dramatically over those of the interwar period.[9] For the first time, industry grew at such a pace, creating such a demand for manpower, that peasants and their sons found ready employment at the new factories and construction sites—and accompanying relief from the burden of rural overpopulation and agricultural underemployment. At the same time, the ranks of the new "socialist" intelligentsia and managerial/administrative cadres grew as the new regimes assumed a range of activities much broader than those of their predecessors. Into these nonmanual "spaces" came the sons of urban workers and even peasants, for offspring of the presocialist white-collar stratum were not themselves numerous enough to "inherit" all of the new positions that socialism created. Eastern Europe remained poor, and life was still grim in many ways. But for the first time, people were conscious of being "on the move."

The investigations of East European sociologists in the 1960s and 1970s have confirmed this break with the past, while supplying more precise quantitative indicators of the magnitude of the transformation. Research on social mobility in the socialist states has been diverse in format and rich, if sometimes unsystematic, in results.

The most useful are studies based on national samples of a country's population, and, except in the case of Romania, national samples yield the data reported in table 7.1. Such studies are far from the only sources of information about social mobility in Eastern Europe—a wide range of data derived from subnational studies, based largely on urban samples, also exist. Yet while subnational data are useful for many purposes, national surveys would seem to be more appropriate for inquiring into the magnitude of *national* social transformation.[10]

In addition, looking cross-nationally at such data raises problems of comparability, although, for our purposes, these appear relatively minor. Where necessary, data have been aggregated into three broad categories—nonmanual, manual (nonfarm), and peasant. (Some of the

TABLE 7.1. Intergenerational Social Mobility
(in percent)

	Manual to Nonmanual	Worker to Nonmanual	Peasant to Nonmanual	Peasant to Worker
Bulgaria	13.5	22.6	10.1	49.8
Czechoslovakia	29.0	35.9	20.6	50.3
Hungary	17.2	27.5	10.7	48.8
Poland	16.9	27.6	10.3	33.7
Romania (estimate)	20.0	37.4	14.3	41.1
Yugoslavia	14.5	27.9	10.7	25.5

SOURCES: BULGARIA: Atanas Atanasov and Aron Mashiakh, *Promeni v sotsialnata prinadlezhnost na zaetite litsa v Bulgariia* (Sofia, 1971), a 3 percent sample of employed males and females in 1967; CZECHOSLOVAKIA: "Intergeneracni mobilita v profesionalni sfere," in Ceskoslovensky Vyzkumny Ustav Prace, *Socialni a profesionalni mobilita pracujiciho obyvatelstva CSSR* (Bratislava, 1972), a sample of males, 1967; HUNGARY: Rudolf Andorka, "Tendencies of Social Mobility in Hungary: Comparisons of Historical Periods and Cohorts," (Conference of the Research Committee on Stratification, International Sociological Association, Geneva, 1975, mimeo.), a 0.5 percent sample of the male population, 1973; POLAND: Krzysztof Zagorski, "Changes of Socio-Occupational Mobility in Poland: Methodological Issues and Preliminary Findings," (Warsaw, 1975, mimeo.), a survey of ca. 72,000 male and female respondents aged 15–69 in 1972; ROMANIA: Honorina Cazacu, *Mobilitate sociala* (Bucharest, 1974), *two* surveys, one in Bucharest and one in a rural commune, totaling 1,116 respondents, in 1970, and weighted by the current author in accord with the 1970 urban-rural population proportions to yield this estimate; YUGOSLAVIA: Vojin Milic, "General Trends in Social Mobility in Yugoslavia," *Acta Sociologica* (1965), 9(1-2); a survey of 8,707 males and females in 1960.

NOTE: Figures in table represent the percentages of respondents born into a particular socio-occupational stratum who themselves have moved into a different stratum.

studies provided *only* this trichotomous classification.) Nonmanual includes both "intelligentsia" and white-collar employees. Nonfarm manual ("worker" in table 7.1) encompasses manual workers employed
outside agriculture—i.e., industrial and other workers, as well as both
cooperative and independent artisans. "Peasant" covers all manual
workers in agriculture, whether collectivized or (as in Poland and Yugoslavia) independent. In sum, and at this level of *gross* distinctions,
the categories are as similar as we are likely to be able to make them
in any investigation of cross-national data.[11]

The data in table 7.1 reveal the magnitude of the mobility between
broad socio-occupational categories. These figures indicate "outflow,"
i.e., the percentage of sons (or sons and daughters, in the case of mixed-
sex studies) of fathers in a given category who themselves move to a
different category. The first column gives the percentage of offspring of
manual fathers (workers or peasants) who have attained nonmanual jobs
themselves. Variation in the figures is wide, from nearly 30 percent for
relatively developed Czechoslovakia to less than 15 percent for backward Bulgaria. The second and third columns decompose the data of
the first into two component parts, showing separate outflow figures
for worker and peasant offspring. It is evident that, in socialist countries
as elsewhere, workers' children, generally raised in an urban and more
modern, complex environment, have an advantage over peasant children
in the competition for the desk job and a white collar.

It is the fourth column, however, which tells the real story of Eastern
Europe's social transformation: intergenerational mobility within the
manual category, the movement of peasant offspring from farm and
village to factory and city. Initially constituting the majority of the total
population in all countries but Czechoslovakia, the peasantry yielded
up nearly half its offspring, on the average, to form the new working
class, to create the social drama of a new life, a new world. As the Polish
poet Adam Wazyk wrote of the process in 1955, "From villages and
little towns, they come in carts / to build a foundry and dream out a
city."[12]

There occurred, then, a critical break with the past, the shattering of
many old, local, primordial ties. A new *fluidity* came to characterize
East European social structures. Mobility expanded the range and volume of opportunities for social advance; it did not make "equal" opportunities, nor did it provide equality of condition or result—to which,
in a broader sense, socialism was committed. But mobility did make
for the *appearance* of greater equality, and for the reality of a more
promising structure of opportunities in expanding economies.

Perhaps it is worth emphasizing that, at least by the gross measure of *manual-to-nonmanual* mobility, the socialist states are not particularly dynamic in comparison with Western industrial and semi-industrial states (where data tend to be the most readily available). Thus, the average manual-to-nonmanual rate for the six countries treated here is 18.5 percent; a similar average for eleven "Western" countries, using studies between 1949 and the mid-1960s, equals 23.8 percent.[13] Ranges within the Western data are also wide (from 17.1 percent for Italy in 1963–64 to 30.8 percent for a sample of U.S. males in 1962), but in general the Western states "outperform" their socialist counterparts on this measure. The reason is clear. The greater degree of economic development in the Western states created a more "modern" starting point—that is, the fathers' occupational distribution includes a much smaller share of peasants/farmers on the average in the Western than in the socialist states. A relatively large peasant-origin stratum thus restricts short-term manual-to-nonmanual mobility, since the next "move" of children of peasants is typically (and given the nature of economic development, almost necessarily) into manual work *outside* agriculture.

But this too is "upward" mobility—indeed, it is the primary social transformation wrought in the backward East European states, as noted above. Its magnitude may best be understood by attention to the fact that, on average, 27.1 percent of all respondents in the six socialist states—of the total populations of the original samples—are "workers" born into the peasant stratum. Data for seven, generally better-developed Western states show, on average, only 13.7 percent of total respondents in this "farm-to-factory" category.[14]

THE SOCIAL CONSEQUENCES

Viewed against the background of historically low aspirations, frustration, and backwardness, the recent transformation of East European societies through mass social mobility, even if at a rate lower, *en gros*, than that of some Western states, takes on its full meaning. One side of the picture drawn by socialism showed initial declines in living standards and many other aspects of the quality of life. Yet socialism also delivered the opportunity "to make something of oneself"—which contrasted sharply with the eternally "peasant" character of the presocialist Balkans and the seemingly unbridgeable gap between the gentry/upper class and the common worker and peasant in Hungary and Poland.[15]

Socialism, as a "principle" of system-organization, claimed and received credit for the transformation. If not yet "legitimate," the East European regimes could nonetheless point to their "effectiveness"—a base from which legitimacy can accrue.[16]

In a strict sense, however, socialism *as a principle* had almost nothing to do with producing a new, more dynamically "equal" society, a factor which has made the interpretation of social mobility under a revolutionary socialist regime a matter of some political sensitivity. The point is that economic development of the sort important here can be promoted by regimes of quite different political-economic colorations. Mass mobility is a product of the "demand" generated by economic development, not of the new "openness" of a revolutionary socialist regime. To be sure, the ascent of activist ex-peasants and workers to the few positions of real political power is connected with the "revolutionary" element, but the very scarcity of such positions insures that only a small portion of the population is so benefited. Thus, in a 1957 address to an international audience, the late Polish sociologist Stanislaw Ossowski asserted that

> one of the immediate aims of the leaders of the socialist states was to reach the level of more advanced capitalist countries in industrialization, urbanization, development of communications, and mass education. All these processes imply an increase in social mobility in socialist countries as well as elsewhere, *and since they were induced by social revolutions we can therefore postulate a plain causal relation between social revolution and this increase of social mobility.* But it is the "social-economic expansion" and not the revolutionary introduction of a socialist order which can be considered a necessary condition of this increase. Increased mobility of this type could have been accomplished also if the capitalist system had persisted: it would have been done, e.g., with the help of schemes like the Marshall plan [emphasis in original].[17]

Clearly, Ossowski took a quite nonideological view of the linkage between socialism and the increase in general social mobility. But such clarity of vision is ideologically inconvenient, and the credit due a socialist regime for benefits and opportunities bestowed on the population is a sensitive matter. Thus, when the posthumous multivolume edition of his complete works was published subsequently in Poland, the last sentence of the passage quoted above was replaced by the more innocuous "The introduction of the socialist order through revolution and the accompanying 'social-economic expansion' is a necessary condition of this growth."[18]

This sensitivity is understandable when one considers what the outcome might have been had socialism been less successful in promoting economic growth and therefore social mobility. Table 7.2 clarifies this by use of a technique whereby the intergenerational mobility attributable to economic growth (i.e., to changes in the structure of employment) is "eliminated" from the net data in table 7.1. The figures in table 7.2 represent that mobility which would have occurred solely as a result of the *random* movement of persons in the occupational structure. These rates, reported in the same manner as in table 7.1, thus reflect what "might have been."[19]

The figures are sobering. Had socialism not promoted development, or only moderate development, manual-to-nonmanual mobility would have been minuscule—birth in a toiling family would indeed have been a sentence for one's lifetime. Similarly, peasant-to-worker mobility would have been but a pale reflection of that which actually took place, leaving the vast majority of peasants locked in the cycle of hard work, underemployment, and poverty. If these random figures, rather than those of table 7.1, had been the reality, would the postrevolutionary socialist regimes, after promising so much, have enjoyed the relative stability they did? Indeed, one would have to doubt it. Mass mobility

TABLE 7.2. Intergenerational Social Mobility: Hypothetical Rates Assuming No Change in Occupational Structure
(in percent)

	Manual to Nonmanual	Worker to Nonmanual	Peasant to Nonmanual	Peasant to Worker
Bulgaria	4.6	11.1	2.0	14.9
Czechoslovakia	6.5	14.1	4.1	27.1
Hungary	4.3	8.3	1.8	23.8
Poland	5.3	10.7	1.9	16.1
Romania (estimate)	4.2	12.7	1.4	10.7
Yugoslavia	5.3	14.2	2.8	11.3

SOURCES: see Table 7.1.
NOTE: Figures in table represent hypothetical percentages of respondents, born into a particular socio-occupational stratum, who *might* have moved into different strata in the absence of economic growth and development. On methodology, see note 19.

upward, from peasant to worker, from manual to nonmanual, generated credits which the regimes badly needed.

It was, finally, by *mobility* that the overall decline in living standards, occasioned by forced-draft, high-reinvestment industrialization, was masked and deprived of some of its explosive potential. My earlier description of "worsening situations" is accurate, but must be understood in the context which mass mobility imparted to it.

The "Warsaw intellectual" was indeed poorer in the early 1950s than in 1938—but he was not the same person. By the early 1950s, the social stratum for which we let him stand was heavily populated by *novi homines*, sons of workers and peasants, recruited to form the beginnings of the new socialist intelligentsia. "Hereditary" intellectuals were on the decline as a proportion of the total stratum. The new arrivals brought with them old frames of reference. Prewar, presocialist living standards and the shortfalls from these were irrelevant, for the life, perquisites, and prestige they now enjoyed were incomparably more exalted than what their worker and peasant backgrounds would have led them to aspire to.[20]

The Budapest worker, by the early-to-mid-1950s, was also disadvantaged in material things compared with 1938—but neither was he the same person. Increasingly, he was not a holdover or child of the smaller, "core" urban proletariat of the presocialist years, but an ex-peasant. In Hungary, as elsewhere, the old small working class was "swamped" by peasant recruits into a rapidly expanding socialist blue-collar stratum. As Zygmunt Bauman has put it in regard to Poland:

> A relatively meagre group of pre-war industrial workers, who remained workers in spite of all mobility opportunities opened by the revolution, suffered an almost continuous deterioration of their living standard. . . . But [they were] dissolved in a vast mass of peasant migrants, to whom the living conditions they met meant a genuine improvement in the standards they had known.[21]

Life was grim in the factories, workers' dormitories, and overcrowded housing of the new cities, but through peasant eyes it was the city, it was the life many had unsuccessfully sought in the 1930s, only to return to harsh labor or enforced idleness in the countryside. And peasant eyes were the eyes of a growing proportion of the working class. Like the new intelligentsia, the new workers were conscious of being upwardly mobile.[22]

Finally, what about the peasantry itself? Here our focus changes, for people are not upwardly mobile into the peasantry, the bottom stratum of East European society. The peasants probably had the least to be "grateful" for, the smallest debt to the new regimes. Of course, isolation, ignorance, and tradition all make for quiescence, moderating a peasantry's potential for generating serious instability. Yet more fundamental, while nonmanual and industrial worker strata were growing in numbers and as proportions of the total population—and growing by adding upward mobiles with a stake in the new social order—the peasantry's absolute and relative size declined. And it declined through the outflow of the young, the male, the adventurous, ambitious, and talented, not through the exit of industrial recruits "representative" of the entire peasant stratum. To oversimplify somewhat, the "natural leaders" of any peasant mobilization were co-opted by economic change and left the stratum of their birth to be upwardly mobile. It mattered far less whether those who remained were disgruntled or not, or even whether agriculture eventually was collectivized or left private, as in Poland and Yugoslavia. The "dynamic" left the countryside in either case—as they continue to do.

Thus, the impact of the deprivation socialism brought, measured in average indicators, was absorbed by a process of mass social mobility which, emphasizing "upward" flow for individuals, changed the size, importance, and "inhabitants" of social strata. The decline in living standards and mass social mobility were the contrasting sides of the same picture,[23] each a result of the industrialization process which socialist regimes set in motion.

Such is the "retrospect"—the history of processes and changes now accomplished, or at least beyond certain critical stages of development. If the factors and processes discussed here indeed contributed in past years to a rather remarkable political stability in socialist Eastern Europe, their consequences and the form they are now taking suggest some rather different implications for the future.

THE DEFERRED COSTS OF SUCCESS

Both socialist publicists and Western analysts have recognized the "maturing" of East European socialist societies—their passage, hard to date precisely but evident in result, from the revolutionary and postrevolutionary phases of system building to the tasks of system maintenance. From this maturity observers also have inferred an increased stability. This judgment may well be warranted, for certainly the years of great decisions, grand alternatives, and heroic transformation of old societies into new are past. But there is, perhaps, another meaning of socialist maturity.

Ironically, the very success that socialism achieved in fostering social mobility has now given rise to possibly serious, if unanticipated, costs. This mobility produced a onetime social transformation, spread over several years, but at a pace which cannot be duplicated. Most East European socialist countries are now entering a critical period of transition: to slower economic growth, with the resulting implications for manpower "demand" and social mobility; and to a gradual, yet seemingly inevitable shift in the social and demographic composition of all three major social strata.

First, the better-developed economies of Eastern Europe no longer grow so rapidly as to demand mass reallocations of labor across manual-nonmanual and agriculture-industry lines, although less-developed Bulgaria and Romania may still have some "room" in this regard. The various white-collar bureaucracies have grown, multiplied, and stabilized somewhat in size. While the industrial blue-collar work force in some countries is experiencing a manpower shortage, no longer does the peasantry, now a much smaller stratum, provide a pool of underemployed manpower upon which industry can easily draw. Eastern Europe has a larger nonmanual and industrial worker population and a smaller peasantry than ever before. These facts testify to the social transformation which has taken place: they also suggest less "slack" in the demographic structure than existed in, let us say, 1949–50. That is, given the socio-occupational structure that now exists, and the persistent difficulties which the East European economies have suffered with respect to automation and computerization, prospects are dim for a manpower demand of the sort which could generate another rapid expansion in the size of the nonmanual sector and the working class, thereby providing the space for future substantial upward mobility. These economies are no longer as dynamic, and though today able to afford more "material stimuli" to their consumers, they are deficient in the spur they can provide to social mobility.[24]

This deficiency extends, moreover, to the second aspect of transition. The "frames of reference" with which members of the major social strata assess their experience and structure their aspirations have undergone a gradual and continuing process of change which parallels that taking place in the composition of those social strata.

The East European intelligentsia, for example, still include a heavy proportion of those whose first referent was a worker or peasant family. But another, different component seems to be on the increase: "second-generation" socialist intelligentsia who have, thanks to education and familial preparation, "inherited" their status from their parents. The ranks of the first-generation socialist intelligentsia grew by external recruitment (upward mobility)—for both demographic and political reasons. Today, however, the number of intelligentsia is not increasing rapidly, and the supply of children in current intelligentsia households is more nearly adequate to fill the available positions. This stratum, therefore, is approaching the point where it can "replace" itself intergenerationally through internal recruitment.

What does this imply? First, it would seem that the present socialist intelligentsia possess frames of reference no longer so favorable to stability as it is defined by their regimes. The status, material rewards, etc., of these individuals are not ones they can contrast to those of earlier worker or peasant milieux and feel lucky and grateful for having "made it"—for they have grown up in intelligentsia families themselves. Their frame of reference is that of the intelligentsia. Their judgments regarding the adequacy of their pay, perquisites, direct occupational satisfaction, and the whole quality of their lives are made from an intelligentsia perspective. They are doubtless less easily satisfied.

The intelligentsia cannot be "bought off" with the promise of mobility, for they already are the most advantaged category of society. Their expectations as intelligentsia are important, and there is no guarantee that their regimes can continue to meet these expectations as successfully as in the past. This is, first, a question of material expectations. That they do and *should* live better than workers and peasants is something the intelligentsia take for granted.[25] More critical, increased access to the West with its higher material standards affords the socialist intelligentsia a completely different point of reference, against which their standard of living is still quite low. This, certainly, disturbs some, who see their lower rewards as the result not only of the relatively poorer economies of their countries, but also of government policies which are failing to generate the growth necessary to raise those standards. Thus, the intelligentsia can frequently be found favoring some kind of market-related economic reform and increased income differentiation, as was the case in Czechoslovakia in 1967–68[26] and as is still true in Yugoslavia among those whom Svetozar Stojanovic calls "anarcho-liberals."[27]

But material concerns are not the only ones regarding which the present intelligentsia's aspiration may go beyond regime capability, or willingness, to deliver. It would be going too far by a great deal to say that the intelligentsia are disaffected or politically "oppositional"—most, it seems clear, still perceive that they have a stake in the status quo and therefore support it. Yet some—among them a good number of the second generation—*are* disaffected politically. Whatever limits on political perception and conventional belief they have transcended to arrive at an oppositional stance, those limits have not been the consequence of birth and early socialization in the working class or peasantry. The students who contributed to unrest in Poland and Yugoslavia in 1968, and also to the Czech reform movement, included many "cadet" members of the second-generation socialist intelligentsia; the same is true of the Hungarian "new left," the groups of dissenters developing in Poland since 1976, and Charter 77 supporters in Czechoslovakia. The angles from which they have criticized their regimes are diverse, ranging from "liberal," civil-rights-oriented stances to quasi-Maoist condemnations of the new "materialism," economic inequality, and general "slackness" of socialist consumerism. Such dissensions do not yet present East European politicians with a major problem. But as the older, first-generation socialist intelligentsia are replaced—to a large degree, *literally*, by their children—it seems likely that there will be a proliferation of more critical orientations, a multiplication of "points of view" from which contemporary East European socialism appears morally deficient.

These are children of a certain "affluence," possessed of a rather secure status and many advantages which their parents' success afforded. Like such children in the United States and Western Europe in the 1960s, many are critical and rejecting in their attitudes toward the system they live in.[28] For many, this is but a phenomenon of youth, while for others, something more fundamental. Western countries generally have proven resilient and adaptive in dealing with the strange mix of generational discontents and real politics which the "student revolt" presented. Whether the less resilient East European states can do the same with their younger intelligentsia remains to be seen.

The dissatisfactions of the second-generation socialist intelligentsia thus present a complex picture. Concerns with material status and a place in the social hierarchy, which are essentially "selfish" concerns, mix with aspirations for a greater role in structuring social priorities in a more egalitarian direction, or (and these are far from the same) for a more libertarian political order. The intelligentsia are, and are likely to remain, divided as to the *desiderata* of politics. As for the sources of these differences, there is little of precision which may be said. One expects, and finds, more dissidence in general in the humanist and social science sectors, where roles are more "marginal" to current regime objectives, than among the technical intelligentsia, although this is true of many Western states as well.

Our judgments must be tentative. At present, the intelligentsia do not represent, on the whole, an authentically destabilizing force, but the social trends sketched above scarcely point to a more stabilizing role for this stratum in the future. While the intelligentsia are not, surely, the gravediggers of socialism, they are unlikely to be its chief comforters in its middle age.

WORKERS' PROSPECTS

The socialist working class presents potentially even more disquieting prospects. Working-class "consciousness" and combativeness, a proletarian awareness of a commonality of interests, is not something usually expected of workers most of whom are "just off the farm." Bauman's comments, quoted earlier, provide a persuasive rationale for the relative quiescence and lack of effective organization among the workers of the 1950s in Poland, Hungary, and elsewhere. But today's working class is also increasingly hereditary in composition. The sons of ex-peasants, who themselves have known only industrial-urban life, are now coming to replace their fathers behind the benches and machines.

This is potentially important in two ways. First, many such sons do not want to follow their fathers. The sons' aspirations, nurtured by the earlier movement of mobiles into a rapidly growing intelligentsia, are to "higher things." These children are almost as likely as intelligentsia offspring themselves to desire a university education.[29] Yet their working-class backgrounds leave them less prepared for the competition for university places.[30] Their opportunities to "succeed" are fewer because places in universities have not grown at the same rate as has the output of secondary schools, and for those places which are available, working-class children now compete with those of first-generation socialist intelligentsia eager to see their own offspring succeed them. Nor does the intelligentsia stratum itself grow fast enough to generate "empty space." If yesterday's recruits to the working class were peasants ready and eager to leave the monotony of the village and happy with their destination, today's are more often people who have grown up in the working class and who are disgruntled at their failure to rise above it.

Second—and related to this—there exists in Eastern Europe now more than ever before the "social base" for working-class consciousness.

Increasingly, the frame of reference for members of this large class which socialism itself created is that of worker rather than of peasant. The regimes can claim no particular credit from most new recruits to blue-collar life, for the latter have not been upwardly mobile from the peasantry. Today's industrial recruits undoubtedly view working-class rewards and life more critically.

To demonstrate conclusively that the chances of working-class offspring for upward mobility are *declining* requires data of a precision we do not now possess—indeed, such data are likely to become available only after the fact. But recent data do show class-related patterns of access to higher education, with worker and peasant offspring being markedly underrepresented. Perhaps the best data come from Poland,[31] but more fragmentary findings from other socialist states also illustrate the problem. One Yugoslav writer explains the situation succinctly, observing that "a manual worker's child today has on the average at least nine to ten times less chance to become a professional than a child of a university trained person or manager."[32] Higher education is, of course, the path to becoming a professional. Whether, in fact, this path is becoming increasingly closed to working-class sons and daughters or is merely stabilizing at a certain level is less important, perhaps, than the fact that many workers appear to *believe* that the former is the case.

Thus, there may be emerging in Eastern Europe a critical element of "class politics"—that few believe their lot can be improved by individual effort and mobility upward, while many believe that they can only improve their lot collectively. Something of this presently exists in Yugoslavia, which has thus far accommodated it fairly effectively. A similar development may be perceptible even in "quiet" Hungary. There, some of the differentiated material stimuli of the New Economic Mechanism, which has been in effect since 1968, have been reduced in response to working-class resentments, and factory managers occasionally have been exposed to varieties of militancy over bread-and-butter issues (which any convinced Leninist would have to denounce as "trade unionism"). Poland, of course, is the most obvious site of "class" sentiments and action. In neither 1970 nor 1976 did Polish intellectuals assume their traditional role as the initial leaders of oppositional politics. Polish workers, *for their own reasons* and not those of the intelligentsia, have taken to the streets (and taken up the rails) in militant outbreaks which appear qualitatively different from those of the 1950s. In general, East European workers are not as easily satisfied as ex-peasants might be, and they are organizationally more astute. Moreover, in Poland they have linkages with dissident intelligentsia, linkages of the sort that seemed to be missing, until too late, in the Czechoslovak Spring of 1968.

The East European regimes thus have reason to be seriously concerned about workers—the largest single class, the product and presumably foundation of socialism. Official rhetoric still makes them the "leading class." Yet in taking to the streets in violent protest, Polish workers at least have demonstrated a clear belief to the contrary. To be sure, such action is not yet common, and to look at the working classes of the socialist states is not to see a mass of blue-collar *enragés*. Certain kinds of material demands can still be met fairly readily by regimes anxious to maintain stability. Others may be articulated, however, which are much harder to accommodate, touching as they do on the routine and subordinated quality of activity at the workplace itself.

In sum, the combination of the growing complexity of the blue-collar work force and demographic trends which point to fewer peasant recruits entering that stratum poses problems for regimes and workers alike. Reforms to increase economic efficiency may be in the offing, but while these may moderate some of the problems of the more skilled, productive, and energetic workers through enhanced economic incentives, they also may increase the dissatisfactions of those with lower skills, as reform serves to decrease the stockpiling of surplus labor in many factories. Though workers, on the whole, are not yet notably "politicized," some economic measures may push them in this direction. And regimes must, in a sense, deal with the workers they have. They no longer can seek large inputs of new and relatively docile recruits from the peasantry.

What, then, of the peasantry? Here some rather different observations are warranted. After years of a depressed material life, the peasants of Eastern Europe have benefited recently from economic policies which have increased their rewards, upgraded their social welfare, and, in Czechoslovakia and Hungary, raised their average total earnings to nearly those of the average industrial worker. The peasant is still at the bottom of the social structure, but the bottom is not so low as once it was. The gap between it and the industrial "middle" of society is less wide.[33]

At the same time, this stratum remains one into which an individual is *born*—people do not aspire to "join" the peasantry. Whatever the improving economic conditions, the young and ambitious still aspire to leave the countryside. Many do, and the peasantry continues to be relatively "old," feminized, and less "dynamic" in comparison with other strata. It is also, given the past and ongoing processes of outward mobility, proportionately *smaller* than ever before.

Those who remain in the peasantry may have reason to credit the state with considerable improvement in their lives as peasants. Yet the paradox in the general situation is evident. On the one hand, the intelligentsia and worker strata have grown in size and social significance just as their changing composition has made them potentially less quiescent. On the other hand, the peasants, despite their eternal grumblings, are probably less likely than ever to furnish the material for a *jacquerie,* yet are fewer in number than ever before, thus minimizing their supportive influence on general sociopolitical stability. The intelligentsia and workers, derived initially from the peasantry, will determine the degree of that stability, while the peasants, once the social bedrock of the presocialist regimes and—despite the fact that they were isolated and difficult to mobilize—a source of stability in the early years of socialism, have now been bypassed.

TOWARD THE FUTURE

Ideally, one would like to conclude with a package of specific, if somewhat hedged and qualified, predictions. This can hardly be the case here, for we already have speculated a good deal on seeming trends which, by their very nature, cannot yet be demonstrated sufficiently by empirical data (although the data at hand certainly do not indicate countertrends).

Perhaps it is enough to state that we have identified certain *tendencies,* inherent in the demographic process of industrialization and consequent social mobility in "medium-backward" countries—tendencies which are especially acute in most societies in Eastern Europe, where the political-institutional framework and mode of economic organization have been "borrowed," semiartificially, and hence suffer the burden of still-questionable legitimacy. These social trends contain a serious problematic potential. While they do not, in themselves, presage upheaval, they do complicate the problems of social management with which the socialist regimes of Eastern Europe, now well beyond any "heroic" phase, must cope. One can predict these complications—one cannot predict the downfall of systems.

The problems focused on here are consequences of economic development and, not surprisingly, seem most pressing in the better-developed socialist states, which to date have had varying success in dealing with them. Thus, under the New Economic Mechanism, Hungary has sought, fairly effectively it seems, to enlarge the "pie" for intelligentsia, workers, and peasants alike. Its bread-and-butter politics, so far not subjected to any stern reining-in from Moscow, are redolent of Chicago's—"Nobody gets everything, everybody gets something, nobody gets nothing." Similarly, Czechoslovakia's "normalizers" have considerably sweetened the pill of 1968 with a consumerism supported by Soviet economic transfusions—a fact which perhaps explains why the echoes of Charter 77 have been soft indeed, especially among workers. Poland, failing once again in 1976 to rationalize its price structure after listening to both the economists' "efficiency" case and public opinion researchers' warnings about mass reactions (and attending more to the former),[34] also needs and benefits from Soviet economic aid in order to maintain social peace. Nevertheless, the Gierek regime may well have encouraged public militancy with its gingerly treatment of those dissidents in the civil rights movement and on the Workers' Defense Committee, and by the recently declared amnesty of so many of the participants in the 1976 disturbances. Yet perhaps the government could do little else, considering how seriously the regime's legitimacy is challenged already.

The Romanian and Bulgarian situations, in contrast, present generally less threatening prospects to the Ceausescu and Zhivkov regimes respectively. The socioeconomic processes with which we have been most concerned here have not yet run their full course in the relatively less developed Balkan countries. Ceausescu's personalistic style, combined with nationalist rhetoric and policy, evidently is quite palatable to a Romanian population which is still largely peasant in origin. Manifestations of dissent, such as that by the writer Paul Goma and a few others, are relatively infrequent and are focused on issues unlikely to evoke broadly based sympathetic concern or understanding. Bulgaria, for its part, remains the seeming archetype of socialist stability, mixing growth in a few industrial sectors with the profitable pursuit of certain types of specialized agriculture. While it is probable that these states too will confront some of the problems of their more developed neighbors, they will do so later (and by then, perhaps, will face these problems in altered form).

Yugoslavia, as in so many other spheres, constitutes a rather special case, for its political development has resulted in a certain flexibility in dealing with the consequences of mobility in a recently quite backward nation. Yugoslav economic policies, and a measure of political innovation, have provided an escape valve for those peasant mobility aspirations which exceed the domestic economy's capacity for satisfaction: the export of industrial workers, as *Gastarbeiter*, to capitalist nations in northern and central Europe. There is militancy among Yugoslav workers, but thus far the system seems to have accommodated it reasonably well—as it has the aspirations of many of the intelligentsia. That Yugoslav intellectuals are often vocal in their criticism of the regime should not divert one's attention from the fact that "permissible" dissent there runs wider and deeper than elsewhere in Eastern Europe. The threats to Yugoslav stability for the most part are rooted outside the set of problems considered here.

Over the long term, and in the light of the trends I have outlined, more destabilizing tensions may be anticipated in Eastern Europe. Of course, I have directed no attention to other problems which these societies face—energy dependence, growing indebtedness to Western states, etc. But these and other factors may well reduce the capacity of these regimes to deal effectively with the tensions I have discussed. Furthermore, it is by no means clear that the USSR, increasingly feeling the pinch of a sluggish economy and constrained by the specter of slowdown and retrenchment, will provide the material wherewithal for the East European regimes to moderate the tensions. Although such has been the policy of Leonid Brezhnev, one should be wary of assuming that his successor(s) will continue along the same path.

This does not mean that the USSR would not readily move to restore order by use of force, should an East European state experience a destabilizing crisis as a result of these or other tensions. At present, Poland appears in the most precarious position. The Polish regime seems to lack a legitimacy it can develop only by proving itself effective, while such effectiveness requires that the public endure some strong economic medicine. Yet the Polish masses evidently would accept such a prescription only if they accorded the regime a basic confidence and/or legitimacy based on qualities *other* than material effectiveness. This is a legitimacy that the Poles do not now widely appear to concede.

It nevertheless seems clear that Soviet intervention is the *last* thing Brezhnev, Gierek, or Cardinal Wyszynski would want, whatever their differing perspectives. The dilemmas which these leaders face today may well confront future East European leaders and their Soviet counterparts, for while Poland may be "unique," not all of its problems are.

EIGHT

WORKERS AND INTELLECTUALS: A DISSIDENT COALITION?

Judged by the ultimate test of success applicable to states—survival—the East European Communist regimes have succeeded. All past the age of thirty, they have now achieved a measure of security after an early period marked both by severely compromised legitimacy and identity as Soviet-sponsored and -controlled regimes (as all save Albania and Yugoslavia have been) and by the threat of a "rollback" by a West then preponderant in the international power balance. Still dominated in many matters by the USSR, each regime nonetheless strikes, in characteristic ways, a balance between persistent elements of national identity and the effects of thirty years of Soviet-initiated change.

None, however, has escaped internal protest and criticism, dissent and opposition. The sources of this opposition have been diverse. Segments of the intelligentsia seem to be in a state of permanent dissent, finding as much to despise in the current regimes as their forebears did

Originally published as "Dissent in Eastern Europe: A New Coalition?" *Problems of Communism* (January-February 1980), 29(1): 1–17.

in the interwar regimes of elitist Poland and Hungary, "bourgeois" Czechoslovakia, and the unstable Balkan states. Workers too have registered discontent, but the potential impact of their larger numbers has been reduced by the episodic quality of their activity. For the most part, the new working classes have remained quiet—their outbursts leaving only memories of riots, marches, and crudely lettered banners, but no literature, no organizational heritage, however loose.

Regimes have prospered from this situation, wherein generally only the intelligentsia seemed to require constant collective political surveillance. But things would grow less favorable were the future to produce a more politicized working class, and if linkages of an enduring sort were to be established between workers and the more articulate intellectuals. This chapter shall examine—in the light of past events and current politics in Eastern Europe—the possibilities of the development of such linkages.

WORKERS AND THE WORKERS' STATE

Though East European Communist parties assumed power in the 1940s in the name of the "workers," the dependence of these parties—as organizational entities—on this social base was minimal. Highly disciplined, centralized organizations, the Communist parties found their *raison d'être* in the acquisition and retention of absolute power, not in the direct representation of worker aspirations. What Richard Lowenthal has said of the Soviet party is equally true of its later imitators:

> The Russian Bolsheviks' presence of being a working-class party had never been true either, even when industrial workers constituted the majority of their membership—because their form of organization made them independent of the actual support of the bulk of the working class and enabled them to change their "social basis" as occasion required.[1]

Liberated as they were from any mass social base, the East European regimes, backed by Soviet power, were able to a large degree to insulate themselves from popular demands, to suppress their very expression. The reality was party domination of all classes, including the workers, and preemption by the party of all organizational space between workers and the polity through dominance of the trade union organizations, "production conferences," and other organs at the factory and higher levels. Add to this formidable array of party control instrumentalities the police apparatus, especially at its high-Stalinist peak, and the quietude of the workers is not difficult to explain.

Yet all these were not the only factors contributing to the relative absence of worker militancy and dissent during the "gray years" of Stalinism. As I have argued elsewhere,[2] the impact of rapid economic modernization and industrialization on the working class also contributed greatly to its political "neutralization." True, the "takeoff" into "planned" industrialization in the late 1940s, with its high reinvestment rates, depressed the living standards and real incomes of most social groups—including many elements of the working class—to a point lower than that of the last years before World War II and lower than the level achieved in the first few years of reconstruction after World War II, but the result was not that destabilizing with respect to the working class. This was because the working class itself was undergoing rapid change. It grew in size as a consequence of the recruitment of peasants (which in turn eased the traditional problems of rural overpopulation and underemployment). "Hereditary" proletarians became a minority in workers' ranks. Moreover, the demand for present and future managers and professionals of presumably "healthy" social origin generated a flow out of the ranks of the working class, especially working-class children, into the new socialist intelligentsia, the new political and economic bureaucracies. Despite the regimes' continued rhetoric extolling proletarian virtue, the participants in this movement out of the working class experienced it as upward mobility.

The working class thus was open at both ends. At the top, the ambitious, intelligent, and even opportunistic—from whom working-class leaders have always tended to come—were co-opted into the new privileged groups. At the bottom, peasants and their offspring, unused to city life and industrial discipline but eager to escape the harsh rural life, entered in increased numbers. It made little difference that the new socialist intelligentsia of, say, 1952 did not live as well as its interwar predecessor, or that skilled workers in the Warsaw or Budapest of the same year worked longer for less than their counterparts in 1938. The frame of reference of the members of the new intelligentsia was that of the working class from which they had risen; that of the new workers, the peasant world they had left. For both, their new status yielded satisfactions, psychological and material, which gave them a "stake" in the system, a reason to feel that what had befallen them could not have come under the old regime.

This state of affairs profoundly affected the psychology of the working class and the probabilities of its developing "class consciousness" in the classic sense. For the peasant, mobility into the working class—into the urban environment, to a job with bounded hours, steady work, and regular pay—represented an *individual* solution. For working-class offspring not content to settle for their fathers' status, the expansion of educational opportunities and the demand for professional cadres held out the prospect, once again, of individual advancement. These high-mobility prospects militated against a readiness to seek *collective* solutions to problems—a readiness more likely to arise when individuals are convinced that their membership in a particular class is a "life sentence."

However, the prospects of mobility have been diminished in recent years. The intelligentsia is not expanding at the rate it did during the "heroic" years, and the rate of growth of the working class has slowed with a decline in fertility and the drying up of the peasant labor pool. Although the offspring of today's intelligentsia possess inherited advantages in their quest to reproduce their parents' status, working-class youths face diminished prospects for advancement, for their numbers and educational aspirations have grown faster than university vacancies. Working-class youths of today also must view their social status differently than their fathers did theirs, i.e., from the more critical perspective of the working class itself rather than as ex-peasants. The chances are increasing that these youths will be forced to remain, against their will, in their class of origin.

Thus, there have appeared to be better prospects for the emergence of a proletarian class consciousness. Some saw such a development foreshadowed in the Polish events of 1970 and 1976, the Romanian strikes of 1977, and other protests. But the question of whether the "new" activism means anything more fundamental than the spontaneous and ad hoc disorders of 1953–56 is a complex one, and even Marxist dissidents have expressed doubts. For example, the Hungarian Andras Hegedus has voiced concern that in the Polish protests of 1970 and 1976, "it was not the demands of the workers as producers . . . but as consumers which came to the front,"[3] and he has argued that the experience of the past has turned workers toward the maximization of wages and the minimization of work to the exclusion of other concerns.[4] Ernest Mandel has called Marxist dissidents to the task of helping the working mass become "politically active and conscious," but has noted that the "higher level of job security and much lower work rhythm" which workers enjoy in socialist economies versus their counterparts in capitalist economies will make this difficult.[5] It is, indeed, difficult to deny that workers' demands have been "economistic."[6]

Whether these demands and those who express them should therefore be written off as of little potential significance for political change is another question. True, in the past, there has been little inclination on the part of workers to merge their particular demands with broader demands voiced by intellectual dissidents for liberalization of economic and political life in Eastern Europe. But is this still the case? To answer that question, one must first examine the record in an attempt to understand better how and why the activities of these two groups have diverged.

DIFFERENT WORLDS, DIFFERENT CONCERNS

The dynamics of Communist politics over the last three decades have unquestionably shown that a wide gap still separates intelligentsia from workers. At most critical junctures, cooperation between them has been the exception rather than the rule.

Poland provides much to ponder in this regard. In 1956, each group contributed to the upheaval of the Polish October, but in different and uncoordinated ways. A rebel intelligentsia and studentry made their impact felt in the pages of *Po prostu* and other journals, as well as through a "revisionist" element in the upper councils of the Polish United Workers' Party (PUWP) itself, paving the way for the return of Wladyslaw Gomulka. Although little contact existed between this intelligentsia and Poland's workers, expressions of dissent by the latter —the riots in Poznan and elsewhere and the rapid growth of workers' councils in the factories—were perhaps even more critical than actions of the intelligentsia in convincing the regime hierarchs that substantial accommodations would be required to restore social peace. In these actions, workers were returning to the tactics used less successfully almost a decade earlier to defend themselves against fundamental changes heralded by the absorption of the Polish Socialist Party into the PUWP.[7] In the context of early 1957, contemplating the tragedy that had befallen their counterparts in Budapest, both the intelligentsia and the workers of Poland could convince themselves that they had "won." Nevertheless, each Polish group had acted separately to achieve its results.

In the Polish crises of 1968 and 1970, there were not even simultaneous actions by both groups. In the first crisis, the intellectuals and students found themselves quite alone. The workers showed no disposition either to identify with the quest of the intelligentsia for greater freedoms of its own or to be greatly concerned about the "anti-Zionist" binge of 1967–68, in which Gomulka struggled to retain his grip on power against the challenge of Mieczyslaw Moczar and at the same time "cool" the intellectuals. In December 1970, the situation was reversed. Precipitous price rises brought the workers into the streets and fire-bombs into party headquarters, but a dispirited intelligentsia expressed little active sympathy with bread-and-butter concerns of the workers. Thus, the spheres of workers and intellectuals, in dissent as in everyday life, continued to be separate in Poland.

What did the events of 1968 in Czechoslovakia tell us about worker-intellectual relations there? A decade later, there still remain questions about the degree of collaboration across class boundaries in the Czechoslovak reform movement of that time. To be sure, in March 1968, the philosopher Ivan Svitak told a group of mine workers in Ostrava that "the best guarantee that our process of regeneration will be socialist and democratic in nature lies in the alliance of workers and intellectuals, that is to say in you, the working class."[8] But such an alliance did not arise swiftly. Some support for a central reform demand of the intelligentsia—a free press—came in the form of "workers' committees for the defense of press freedom," which emerged first in the Ostrava region and then elsewhere. Still, neither the mandate nor the procedures and activities of such committees were ever clear. As one analyst put it, they could be regarded only as "a worthy initiative which, although promising spontaneous working class action and an alliance between workers and the intelligentsia, did not in fact go very far."[9]

Moreover, the attempts of the reformers to "sell" the nation on the dual package of political and economic reform encountered a mix of worker apathy and resistance. This response reflected the success of a government policy that, since 1948, had attempted to drive a wedge between the workers (who were exalted in almost cult proportions in official rhetoric) and the intelligentsia (oft derided). This divisive view had "infected the party as a whole and all levels of society."[10] Under Antonin Novotny, the regime continued to play on worker "prejudices and disdain for intellectuals."[11] As the events of 1968 unfolded, Novotny partisans denounced the reformers as "radicals" who sought "to rob the working classes of what they had achieved in 20 years' hard work." Indeed, the reformers' call for discipline and productivity—in addition to appeals for greater civil freedom—did seem to threaten the extreme egalitarianism of reward and the degree of security workers had achieved in jobs they performed with minimal effort. Furthermore, the same persons who had crippled implementation of the New Economic System shamelessly blamed its architects for the sorry state of the Czechoslovak economy in 1968.[12]

Whatever the distortions in such demagoguery, both the political emphasis of the reform and the social background of its vocal proponents made it seem alien to some, perhaps a majority, of the workers. Gordon Skilling describes the situation:

> The workers were often unhappy with the prominent part taken by journalists, scholars, and writers after January and feared a "hegemony" of the intellectuals. . . . The economic reform itself was viewed with considerable reserve, and even opposition, raising as it did the specter of unemployment and by its emphasis on productivity and qualification, threatening the "equalization" of income under previous wage policy. The so-called workers' policy in the past had given them, they felt, "social security," assuring them both employment and a minimum and stable standard of living, and affording certain sectors of the working class a privileged position. Such attitudes were fostered by trade union and party functionaries, often of working-class origin, who saw their own positions endangered by reforms and speaking in the name of "their" class, inculcated the workers with their fears for the fate of socialism.[13]

As a consequence, no firm "coalition" of workers and intellectuals emerged in Czechoslovakia until August 1968, when the Soviet-led invasion persuaded the two groups to look beyond class or occupational interests. The effect was similar to the temporary unification of views wrought by invasion or the threat of it in 1956 Hungary and Poland. However, it was not long before workers and intellectuals returned to uncoordinated pursuit of their respective and disparate goals.

Let us look more closely at these differing sets of aspirations. Many members of the intelligentsia, despite the group's generally successful accommodation to the socialist system and benefit from it, incline toward liberal reform for reasons both of self-interest and of principle. Decentralizing, market-oriented reforms of the economy promise rewards for scarce skills and knowledge. The intellectual is likely to see his specialized competence as "scarce" and to anticipate greater rewards in any move away from the "compression" of pay differentials common in command systems. "Marketization" also promises broadening of the range of goods, services, and housing available to the many intellectuals and professionals who are already well paid. Greater freedom to travel abroad offers the prospect of new earning opportunities, as well as professional growth.

More fundamentally, liberal intellectuals are attracted by the prospect of a more generalized "freedom," which would permit them to go where facts, theory, and the thought process lead. While virtually no large organization anywhere completely guarantees the specialist such autonomy, the politicization of broad spectra of life and the pervasiveness of the party apparatus in research institutes and universities (as well as in the factories and farms) in Eastern Europe tend to reduce such autonomy to a minimum. Intellectuals look to reform to bring a freer, looser, "decompressed" political environment, which they see as benefiting not only themselves but other classes as well.

But other classes—the working class the largest among them—have their own priorities. As Alexander Matejko puts it, for the intelligentsia "political freedom was and is a primary need, whereas for the blue-collar workers it is only a secondary need."[14] Indeed, given the social and economic history of the East European working classes, preoccupation with more mundane concerns—an adequate material existence and security of employment to undergird it—is no surprise.

And, whatever the ultimate consequences for productivity and efficiency, socialist economies have provided "full" and secure employment—often through an overstocking of labor, which creates a full-paid "underemployment" wherein individual workers do not work hard and many husband their energies for other, more remunerative "private" work.[15] However modest the general living standards may be, wage and welfare policies have provided a "floor" below which one cannot fall, whether one is diligent or not. These policies have also in some measure kept down top earnings, in response to and reinforcing egalitarian sentiments among workers.

Prescriptions for economic reform, particularly the emphasis on increased efficiency and a tighter tying of reward to performance and to scarcity of skills, seem to menace many worker interests. Unskilled workers fear the stated preference for skilled workers; lazy workers, the endorsement of the industrious and energetic; those in unprofitable factories, the possibility of closings and layoffs; and all workers, a new and more demanding tempo of work.

The need for financial and psychological "belt tightening" among some portion of the working class in the short run lessens the receptivity of workers to the long-run reform promise of a more productive economy and an overall improvement in living standards. Promises of a greater role for workers in management—a change itself generally envisaged for later stages of the reforms—run up against worker coolness to contemporary forms of "participation" and perhaps some preference for revitalization of the trade unions as defenders of workers' interests against management.[16] As Matejko observed in the Polish context, "Intellectuals, who may advocate reform, cannot count on the immediate support of the blue-collar workers."[17]

Through the early 1970s in Eastern Europe, then, the concerns of the dissident intelligentsia sparked uncertain response at best among the workers. The working class, when it showed signs of dissent and revolt, generally acted independently of the intelligentsia, manifesting different timetables and priorities. Such outbursts were episodic and lacking in organization. There was little evidence of any alliance between intellectuals and workers.

PROSPECTS FOR A COALITION

Events in Poland, beginning in June 1976, have raised at least the possibility of a significant change in the general pattern just described. However, the Polish case must be judged against the backdrop of developments in other East European states to determine whether it is unique or symptomatic of a major new trend in the area.

As the summer of 1976 came to Poland, things seemed to be proceeding according to form. For example, there had been little worker participation in the protests that had been voiced by Polish intellectuals in late 1975 and early 1976 over proposed changes in the Polish constitution that would further strengthen regime controls and "cement" relations between Poland and the USSR.[18]

But an unprecedented sequence of events began with the riots by workers in Ursus, Radom, and other locales after the June 25 official announcement of sharp price increases. As in 1970, the workers acted on their own, responding to bread-and-butter issues of particular concern to them (in the process bringing both a rollback of the price rises and police repression). This time, however, the intellectuals came to the support of the workers in a most untypical fashion. On June 29, an open letter to the Polish parliament (the Sejm) from fourteen intellectuals denounced government reprisals against the workers who had rioted, and observed that "on the agendum is the establishment of a real representation of the workers."[19] This was followed on July 11 by Jacek Kuron's open letter to Italian Communist party secretary-general Enrico Berlinguer, calling for Eurocommunist support for the Polish workers' cause,[20] and then throughout the summer by further protests on the workers' behalf. Finally, in September, there emerged a Workers' Defense Committee (KOR). This group, which included a broad spectrum of mainly Marxist intellectuals, from Jerzy Andrzejewski to Jacek Kuron, promised economic, legal, and medical assistance to strikers' families; called for an amnesty; and demanded investigations of police brutality during and after the riots.

The creation of this "bridge" across the gap between worker and intellectual reflected, perhaps, a reassessment of the paths to, and potential for, political change in Poland. Indeed, the young Polish historian Adam Michnik, a veteran of the struggles against intellectual repression in 1968 and subsequently a member of KOR's directing committee, had earlier urged intellectuals to appreciate

> the power of the workers who, by their firm and resolute attitude, have already wrestled some spectacular concessions from the government. . . . without any doubt it is of them that the government is really afraid; it is the pressure of this social class which is the sine qua non of the evolution of national life towards democratization.[21]

The proworker activism of KOR fostered by implicit support from the hierarchy of the Catholic church, by occasional spontaneous open letters of protest from workers,[22] and by the gingerly quality of the harassment by a regime concerned above all with "muddling through" a time of trial proceeded along the lines KOR had laid out for itself. To be sure, KOR remained an organization of intellectuals who had decided to defend workers' interests—not a joint organization of workers and intellectuals as such. The degree of unity between the two groups with respect to demands and views must be regarded as questionable—despite Michnik's statement that "within one year, we have succeeded in creating an extraordinary unity among intellectuals, students, and workers."[23] Still, the dissenting intellectuals had learned the importance of joint action from the events of 1968 and 1970.

The government, aware of the significance of such action, attempted at various junctures to discredit the intellectuals of KOR before the workers. For example, a speaker at a Socialist Youth Union conference in February 1977 stated that "in 1968 these people [the intellectuals] expressed their contempt of the working class. They don now the garb of defenders of workers."[24]

The year 1977 saw some significant, if partial, successes for KOR and its causes. By late July, less than thirteen months after the Radom-Ursus riots, all the jailed strikers had been released. KOR also was eventually able to achieve some measure of cooperation with a new organization, the Movement for Defense of Human and Civil Rights (ROPCIO)[25]—a group with a non-Marxist and more traditionalist orientation. At the end of September, KOR reconstituted itself as the "Committee for Social Self-Defense-KOR" (KSS-KOR).[26] Its earlier, more limited objectives partially achieved, the group took on some new, more general goals, committing itself to "supporting and defending all social initiatives aimed at implementing human and civil rights." While these more "global" objectives (like the renaming of the committee) might to some degree have blurred the earlier commitment to specifically workers' causes, KSS-KOR announced a new *samizdat* journal, *Robotnik* (The Worker), designed to support a unified defense of workers' interests, promote independent representatives of the workers in place of the "moribund" official trade unions, and work for greater worker control over matters such as factory conditions and housing.

The Polish situation just described was unique in Eastern Europe at the time—not at all with respect to the existence of dissent, but to the degree that it provided signs of a bridging in some measure of the old gap between workers and intellectuals. With regard to the latter phenomenon, the situation elsewhere in the area was quite different. This is clear from a brief review of the state of affairs in Czechoslovakia, Romania, and Hungary.

After roughly eight years of "normalization" under Gustav Husak, dissent resurfaced in Czechoslovakia in January 1977 in the form of the Charter 77 manifesto. The "chartists" formed no committee as such and coalesced around no set of crises such as the June 1976 events had provided for their Polish counterparts. The political and economic scene in Czechoslovakia was very different from that in Poland. In Prague, there was an unpopular government, but one that felt itself rather more firmly "in the saddle" than did that of Poland's Edward Gierek. This sense of security was due to Soviet support, political resignation on the part of the populace, and a different set of economic facts. "Consumerism" had flourished in Czechoslovakia, sweetening the bitter pill of "normalization."

Thus, there was unfertile ground for the seeds of protest, and by all indications, mass response to the chartists has hardly been overwhelming. To be sure, the number of signatories grew rapidly from the initial 250 or so (by mid-1978, to more than 1,000 signatories), and at each phase those identifying themselves as workers grew as well. But the total of the latter never reached the point where it was more than a modest minority of all signers. Moreover, some portion of the "worker" signatories were former students or former members of the intelligentsia—precipitated by political reprisal into the working class—rather than "authentic" proletarians.[27]

Basically, the chartists have lacked an issue broad enough, and conditions appropriate, to galvanize other groups. Their problem is not so much one of integrating intelligentsia and worker interests as of finding any significant mass base willing to offer support. Conscious of this isolation of dissidents, and probably prepared to face the subsequent protest from the West, including the "Eurocommunist" parties, the Husak regime in late 1979 went ahead with the trial of six activists connected with Charter 77 and the Committee for the Defense of the Unjustly Persecuted (VONS), and on October 22–23 sentenced five to a total of nineteen and a half years' imprisonment (the sixth to a suspended term).[28] Those convicted ranged from the writer Vaclav Havel (four and a half years) to Dana Nemcova, a mother of seven (two years, with a five-year suspended sentence)—an outcome probably inconceivable in Poland, where volatile public moods are an element with which Gierek's regime must reckon. Dissent in Czechoslovakia thus remains a virtual monopoly of the highly committed, and the meetings that since 1978 have occasionally taken place between Czechoslovak dissidents and some of their Polish KOR counterparts may indicate that the former have more in common with the latter than with any significant segment of their own countrymen.[29]

In Romania, 1977 saw manifestations of dissent by both intellectuals and workers, in characteristically differing and isolated forms. Early in the year, the writer Paul Goma's letter of support to Pavel Kohout and the Czechoslovak chartists emerged, followed by the "Letter of the Eight"—a protest from Goma, his wife, and six others calling on Romania to honor the human rights prescribed in "basket three" of the Final Act of the Helsinki Conference on Security and Cooperation in Europe.[30] The regime combined harsh denunciation of the dissidents with permission for a significant number to emigrate, even as the number of signatories to the Letter of the Eight grew. Significantly, the document said little specific about workers' interests and rights, and it is unclear if many of the signatories (whose number reached approximately two hundred by mid-November 1977)[31] were workers—and if so, whether their protest was motivated by class or by ethnic interests (the original signatories included a number of ethnic Hungarians and Germans, whose complaints against the regime could have to do mainly with Ceausescu's policies of cultural homogenization).[32]

Goma was arrested in April 1977, released the following month, and then "exiled" to Paris later in the year. This combination of intimidation and enforced emigration has been used by the Bucharest regime to contain what, so far, seems to be a relatively small problem, involving mainly intellectuals. The chances that such policies would generate mass reaction must have appeared slim in a Romania where (in contrast to Poland) virtually no historical precedent existed for the recognition of the intelligentsia as the "conscience" of a nation in adversity.

Far different in implications were the disorders in Romania's Jiu Valley in July and August 1977, which saw thousands of miners strike on issues involving a new pension law, poor food, forced overtime, and poor equipment.[33] These were "workers' issues," and the regime's response was rapid. State and party chief Nicolae Ceausescu visited the area on August 3, promising reforms and announcing a 5 percent pay raise, and, for the moment, he at least partially defused the situation.

The workers had acted on their own, and in the wake of their action, Bucharest intellectuals generally remained silent. Reports are still vague, but it seems clear that, in the aftermath, many miners were fired, "delegates" of the spontaneous strikers were arrested, and activists were deported back to their native villages.[34] Yet neither workers nor intelligentsia organized effectively to press for amnesty of the sort achieved in Poland in 1977.[35] While Goma did observe later that "workers are the main victims" of internal repression in Romania,[36] Romanian intellectuals have yet to develop a "critical mass" of open dissidents who might, in the Polish fashion, seek contact with a working class at least segments of which have shown a readiness to fight.

The resolution of the 1977 crisis in the Jiu Valley followed a fairly traditional pattern for "personalistic" rule in a Communist state (which is more pronounced in Romania than in any other East European country): the appearance of the leader "on the scene" to cool tempers and to signal that cries had been heard at the top, who then moves to "crack down on the leaders [of disturbances] and introduce quick palliatives for the area's population as a whole."[37] So far, such a strategy seems to have minimized sustained dissent and to have prevented a bridging of the gap between the intelligentsia and the workers in Romania.

Hungary's situation is different yet. Janos Kadar's delicate political management and the fruits of the New Economic Mechanism (NEM) have generated a legitimacy for his regime which could scarcely have been predicted from the perspective of 1956. Hungary today combines a rather liberal internal regime and a population generally satisfied and thus "resigned" to realities as they are. What this has meant is that, for some time, links of the dissident intellectuals to the working class have been "next to nonexistent" (though their moral links to dissidents elsewhere were manifested in the protest of more than 250 Hungarian intellectuals against the trials of Czech dissidents).[38]

Having no "issue" to take to the working class, Hungarian dissidents have, for the most part, dealt with questions (the quality of life in socialist society, the measure of egalitarianism appropriate to socialism, consumerism and its implications) which reflect both a rather low degree of crude political repression in Hungary and the "new left" orientation of some of the dissenters. The writings of the Budapest dissidents have been complex, dense, and aimed at other intellectuals. Manifestos and broadsides have not been their métier.[39] Rather, their aim seems to be the diffusion of ideological alternatives, the starting among potential allies in the intelligentsia of a process of thought which goes beyond acceptance of the current rather comfortable situation. Two volumes of *samizdat* essays which appeared in 1977, *Marx in the Fourth Decade* and *Profiles*, indicated some movement away from Marxism among some of the dissidents. (A subsequent Polish compilation of selections from these two volumes prepared at the request of Adam Michnik represented another instance of cross-national cooperation among Eastern Europe's dissenting intelligentsia).[40]

Thus, dissent emanating from the intellectuals has not spread far outward into Hungarian society. The relative self-confidence of the Kadar regime has allowed it to deal with the dissidents in a relatively civilized manner. Expulsions from the party have been followed by enforced emigration, either permanent or of indefinite duration. Ivan Szelenyi and Gyorgy Konrad were dealt with in such a fashion in 1974. Similarly, in early 1978, Gyorgy and Maria Markus, Ferenc Feher, and Agnes Heller were sent off to the West with little rhetorical flourish or denunciation—indeed, with official statements verging on regret.[41]

For all the differences in national situations in Eastern Europe, there does appear to be emerging one common theme in the dissident intellectuals' views of workers: explicit support for freely elected trade unions and for the workers' right to strike. In a very real sense, the intellectuals have accorded legitimacy to the workers' "economistic" demands. Thus, the "Letter of the Fifty-nine" to the Polish Sejm on December 5, 1975, spoke of the "freedom of work":

There is no such freedom while the State is the sole employer, and while Trade Unions are forced to conform to the administration of the Party, which actually wields the power in the State. In conditions such as these—as the events of 1956 and 1970 testify—any attempts to protect the workers' interests are threatened by bloodshed and can lead to serious outbreaks of violence. For this reason employees must be assured their freedom to choose their own trade representation, which is independent of both State and Party. The right to strike must also be guaranteed.[42]

In like vein, Andras Hegedus regards the increasing tendency of trade unions to defend particular workers' interests at the factory level in the NEM period as a desirable development.[43] And Jiri Pelikan, speaking no doubt for many like-minded Marxist and non-Marxist veterans of the Prague Spring and Charter 77, makes an element of his "common platform" for the Marxist opposition in Eastern Europe the guarantee of "the autonomy of trade unions in defense of workers' interests which can, even in a socialist society, conflict with the interests of State power."[44]

Although the "programmatic" aspects of the liberation of trade unions from state-party control are vague (perhaps the intellectuals look to the workers to make their own arrangements?), the important matter is the evident unity among dissident intellectuals, *including* Marxists, regarding the right of independent unions to defend workers' interests in a "workers' state." This seems to represent a serious response to the workers' concerns and view of the world.

Beyond this, however, there is little else, except a conviction concerning the necessity of cooperation between intellectuals and workers. The intellectuals recognize that they need the workers as a broad social base supporting change, and they see the workers as needing the intellectuals to provide continuity, the persistence in opposition which will break the pattern of "outburst-repression-concession-stabilization" which has characterized conflict between workers and regimes in the past. Thus, Pelikan observes that the socialist opposition "should see to it that outbursts of workers' struggle do not lose impetus after a few economic concessions and that a united front of workers, progressive intellectuals and youth unremittingly challenge the bureaucracy."[45] Similarly, KSS-KOR observes in its 1978 "Appeal to Society" that the concessions that "social pressure" forced out of Polish authorities in 1970 and 1976 were "short-lived." Indeed, "in no time at all, the authorities took back from the disintegrated community what it had obtained. Only steady, broad, and organized pressure can counteract this."[46] "Organized" pressure implies, above all, functional linkages between intelligentsia and workers.

But whether these perceptions are being realized in action is another story. The current situation differs from country to country. Hungary's smooth political surface conceals what, for the time, is likely to be a smooth reality as well. Kadar's talents for political management remain evident. In Romania, the Jiu Valley is seemingly quiet, and Bucharest offers little of an intelligentsia core likely to provide support and ideological articulation of worker demands. So far, the Bucharest regime has taken tough measures toward the Free Labor Union (SLOMR) formed in February 1979.[47] The Charter 77 group in Czechoslovakia has manifested courage but on balance has failed to bridge critical class and ethnic cleavages. Slovaks, workers, and peasants have stood aside, and the Husak regime in late 1979 imposed harsh sentences on major spokesmen of the movement.

In Poland, to a greater degree than elsewhere, action has followed rhetoric. When KSS-KOR announced in November 1977 that a "cell" of its journal *Robotnik* had been formed among workers in Radom to struggle for workers' interests, one analyst in the West viewed the event as the "first concrete evidence of institutionalized links between the workers and the intelligentsia."[48] Yet even here one cannot be sure how "institutionalized," how durable, such links will prove or whether intellectuals can keep workers', and therefore mass, concerns in the forefront of their activity.

Clearly, Poland remains for the present the most critical testing ground for the viability of a worker-intelligentsia alliance. On the workers' side, there are signs of more purposeful organizational work, as witnessed in the foundation of workers' committees to push for the creation of free trade unions, first in Katowice in February 1978, and then in the Baltic coastal cities in late April of the same year.[49] This trend continues in the founding of another free trade union committee, in Szczecin in October 1979.[50] There have been some rural echoes of this organizational activism in the emergence of peasant dissent in the Lublin area,[51] and later in Grojec.[52]

Bread-and-butter issues, centering at first on new peasant pension laws, expanded into demands by peasants for what amounts to a veto power over legislation affecting them; in the words of the Grojec activists: "Nothing about us—without us."[53] It is of interest that there was even a heavy worker flavor in the peasant dissent, for a large proportion of the activists were "peasant-workers" with one foot in the private sector and the other in socialist industry.[54] As for the intellectuals, both KSS-KOR and ROPCIO have commented favorably on the new worker activism and have reported with concern reprisals against working-class activists and their families.[55] Moreover, 1978 also saw the foundation of the Society for Educational Courses (TKN) and its "Flying University" among Polish students, which among its many themes included sensitization of the students to the interests of the working class of Poland.

The Polish context, of course, cannot be fully appreciated without reference to the role of religion and mass religious consciousness. To be sure, religious issues—freedom of belief and ritual—have served to mobilize workers and peasants in other East European states, and in the USSR as well. In general, such issues seem of greater concern to non-intelligentsia groups than do the general issues of liberty which mobilize the intellectuals. In some states—for example, Romania—the "action" has been with religious minorities, typically Protestant groups, and religious divisions in the society have blunted the potential impact of such dissidence. Poland, however, combines a virtually universal nominal Catholicism with high levels of religious observance and an articulate and organized Catholic intelligentsia that is in touch with the secular intelligentsia. To top things off, a Pole, Karol Cardinal Wojtyla of Krakow, has now ascended to the papacy as John Paul II. Catholicism thus provides an alternate—and more authentic—focus of national identity for Poles than the state or its ideology, as the mass response to the June 1979 papal visit to Poland once again reaffirmed. In such a situation, the support that the church offers to intelligentsia seeking freedom of expression and to workers seeking economic justice, as well as the moderating influence it exerts with respect to the way in which demands for the latter are expressed, places it in a position of strength vis-à-vis a regime which, paradoxically, is dependent on the church's acquiescence in many important areas. Consequently, the church will remain a critical actor in Poland.

No other East European state currently faces the "mobilization," albeit quite partial, of such a diversity of social strata and groups, as does Poland under Gierek's government.[56] At the same time, this very diversity creates problems of cooperation. Factory conditions and price subsidies on foodstuffs are matters of more direct concern to workers than to the intelligentsia, whose work environments differ from those of laborers and who expend a smaller proportion of their budgets for food than do laborers. The preoccupations of peasants, as producers of food the others consume and as both beneficiaries and victims of their own private-sector status, are not the same as those of either the workers or the intelligentsia, but the peasants tend to have more in common with the former than with the latter. While the intellectuals feel a political pinch, the workers and peasants feel an economic one.

The differences in perspectives between workers and intellectuals are evident in a 1978 KSS-KOR document analyzing the state of Poland's economy.[57] The independent-minded economists who drafted the document see the big picture—the irreconcilabilities inherent in the consumption aspirations of Polish workers, the shortages, a huge foreign debt, and the costs of price subsidies. Shortages cannot end, pay packets grow, and subsidies continue, all at the same time. To the worker, however, the "big picture" is vague, and the problems of the moment are paramount. The foreign debt means little to him, even if it ultimately affects his prospects in profound ways, and he fears the message of "belt tightening" implicit in the KSS-KOR document. This conflict in perspectives does not bode well for the construction of firm and lasting linkages between intelligentsia and workers in the years to come.

THE OUTLOOK

Indeed, it may be that the conflict between the relatively egalitarian attitudes of workers, fostered if not completely satisfied by thirty years of Communist rule in Eastern Europe, and the more meritocratic convictions of the intelligentsia is insuperable. Likewise, conflict between the concrete, here-and-now issues that concern the workers and the more abstract strivings for "freedom" that motivate intellectuals may not be resolvable. This is a pessimistic assessment, but one shared by a number of observers of worker-intelligentsia relations in the East European societies.

For example, Zygmunt Bauman—analyzing the interplay of class structure and bureaucratic power in the Communist states—concludes that the workers, holding suspect the reformers' calls for greater play of market forces,

> see in officialdom the only body called to defend them against mounting deprivations in the market sphere. A sort of alliance between the party and the workers against the managers and professions (... the most privileged classes in market terms) asserts itself more often than not as a persistent mark of the ... power structure.[58]

Similarly, two Hungarian dissidents, writing under the pseudonym "Marc Rakovski," note how the "elite of the ruling class ... presents itself as the protector of the working class against those strata [the economic and technical experts and the lower- and middle-level managers] which are trying to enrich themselves at the latter's expense."[59] The Hungarians Gyorgy Konrad and Ivan Szelenyi, now émigrés, push their analysis a step further to argue that the intelligentsia—far from serving as a mediator between workers and the political elite—is on the road to becoming the dominant group within the ruling class, the intellectuals' possession of "teleological knowledge" giving them a claim to preeminence in a system of "rational [i.e., non-market] redistribution." Intellectuals who defend the workers, then, take on the character of "defectors" from their own class.[60]

These general formulations may seem overly abstract, too simple, when held up against the quite complex realities of 1956, 1968, 1970, and 1976. Yet the "pessimism" of the Bauman-Rakovski view has much to support it, on the evidence. Workers' coolness toward the Czechoslovak reform package in earlier 1968 was transformed into support of a generalized sort after the Warsaw Pact invasion, but worker resistance, as long as it continued, focused more and more on the sort of economic issues embodied in the trade union charter and statutes adopted in March 1969 rather than on broader issues of participation in management and the expansion of civil freedoms. And while the firebombing of PUWP offices at first glance hardly seems the sort of act that workers who "look to officialdom for redress" from economic grievance would perpetrate, it is a form of communication with the locus of power, with the party. In the absence of institutionalized nonviolent mechanisms, it is a way of telling the party that the "social compact" between the regime and the masses is being violated. Workers have not looked to intellectuals for redress, whether or not they view them as a group with opposed interests.

Economic issues are the ones that will continue to catalyze workers' direct action. Thus, one can expect more localized protests at the factory or industrial-branch level when earnings appear endangered by upward revision of output norms, or by the tying of wages more tightly to productivity, and broader protest when price rises threaten purchasing power.[61] Either may be precipitated within one of two more general situations: relatively constant working-class material expectations whose fulfillment is threatened by stagnating economic conditions, or rising expectations fed by a record of recent substantial progress but impossible to fulfill without the sort of modifications in the social compact workers are unwilling to countenance—namely, a sacrifice of security and/or of slow and undemanding work rhythms for heightened reward for the skilled and diligent.

In all of these circumstances, there is little of the evident political content of issues dear to the hearts of the intelligentsia. The political issue that KOR seized upon at its foundation was the repression of workers after protest had occurred—a protest that had succeeded in securing a rapid rollback of the 1976 price rises before pro-worker intelligentsia activity had even surfaced. Unquestionably, worker-intellectual cooperation can develop around the relatively "narrow" political issue of specific antiworker repressions—to which KOR's call for amnesty and restoration of jobs, as well as its welfare work among families of the imprisoned and fired, was an appropriate and well-received response. However, mobilization of the large mass of workers for the long haul has proved difficult. With the goals of amnesty largely achieved by the summer of 1977, Polish workers seem to have settled into a relative passivity. This is not to deny the significance of *Robotnik* or of the "free trade union" committees. Rather, it is to emphasize that by now, more than three years after 1976, a more mobilized working class would have spawned more such committees, more *samizdat* clearly its own, and, perhaps, more of its own organizational initiatives for at least tactical cooperation with sympathetic members of the intelligentsia. This has not happened.[62]

To their credit, the Polish and Czechoslovak dissident intelligentsia have focused on immediate worker concerns by generally continuing to advocate free trade unions for the workers and downplaying any appeal for the more conceptually elaborate, and practically difficult, mechanisms of worker participation in management, to which workers, finding it hard to envision their representatives on both sides of a bargaining table, have generally remained cool. Still, the divide between the groups remains wide. The KSS-KOR economic analysis mentioned earlier, as a document of the intelligentsia, takes into account the long-term implications of Polish economic problems in a way that Polish workers, self-organized to defend their own interests, could not—and under the current circumstances, perhaps should not—be expected to. The ability of intellectuals to articulate complex proposals, to be "objective" and to strike a balance between the claims of various groups, to persist in commitment over the long run to work for political change, distinguishes the intelligentsia as a privileged, even if dissident, element, and distinguishes it from the working class as well. The contrasts are highlighted by Rakovski:

> Even among themselves, the members of the working class are not linked by a network of communication comparable to that which serves as the basis for the circulation of samizdat. This kind of communication is not a natural part of the lifestyle of the worker. To establish an opening through which the underground can commu-

nicate with the workers, the workers themselves must reach the stage of organized class struggle and institute, at least at factory level, associations which can then be stabilized. Then these organizations would be able to interact with the underground. But in Soviet-type societies, the working class is as incapable of organizing itself as [is] any other social group. While the rare moments of cataclysmic crisis in the system give rise to strike committees and workers' councils, these organizational results of popular uprisings never succeed in consolidating after normal reproduction has been reestablished. In such circumstances, to a working class which is deprived of its organizations, the ideas of the underground are not social facts, or else they are the particular business of an alien group.[63]

For the present, then, both the factual record and some of the analytic perspectives on socialist societies explored here warrant a good deal of pessimism about the maintenance of worker-intelligentsia coalitions as sources of major change in Eastern Europe. It is, of course, not beyond the realm of possibility that an intelligentsia-worker alliance might take shape despite the existing conflicts of interest between the two groups, and that this sort of an alliance would constitute a unified force for change. Such a development would require not only mutual recognition of opposing interests but also an agreement to "rise above" their conflict until mutual cooperation brought about institutionalized political mechanisms (now absent) through which it could be channeled.

This kind of an agreement would amount to a recognition that a civil society—freer politically and less centralized economically, and therefore probably more inegalitarian yet more productive as well—would achieve no final resolution of conflict, because such is impossible. In addition, both groups would have to acknowledge, explicitly or implicitly, that freedom and equality are in conflict, and that a new balance must be struck between them. It is important to understand, however, that the factors promoting such coalitions are weak. Moreover, the considerable repressive capacities of the Communist regimes are still a major element limiting the abilities of groups to organize politically for their own ends—and the USSR remains, judging by its actions in Afghanistan, quite ready to apply whatever forceful measures it deems necessary to guarantee the status quo in its East European backyard.

If prospects for the immediate future are dim, what of the longer term? Two points—a contingency and a trend—are worth noting. The contingency is the possibility that strong agitation for reform, emanating from and supported by either intelligentsia or workers, might result in a regime crisis sufficient to create, as just noted, the threat or reality of Soviet intervention à la 1968. Such circumstances provided the catalyst for worker-intelligentsia cooperation in that year in Czechoslovakia, and if the Polish situation deteriorated in the 1980s, they would probably do the same there. But this sort of catalyzing crisis, "resolved" in the end by Soviet power, ultimately entails drastic limitations of freedom for further actions by either group. The general defeat of reform and change is the greater fact; the final union-in-crisis of workers and intellectuals, the lesser one.

The trend involves the changing composition of the working class in the East European states. From its immediate postwar configuration— a small group composed of the surviving old proletarians—the working class expanded in size through the absorption of upwardly mobile peasants generally content with a lot far better than that of life in the villages. In the current third phase, a differentiated working class is, in its skilled and semi-skilled components, increasingly populated by the children of the ex-peasants who made the transition from village to city, i.e., by people who have grown up in the working-class milieu. As the average educational level of working-class youth rises and as many find themselves remaining in the working class because of limited numbers of places in higher education, their receptivity to ideas of an abstract sort, to the programmatic language of the dissident intelligentsia, may grow. Certainly the several years more of education that younger workers possess in comparison with their parents may help render the ideas of intellectuals more intelligible. A sufficient supply of such workers with a new class consciousness might provide the basis for the genuine working-class organization presently lacking.

The diversity of the present situations, country by country, presages a likely diversity in the future interplay of the forces discussed here. Stabilization is possible, if improbable, in Poland—just as exacerbation of the situations in other states to a "Polish" intensity is conceivable, if unlikely. Events often make fools of those who predict and project. For example, religion and nationalism, rather than a developing interclass cooperation, may prove the main challenge to the East European regimes in their fourth and fifth decades. What does seem probable, however, is that they will not pass through the 1980s without facing new tests of their durability.

NINE

WORKERS AND POWER

Marxism placed the worker—its sole creator of material value—at the center of its analysis and calls to action. Born of the industrial revolution and capitalism, dispossessed of all but the labor power that was his to sell, no longer (as his peasant forebear) woven into the more intimate servant-master relationship with its overlay of traditional obligations and reciprocities, but confronting impersonal "capital" in uneven contractual relationships, the worker was the exploited of the present, the revolutionary of the future. That future, achieved, would see proletarian triumph through an exercise of power ("dictatorship") by the working class, against exploiting classes (the bourgeoisie) but in favor of all men's "true" interests; so evident that, after a transition period, the problems of power, control, the segmentation of man's life between work and other roles, would also dissolve in the construction of a new society.

History has played both Marxists and workers false. Marxism has

Originally published in Jan F. Triska and Charles Gati, eds., *Blue-Collar Workers in Eastern Europe* (London: Allen and Unwin, 1981), pp. 157–172.

yielded "workers' states"—as yet no Communist societies—not in the states where capitalism had run its course and done its historic work, but where it had hardly begun. It became the ruling ideology, with various national adaptations and distortions, not where large proletariats had been concentrated, but over societies where peasantry dominated —first Russia, then the states of Eastern Europe. Rather than basing itself on the industrial civilization laid down by capitalism, Marxist rule faced the task of creating a socialist variant of that civilization on an underdeveloped base.

The results, diverse as they run from East Berlin to Vladivostok, look little like any nineteenth-century design. No aspect of these societies, save propagandists' rhetoric, approaches the utopian. Power is radically concentrated in leaderships which, in addition to traditional instruments of political control, hold the economic fate of individuals in their hands through far-reaching state ownership and centralized management of productive resources. In none do living standards equal those of the countries of developed capitalism, among the latter those very states where Marxist expectations predicted the revolution would first come. In none does the diversity and liveliness of cultural and occupational expression rival the advanced societies of the West, much less resemble that arcadia where a man might practice a craft, farm, and criticize all in the same day.

All this means that workers are still a distinct group in Marxist socialist societies—takers rather than givers of order, specialized in their work functions, performing these distinct from other aspects of their lives. Lacking workers, socialism created them through industrialization—and created workers of a sort not readily distinguishable, for many purposes, from their counterparts under capitalism. These workers "fit" in a system of stratification—the patterned, unequal distribution of material goods, power and prestige, and opportunities to achieve these—advantaged compared with some groups, disadvantaged vis-à-vis others. Exalted as the leading class by regimes still tied to nineteenth-century rhetoric, they are, along with the vast majority in socialist society, among the led.

Thus, the problem of power reasserts itself in the situation of the socialist industrial class. Power is neither equally distributed among all (and hence not "power" at all), nor is it all in the hands of the workers after thirty-five years of socialism in Eastern Europe. It is a multifaceted problem, involving the sorts of resources workers possess to assert power versus other groups, the regime, or both, the liabilities and weaknesses of the workers as a power group, and the institutional-ideological constraints of the systems they inhabit. The assertion of working-class power, directly and indirectly, has a history as well, combining success and failure, which we will review later. Finally, the present state of worker "consciousness," assertiveness, and degree of cooperation with other forces needs to be assessed to project possibilities for the future.

The present chapter attempts to do all this, in a general way. Much of what follows is summary—specificity in single-country situations has been sacrificed in an attempt to isolate and discuss some general themes. Much is also speculative, not lending itself easily to documentation—hence, a relative paucity of reference. It is offered, in a serious way, as an introductory look at workers as a power group in socialist societies, since other chapters in this book deal in much greater depth with both individual issues and distinct national patterns.

POWER POTENTIAL AND RESOURCES

Save in Czechoslovakia and the German Democratic Republic (GDR), the leaderships in East European socialist states faced, at their inception, a deficit of workers—the group supposedly providing a natural support base for socialist politics and policies. Inheritors of under- and semi-developed economies disrupted by war, they sought to establish rule over societies where the peasantry's demographic weight ranged from preponderant (Poland and Hungary) to overwhelming (the Balkan states). Stabilizing that rule to a certain degree, with significant Soviet aid and control, they set about the task of transforming societies in the image of their regimes—the creation of workers to inhabit and justify a worker's state.

They succeeded. Throughout Eastern Europe today, the workers constitute the largest class or stratum—outnumbering the peasantry and white-collar groups and, in some states, amounting to a majority of the population. This numerical predominance of the blue-collar industrial work force bespeaks both success and failure in socialist economic performances. The successful mounting of industrialization strategies in the late 1940s to early 1960s drew off the underemployed surplus from agrarian labor pools, added them, frequently at high social cost, to the burgeoning urban factory labor forces, and generated professional and administrative cadres of greatly increased size through the recruitment of ambitious adults and youth from worker and peasant backgrounds. Failure, however, is registered in the fact that no socialist state economy has yet passed through the "second industrial revolution" or the move to a postindustrial society, wherein more than half of the labor force produces neither finished goods nor crops, but renders services: a society wherein the tertiary sector is dominant.

Faulting the socialist regimes on this point may be unfair, since it is not clear that they have aimed at such an outcome, but not entirely so. References to the scientific-technical revolution, the various theories of "developed socialism" in futurological rhetoric, indicate some end point not yet arrived at. The socialist economies have proven poor at the substitution of capital for labor, of technological and management resources for capital, and slow to adapt to the challenge of increasing materials cost, decreasing labor force growth rates, etc. All this contributes to the situation wherein workers make up the largest social stratum; one less mechanized and skilled, all in all, than its counterparts in Western Europe and North America, but larger versus the society as a whole.

Thus, a prime power resource of workers is that of their absolute and relative numbers. Whether this potential is actualized is not at all a simply answered question in politics, where no institutions provide for the regular and legitimate exercise of workers' "class power." But it is well to contemplate certain aspects of the matter of numerical strength. First, it makes workers the largest "constituency" group in relation to general regime policies; for good or ill, workers (and their families) make up a majority or near-majority of all persons affected by particular policies. Not one group among several ("workers, peasants, socialist intelligentsia... ") groups, the workers are, from some viewpoints, *the society*, or as close to it as any group is likely to approach.

Second, whatever the differences in social perception and expectations formed among the different social strata, working-class size guarantees that any views peculiar to, but adequately diffused among, this class become major elements in the political psychology of regime-society relations. "What the workers think" *en gros* assumes an importance beyond "what the intelligentsia think" in certain ways. Any development of a combative class consciousness among workers, expressed finally in organizational forms which facilitate their ability to negotiate with the state, would be profoundly consequential. On the other hand, a fundamentally apolitical, "economistic" orientation on the workers' part—a failure of class consciousness to develop—is also a social fact of political importance.

Beyond numbers, the location and function of the working class or stratum in the society and economy confer upon it several potential strengths. The day-to-day functioning of industrial societies depends on an immensely complex set of interactions, exchanges, activity patterns predictable and persistent—and "workers," broadly conceived as including not only manuals in industrial production, but also those in energy production and distribution, transportation, waste removal, etc., stand at a number of the most critical points in the pattern. True, they are not potentially "independent" of the economy to the degree that peasants—direct producers of the means of subsistence—may be regarded so (although the dependence of today's peasants in socialist states on many items from the market places some limit on their ability, even in extremis, to withdraw). But compared with the intelligentsia and many administrative cadres, a "withdrawal of services" on the part of workers will be felt by the whole society much more readily. Universities, schools, publishing houses, even a broad range of government offices, might close with only moderate immediate effects on the daily life of citizens—in the West as in the East. But they all depend on the operation of human and goods transport, the flow of electricity when a switch is turned, the removal of garbage, in a direct and everyday way.

The potential, then, of large-scale strikes and disruptions by workers is immense. It has been actualized, to degrees moderate compared with the logical extremes it might reach, in Poland (1956, 1970, 1976) most frequently, and less so in other states. The potential has led to more response from regimes than has intellectual dissent, measured by reallocative decisions, changes in leadership composition, etc. But as yet it has left the design of regimes unchanged. This points to some of the limits on working-class power and the exercise thereof, to be considered in a later section.

Workers' relatively high degree of concentration—the ecology of the medium-to-large-size factory, mine, etc.—amplifies the likely simultaneity of actions and responses, and provides a possibility of spontaneous organization greater than office work or agricultural labor typically afford. This is an old point, well appreciated by the Marxist propagandists and organizers of the past who found proletarians so "reachable" in the large bureaucratically managed factories which succeeded the smaller-scale, often family-owned and -managed workshops of earlier stages of industrialization. The factory, the shipyard, the mine—a physical property which is also the locus of complex activities involving large numbers of persons—offers a base for rapid diffusion of rumors, complaints, reactions, an audience for those who will at critical times speak out uninvited. This is the workers' natural habitat.

Finally, the element of myth is a critical potential asset in the inventory of working-class power. What one analyst has called the "legitimacy myth" of socialist regimes—that they draw their mandate, legitimacy, and support from the working class, whose interests they articulate and advance[1]—makes working-class perceptions of the rough "justice" or effectiveness of the system extremely salient for those regimes, however they may seek to control the behavior and manipulate the perceptions. From no quarter are regimes so vulnerable to populist appeals to their own professed ideals as from those who can conceivably be seen as representative of, or at least rising from, "the workers." The countervailing realities of the workers' real place in the system of social, economic, and political rewards—hardly a leading one— do not matter here.

True, such a background is disadvantageous with respect to access to higher education at the most elite universities and institutions. True, there is less of the regime rhetorical populism (epitomized perhaps by the Novotny period in Czechoslovakia) which castigated the instability and ingratitude of intellectuals, and on occasion the recalcitrance and truculence of peasants, while extolling proletarian virtue. But the elements of charade have not been acknowledged as such: no regime has yet declared that its critical, legitimating support lies domestically in its intelligentsia and managers, or its peasants, or in any other stratum save the working class. None *can*, without abandoning the ossified and confining set of symbols and catch phrases they have grown so used to. And to do so would be an act taken as something serious indeed by workers who, while aware that materially and in power terms they do not lead, are not by that reason likely to take any forced move out of symbolic center stage with equanimity.

WORKERS' LIABILITIES: LIMITS ON POWER

Many entries can be made in the debit side of the ledger of workers' political power—some of these the mirror images of some of their elements of power potential, others factors that in a more direct way inhibit their development of effective power.

Large numbers, diffusion across the landscape of cities and factories and across various social boundaries within the working class (skilled, semiskilled, unskilled categories, as well as divisions by industrial branch), all complicate any possibility of effective worker organization—especially in a hostile political environment. Intelligentsia organizational capacities are limited enough, yet much greater than those yet manifested by workers; here, the smaller numbers and freer communication of the former play a role. And while regimes such as Poland's seem to have settled, grudgingly, for a certain amount of unofficial but permanent self-organization on the part of the intellectuals, they have typically cracked down harshly on any sign of working-class attempts at self-organization.

Weakness also stems from a relative lack of ideological and conceptual resources. Working-class movements have not, in the past, elaborated their own ideologies to give meaning and shape to their activity—they have received or adopted them, generally from upper-class "defectors" or intellectual allies. Given the degree of control socialist regimes exercise over intelligentsia-worker contacts, passing on a new ideology to the workers will be difficult. It may indeed be, as a recent provocative analysis argues,[2] that only "traitors" to the class interests of an intelligentsia which enjoys many rewards under socialism will make such an effort.

A further complication is that socialist workers live in systems whose ideology decrees that workers themselves are the leading or ruling class. This "myth" constrains the regime in some sense, but it also constrains the workers. Workers' riots are serious, and taken seriously by the regimes, but the myth which "helps to attain momentary success" by riots "creates difficulties in developing protracted, lasting action by the workers: it is very difficult to fight for something that nominally exists," in the words of one Polish analyst.[3] Similarly, the conceptual-psychological problems of developing a sustained opposition against a regime which claims to base itself on the class in question has tended to leave class consciousness at a rather simple level:

> This class consciousness does not go beyond the level of a primitive "us and them" distinction. This kind of distinction, because of its non-differentiated character, can only be used to orient social behaviors among the interest relations of the groups concerned in the workplace and the living area, where all that is needed to decide who belongs to "us" and who belongs to "them" is to interpret the typical activities and material symbols (clothes, etc.). On a broader scale, this turns out to be an empty interpretative framework without practical consequences in any situation other than the extremely rare cases of mass riots, which are quickly crushed. In order to reach a point where there is solidarity and extensive co-operation, in order to realize an overall social programme, the classes need to institute their own

political and economic organizations. But in Soviet-type society, none of the social classes is in a position to organize itself.[4]

To these liabilities can be added the relative lack of information at workers' disposal about issues that affect them—their dependence, in a real sense, on a regime's willingness to "share the facts" with them. This is rarely manifested except in those times of crisis when, accommodating some worker demands with concessions, a leader may point to grim economic information dictating the need for workers to limit the scope of their further demands, "understand" the delicate situation of a leadership placed between popular demands and Soviet concerns, and go back to work. East European workers live in a world of economic mystification, flooded with information about inflation and unemployment in market economies (as well as high income-tax rates) in the West, but less knowledgeable about their own situations. Few understand the trade-off of shortages for inflation, few realize the extremely high (and regressive) reabsorption of purchasing power through the hidden "turnover tax." Few, in sum, understand how the system taxes its subjects, taxes away what it has "given."

The exigencies of working-class life, finally, impose somewhat restricted frames of reference and time on workers as participants in politics. Given the presocialist political cultures of most of Eastern Europe, and the experience in the thirty-five years since World War II, it is not patronizing to note that workers have shown less concern with the intelligentsia's agenda of dissent—civil liberties, freedom to travel, to publish, etc.—than with bread-and-butter issues. Material grievances can be, and have been, accommodated by regimes, often swiftly, when disorder arose—"cooling" the situation until the next crisis. These episodic material concessions, however, limit workers' motivation to settle into the long fight, the protracted struggle, and help give worker protest its own episodic, short-lived quality. While most intelligentsia have been "bought off" by a combination of job security and material rewards, the dissident intelligentsia's demands are not subject to easy accommodation, nor so time bound that concessions offered would automatically lead to a moderation or cessation of political activity.

Thus, working-class liabilities are considerable. They would weigh heavily in an open political system; they do so all the more in systems whose design excludes spontaneous participation, and whose leaders are committed to maximizing control and monopolizing effective political power. The range of tolerance-to-repression is a wide one in Eastern

Europe. Yugoslavia's "openness" is unique, as are its economic and political designs. Poland and Hungary are "liberal"—the former more through the sheer difficulty of maintaining control over the feisty mix of church, mass nationalism, and an eternally belligerent intelligentsia than through any regime leanings; the latter because Kadar's deft political and economic management is complemented by a popular response, which itself has shown consciousness of the utility of moderation. Czechoslovakia remains repressive, its regime designed to contain the elements of a political culture incompatible with state socialism, and prevent even at high cost the repeat of the 1968 experience. Romania and Bulgaria also cluster at the repressive end of the continuum. But for all the differences, it should be noted that "liberalism" perceived in any of these states is defined by the negative reference point of the Soviet Union. All are illiberal, repressive by any West European standard, and thus in all any independent assertion of power by workers is a matter of uphill struggle, a fight where challengers to the current order are likely to be overmatched.

ACTION DIRECT AND INDIRECT

How has the balance between workers' resources and liabilities been struck in action? The answer—general as it must be, given space constraints here and the more than thirty-year history of worker-socialist regime relations—has two aspects: first, touching those actions emerging from and remaining essentially of the workers, and second, referring to those actions where workers have operated in concert with other groups (primarily the intelligentsia).

Direct worker action has ranged from the smallish in scale—many of these remaining largely unknown outside the country or area of their occurrence—to the "high points" of their involvement in Berlin (1953), Plzen, Poznan (1956), Budapest (1956), the Polish outbreaks of 1970 and 1976, and the Jiu Valley miners' strike in Romania in 1977. Many of these have involved spontaneous protests on economic issues. "Speed-ups" via an upward ratcheting of work norms threatened real incomes of workers, or changes in the price structure of everyday consumption items jeopardized living standards. Reactions to these, in turn, have ranged from factory sit-down strikes to street riots, from swift, episodic and almost wholly unorganized actions to those more lengthy, wherein committee structures have emerged to negotiate with leaders local and national.

Not all, however, have been simply economic in their base—some of the worker militancy in Poland in 1956, for example, and also in Hungary in the same year emerged and simultaneously took on a political character only as they became linked to national agendas against Soviet domination. In the "reform" of Czechoslovakia of 1968, worker support—moderate in the early period of the reform movement, since the economic package of the reformers seemed to threaten as much as it promised workers in the economic sphere—only took on the character of politicized direct action after the Soviet invasion. Indeed, instances of worker-intelligentsia coordination (as opposed to parallel and anti-regime action) seem in general to have arisen in response to real or threatened Soviet intervention to restore a "balance" in favor of unpopular regimes destabilized by social forces beyond their control (see chapter 8).

The history of worker action also encompasses important elements of change in the composition of the industrial blue-collar world and the underlying nature of regime-worker understanding of their mutual relationship. The early postwar periods—those of coalition or "popular front" governments in most states and policies of economic reconstruction—saw the survivors of the old prewar working class making up the new. In Czechoslovakia, this amounted to a large, experienced proletariat used to "politics" in a competitive sense—though heavily under Communist influence. In Hungary and Poland, much smaller, old proletariats, heavily affected by the war, reemerged. The Balkans, of course, boasted little by way of a recognizable working class or stratum at all.

This situation changed rapidly, as the industrialization drives inundated the surviving core of seasoned industrial workers with a massive inflow of new factory recruits from the peasantry—recruits whose level of political consciousness, whose attitudes toward the new industrial environment, and whose traditional modes of relating to authority (patron-client relations and bribery) little disposed them toward political action of a "classic" proletarian sort. Whatever political intelligence and capacity for action survived among the experienced workers was overcome by the readiness of regimes to resort to coercion during the period of rapid industrialization, and by the peasant influx—a "labor draft," cushioned from the general fall of living standards in this period of high investment rates and beggarly distribution by their move from the uncertain countryside to the better rewards of working life in the factories, and to the urban world hitherto seemingly closed to them (see chapter 7).

Thus, tendencies toward worker rebellion underwent some moderation. The new working mass, albeit heavily pressured in the earlier 1950s, was not a working class—it had been assembled too swiftly, from the "wrong" components, to coalesce into a conscious, interest-seeking collectivity against managers, bogus trade union bosses, and the regime at large. The outbursts of the early 1950s left little or no organizational heritage. Suppressed and defused in various ways in the GDR, Czechoslovakia, and Poland, they were also easier to contain because the mass social mobility which saw peasants enter the working class also saw many ambitious workers and their sons, who might have provided leadership for their class in a different situation, co-opted into the white-collar managerial-administrative world—and ready to use the rhetoric of the "workers' state" against the workers.

However, Eastern Europe's working strata have been, since the late 1950s or early 1960s, moving away from this pattern. The new workers of today are fewer, year by year, since the peasant labor pool is largely exhausted and in any case declining rates of industrial growth demand smaller increments to the working class. Those new workers are, increasingly, sons (and daughters) of workers. Hereditary recruitment has become more common as mobility out of the working class has slowed, with the stabilization of the status advantages of socialist elites and their inheritance by their offspring. Over the long term, then, the trend moves toward a more hereditary working class, wherein the young cannot look toward solving status problems on an individual basis through mobility—as many did in the past. Instead, they face the prospect of achieving satisfactory rewards as workers: the beginning, at least, of class consciousness and politically important insofar as it translates itself into action.

This changing working class, whose composition departs further with each year from the "yesterday's peasants" image familiar to analysts in and out of Eastern Europe, is also a partner of sorts in a "social contract" agreed upon in various states at different times, still valid in those countries where it has been reached, but subject to increasing strain in the years to come. Its terms are specifiable at a rather general level. The "people," but workers most specifically, will forswear political challenge and organized expression of discontent, will work (regularly if not always well), and generally remain quiet. The regime, in turn, undertakes to avoid broad-scale terror or coercion in everyday administration, and promises to provide (and to take credit for) moderate but steady increases in the living standard, to secure employment, and to shield workers from the psychological status consequences of a too evidently differentiated reward system which would underline the disadvantages of this "leading class."

This social contract was not always in effect. It has been broken on the regime's side, from time to time, by the drift of central investment policies. It has barely been reached in some states. Still, it is a critical element in worker-regime relations, and to its fate are tied the probabilities of direct worker action in the 1980s.

Without distorting history too much, one can probably find the social contract first in Czechoslovakia—where Novotny's rule fell harshly indeed on intellectuals and "nationalists," "cosmopolitans," etc., but where workers were exalted rhetorically and compensated economically by Eastern Europe's most egalitarian economy. The large working class benefited from this, and the early date of the contract was facilitated by a well-developed economy which allowed the regime to "make good" on its side of the bargain.

Poland and Hungary—cases of "medium underdevelopment," with initially small working classes—showed a different pattern. In the former, the contract dates, really, from the latter period of the Gomulka honeymoon after the Polish October of 1956—perhaps 1958—when it became clearer which concessions of the immediate postcrisis period would remain, and which (active workers' councils in the factories, for example) would be gradually dismantled by the regime. In Hungary, Nagy's post-Stalin New Course offered a broad contract, victimized by the byplay of Kremlin and Budapest politics in the 1953–56 period. The 1956 debacle eliminated all hope of a renegotiation until 1961, when Kadar implied the broad terms of the one which remains in force today with the statement "He who is not against us is with us."

In the Balkans, Yugoslavia's contract remains unique—so unique that its pattern and terms deserve a separate consideration we must forgo here. In historically underdeveloped Bulgaria and Romania, but especially in the latter, it is not clear that one has, in the sense of the earlier discussion, yet been "negotiated." Bulgaria remains quiescent, accepting its rather profitable "market garden" role within CMEA (as it did once before in the Ottoman Empire), orthodox politically and close culturally to the Soviet Union. But in Romania, alone among the states considered here, the rhetoric of sacrifice today for the benefit of one's children and grandchildren, long abandoned elsewhere, remains. In place of the social contract in conventional terms, Ceausescu has imposed stern discipline, short rations, and a personality cult, but compensated the population by offering the psychic rewards of a strident nationalism and "independence" from the Soviet Union. In its formation, the Romanian working class is perhaps a phase behind the Polish and Hungarian, heavier in ex-peasants, and thus not yet as acclimated to the sorts of demands its counterparts elsewhere express. But the Jiu Valley events of 1977—among a relatively well-paid group of workers—signal for perhaps the first time that Ceausescu's formula is losing its potency, that economic demands are moving toward center stage.

The social contract, of course, represents a secularization of the legitimacy claims of the East European socialist regimes but does not insulate regime-worker relations from strains of two sorts. The first is the cyclical character of compromise between "doctrinal" growth goals and consumption pressure in the socialist economies, most manifest, in the estimation of one analyst, in Poland.[5] The Soviet-style "heavy metal" bias of socialist economic planning, and consequent favoring of reinvestment over consumption, generates low living standards and dissatisfaction. Disorder results, and (for the first time) social contracts are offered, grudgingly, in crisis situations. Amelioration of wages and consumer goods stabilizes the situation, economic activity picks up; more absolute funds may even become available for reinvestment, but represent a declining percentage of national income. The state looks with concern at such figures, and, reassured by evident stability, turns the screw toward depression of consumption and increase in investment, since it still regards "personal consumption as a cost of growth rather than the ultimate goal of growth."[6] This violates the contract, leading to worker reaction—as in Poland in 1970 and 1976—especially when changes in price and subsidy mechanisms represent the visible leading edge of a change in economic course. As long as the strong doctrinal resistance to treating consumption as the ultimate rationale of production persists, the cyclical strain on the social contract will recur as well.

The other strain—of a different sort, and not one to detain us here—is connected with regime moves, "pushed" by generally pessimistic economic diagnosis, toward market-type reforms. Though of generally less than a wholesale or consistent sort, such reform programs have demanded profitability at the factory level, more efficient work, a closer tying of reward to performance, and output at the individual level—all of which threaten what workers see as valuable elements of the social contract. The costs come in the short term; the rewards (of a more productive, affluent economy with more to distribute) are located in the more remote future. Violent worker reaction has not followed the announcement of reform programs, which rarely seem to reach reality in anything like original form (whereas price increases are provocative, simple announcements). But coolness toward these economic designs is a characteristic reaction, as noted above in the case of Czech workers in 1968; in this sense, workers can exercise a certain considerable "braking" influence on the process of introducing even benign alterations in the social contract.

Maintenance of the social contract will grow even harder for regimes in the 1980s. The economic slack available in earlier years when manpower and capital could be treated as plentiful, and Soviet-supplied energy was cheap, is gone. The future is bleak—as is the present—in a Poland where 1979 recorded minus 2.0 percent growth. Poland is not unique. Rising energy costs, unfavorable alterations in terms of trade, and other factors expose East Europeans not only to stagnating consumption and shortages—familiar enough from a decade ago—but also to the new and unsettling experience of inflation. It will be surprising indeed if the next decade does not see instances, with whatever outcome, of workers directly protesting regime "non-compliance" with contractual terms it can no longer meet but is unwilling to revise with respect to the demand that workers forswear organized protest.

Direct action, however, does not exhaust the manifestations of workers' power. Indeed, the whole texture of socialist industrial life reveals the sort of power constantly exercised by the workers in a nondirect way—not so much to improve conditions, as to guarantee that they do not worsen.

In an unorganized but rather unanimous way, workers have limited their "contribution" to the state-owned economy by a slow rhythm of work—one among the causes of low labor productivity in the socialist economies. At the factory level, disagreement over the social contract's concrete terms arises when managers—truly men in the middle—attempt occasionally to speed up work in response to downward pressures. Workers respond to the threat by further absenteeism, simulating compliance through "faster" work which produces an excess of reject goods, and other forms of sabotage and withholding of effort.[7]

In many industries, workers' low in-factory effort and productivity reflect a husbanding of energy for work outside the state sector. The worker who "moonlights" in the service-repair sector of the "second" economy contributes to the economy, but at the same time asserts a certain amount of power: that conferred by his particular skill or access to materials/facilities which allows him to operate in the market as well as in the nonmarket state sector of the economy. It may well be that on the whole, workers are dependent on the insulation statist-planned economies provide them from the disciplines and uncertainties of the market—and are thus unlikely allies for reformers whose aim is further efficiency and differentiation of reward via marketization.[8] But this in no way precludes a rational, opportunistic participation at the same time in an illegal but tolerated labor market, where the ability to charge what one's skills will command generates the higher return per hour of work. Workers' "market position" differs here depending on branch of industry and function—some are better placed than others, having a specialty of the assembly-repair sort that allows the development of maintenance skills salable to those with broken plumbing or appliances, and access to necessary spare parts. But a huge number, in one fashion or another, find a way to participate, insuring themselves against complete state-sector control. The power workers assert here has several components: their own marketability, the demand for various "second" economy services by a population ill-served by the state sector, and the state's recognition of its own inefficiency in the service area and unwillingness to use sufficient coercion to bring this economic activity under control.

A related but distinct element of worker-regime relations is the victimization of enterprises via theft. The rather massive "inventory shrinkage" in factories is attributable partially to goods being re-channeled as raw material into the shadow service sector, and partially to simple theft for use or resale. In either case, the practice is common, the workers' attitude toward such activity tolerant. The quantum of repression necessary to prevent such theft is evidently too high—since the practice is so massive and involves a group whose morale must be kept above a critical minimum—to be seriously contemplated.

Theft of this sort is hardly an articulate political statement, but it does reflect political and economic costs the state incurs through a combination of political dogma and practice. Sole or near-sole proprietors of the national wealth, socialist regimes have made themselves ready victims of those who have no other source to steal from, and who can rationalize their behavior ("He who steals not from the state steals from his family"; "They pretend to pay us, and we pretend to work") in a populist fashion, with a touch of redistributive rhetoric. The gap between real status and idealized status as "leading class," the politicization of welfare issues when the state is governor, sole employer, and welfare agency all in one, and the appeal of redistribution from an impersonal, distant employer/controller ("What belongs to the state belongs to no one") all promote such behavior among workers. The state, facing the problem of numbers, discipline, and morale, can do little to decisively alter it.

PROSPECTS FOR POWER: THE FUTURE

Some of the present patterns, especially the more "apolitical" forms of action just described, will clearly persist into the indefinite future. More organized, politicized varieties of protest face less certain prospects.

Independent, organized action is, thus far, in its infancy. "Free trade unions," established in Poland and Romania, are a striking form of such activity. These are, of course, "mass organizations" only in potential —at the present phase, they represent the only sort of organizational initiative which workers have taken. Their nature—recognizing the existence of inherent conflict between socialist workers and socialist "owners"—is itself important as an element of demystification of the nature of worker-regime economic and political relations. There is, no doubt, something utopian about the formation of interest-articulating organizations, according to a free-society model, where regimes exclude such bodies as *de facto* unnecessary, and therefore subversive. Trade unions faced a long struggle toward legitimacy in Western market systems as well, a fact not to be underestimated—but the dissident free unionists in Eastern Europe operate under political game rules aimed against all unofficial organization, and in an environment which provides trade unions of a nonindependent sort, presented as serving the workers' legitimate interests.

Repression has been decisive and harsh against worker activists. In Poland, Kazimierz Switon and others have been tried on various criminal charges and intimidated in extrajudicial ways, and have generally faced a different response than have many dissident intellectuals whose recurrent forty-seven and a half-hour confinements (just within the time limit for formal charges) have become regular parts of their lives. This is especially true of trade union activists, but in general workers who get a "ringleader" label in the context of militant action are high-probability candidates for stern measures. In Romania, concessions were granted the Jiu Valley miners, but a surgical repression of those identified by the regime as organizers followed. The probability of similar action has no doubt helped limit any positive workers' response to the Charter 77 group in Czechoslovakia.

None of this at all precludes further outbursts of worker militancy touched off by discrete events—the most typical scenarios of protest. But evidence thus far strongly suggests that episodic uprising and violence is "manageable," and does not readily convert itself into more stable organizational forms suited to long-run struggle. The most striking fact emerging in a thirty-five-year review of workers' political activity in Eastern Europe, even allowing for the massive coercive resources of the regime, is how little organized activity there has been.

If workers acting alone have accomplished little of a lasting sort, what are the prospects for collaboration between this most numerous and potentially powerful group and the better-organized dissident intelligentsia, whose activity has been less episodic? One may make optimistic projections, and construct a future view of sustained worker activism with intelligentsia guidance and support, though not control. But in doing this, one assumes away a number of problems important enough to make such projections extremely questionable.

A large gap still separates the concerns and perspectives of workers and intelligentsia. Not even the initiatives of the KOR in Poland in the period immediately after the 1976 events—so different from the do-nothing, faintly contemptuous attitude of the intelligentsia in the wake of the 1970 crisis—have generated a sufficient worker-intelligentsia bridge to sustain any large-scale working-class organization or commitment. The intelligentsia is inclined to take a long-term perspective, to analyze, to seek interrelationships, to place reform in a broad context of political and economic measures. Their day-to-day bread-and-butter concerns are, obviously, of a less pressing nature than those of the workers, and their relations to power are more ambiguous. The workers' very real, and at any given point primarily economic, concerns do not in general find expression in questions about the linkage of economic problems to the nature of the political system. Hence, the economic reform proposals with which workers have come to connect reformist intelligentsia have often been unattractive to workers. The combination of political liberalization and typically greater industrial discipline and differentiation of reward does not seem a "necessary" one to workers (a) not ready to connect their economic grievances to the political system (as opposed to the perceived performance of individual leaders), and (b) likely to perceive the burdens of the "short-run" early reform period as falling particularly upon them.

Thus, while recognition of the legitimacy of workers' economic grievances as ground for political action, and endorsement of trade union action as a fitting response (as opposed to earlier concentration on "workers' council" schemes), says something positive about the widening political and ideological perspectives of the intelligentsia, it has not been sufficient to build a worker-intelligentsia coalition, nor to set into motion self-sustaining organizational activity among the workers; either of which would provide possibilities of converting workers' potential power into real ability to exert pressure on regime decisions and activity.

To leave the matter here, though, would be to ignore two longer-term factors, mentioned earlier, whose operations may conduce to greater worker power, or (equally significant) diminution of regime power.

First, the continuing trend toward a hereditization of the working class draws attention to the changing perspectives with which workers must view regime performance. To expect a mass of ex-peasants in factories and construction sites to act as a class is to expect too much. The large number of recent arrivals from the countryside, and the upward exit of many experienced workers to administrative work, kept the working population fluid. These factors no longer operate on the scale of the past, and the increasing working-class inheritance rate guarantees that more and more workers will view their rewards and demands from the perspective of urbanites used to factory life. The working stratum can, slowly, become a "class," and with this, become more demanding and hard to satisfy. Such a process of conversion is a long-term one; classes are not made overnight. The process described here, the product of declining mobility rates, is not completed; in some limited measure, regime policies *can* retard it. Analytically, we may be posing questions about the (lack of) workers' political action too soon.

But, second, it is not too soon to note that Eastern Europe's grim economic prospects raise the specter of regimes' declining powers to honor their side of the social contract with the workers. The multiple woes of overcentralization critically affect the ability of these economies to respond to the new problems of soaring energy costs, labor shortage, and mounting hard-currency debt. "Designed" to run on a diet of cheap energy, plentiful resources, and abundant labor supply in a context of isolation from the cyclical swings of Western and world markets, they now live in a world less favorable in the supply of factors of production, and are more enmeshed in relationships with Western economies.

East Europeans have long known shortages—but have, overall, seen significant increases in their living standards over the past decades. Expectations have risen (though not in a revolutionary manner), and, though the shortages now affect less critical items, they are still present. Some of the more affluent life enjoyed in the better-developed East European states emerged with the general process of economic growth out of poverty and political adjustments made in favor of consumption. More recently, a good deal has depended upon imports of Western plant and finished goods. The debt incurred is large, the prospects for continuing imports at anything like the levels of the early mid–1970s quite remote; for controlling consumption is once again a central problem, from the viewpoint of economic planners and regime leaders. This new countertrend promises rough times ahead, as heavy price subsidies are reduced on various items to redirect and restrict the habits socialist consumers have developed over the last ten to fifteen years.

What socialist workers face in the future may well be the volatile and quite unfamiliar combination of shortages and inflation, as low-growth economies retrench. There will be, of course, attempts to "cushion" these effects, especially for the blue-collar stratum. But it will be difficult to find the maneuvering room to do much cushioning. Food, fuel, clothing, all grow more expensive—a price rise or cutoff of luxury items generally not consumed by workers will not suffice to assure that average workers' wages will buy a satisfactory share of life's necessities.

Not all the socialist economies have these problems at the same level of intensity; not all populations have a history of reaction similar, say, to that of the Poles. But it is clear that the regimes face increasing difficulties in honoring their guarantees to the population. From this may come, in the 1980s, hitherto undreamt-of levels of unrest, exacerbating problems of internal political stability. Whether growing class consciousness and the economic weakness of regimes will deal workers more political power, what organizational forms (if any) that power may assume, and what the consequences will be for the regimes and their Soviet guarantor are perhaps the most important questions the East European states will face in the next decade.

TEN

THE SUCCESSOR GENERATION

The people born in Eastern Europe since the onset of World War II—apart from those still children—range in age from the early forties to late teens. To an observer from the West, they are a mix of the exotic and the familiar. The older members of this "successor generation" bear lingering childhood memories of Stalinism; the younger see the Hungarian Revolt of 1956 as a piece of history before their time, the Prague Spring and Soviet invasion of 1968 as dim events in their childhood. (For Poles, it is perhaps too early to record the significance of the martial law imposition of 1981—which came after this chapter was written—except as another event in a turbulent political history.) The political history of Eastern Europe is punctuated by such events, but political life as it is lived by East Europeans is also "everyday" life—its peculiarities alien to Westerners but part of a familiar, sometimes banal, picture to those who exist within its frame.

War, and later Communist regimes, came as cataclysms to the older

Originally published in Stephen F. Szabo, ed., *The Successor Generation: International Perspectives of Postwar Europeans* (London: Butterworths, 1983), pp. 141–166.

generations, whose memories and experiences extended back to the interwar years of parliamentary democracy in Czechoslovakia, authoritarian rule in Poland and Hungary, and the squalid, unstable politics of Yugoslavia, Romania, and Bulgaria under their kings. While American military and economic predominance insured the reemergence of Western Europe's economic dynamism and supported the further development of the democratic tradition in its political systems, Soviet hegemony in the "other half" of Europe brought Stalinist regimes and rapid development of the heavy-industry base and, with them, depressed living standards and high rates of social mobility that changed the face of East European societies. Rejected in Yugoslavia, somewhat modified by events in the western part of Eastern Europe, the Soviet model was initially imposed on these diverse societies for security and doctrinal reasons—and has been perpetuated by Soviet willingness to use a whole variety of means, including force, to maintain it.

It is in *this* world, of socialism and Marxism-Leninism as ostensibly "ruling" ideologies, of the military and economic alliance with the USSR of peoples who for the most part find little to admire and much to despise about "Russia," of nationalism deeply felt if dangerous to express, that the successor generation has emerged. However compliant or subversive their attitudes and values, however simplistic or sophisticated their thinking about politics and economics, these people have been shaped in the period of socialism. Their adjustment to the reality that surrounds them, their readiness to strive to change it, emerge not from contrasts between today's life and a world that vanished in September 1939 but from their experiences in systems that, while subject to changes and oscillations on liberal-repressive and consumption-re investment dimensions over the past thirty years, remain largely unaltered in their fundamental aspects.

One would like to promise answers to a whole host of questions in this chapter about the desires, values, political convictions, and worldviews of East Europeans of the postwar era, to guarantee a nicely wrapped package that could be stacked alongside those of the West European nations for comparison. Such cannot be—an early warning of the reality of the East-West divide and its impact on information available—but we can go more than a little way toward outlining *some* answers, at least. They will refer, mainly, to the three historical states (excluding the GDR) that make up Eastern Europe's "west"—Poland, Hungary, and Czechoslovakia. History has made these nations and peoples a part of "Western" culture, of Christianity in the Catholic or Protestant modes, and of the Latin alphabet. The bench-marks of Middle

Ages, Renaissance, etc., mean here much what they do in lands further west, and distinguish them from the Balkan lands and Russia itself, whose area is heir to an Eastern tradition mixing Mongol and Ottoman conquests, a Christianity derived from Byzantium, and a different set of historical periods and experiences. We *know* more of these peoples; we have, perhaps, more by way of a common yardstick to judge the nature of their successor generations against the West's than we possess for the people of Bulgaria, Romania, and the southern/eastern reaches of Yugoslavia; hence my concentration on them.

The concept of "generation" is a slippery one, of differing utility depending on one's purpose—in a sense it is a "pure" concept, quite imaginary, since people are born all the time, rather than on some cohort-by-cohort schedule. Experience, however, has been the rationale for use of the term in many contexts, including ours here—the successor generation differs from all *older* groups in its freedom from direct experience of prewar and wartime conditions. I shall be dealing with a broad range of ages here, but all of them are "products" of the experience of the postwar socialist period. It is time to draw the broad outlines of that experience for Eastern Europe's successor generation.

ORIGINS AND EXPERIENCE

The successor generation emerged in an East European landscape unfamiliar to its predecessors, one in the process, and then in the completion, of radical social, economic, and political change. It has been formed, mainly, in the period of stabilization ("normality") of the socialist political order.

This means, of course, that it knows nothing by direct experience of the interwar period of "independent Eastern Europe," a historical interlude (1918–1939) that was hardly more than half as long as the postwar period of the Soviet-sponsored socialist regimes. But further, it means that the successor generation is by and large somewhat removed from the most intense experiences of Stalinism as political catastrophe, and from the complex of rapid changes in economy and society from the late 1940s to the mid-late 1950s of which its elders were victims and beneficiaries. Paramount among these were rapid Soviet-style industrialization and the concomitant phenomena of mass social mobility and alteration of living standards. The details of these have been dealt with elsewhere (see chapters 7 and 8)—at present, what should concern us is their quality as formative experiences encountered by "elders," but largely missed by the successor generation.

East Europeans born between 1925 and 1935 faced ten to fifteen years of wrenching transformations of a world in postwar flux (and wartime destruction). Little could they have understood, at war's end, how radically different the "new way of life" would be from the pre-1939 years of peace—although the experience of war itself, the total disruption of societies and economies, fostered a belief that there was "no going back" to the life of prewar days. In Poland, Hungary, and Czechoslovakia coalition governments of a sort, with growing Communist domination, undertook the tasks of restoring shattered economies and mobilizing resources to produce the minimum of life's necessities. Land reform broke up the large Polish and Hungarian estates and swept away the influence of the "gentry"-type upper classes. Disrupted industry was put back into motion where possible, and in Poland the "great migration" of Poles from the eastern lands claimed by the USSR, across the core of the nation into the western and northern territories detached from the former Reich and emptied by the expulsion of Germans, changed the landscape.

Living standards improved in these early postwar years, but as Communist regimes consolidated themselves and set about economic development on a Soviet model, the upward trend gave way to something quite different. Beginnings of agricultural collectivization—to force the production of a "surplus" and extract it from peasants at low to "zero" prices—and grandiose schemes and commitments of resources to rapid, heavy industrialization radically lowered living standards. Not yet recovered from war, people experienced the onset of proletarian dictatorship as a lowering of peasant living standards, a decline of working-class standards to a point lower than workers of the late 1930s had endured in the "bad old days" of authoritarian regimes. High reinvestment rates left precious little for consumption, while the heavy-industry focus of development and the depredation of agriculture promised little improvement for years ahead. For the intelligentsia at one end of the social spectrum, for peasants at the other, and for the workers in the middle—the proletariat in whose name "revolution" had been made—material standards were, in 1950, worse than they had been under the old regimes.

Although victimized in this sense, those who preceded the successor generation were in many cases also the beneficiaries of mass social mobility. Economic development required a great expansion of bureaucracy and a growth of industrial worker cadres. Offspring of the smallish urban industrial proletariats—and younger workers themselves—ascended through political sponsorship and rapid training to the administrative and professional ranks (the first-generation socialist intelligentsia), along with a smaller group from the peasantry. The latter, for the most part and in the millions, left the land via the push of collectivization and the new pull of factories growing everywhere by the rhythm of the "Plan," and became workers, rapidly outnumbering the core of experienced urban blue-collar workers. This mobility served in a sense as a shock absorber to the general lowering of living standards: the young (recently working-class) manager or director felt the heady experience of power, prestige, and material benefits beyond those of the people who took his orders. The new workers—fresh from village and farm—felt the contrast between that life and the urban industrial world, reflecting the distance they had traveled, and were by and large glad they had made the trip. Their standards were those of the classes they had left, not the old standards of the classes they had now entered.

By the late 1950s, this transformation of agricultural to industrial societies was well advanced, if not complete. And it was into this world that the successor generation came as adolescents and young adults— one in which the great transformations were either childhood memories or prebirth history. As adults, its members have been neither victims of Stalinism and the short rations of pell-mell industrialization nor beneficiaries of that profound and rapid burst of mass mobility that swelled the size of nonmanual intelligentsia strata, made the industrial working class the majority of the population, and reduced the size of the peasant/agricultural sector drastically. Their world has been a more settled one, and this has shaped their consciousness in profound, if not always predictable, ways. No massive "national tasks" have captured the energy or enthusiasms of the postwar generation—except perhaps for the very oldest of its members. No memories of poverty, combined with real enthusiasm over writing new lines on a tabula rasa, of building a new socialist society, evoke bittersweet thoughts, as they do for the elder generation.

Increasingly, the successor generation has been formed in the environment of educational institutions, including universities. In prewar Eastern Europe, the legacy of underdevelopment and the social/economic/academic selectiveness of secondary education passed very few youth through to higher education—according to one survey of official data, only 50,000 students in higher education in Poland in 1939, 13,000 in Hungary in the same year, and about 29,000 in Czechoslovakia in 1935–36.[1] The development goals of the regimes—the desire to mobilize talent from the working class and peasantry in the formation of a new socialist intelligentsia—led to a rapid and tremendous expansion of higher education: by 1970, over 330,000 Polish, 86,000 Hungarian, and 107,000 Czech students were in higher educational institutions, though a fair number of these were correspondence or evening students.

The numbers have grown further since, though not sufficiently to keep pace with the number of students finishing secondary school and desiring higher education. What has happened, in essence, is that a larger number of East Europeans are in an organized, age-specific environment than ever before, in a social situation where both attitudes and insights different from those of elders or youth not in universities may develop. The political effects are, as yet, unclear. University students also enter the bureaucratic/organizational side of life and learn the limits and opportunities of socialist systems; the lessons may be unwelcome, but they show a tendency to "stick," at least in behavior. The understanding reached by teenage years, that political life operates in a statist bureaucratic economy in which the individual's concerns are low priorities, tends to engender a "privatism" of aspirations and concerns among the successor generation. The point is to survive and prosper within a system seemingly quite resistant to change.

Indications that youth place personal happiness, interesting work, and comfortable living standards at the top of their lists of desiderata provide an occasion for political writers to deplore the lack of public-spiritedness, social concerns, or great aspirations in the service of socialist ideals. But these are themselves insincere complaints. Given the alien provenance of the state-socialist systems, the continuing dislike of things Soviet/Russian in Eastern Europe, and other factors that make for a poor fit between regimes and societies, this privatism is about as good a "deal" as the regimes can expect to secure political stability. When masses of the successor generation become politicized and move beyond their private concerns, as the example of Poland in 1980–81 shows, it is likely to be against the regime that their energies are directed.

In this relatively stable environment, patterns of inequality have solidified as well, clashing with career and social aspirations among successive young cohorts of a generation nourished on the tales of the mass mobility of the earlier period of socialist construction.[2] A sizable gap separates intelligentsia from workers, and both from the remaining peasantry. Slowing of economic growth dictates slower expansion of the intelligentsia and a stabilization of the working class; the "pull" factor in social mobility has weakened drastically, and with this weakening has come an increasing hereditization of status. Fewer new "places" in the intelligentsia mean less demand and space for ambitious and talented working-class offspring to move up; conversely, the supply of intelligentsia children, with the cultural, motivational, and other advantages in competition for top slots that they derive from their milieu, comes closer to meeting the total demand for new members of the intelligentsia. As growth slows, those born into the intelligentsia may be somewhat more likely to remain in it; those born into the blue-collar world are clearly more likely to find it a lifetime location.

Attaining intelligentsia status is a desideratum—hence intelligentsia children who reproduce their parental status "win," pleasing themselves and their parents. Those of working-class origin—at least that substantial group oriented toward upward mobility—who reproduce their parental status are, in some sense, "losers." There will be more of these, and out of this trend has already developed the core component of class consciousness, a conviction of a common "workers' lot" unlikely to be changed by individual mobility and therefore calling for collective action. Workers, as in Poland, have greater reasons than in earlier years of socialism to assert their interests as workers, to feel that their claim to a share of society's resources must be made as a class claim. This does not preclude cross-class cooperation, as in the unprecedented degree of intelligentsia-worker coordination that, in Poland in 1980, aimed at advancing political and economic goals sought by both. Indeed, this cooperation may have depended on workers developing a measure of self-organization sufficient for coordination purposes.[3]

The problems, opportunities, and "interests" (in the narrow sense) of the two classes are nevertheless quite different. One can argue that opposition between workers and the intelligentsia is as deep or deeper a reality than communality, or take the view that the intelligentsia's opposition to the political leadership redounds to their own and also to the workers' benefit.[4] If this is so, it is not "bad," but represents, simply, the maturation of the socialist systems, the phase in which the successor generation, with its greater internal variety, has come to be statistically dominant, and in which the apparent unanimity, imposed earlier on societies in the throes of change, can no longer be sustained.

"Class" may divide, but common culture and nationality may unite the successor generation. Certainly the modernizing forces in the postwar period under socialist regimes, especially the expansion of education and media participation, have made identification with such larger concepts and collectivities as the "national" culture and the "nation" possible for people whose earlier perspectives were limited to the traditional village and family. As a recent review of years of Polish studies of social attitudes and values indicates, most people seem to be distributed on a normal curve: few group at the extreme ends, and most hold a particular value at the medium level of intensity, even given disparate occupations, educational levels, etc., with the Polish nation itself a critical point of identity.[5]

A chapter of moderate length cannot hope to give full expression to all the elements of commonality and diversity in the collective consciousness of the successor generation. What follows is an attempt to "catch" and explore elements of its view of itself, of other nations, of desirable political orders, and of the contours of the futures it faces.

SELVES AND OTHERS: IMAGES AND STEREOTYPES

Years of effort have been invested in official attempts to reshape the collective self-images of East European peoples and their images of other nations. Through the education system, youth organizations, the media, and other channels, regimes have sought to implant, from early youth onward, suspicion and reserve (if not outright hostility) toward the United States and West European nations, and positive attitudes toward the USSR and the other East European states. This exercise in the reformation of consciousness has aimed as well at reshaping the conceptions of Poles, Hungarians, Czechs, and others about the meaning of their past, and the relevance of their diverse political traditions. It involves condemnation of those elements the regimes find "uncomfortable" and enthusiastic endorsement of the new elements that lock them into their own domestic political and economic orders, and into the bloc and their relationship with the USSR.

All this amounted to a daunting task. Polish, Hungarian, and Romanian Russophobia cut deep in the interwar period, while traditions of heroic individualism and elitism remained alive in the first two states. The Czech bourgeois tradition, supported by the stable parliamentary political life and high economic development of the interwar years, distanced it from Russian/Soviet traditions. History, however, also left it (until 1968) less marked by Russophobia. Bulgaria, probably, was seen by the Soviets as a lesser problem, with its linguistic and cultural closeness to Russia, and the latter's role as its sometime defender against the Turks. For all Eastern Europe, the USSR sought to promote anti-German feelings; easy enough in the wake of war, but an objective complicated after 1949 with the establishment of the East German state and the consequent need to sell its citizens as the "good" Germans, and their state as the natural inheritor of the democratic/left Weimar and German Marxist traditions.

Too much, however, should not be made of Soviet-sponsored attempts to make East European nations and peoples "like" each other or to feel commonalities independent of their roles as Soviet "allies." The emphasis has been, rather, on bilateral relations of each East European people to the "Soviet people," as exemplified in their state, the USSR. Historic Polish-Hungarian feelings of sympathy were no asset, Czech-Polish coolness no liability, from the Soviet viewpoint.

The degree to which these objectives have been achieved among the successor generation is moderate. A decade ago, one writer on East European youth noted that their "hatred of Russia...has to be seen to be believed."[6] This assessment is reflected with somewhat more complexity in data collected (anonymously) for Radio Free Europe Audience and Opinion Research (hereafter RFEAOR) by a West European polling organization from East Europeans visiting the West—a creative enterprise which, under difficult conditions, supplies a surrogate for surveys of convictions "at home."[7] The data that follow express "stereotypes" held by Poles (October 1966–April 1967), Hungarians (July 1966–May 1967), and Czechs/Slovaks (polled between April 1965 and May 1967, and others between August and December 1969, after the Soviet invasion of 1968).[8] Interviewees were provided with a list of characteristics and asked to mark those they felt applicable to the people in question. The figures for younger respondents in these surveys did not diverge significantly from those for older people.[9]

EAST EUROPEAN VIEWS OF RUSSIANS
AND AMERICANS

Table 10.1 reflects the striking failure of attempts to propagate overwhelmingly positive images of Russians and negative ones of Americans. Across the board, Russians "outscore" Americans on the negative characteristics and lose to them on the positive—with the exception of bravery, on which Poles and (pre-invasion) Czechs score the Russians higher. Far from exemplifying a model of a mature socialist way of life, Russians are regarded as relatively backward and cruel, as lacking in intelligence, practicality, and generosity vis-à-vis Americans—and also (see below) vis-à-vis the Poles, Hungarians, Czechs, and Slovaks. Poles and Hungarians are generally more negative on Russians than are pre-invasion Czechs and Slovaks, reflecting the latter's lesser tendency to draw bold stereotypes (even about themselves), and their lack of historic bad feelings toward a Russia that had not dominated them in the past. But, as it had for Austria and Hungary in the past, "Russia" became part of Czech and Slovak history with a vengeance in 1968, as the postinvasion collapse of all positive ratings and explosive exacerbation of all negative ratings show. With 66 percent seeing Russians as cruel, 80 percent as backward, and only 6 percent and 4 percent as brave and advanced, the USSR commands neither friendship nor respect—only the acquiescence of people with no alternative.

There is no reason to think that the years since these surveys have radically altered these views. The USSR has not reinvaded Hungary or (at the time of writing) intervened in Poland. If the Soviets score any points, it is for what they have not done, not for any positive acts. This is surely insufficient against the backdrop of deep Polish and Hungarian antipathies, and the trauma of 1968, which Czechs and Slovaks will not forget in this century.

TABLE 10.1. East European images of Americans and Russians (% selecting given characteristic)

Characteristic	POLES		HUNGARIANS		CZECHS/SLOVAKS		
	USA	USSR	USA	USSR	USA	USSR[a]	USSR[b]
Hard-working	64	52	53	23	59	44	11
Intelligent	66	37	51	13	68	30	4
Practical	63	27	71	26	74	19	5
Brave	46	56	29	27	36	63	13
Peace-loving[c]	61	41	41	28	58	47	6
Generous	60	29	63	8	66	30	10
Advanced	76	22	52	17	72	32	4
Backward	5	53	1	49	1	49	80
Conceited	42	59	32	44	—	—	—
Domineering	21	59	11	58	22	39	65
Cruel	9	46	6	49	3	32	66

SOURCES: Radio Free Europe Audience and Opinion Research (RFEAOR), "The Polish Self-Image and the Polish Image of Americans, Russians, Chinese, Germans, and Czechs" (Munich, 1969); "The Czech and Slovak Self-Image and the Czech and Slovak Image of Americans, Germans, Russians, and Chinese" (Munich, 1970); "The Hungarian Self-Image and the Hungarian Image of Americans, Russians, Germans, Romanians, and Chinese" (Munich, 1970).
[a]1965–7 survey.
[b]1969 survey.
[c]"Freedom-loving" in Polish survey.

EAST EUROPEAN IMAGES OF SELVES AND NEIGHBORS

What did the same people think of themselves, as Poles, Hungarians, etc? What of each other, and what of the other historic "external actor" in the area—the Germans? The responses in table 10.2 reveal an interesting mix of similarities and differences.

Poles

Poles rate themselves high on intelligence, bravery, love of freedom, and generosity (a set of qualities not inconsistent with a "gentry" ethos still alive in many ways) and more modestly on hard work and practicality. Poles rank Germans predictably high on negative emotional qualities, low on generosity, but high on the (emotionally neutral) practicality and hard work dimensions. Their views of Czechs are similar; however, Czechs are not seen high on the negative qualities (domineering, cruel) or as brave—only 9 percent rate them as such.

TABLE 10.2. East European Images of Selves and Neighbours
(% selecting given characteristic)

Characteristic	POLES			HUNGARIANS			CZECH/ SLOVAKS[a]	
	Selves	Germ.	Czech.	Selves	Germ.	Rom.	Selves	Germ.
Hard-working	54	81	69	69	82	8	62	78
Intelligent	74	54	54	74	71	11	69	64
Practical	29	71	69	43	67	18	49	78
Brave	84	32	9	79	57	4	34	42
Peace-loving[b]	92	28	32	67	20	15	84	19
Generous	64	9	9	68	13	4	28	16
Advanced	56	53	58	49	38	14	58	47
Backward	13	3	9	8	1	61	18	2
Conceited	30	73	44	23	57	37	—	—
Domineering	5	48	10	4	30	40	4	74
Cruel	5	70	9	3	35	46	4	45

SOURCES: see table 10.1.
[a]Pre-invasion sampling
[b]"Freedom-loving" in Polish survey

This all fits with more traditional, impressionistic perceptions of the Polish psyche and its enduring elements. Coolness and hostility toward Germans has ample historical precedent; so does the respect for German abilities (frequently turned against the Poles) reflected in the figures. Despite the fellowship of a western Slavdom sharing a Latin-Christian tradition, Poles and Czechs are not "close"—it might almost be said that Poles have regarded Czechs somewhat contemptuously, as a hard-working, calculating "nation of shopkeepers," devoid of any strong aggressive tendencies but also of bravery, of the capacity for "grand" gestures. Poles might readily contrast their resistance in 1939 to the Czechs' capitulation a year earlier, and find an echo in the Czech nonresistance in 1968 compared with their own projected readiness to resist Soviet invasion themselves in the turbulent atmosphere since 1976. Czechs will for their part remember that Poland participated in the 1938 Munich partition, excising the small Teschen area. From their own perspective they are likely to think of Poles as given to ill-conceived romantic/heroic gestures and defeats—again not without some accuracy.

Hungarians

Hungarians are not unlike the Poles in their collective self-image, though rating themselves rather higher on hard work and practicality. The complex of high ratings for bravery, intelligence, and generosity complements their own aristocratic tradition—the only other authentic one in Eastern Europe. History too is reflected in a somewhat less negative view of Germans. One recalls their long acquaintance with Germans and their culture in the days of the Dual Monarchy and the fact that Hungary was a German ally during World War II.

In contrast, dislike and contempt emerge in the stereotype of Romanians, in a manner that could hardly be more direct: low marks on positive characteristics, high on negative. To the Hungarians, Romanians seem craven, cruel, and backward. It is an image composed of many elements. For practical purposes, the border between the two nations is also perceived as the one between the western part of Eastern Europe (Protestant/Catholic, Latin alphabet, experience of the Renaissance, Reformation, etc.) and the eastern segment (Orthodox/Islamic, Cyrillic alphabet, long Ottoman domination). Despite their Romance language and adoption of the Latin script (after centuries of Cyrillic), Romanians are "Balkan." The state boundaries, as an enduring legacy of World War I, leave over one million ethnic Hungarians in Romania:

a human and territorial irredenta, and still a sore point for Hungarians. The feeling is further exacerbated by the contrast between Romania's repressive regime and the relatively liberal internal order in Hungary under Kadar—though few Hungarians seem concerned about the vigorously repressive policies their grandfathers pursued toward Romanian minorities in the Austro-Hungarian state before World War I.

Czechs/Slovaks

Czechs/Slovaks seem, against this background, rather singular peoples, both in self-conception and in their views of others. Theirs is a less self-congratulatory image: in their own mirror, they are neither particularly generous nor brave, but are high on the "peace-loving" dimension. This shows both a tendency to be less stereotypical in their views of themselves and other nationalities, and also some feeling that Czechs and Slovaks are not particularly high on "heroic" virtues. There is, in general, a peculiar realism here about the collective national self, in the sense that the Czech self-image finds reflection in some traditional views of their neighbors. Alone among the groups, the Czechs and Slovaks rated another nationality—the Americans—overall more positively than themselves.

These data, along with more impressionistic observations, indicate that the peoples of Eastern Europe remain distinct, unhomogenized by socialism, no better inclined toward Russia/the USSR than in the past. Given their small deviations from the general picture, the members of the successor generation seem more part of a national consensus than separated from their elders by any marked gap. Why this is the case is not immediately obvious, but one may well speculate that the pressures under which East Europeans have lived, the contrast between the "authenticity" of historically rooted national feelings and the artificiality of Soviet bloc alliances, have put a premium on the passing on of convictions and general perspectives from generation to generation. If it has been a priority of the elders to accomplish this, the successor generation shows little evidence of their failure.

POLITICS

Action or Acquiescence?

No pat formulas—neither wholesale rejection of all that Soviet-style socialism has brought, nor complete accommodation to it through indoctrination from the cradle and consequent inability to conceive of any alternative—can characterize the political perspectives and convictions of East Europeans of the successor generation. Yet there are temptations to overgeneralize, fed perhaps by the fact that the postwar generations have had little chance to speak for themselves. One such temptation is to conclude that apoliticism is the "politics" of the successor generation. The anxiety of those aged twenty-five to forty to "get on" with their lives, the consumerism of a generation seemingly enmeshed in a youth culture of clothes, rock music, etc., draws one, understandably, toward such a conclusion. In this, one follows some East European commentators on youth, like Czech critics who complain periodically of the weakness of ideological training that leaves the young corrupted with a petit-bourgeois attitude and taste[10] or Hungarians who noted in 1976 the fad for clothing with American flags, T-shirts with slogans, etc.[11]—giving the lie somewhat to an earlier claim that among Hungarian youth, "fashion and taste . . . dance and dress fads are becoming less and less important in the scale of human values."[12]

The concerns of foreign observers and domestic commentators differ, of course. The latter would rather live with apoliticism than with a mobilized public pressing its demands on the state; the former, in many cases, would cheer such a development. In any case, two factors have a large influence on how "apolitical" the youth and early middle-aged will be; first, the degree to which the current "system" seems reasonably satisfactory, given perceptions of realistic alternatives; and second, the degree to which open expression of political opinion or direct political action promises to have some positive effect.

Kadar's Hungary provides a case of a relatively liberal regime in political terms, and an effective one in the economic performance and living standard it has provided. These have sufficed, given Hungarian expectations, to make for a quiet, manifestly apolitical populace—youth included. Since the 1960s, especially since the economic reform of 1968, the regime has relied more on positive incentives, less on threats. Interestingly, much of what little dissent there has been in Hungary took a "new left" orientation, complaining of embourgeoisement under Kadar's "goulash socialism." General satisfaction and unwillingness to rock a fairly comfortable boat have led to a marginalization of dissent, to the point where one specialist has coined the term "para-opposition" to indicate the peculiar mode of coexistence between regime and critics.[13]

This, of course, is not the whole story of the successor generation. The Soviet invasion of 1956 and the crushing of the Hungarian Revolt are still limiting facts. Hungarian political consciousness and demands take into account that theirs was the first test in which the USSR demonstrated the "irreversibility" of socialism. In this sense Hungarians are realists who have been socialized in a quite effective school.

For the Czechs, the recency of a similar experience explains much of the quiescence. The current system can hardly be satisfactory. Many of the successor generation were active in the Prague Spring, indicating how unacceptable they found its pre-1968 Novotnyite predecessor. But Husak's regime and its Soviet guarantors tolerate little and show no "give." Apoliticism is a reasonable response to such a situation; open expression of dissent is dangerous, and attempts to change the situation are met with repressive measures that make them seem hopeless. The failure of the Charter 77 movement to generate any substantial mass support says much about the general assessment of the likely result of independent political action.

Obviously, the Polish situation of August 1980–December 1981 could hardly have been more different. This reflects a different "correlation of forces" from the other two cases. For a sufficient number of Poles— the majority of whom are of the successor generation—the "system" is quite unsatisfactory in political and economic terms, a fact having to do with the scale of Polish demands as well as with the actual economic performance and measure of internal liberalism of the regime. Unlike in Hungary and Czechoslovakia, in Poland the costs of free political expression have been low and the chances of positive outcome from action have been moderate to high. The chronicle of socialist Poland is one of mass action that has brought change even if, in the end, not as much change as people wanted: in 1956, the restoration of Gomulka and the exit of the Stalinists; in 1970, the exit of Gomulka and an end to price increases; in 1976, recission again of the major portion of price rises; and in 1980, the political demise of Gierek over this and other economic and political issues.

Neither in 1970, 1976, nor 1980 was Poland spectacularly repressive by East European standards, but the Polish boiling point is a low one. This is a matter both of experience and national character. Poles have received "positive reinforcement" for each mass action, and have not been brought to heel by Soviet invasion. Herein lies one key, at least, to their difference from Hungarians and Czechs, which is not a matter of chance. Polish society was never completely "Stalinized." The church's unique strength, its maintenance of independence as an institution and its role as a focus of national identity, carried it through the years of Stalinism. Other specifics might also be cited, such as the strong national consensus on a core of common values,[14] but this recital is sufficient to make the point of Poland's capacity to resist the designs of the regime.

Expectations

These differences are reflected as well in some further research sponsored by Radio Free Europe in 1970–71. Czechoslovak, Hungarian, and Polish visitors were asked about their expectations regarding political developments in the 1970s in their countries.[15] (The Polish sample was supplemented by an additional polling in 1971 after the fall of Gomulka.) Five alternative lines of development were presented to the interviewees; the results are shown in table 10.3.

Mindful of the temporal setting, the Czech responses make eminent sense—"normalization" was in full swing, the regime showed the hardline tendencies of the second alternative clearly, and the people, in response, were cultivating their own "gardens," as the first alternative implies. Few saw popular pressure as a promising prospect in 1970. Hungarians, two years into their economic reform, were more optimistic overall, but showed little feeling that popular pressure would be the engine of change. The one-third who felt the regime would grant more freedom were optimists, while those who saw less public pressure for freedom and more privatization did not necessarily predict less freedom

TABLE 10.3. East Europeans' Political Expectations, 1970–1971

| | | | POLES | |
| | CZECHS | HUNGARIANS | 1970 | 1971 |
Development	%	%	%	%
Less public pressure for freedom— more pursuit of selfish interests	42	30	20	6
Regime will return to a harder line	35	21	26	13
Regime will grant more freedom	14	33	30	55
Popular pressure will change the system	3	5	10	25
Communism will gain ground	3	9	7	0
Other answers, don't know	3	2	7	1

SOURCE: RFEAOR, "Czechoslovak, Hungarian, and Polish Expectations About Domestic Political Trends in the 1970s" (Munich, 1972).

thereby. Poles, however, both before and after December 1970, had more faith in the efficacy of public pressure and also saw a new regime as likely to grant more freedom.

Those in the successor generation were more optimistic, a decade ago, than their elders. Of Poles under twenty-five in 1970, 40 percent saw the regime granting more freedom (versus 30 percent of the total sample). In Hungary, 45 percent of those twenty-five and under expected the regime to grant more freedom. Czech youth were not so positive: those under twenty-five selected a "harder line" in 31 percent of the cases (less than the average), but made this up in the "resignation" alternative of "less public pressure" picked by 48 percent.

The youth of 1970 now make up a good portion of the 1980s successor generation. The last decade's effects are not ones that can be measured with data of the sort just discussed, but some observations may be made. Czechs, *faute de mieux*, pursued their own private affairs in the 1970s and have continued to do so, a pattern that probably is "natural" to those who have come to adolescence/adulthood in the thirteen years since the Prague Spring ended. Few probably expect more freedom, fewer that popular pressure will achieve it, and fewer yet are likely to feel that Communism will find greater public acceptance.

Hungarians in the latter 1970s faced the prospect of slowed economic growth and rising prices, under a regime that showed no clear movement toward repression or liberalization. Many of those to whom I spoke in Budapest in the autumn of 1980 expressed concern that Polish events, if they led to Soviet intervention, would make further economic reform of a decentralizing sort—then on the state's agenda—difficult. One might guess that the first and second alternatives would have been selected by somewhat more respondents in 1980 than a decade earlier.

The year 1980 saw the outbreak of the Polish crisis still not wholly resolved, and exacerbated by the December 1981 imposition of martial law. Its roots, lying in part in the expectations of the older members of the successor generation (who have been heavily represented in the leadership of Solidarity, KSS-KOR, and other groupings), were reflected to some degree in the 1970–71 data. In the Gierek "honeymoon" period, more than half the respondents expected more freedom from the regime (a healthy 30 percent had the same expectation before Gomulka's fall), while one in four expected popular pressure to bring change. Gierek's failure to push political reforms was balanced in the first half of the decade by a growth in living standards financed through heavy Western borrowing. Economic danger signs led, *inter alia*, to the attempt to raise prices in 1976. This move confronted a public "expecting better" of the regime and inclined to see public pressure as an effective means of imposing a veto. The years 1976–1980 were a long slide downward for the Gierek regime. Workers' consciousness matured, and linkages developed between workers and dissident intelligentsia that were critical to the mobilization of exactly the sort of organized public pressure that broke through the crust of official politics in 1980 (see chapter 8).

Political Convictions and Preferences

What beliefs motivate action or underlie quiescence in Eastern Europe? What is acceptable about these regimes? What would people of the successor generation, given their limited experience of other sorts of regimes, change if they could? Answers to these questions, while approximate, suggest which elements of the political/economic environment seem "natural," as well as indicating broadly held political convictions that strain against the bounds of the permissible under the current system.

Socialism, one can say, is accepted as permanent and desirable. But this acceptance accommodates a generalized, lower-case variety of socialism, not necessarily Marxism, Leninism, or anything much beyond a conviction that state ownership of large-scale industry, etc., accords better than unfettered capitalism with the public interest. At a minimum, it is not clear that this goes much beyond left social democracy. Polish students in the late 1950s affirmed their acceptance of socialism, conceived in roughly this way: "some form of socialism" was approved by nearly 70 percent in a Warsaw University poll, but 68 percent of the same group said they were not Marxists. On the role/scope of private enterprise, almost 85 percent would not permit it in heavy industry without limits, although a majority would allow it in light industry, retail trade, etc.[16] The majority of those polled must now be near the upper boundary of the successor generation, and little evidence has emerged in ensuing years to suggest that educated Polish conceptions of what socialism means and should mean are today any closer to a Marxist-Leninist definition.

It is the welfare state aspects of socialism and not its Marxist-Leninist elements that are the fundament of its general acceptance throughout Eastern Europe. The postwar generation has grown up in a mesh of state-provided medical care and education, stable employment, and a relatively slow work tempo. Even if the medical care is low-average, education still "overutilized" by advantaged youth, the pay not all one feels one's work deserves, these are gains people are unwilling to forsake.

Here the propaganda of the "bad old days" before socialism has been effective.

Conscious identification with the system, its history and heroes, is a quite different matter, however. Hungarian surveys in the 1970s noted the low political knowledge of youth, with some amusing hand-wringing over more egregious manifestations of ignorance. In a 1976–77 survey of leaders of the Communist youth organization between fourteen and thirty years of age, 17 percent responded that they knew nothing about Lenin, 31 percent said the same about Stalin, and a full 42 percent confessed ignorance of Khrushchev (one thought Stalin had been governor of Hungary, another that he had been the World War II German commander in chief; two had Khrushchev as the American president in the early 1960s).[17] Even allowing for a youthful tendency to twit the pollsters, these figures reveal a remarkable failure of political socialization among young people whom the statistics record as politically "active."

General preference for a welfare state is compatible with a range of different political orientations and political system preferences. One attempt to ascertain where East Europeans would place themselves in a choice of governments across a spectrum was a 1974–75 Radio Free Europe survey of 1,200 Czechs, 1,370 Hungarians, and 1,309 Poles visiting the West.[18] Eight alternatives were presented, grouped in four categories: "democratic socialism" (Austria, Sweden), "democracy" (USA and, for Czechs, the interwar republic), "Marxist system" ("as Marx described it," "as in Yugoslavia," "[your] present system"), and "authoritarian system" (Franco's Spain and, for Poles and Hungarians, their own interwar regimes). The results for the whole sample are arrayed in table 10.4.

In gross terms, democratic socialism in the West European example gains a clear plurality; when combined with classical democracy, a majority emerges. Marxist systems are not totally lacking in support, but each group perceives an alternative Marxism as better than what they have. Hungarians split almost equally on their own Kadarism versus Yugoslavia. (Interestingly, whatever it may mean to respondents, "Marx's" Marxism has little appeal—which suggests anything but a positive response to a highly explicit, "cleansed" ideology harking back to original designs.) Authoritarianism commands little support, though in Poland it scores nearly as many votes as all varieties of Marxist systems. The Polish response draws perhaps on the general feeling that the interwar regime was, whatever its faults, one that served Polish interests.

At the very least, figures such as these remind us why the USSR and its East European client regimes do not countenance free elections. But a closer look allows a better focus on the successor generation compared with its elders. For Czechoslovakia and Poland, separate data in table 10.5 distinguish those aged 14–25 and 26–35—who now represent, roughly, the 20–40 age group. Here, support for authoritarianism tails off markedly among Poles, while Yugoslav-style Marxism picks up votes. Democratic socialism is also a large gainer in comparison with the total sample, while U.S.-style democracy, with which these respondents are unlikely to have as much familiarity as West European systems, loses support among the Czech sample and among the younger Poles. Older people (50+) in Czechoslovakia, by contrast, gave the interwar democracy 44 percent of their votes, and the U.S. system 8 percent. In Poland, the same group was as democratic (U.S. preference) essentially (28 percent) as those aged 26–35, but the prewar authoritarian system received 38 percent. This same group gave 26 percent of its votes to democratic socialism. In Hungary, support for Marxism and democratic socialism dropped among those over 50, with more support for both democracy and prewar authoritarianism.

TABLE 10.4. Political System Preferences of East Europeans, 1974–1975

	Czechs/Slovaks	Hungarians	Poles
Democratic socialism	44	9	40
Sweden	22	16	28
Austria	22	23	12
Democracy	33	16	24
USA	13	16	24
inter-war	20	—	—
Marxist system	15	34	16
as Marx	4	8	3
as now	3	12	7
Yugoslavia	8	14	6
Authoritarianism	0	8	13
Spain	a	a	a
inter-war	—	8	13
Don't know	8	3	7

Source: RFEAOR, " 'The Best Government' as Seen by East European Respondents" (Munich, 1976)
aLess than 0.5%

Thus, these mid-1970s data do show some generational differences, which indicate that regimes will escape nostalgia for the "old days" as the older grow older still. But the gulf between West European democratic socialism and the system in Eastern Europe is as great as that between that system and its democratic (Czech) or authoritarian (Polish, Hungarian) antecedents. With perhaps the partial exception of younger Hungarians, political preferences in the successor generations were in the mid-1970s radically at odds with the current order.

Expressed in confidential circumstances in the West by persons who plan to return, these opinions are, of course, "cheap." Situational factors at home determine how expensive acting on them can be. In Czechoslovakia the costs are assessed as too high, while in Poland, where some might characterize recent state-society relations as ones wherein people neither fear that the state can do much to them nor hope that it will voluntarily do much for them, the successor generation is acting.

A 1977–78 survey of self-placement on a left-right spectrum by Czechs and Slovaks (1,052), Hungarians (1,162), and Poles (1,553) under Radio Free Europe auspices is also revealing (table 10.6), especially when compared with similar West European data (on Belgium, the Netherlands, Denmark, Germany, France, the United Kingdom, Ireland, and Italy).[19] On a 10-point scale, with 1–3 representing the left, 4–7 the center, and 8–10 the right, the East Europeans were less leftist and more centrist than the unweighted average of the eight West European samples. Only in Poland did the left bulk proportionally larger than in the least left West European states—Denmark, Ireland, and Germany. All West Europeans were more "left" than Czechs and Hungarians. Even here, leftist

TABLE 10.5. Political System Preferences, Successor Generation

	CZECHS/SLOVAKS		POLES	
	14–25 %	26–35 %	14–25 %	26–35 %
Democratic socialism	54	52	46	42
Democracy	23	18	14	28
Marxism (Yugoslavia)	25	23	29	21
Authoritarianism	0	1	1	1
Other, don't know	0	6	10	8

SOURCE: see table 10.4.
NOTE: Columns do not always total 100% due to rounding.

Poles selected the "softest" left alternative (point 3) more decisively than the West European leftists. In all three East European samples, only 1 percent selected the leftist extreme, while West European proportions ran from Italy's 10 percent to West Germany's 3 percent.

These results seem consistent with impressionistic observations (recalling that the majority in each of the East European samples was, by the late 1970s, likely to be of the postwar generation). East Europeans are not drawn to radicalism—politics as they have lived it has been too expensive; West Europeans, in fact, express greater rhetorical support for radical leftism and, at the extreme, more contempt for mere "bourgeois" freedom. Stephen Spender notes the attitudes of Western radical students visiting Prague in the *enragé* year of 1968, who expressed such a view of their own freedoms in cautioning Czech students, and quotes the words of a Czech student leader in response: "I have often been told by my friends in Western Europe that we are only fighting for bourgeois-democratic freedoms. But somehow I cannot seem to distinguish between capitalist freedoms and socialist freedoms. What I recognize are basic freedoms."[20] This is no less true today, though Czechs are in no position to pursue the preferences of 1968.

These preferences also confirm the conception of socialism accepted by East Europeans as broad and centrist, not pro-"Communist." Nor does it, at least since 1968 and the Soviet invasion of Czechoslovakia, look to "revisionism" as its salvation, or to an eastward transfer of "Eurocommunism." Reformism by the parties in power is less expected or trusted than in the past, and even where it might be, the Soviet factor imposes a limit on its relevance. As a summary of the RFEAOR survey puts it:

TABLE 10.6. West and East Europeans' Ideological Self-Designations

	W. EUROPEANS (AVG.)	CZECH/SLOVAKS	HUNGARIANS	POLES
	%	%	%	%
Left	23	12	7	19
Center	55	72	79	62
Right	22	16	14	19

SOURCE: RFEAOR, "The Political Self-Assessment of Czechoslovak, Hungarian and Polish Respondents" (Munich, 1979).

"Revisionism" as a purifying force applied to the Communist system from within has always had little echo in East Europe: the wide popular support at critical periods for men like Imre Nagy, Gomulka or Dubcek was rooted in the belief that they stood for less Communism rather than for better Communism.[21]

If, indeed, the attitude toward Communism is "rejectionist," attention in exploring the sources of this rejection needs to be given to religion as well as to the alternative political beliefs just explored. Though the global-universalistic claims of Marxism as a metaphysics have been muted in recent years in an Eastern Europe whose people are too sophisticated for simple presentations of atheist/materialist dogma, it remains the case that the regimes are strategically opposed to religion. "Tactical" compromise may well preempt virtually the whole area of strategy, as in a Poland for the last half decade dependent upon the church for the maintenance of an uneasy social peace. But principles remain opposed and will remain so until regimes alter their stand toward religion. Under the present situation, an examination of the successor generation's religious consciousness is worthwhile.

RELIGION

Religious belief and practice have been the objects of two sorts of assaults in postwar Eastern Europe. There has been a direct assault by Marxist-Leninist regimes committed to the propagation of atheism and a "scientific-materialist" outlook, and an indirect one of secularization, borne by processes of urbanization, industrialization, mass education, and other ruptures of traditional ways. For the postwar generation, these assaults have been simultaneous forces, altering drastically the environment in which older generations emerged.

Atheism, of course, was no major social force anywhere in Eastern Europe, in its Protestant-Catholic "west" or Orthodox-Islamic "east," before Communist rule. Indeed, the relatively lower level of economic development and the stronger grip of traditional styles in the region in the 1920s and 1930s left it less subject to gradual secularization than its more developed Western neighbors. As the example of Poland has demonstrated, even to those totally uninterested in East European affairs, religion is obviously not "dead," or dying. The successor generation and its children, as well as its elders whose formative experiences predate Communism, are readily observable in the churches not only of Poland, but also of the rest of Eastern Europe. But here, generalizations are extraordinarily difficult.

In the eastern states—Bulgaria, Romania, the non-Croat/Slovene area of Yugoslavia—it can probably be said that the tradition of Orthodox subjugation to state power has weakened the church's ability to resist state preemption of religious, educational, and socialization functions. Less developed traditions of theological disputation left the Orthodox churches poorly equipped to counteract the "scientific" thrust of state atheism (much as in the USSR), while the nature and context of Orthodox religious organization left it ill-prepared to form a core of resistance to state encroachment. It is notable that in Yugoslavia the regime shows more concern about the influence of the Catholic church, especially in Croatia, where it remains one of the defenders of national identity against the Orthodox Serbs, than about the Orthodox church.[22] It is, of course, inaccurate to use the old Soviet line that "the only people in the churches are old women" (even in the USSR they cannot be the *same* old women, after over a half century) with respect to this part of Eastern Europe, but it is probably not unfair to say that religion has weakened, and that religious observance may be tied tightly to the life cycle.

In Poland, Hungary, and Czechoslovakia the situation is rather different. Here, the pattern itself is diversity. Poland's virtually universal Catholicism and a strong church institutional presence have proved beyond the state's ability to destroy. Their linkage with mass nationalism, and the increased prestige of the church as arbiter between state and people in most recent times, makes for a strong future. Hungary, ethnically homogeneous, divides between a Catholic majority and a strong Protestant minority. In Czechoslovakia, religion coincides partially with the ethnic divide between historically Catholic Slovakia and the Czech lands, which are divided between Protestant heirs of the Hussite tradition and Catholics. The Slovaks are traditionally religious and somewhat suspicious of the "free-thinking" Czech tradition, while the latter look askance at the Slovaks as a historically rural "priest-ridden" people.

This is the part of Eastern Europe where, in history, Protestantism confronted Catholicism, where Counter-Reformation followed Reformation, where each faith sharpened its dialectical (as well as other) tools, neither quite subservient to the state, and where Catholicism's universalistic and Rome-based "international" quality served to give strength to religion and its appeal. While the regimes have probably been most successful with the antireligious fight in Czechoslovakia (and least so, it goes without saying, in Poland), religion has survived among the successor generations—some might argue, as well as or better than in Western Europe. The threat over the long run probably revolves more around general forces of secularization than around what the state may do in the future.

Data from Poland in the late 1950s are indicative: in 1959, a nationwide sample survey found 78 percent declaring themselves Catholic;[23] the following year, a nationwide poll of youth (eighteen to twenty-four years of age) found 78 percent classifying themselves as religious believers.[24] Studies among Warsaw University students in the same age range (an "elite" group) found a lower share of believers (69 percent) and not all of these churchgoers.[25] This is surely far from an "atheist" socialist intelligentsia in the making. Education and occupation affected religiosity: only 18 percent of unskilled workers in a 1961 survey rated themselves "not believers," while 40 percent of intelligentsia with higher education did so.[26] Nevertheless, declared believers were a majority in each category.

A 1969 RFEAOR survey provides insight into all three countries, and allows some examination of reported religious belief and practice, and age differences in these.[27] The figures summarized in table 10.7 show the percentage of respondents holding that religious beliefs are essential in response to the question "Do you think that one can go through life without religious beliefs?" and the percentage of the same sample who regularly attend church. The under-twenty-fives of the successor generation were clearly less religious than those over fifty, a group that in 1969 was made up of those who came to adulthood in either the prewar or wartime periods. In all cases, more express religious belief than attend church regularly, a pattern hardly unique to Eastern Europe.

National differences appear, with Poles most religious, independent of age, and Czechs least so. The extremes thus run in the direction one might have predicted from more general impressions, although Hungarians score perhaps somewhat higher and Slovaks somewhat lower on these scales than might have been expected. The figures reflect a successor generation in its youth—not very religious, especially in external observance, but hardly persuaded of the overall adequacy of Marxist worldviews, and certainly no less religious than an increasingly secularized Western Europe. In both Europes, education and occupational status, as they rise, tend to be correlated negatively with religiosity.[28]

Clearly, the religious picture is a mix of accommodation and assertiveness. The costs of open religious behavior—exclusion from certain positions, occupations, education—are not small, even in Poland. These have weighed more heavily on some than on others, most lightly on workers and peasants whose opportunities and "risks" in these worldly competitions are less. But principled resistance among those willing to forgo certain prospects is not so uncommon as to be negligible.

Accommodation can also indicate the failure of the maximal program of atheism of the late 1940s to early 1950s. What regimes face, and must now grapple with, is an element of the population that, without being "Christian Socialist" in any upper-case sense, accepts the broad institutional outlines of much of the system but shows a sophistication of religious faith and consciousness with which no regime is well equipped to tangle. Well educated and possessed of high occupational qualifications, these people argue the desirability of a real separation of church and state, wherein religious convictions or lack thereof are equally matters of no concern to the state. A Hungarian journal notes some elements of this phenomenon, quoting the words of one member of a small religious group of students and university graduates that meets once a week in a Budapest parish: "We criticize, and rightly so, West Germany because people with leftist ideas may not teach or occupy public offices. But at the same time we banish religious people from public life or educational jobs, even though they are not right-wing and advocate and consider socialism important."[29]

It is a measure of the differences in the degree of repressiveness of the regimes and in the consequences of open religious profession that this is a Hungarian, rather than Czech, source and situation. In Poland, the totally unique institutional and historical role of the church allows for more activism and assertion, and the possibility, in situations like that of 1980–81, of a further expansion of its freedom of maneuver. Indeed, in the past—notably in the "Polish October" of 1956 and for

TABLE 10.7. East Europeans' Religious Belief and Practice (%)

	POLAND		
	−25	50+	Overall
Religious beliefs 'essential'	42	80	69
Attend church regularly	16	55	34

SOURCE: RFEAOR, "East Europeans and Religion" (Munich, 1971).

years following—the strength of the church, and uncertainty about the sorts of accommodation it might make with the regime, alarmed secular and Marxist reformers who feared moves toward the quasi "established church" status it had enjoyed until World War II. Since 1976, there have been clear signs, admirably outlined in some of the writings of the quite secular dissident Adam Michnik,[30] that believers and hierarchy understand the value of common struggle toward a tolerant society, coercing neither belief nor unbelief, that would include secular intellectuals who no longer work from a principle of "no allies to the right." Religion in the East European states increasingly propels its adherents toward reclaiming those principles of mutual tolerance, imperfectly honored in the interwar period but still part of a Western tradition they share, that state socialism has denied the postwar generation as well as its elders.

HOPES AND FEARS

What does the successor generation expect, what does it hope for and want, from the international environment? Enough disasters have befallen its peoples over the centuries to provoke cynicism. Soviet hegemony in the area is, currently, a limit on expectations for Czechs, Slovaks, and Hungarians, if not so much so for Poles (in the period from mid-1980 to late 1981). By and large it is difficult to imagine postwar East Europeans expecting a Soviet rollback, Western "liberation," or radical alteration of the status of their nations on the international scene.

Desires are a different thing. Nothing save the limits of imagination restricts what one can want. It seems unlikely on the face of it that East Europeans want a "heating up" of the international environment be-

TABLE 10.7. (continued)

HUNGARY			SLOVAKIA			CZECH LANDS		
−25	50+	Overall	−25	50+	Overall	−25	50+	Overall
37	76	61	40	70	58	29	68	45
10	42	24	4	41	20	3	16	10

tween East and West, even if that would promise a chance for national freedom outside the bloc. Crises have a way of producing East European victims rather than winners. Add to this the fact that they are comfortable now with elements of "socialism" in a nondoctrinaire sense, and one might expect their desires to focus around a more open world, a belonging to Europe as a whole (meaning the "West" from which their identity derives), on a basis not of a Western alliance, but of some rapprochement between "East" and West. Hungarians have tasted some of this, Poles also; it would be surprising if they did not want more.

This may in turn suggest why détente has been so appealing to East Europeans—a peaceful mode of relationship between superpowers that would, arguably, facilitate such outcomes. Soviet dissidents, whose domestic political environment was that of a superpower, were more suspicious and critical of détente, seeing it as a tactic for lulling Western perceptions and as a facade behind which repressions could intensify in the USSR, than were East European dissidents, who saw in it more maneuvering room for their governments and also for themselves. Both have, perhaps, been partially right. The Soviet dissidents who have "warned" the West have, given their position, found it easier to perceive a "big picture," to their credit. The East Europeans, by no means to their discredit, have focused on their own nations' concerns and interests, within a context where external Soviet power seemed an immovable object.

Some evidence of this emerges from two RFEAOR polls dating to 1970,[31] asking Poles and Hungarians which of five alternative courses of development in East-West relations they thought likely for the 1970s, and which they most desired. In table 10.8, figures for the desires of the total sample (age break-downs unreported) are followed by assessments of the likelihood by total samples and those under twenty-five. Obviously, few (virtually none) want war or crisis. This, itself, is a change from the early postwar days when there were not a few who saw in the outcome of a Soviet-American conflict their liberation from Soviet control. Desires in general run heavily to rapprochement, with "greater Western influence" second. Hungarians a decade ago were more moderate than were the Poles, less than a year before the increasingly unpopular Gomulka regime fell. "Greater Eastern [Soviet] influence" is almost as unpopular as war and crises.

Wishes may father thoughts, but East Europeans are far less optimistic in their assessments of what is likely to happen. Here the successor generation, however, was more optimistic than the average a decade ago, particularly with respect to the chances for rapprochement rather than increased Western influence. In 1981, one may ask how such expectations have been borne out: the answer is clearly a mixed one. Hungarians are still wary; Poles have seen two crises—1976 and that kindled in 1980—that give cause for some optimism, some fear. Czechs and Slovaks must have found the 1970s a decade of predictable frustration. These hopes and fears confirm much of what has already been reflected earlier in this chapter. They suggest, at the very least, that the official rhetoric of East-West opposition, and of Eastern European "solidarity" with the USSR, reflects little of what is in the hearts and minds of the successor generation or its elders. Whether the gaps between conviction and reality can be bridged in favor of the former is an important question. As with all such questions, there is no ready answer.

Meanwhile, before leaving Eastern Europe's successor generation, let us understand a final, tragic relevance of its current position, a burden of its heritage. It has been the role, or misfortune, of the peoples of the region to be the European "shock absorber" against more despotic systems moving westward from the East—defining, in a sense, the broader East-West division. Relative backwardness, poverty, and weakness have been part of the story. Stronger medieval Balkan states might have repelled the Turks in the fourteenth and fifteenth centuries, radically altering the later histories of the Romanians, Serbs, and Bulgars. Weaker nations would not have thus absorbed the Ottoman expansion, and would have permitted the extension of what became Balkan backwardness further into Central Europe. The weakness and anarchy of the

TABLE 10.8 Desires and Predictions on East-West Relations, 1970

	POLES			HUNGARIANS		
	Desire	*Likely*		*Desire*	*Likely*	
		Overall	*−25*		*Overall*	*−25*
Development	%	%	%	%	%	%
Genuine rapprochement	65	36	40	74	31	45
Greater Western influence	31	28	29	24	18	22
Greater Eastern influence	2	10	12	2	16	12
Growing crises	0	21	15	0	31	19
East-West war	*a*	2	1	0	3	0

SOURCES: RFEAOR, "Polish Expectations, Hopes, and Fears Concerning East-West Relations in the 1970s" (Munich, 1971); "Hungarian Views on East-West Relations in the 1970s" (Munich, 1972).

Polish state in the eighteenth century subjected it to partitions, with Russia a major claimant to its share—yet had it not also borne the seeds of the recurring revolts in the nineteenth century, might not the history of all Europe have been altered in the direction of further westward expansion by the Russian Empire?

Today, save for Yugoslavia and Albania, the region is under Soviet domination—a modern variant of the Eastern intrusion. But the relationship between the dominating power and the states it dominates is a complex one. Eastern Europe is both asset and problem to the USSR —if contemporary Polish trends (despite the move to martial law in December 1981) indicate anything about likely directions of long-term developments, the future balance will tend toward the latter. The geopolitical realities of 1945 dictated this outcome, once again placing a weakened region in the role of victim, but conferring upon it as well the role of a "management problem" for the Soviet Union, which has reduced the Kremlin's ability to extend its hegemony further west. This is, to put it mildly, no small thing: a historic role not chosen, but executed nonetheless. Solidarity, Charter 77, and other dissident movements benefit, of course, from democratic encouragement and support in the West; the benefit to the West from these patrollers and contestants on a far boundary, equally part of the common Western heritage, is less frequently acknowledged or understood. But it is here, in this cause, that the best, most hopeful elements of Europe's successor generations come together.

ELEVEN

FROM UTOPIA TO AUTONOMY: THOUGHT AND ACTION IN THE EAST EUROPEAN OPPOSITION

The last chapter stressed elements of continuity in broadly shared values in Eastern Europe, on the whole, values complicating the regime's quest for complete domination. The current chapter shifts focus from society at large back to the dissident intelligentsia and its thought. Here, however, there is a chronicle of discontinuity over time. Socialism's first twenty years, roughly 1948–1968, appear in this respect quite different from what has followed. In the earlier period, for a significant number of activist intellectuals of Marxist persuasion, life was a struggle between old and new in postwar Europe: between the new socialist order and its promise and its strength, demonstrated by the Soviet Union's emergence as World War II victor, and what was left of the politics,

Originally written in 1981–82 for a planned collective volume that fell victim to various exigencies, this chapter appears in print here for the first time, in essentially original form, with the addition of new introductory matter and a new conclusion.

the psychology, and the culture of the old feudal/capitalist/ bourgeois/clerical Hungary, Poland, and Czechoslovakia of the interwar period. The enemies, through ignorance or malign intent, were diverse: entrepreneurs, landowners, capitalists of the old order (even if gone or expropriated, their estates, their factories, still stood to remind), peasants, and priests clinging to yesterday, refusing to lift their eyes to tomorrow. Yet is was not from these enemies that the intellectuals were to suffer, but, from the late 1940s to the mid–1950s, "their own"—the party *apparats* and the secret police of Eastern Europe's period of Stalinism.

Chastened, disillusioned, but by and large still secular, left, "Marxist" in their thinking, the intellectuals emerged in the mid–1950s to a more critical view of their regimes, a realization of the gulf between the societies they had sought to create and the results of socialism's first decade in power. Still, for the better part of the second decade, they saw opponents on two fronts: on one, the "Stalinists" and authoritarians in the party-state hierarchy itself, even denying *party* "liberals" and reformers the opportunity to work toward the humanization of socialism, and on the other, still, the "right"—those groups, forces, persuasions, suspected of wishing not the purification and liberalization of the postwar socialist order, not even tolerance *for* them within it, but the restoration of the old order, under their own hegemony. No matter that these forces were small at best (with the exception of religion), that the regimes themselves guaranteed no resurgence of the "old right"—they were still present. Their reasons for resistance—the stance of Cardinal Wyszynski in Poland through the 1950s and 1960s, for example—were the "wrong" ones.

Little wonder that, from the side of a nationalist, "traditionalist," religious-based dissent from the realities of socialism, little understanding was shown of the real conflict between the party *apparat* and the revisionists, that it was written off as "a fight between Communists."[1] In Poland's heady October of 1956, the "secular left had . . . two enemies: the central committee of the party, and the Catholic Church."[2] In such circumstances, there is no cause for wonder that the church, and other groups and persons whose quarrel with the regime drew on nonleft, non-Marxist sources, saw no potential ally when it looked across the divide to that secular left.

In socialism's young adulthood—in the last fifteen-twenty years— this *has* changed, at an accelerating pace. Some of the end points have been obvious: the Solidarity of 1980, supported by church *and* secular left, its leader, Lech Walesa, wearing on his lapel the badge of the Black

Madonna of Czestochowa and leaning to listen to the advice of "un-churched" intellectuals drawn from the Worker's Defense Committee (KOR) was the most visible. In this chapter, it is with the shifts in dissident thought underlying the change that we deal.

They are many. Described from the perspective of the secular left (since it is on these that the written record is richer), they have involved a move away from Marxism as the sole basis of critique and judgment to a broader base drawing on concerns with autonomy, participation, legal protections, and civil rights for all. With this has come a loss of faith in any "perfected" one-party regime, an end thus of "revisionism," and a more open exploration of political formulas of all sorts. From a general acceptance of a socialist economy, implying as near a monopoly over economic activity as the state can possess, dissidents have moved to question the effects, and the very concept, of this union of political and economic power. From a concern with the iniquities of the political system which said little of the gap between the Western heritage of Poles, Czechs, and Hungarians and the culture of the Russia which first created that system, they have moved closer to stressing the critical relevance of that gulf—one their ex-opponents of the "right" have well understood.

Both sides have moved toward a center; in the process, the base of dissent in thought, in ideology, in values, has broadened. Tolerance mutually extended and an appreciation of each other's struggles have grown. It is with the Western part of Eastern Europe that we are concerned—with Poland, Hungary, and Czechoslovakia, where these things *are* happening, and with the German Democratic Republic, where for reasons we will explore if not exhaust, dissent remains on a relatively narrow doctrinal base and increasingly difficult to fit into the trends of the last decade and a half elsewhere.

FROM SINGLE PARTY TO CIVIL RIGHTS

The roads along which dissidents traveled to disenchantment with the one-party *system* (rather than simply the dissent from the policies and practices of that one party, which they had all shared) were lengthy. The post–1956 Gomulka stabilization in Poland, withdrawing piece-meal (but no less effectively) many of the gains of October, was not enough to "turn" critics in the direction of wholesale rejection. Adam Michnik, writing in the mid–1970s, observed that neither Polish revi-sionists (Marxist but anti-Soviet) nor "neopositivists" (anti-Marxist but "realist" in their view of Soviet dominance) had broken the link of dependency with the PZPR regime.

Revisionists and neopositivists were at one in counting on changes from above as a way leading to the achievement of their goals. Both were expecting a favourable outcome of the Party's evolution resulting from realistic policies implemented by intelligent leaders. Neither of them even considered reinforcing the likelihood of this evolution by means of constant organized social pressure. They relied on the reason of a communist Prince rather than on the struggle to establish sovereign institutions which could control power.[3]

Even Kuron and Modzelewski's 1964 "open letter," so critical of the regime, did not carry the argument quite in the "rejectionist" direction: while asserting *the working class must organize itself into more than one party* (original emphasis),[4] they "oppose[d] parliamentary regimes"—which a Western critic may find somewhat illogical, until he understands that their goal was a workers' democracy, "the permanent participation of the working class, organized in a system of councils, political parties, and unions."[5] Their ideas were still exclusionary, "left-sectarian" in a sense, and turned primarily on the "real" participation/representation of *one* class, that for which the PZPR ostensibly spoke. This was less than the "broadening" which was to come later, less than the recognition of the need for *autonomy* of social groups.[6]

In Hungary, the "Budapest school" of Lukács' older followers was, during the 1960s and into the earlier 1970s, revisionist to the core, seeing in-system reform as the essential element in responding to what they regarded as the specifically *political* problems of a society already socialist in structure:[7] a stance understandable in the context of the gains won in economics and in the general tenor of life by Kadarism as a species of partial revisionism, under the aegis of a ruling party.

It is typical—and in some senses, quite accurate—to regard the Czech experiment of 1968 and its abrupt termination as the "end" of revisionism, via the realization that the USSR would not tolerate a liberalization even by a ruling party—in Michnik's earlier words, "realistic policies implemented by intelligent leaders"—but would see in this only betrayal; ominous and ultimately intolerable portents of change in East European regimes. But it is well to note that in the pre-August period, criticisms of the one-party system already went beyond revisionism, prefiguring in a sense all that came later in Czechoslovakia, and Poland and Hungary as well.

In April 1968, Vaclav Havel attacked the notion that internal de-mocratization in the party, the licensing of an intraparty opposition, would guarantee society's democratization. Seeing the latter instead as an essential condition of the former, he rejected any compromise of-fering political roles for nonparty "independents," arguing instead that nonparty forces must *themselves* be organized, and for the building of a democratic party to compete with the Communist Party in real elec-tions.[8] Petr Pithart cited the need for a real "autonomy" of political parties,[9] and cautioned against accepting workers' self-management schemes as some component of a "higher" democracy ("What we should be paying attention to is the lower storeys of that democracy. Because it's on them that the house in which we live will stand")[10] when such could in fact be manipulated toward the depoliticization of the workers.

In strident and similar terms, both Ludvik Vaculik and Antonin Liehm acknowledged that the party had started the reform process, and denied it any special credit therefore, since it alone was in control, and it alone (having preempted other groups and forces) had the resources to act. "The initiative and efforts of democratic communists are therefore only part of the debt which the Party as a whole owes to non-communists, whom it has kept in a position of inequality. No thanks, therefore, it due to the Communist Party."[11] Against these words, Dubcek's insist-ence on the party's continued exclusive leading role, his tolerance for hypothetical other parties as long as they were not "oppositional," reads today as quintessential revisionism.[12]

To be sure, such voices were not dominant in 1968. Nor, as the post-August "normalization" proceeded, were those who saw the one-party monopoly as a critical element in the Czechoslovak political tragedy to assume at once the leading role among the dissenters. Skilling[13] and Kusin[14] have chronicled the developments in dissident ideology between August 1968 and the early years of the Charter 77 movement in some detail, and we need not go over that ground at length here. Gradually, the various strains of Czech dissidence "outgrew" positions that could tie them effectively to any notion of a "reformist" single party as the key.

Early on, in the 1969–1972 period, the party purge of September 1969 removed reformist leftovers and thus the *organizational* base for any intraparty revisionism. Outside, dissidents spoke/wrote with various voices, some ideologically exclusive. The underground "Socialist Move-ment of Czechoslovak Citizens" Short Action Program (January-Feb-ruary 1971) warned against too-close collaboration with non-socialist Czech émigrés,[15] and sought to control its *samizdat* production so that "all programmatic, theoretical, analytical and polemical activity is closely linked to the needs of the movement."[16] But the Husak regime rejected equally dissidents of all stripes, in effect totally isolating itself from the dialogue proceeding among its critics. Under such circumstances, the early-mid-1970s saw a development of mutually shared perspectives among the latter, and a relative reduction in the weight of "Communists" linked, historically at least, to the single-party system. As Kusin put it,

> Less communism in theory meant easier cooperation with social-democratic and liberal oppositionists. In fact, the difference in outlook between revisionists and liberals became soon so blurred as to be practically non-existent. It was the ex-communists who made most of the ideological concessions, while the liberals were quite happy to endorse the "socialist" reference in public statements by the opposition, seeing as they did that the term now denoted something else than just a slightly adjusted communism of Soviet provenance. With a measure of over-simplification, one can suggest that opposition in Czechoslovakia became social-democratic in the period from 1973–6.[17]

In turn, the stage was set for Charter 77, whose "styles" and documentary content have, on the one hand, reflected the divergent political *histories* of its signatories, spokespeople, and writers but, more important, on the other, reflected cooperation, forebearance, and ideological tolerance among them. As Zdenek Mlynar put it in 1977, the charter was "not politically monochromatic":[18] the new unity

> is shared even by communists and Marxists who, after 1968, were kicked out of their privileged positions and came to share the lives of working people. The paradoxical achievement of the ruling power has been to force hundreds of thousands of communists to appreciate the significance of political democracy. These people needed a profound personal experience in order to arrive at a profound inner understanding of the inseparability of civic and political rights.[19]

In language very similar to Michnik's ideas on a new evolutionism in Poland, Ladislav Hejdanek characterized the aims of the charter as "not the liquidation of the state—that would only bring us to disaster—but the establishment and systematic extension of social space, which will be extracted from the state."[20] In 1978, the "declaration of Czech independent socialists" stated its demands for political rights as "no more or less than the rights and possibilities available to communists and communist parties in West European countries"[21]—indicating that from an alternative subject to critical analysis and qualified support, liberal democracy had now, in a sense, become the touchstone of the sort of system the dissidents sought. In all of this, the dual themes of rejection of the one-party system and the rapprochement of dissidents of the secular left with "allies to the right" earlier rejected were intertwined.

In Poland, the casting off of revisionism was a clearer process: fewer of the dissidents active from the mid–1970s had so many links with the party, and non-Marxist critical stances were better represented.[22] The arguments about the necessity of "rebuilding of informal social links and the resulting stimulation of public life,"[23] to fight a "totalitarian bureaucracy [which] destroys social links,"[24] were, analytically and programmatically, breakthroughs. KOR's very existence, as well as its words in an "appeal to the nation" on October 10, 1978, demonstrated the belief that it "is imperative to be organized in order to defend one's rights."[25] By this time, the struggle had passed beyond approaching the party as supplicant, or as unsolicited but sympathetic adviser, and turned to opposition, to pressure on the party-regime from without, from "society." As Maciej Poleski wrote: "These tactics mean, however, a final farewell to the dreams of reforming socialism. In no way do we desire to revitalize the existing system. What we want is to manoeuvre the authorities into carrying out the opposition objective. All partial reform must be looked at from this point of view."[26]

Polish dissidents, at least those of the "secular left," had come a long way. Looking back at the 1960s, Michnik recalled the time when the left reformer-dissidents (Kolakowski, Brus, Slonimski, etc.) had not objected to the state's slanders of the church, but saw the church as the enemy "to the other side"—equally with the PZPR *apparat* an obstacle to a humane future polity.[27] In retrospect, the church had behaved better toward the students and intellectuals attacked by the state in 1968 than that year's victims had earlier behaved toward the church.[28] By the mid-late 1970s, this was far from the case—the secular left no longer rejected "allies to the right."

Striking in this respect was the reversal by Jacek Kuron. In the 1964 open letter, anticipating critical reactions from left reformists, he and Modzelewski had acknowledged that while the right no longer had an economic base, "considerable importance must be accorded to *politically right-wing* groupings and currents headed by the Church hierarchy, which hung on to the old catchwords of reactionary ideology"[29] and saw fighting the party's "bureaucratic dictatorship" as "the only effective way to combat the traditional right"[30]—the struggles, on what were in effect two fronts, were "inseparable." By 1976, however, Kuron's diagnosis had changed as to the major source of Poland's ills, and, as he himself indicated, his "ideas on certain points [had] changed considerably during the last 20 years."[31] Nowhere more, perhaps, than with respect to the church, on which he wrote in 1976:

> But the Church in Poland is genuinely independent because it represents a mass social movement while churches in other countries of the socialist bloc are not. And because it is independent, the Church is able to oppose the totalitarian state effectively. This does not in any way mean that the Church has had political objectives at any time during the last thirty years. It means, however, that the Church is bound to oppose the system which restricts individual freedom, a fundamental concept of Christianity and our whole civilization. The Catholic movement, in defense of freedom of conscience and the dignity of the individual, struggles for the universal values on which our national culture is based.[32]

From a worker's democracy he had moved to a broader notion of "social cooperation" to create the possibility of fulfilling *individual* aspirations, even though these might be contradictory,[33] and saw new attractions in the parliamentary systems he had scorned in the 1960s. While it "leaves still much to be desired," in the eyes of the Kuron of 1976, "parliamentary democracy...is certainly the best of all political systems tried thus far."[34] His sensitivity to the relation of people as *workers* to the system of authority still echoed his earlier concerns. Still committed, in any future parliamentary democracy, to work for a "direct democracy" to respond to these workers, he also now cautioned that "without parliamentary democracy any attempt to introduce forms of direct democracy is at the mercy of the state."[35]

Kuron had come to endorse autonomy—of individuals, of groups— and to castigate the regime monopoly of "employment, information, and organizations" as "totalitarianism."[36] The whole spectrum of Polish dissent, whether drawing mainly on the left as did KSS–KOR, or the right-center as did ROPCIO (one of whose members said, "There is no bread without freedom...today, 61 years after the regaining of Polish independence, we have no freedom and no independence and this is one of the reasons why we have no food and no housing"),[37] or later on the whole society as did Solidarity, had reached the point of rejecting any possibility that Poland could continue or achieve a healthy existence under terms the party could ever bring itself to dictate and then live by.

If the multidimensional crisis of Polish political, economic, and social life gave wide scope to the forces of dissent there, the same can hardly be said of Hungary. The problem of the dissident intellectuals of Budapest arises from the *success* of Kadar's brand of revisionism: they reject it not because it "cannot work" to make Hungarian life better, more humane, secure, livable, but because having done so, it is still far from freedom, from autonomy. Most of Hungarian society, most of the intelligentsia, has been co-opted, and the "carrot" rather than the "stick" has predominated,[38] thus distinguishing this scene from Poland, Czechoslovakia, or the GDR. The dissident intellectuals have been "marginalized," and thus have turned their energies to thought and critique, aimed not at persuading the mass, but at pricking the minds and consciences of establishment intelligentsia who may be moved into an oppositional stance.

The burden of that thought and critique is, however, parallel in many ways to that of their compatriots to the north. Beginning as critical Marxists, carrying the heritage of the Lukács school and the notion that *party* reform was the critical necessity, they have gone beyond: a democratic, civil-libertarian order has replaced reformed one-party socialism as the desideratum. As Haraszti put it, "No one should mourn the wasted dream of a forward-moving state socialism that was destroyed ten years ago in August. That dream was the East European disease. The 'hopeless' struggle of the movement for democratic rights constitutes the first real sign of health."[39]

The fight against the "disease" is typically expressed in language more complex than that of Haraszti; Gyorgy Konrad and Ivan Szelenyi's exploration of the temptation state socialism presents for the intelligentsia (for which they were arrested in 1974)[40] and Gyorgy Bence and Janos Kis' joint writing as Marc Rakovski[41] are "dense" works, hardly broadsides aimed at galvanizing support from any medium-to-large-size public. But they do represent critical revelations of a political thought process which has distanced Marxists from Marxism, and hence from any possibility of making peace with a party which demands monopoly power by virtue of representing it. As Bence and Kis (Rakovski) put it,[42] the original articulators of democratic socialist ideals (Marxist) in the Hungarian context saw their objective as a system better than (Western) democratic capitalism, and were not of a simply "legalist" persuasion. They *moved* in the direction of increased emphasis on free speech, civil liberties, "space" between citizen and polity, as they found themselves "marginalized" by a regime which chose this path rather than dialogue.

In such a confrontation, emphasis on "Leninist norms of party life" was rather beside the point. Beside the point too, increasingly, was Marxism—for these Marxist democratic socialists had to fall back, per-force, upon positions which distinguished them less and less from le-galists, or *liberal* dissidents who aimed at transforming the political structure. While the tendency they called "radical reform" was limited to Poland (essentially, the Michnik/"new evolutionism" strain which eschewed "final" states and aimed at pressuring the regime, creating space), there seemed also to be less distance than in the past between the thought of the Poles and that forced by circumstances quite different on their Hungarian counterparts.[43]

Whether Bence and Kis were still "Marxist" or not is rather beside the point (Wlodzimierz Brus, in a review, wrote of Rakovski that "as far as Marxism is concerned he seems to propose saving the theory by abandoning it"),[44] but their examination of the roots of current problems in the dynamic of Hungarian de-Stalinization is not.[45] The latter was a bone of contention between the "diehards" and moderate reformers in the party hierarchy, who sought to use the intelligentsia for its purposes, and were thus more permissive toward them. Two groups of intellec-tuals responded—unaware that they *were* two: a category that wanted more security, better working environment, recognition, and reward (who were to be co-opted by Kadarism) and a second that sought insti-tutional reforms.

By the end of the 1960s, the political rulers had reunited on a program that satisfied the first group, but just as surely rejected the propositions of the second and pushed its members toward marginalization: not a return to Stalinism, but a refusal to allow "autonomous" representation of the interests of would-be institutional reformers, a dilution of the Kadarite monopoly.

This is the point—the one-party system's denial of the right to po-litical action outside of its (even loose) control; the temptation serving and directing its monopoly presented to intellectuals eager for the power they would enjoy as "redistributors" in its nonmarket economic design (Konrad and Szelenyi's critical point).[46] It is this which has driven Hun-garian dissidents who generally began in revisionist intellectual envi-ronments to reformulate attitudes in opposition to the single-party principle and favoring a broader diversity of views: the act of free expres-sion of all and any "non-official" views became *itself* desirable.

Even the most ancient and reactionary myths have a clearly positive role ... since they in fact multiply the number of patterns of thought ... [and] relativise the official ideology's *Weltanschauung* ... every oppositional ideology ... if it does in fact transcend the official framework of communication and social discussion, implies a deep democratic content.[47]

More, probably, than in the other countries, the Hungarian dissidents have thus isolated some of the temptations and dangers of a Marxist perspective linked with the possession of irresponsible power, or close to that power, which tends to close off or fail to attend to alternative diagnoses of the state of polity and society. Haraszti echoes Konrad and Szelenyi in arguing that with the victory of the party, the directing, planning, and organizing intelligentsia became "ruling class," *became* the state, and their *revolutionary* Marxist ideology became meaningless.[48] They may not, in fact, "like" this—but they are saddled with it. "The planners themselves desire the support of public opinion instead of dogmas; but it is precisely to the destruction of individual autonomy in the Marxist transformation of society the planners owe their power."[49]

Even Andras Hegedus, unique in his status as the only ex-Prime Minister in a socialist state active as a dissident critic, sets his analysis in terms which deny the adequacy of any revisionism: while "serious forces" in the leadership want a rational extension of the NEM, he observed in 1979, "it is another thing whether or not the political leadership will tolerate the formation and existence of autonomous movements, without which significant social reforms are unthinkable."[50] It was "another thing," indeed, for a single party which tolerates "autonomous movements" *is* no longer, or for so long as it does tolerate them, the possessor of the monopoly which its singularity was meant to guarantee.

With the exception of the GDR, to be treated later, a loose but rather consistent dissident ideology thus emerged in Poland, Czechoslovakia, and Hungary. Born of experience, and of an end to the divide between critics from the left and the right, it rejected the *design* of a system which had distorted the root meaning of the word "party" into claims of totality, and claimed the rights of people of varying persuasions to speak, write, be heard and read, and organize themselves to convince others of their ideas, priorities, claims. No longer petitioners, dissidents were no longer content to wait in the anterooms of power; not desiring to enter the inner sanctum, they would attempt to affect what was decided there. In all of this, an emergent stress on a Western civilization heritage grew in importance.

AFFIRMATION OF THE WEST

At various times in the twentieth century, spokesmen for virtually *every* East European country (predominantly those of the traditional/conservative sort) have held their nation up as the last bastion of Western civilization, the easternmost outpost past which "Asiatic" Russia, Tsarist or Soviet, commences (or, to some degree, the southeasternmost, past which the world of Islam begins). This, of course, amounted to competition: a Romanian claim that its Latin culture marked the Western border would be scoffed at by a Hungarian who regarded *his* country as the outpost and Romanians as quintessentially Balkan, as part of the "other," non-Western world. (But then, for Metternich, "Asia" began a little beyond Vienna's eastern gate—little comfort to Hungarians—and for Chamberlain in 1938, the Czechs and Slovaks, in their democratic state, were faraway people of whom he "knew nothing.") Many things were entangled here: language, religion, "culture" and life-style, economic development. One thing was constant: an "investment," by at least a significant segment of the "conscious" upper and middle classes, in a self-identification with Western civilization, perceived as something coherent, distinct from, and better than the East.

This theme finally returned to East European dissent after an absence, partial but important, over perhaps the first two decades of socialism. "Partial" is the qualifier because traditionalists, nationalists, and religious resisters of the new regime did draw on these sources of Western identity. But in dissident thought and ideology, these sources did not make the running. In the dissident lead were those of secular/left/revisionist orientation, who made little of the "Western" identity of their societies, of the lack of fit between culture and history on the one hand, and the Russified Marxist political system on the other. The "why" here is a big question, but not necessarily one we need try to answer fully. The revolutionary commitment many preserved as they went into dissent tinged past national history with mainly negative tones. Their Marxism, if not deracinating, was rather insensitive to national heritage (both their own and the Russian), and their stance, as we have seen, was exclusivistic—in dissent, "no allies to the right."

It is "not accidental" that dissent specifically Western in its cultural base has emerged in Poland, Czechoslovakia, and Hungary. These are, after all, nations and societies of the "West." Their traditional civilizations and high cultures, alphabets, forms of Christianity, and the political aspirations, if not competences, of their historic elites derive from Western roots. "Middle Ages" and "Renaissance" have a meaning here, as they do not further east and south. This is true of the Reformation and Counter-Reformation as well—Poland remained Catholic, Hungary and the Czechs and Slovaks divided between Catholicism and Protestantism, but in none of the three is Eastern Orthodoxy or Islam a major component, as it is in the Balkans and historic Russia. The sense of an alien *source*, alien design in their current political regimes, and an alien guarantor of those regimes in the contemporary Soviet state should naturally be more pronounced there than in Bulgaria and Romania, which lie in whole or large part to the other side of a line separating the worlds of a Western and Eastern civilization.

The Soviet invasion of Czechoslovakia, more than other events, reintroduced this critical distinction and intensified its meaning. Ivan Svitak had earlier addressed the issue of the country's own Communist party's capability to transform itself in squarely Western terms of judgment.

Is the Communist Party still at all capable of making decisions about national and state questions in line with the basic rule of European politics, which have been applied since the French Revolution, that is, to ask the people's will before acting and to respect the sovereignty of the people as the basis of state power superior to personalities and all institutions, not excepting the Communist Party? If it is not, then it must give up its intention of preparing constitutional and other basic changes in the structure of the old power system, and on the contrary ask the people what the basic rules of the democratic game are, so that they have a chance to vote for their real representatives.[51]

Looking back to the first day of the invasion, the novelist Milan Kundera was to talk, chillingly, of a

visceral horror [that] did not come from the fact that Dubcek's reforms were finished, but from what could be sensed behind the faces of the Russian soldiers, from that strangeness of a civilization that thinks differently, feels differently, has a different destiny, lives in a different historical time—a civilization that came to swallow us up into its own eternity.[52]

Nor were these words simply the atmospheric response of a creative writer to his nation's tragedy. Kundera also made a point of the gap between the native culture and the imposed political system, the tension between them which contributed so much to the impetus for reform, and the frustration flowing from what he saw as the West's failure to understand.

> The greatness of the era of the '60s and the Prague Spring does not lie in the politics of the times (which were incompetent and destroyed everything in the end), but with the culture. Culture in the broadest sense of the term: not only the arts and sciences, but the overall behavior of the people, its tradition of tolerance, of humor and of freedom. This culture attacked the imported political structure in order to fill it with its own contents, to invest it with another meaning.... The West, which is no longer capable of conceiving of this culture as anything other than an appendage to the political system, never understood what happened in Czechoslovakia before 1968.[53]

Realization of the breadth of the gulf came late, perhaps, to Czechs and Slovaks. Historically, their problems as peoples were, respectively, with Austro-Germans and Hungarians, with Russia a distant Slavic "well-wisher." Masaryk's image of Russia had emphasized the thread of progressive tradition there; the people he led were perhaps less discriminating in their image. The Communist coup of 1948 was ostensibly "domestic"—no Muscovites arriving in Soviet baggage trains—but guaranteed what it had taken by Soviet power. Czechs and Slovaks were not historically Russophobic (see chapter 10); in the interim years of their parliamentary democracy, they on the whole underestimated the gap between their culture and political system and the regime of terror and mobilization Stalin presided over in the East. (As Pithart noted ironically in 1968, in its twenty years "the First Czechoslovak Republic, which no one wants to return to today because of all its other faults, sentenced, as far as I know, only eight people to death.")[54]

Russophobia in both harsh and more measured form had deeper roots in Poland. Yet again, the *open* discussion of the "Western" quality of Poland as an element in "secular left" dissent emerged fully only after some years of revisionist critique. Externally, one found it in the writings of the poet Czeslaw Milosz;[55] internally, the words of Andrzej Szczypiorski, written at "flood tide" after the Pope's visit to Poland in 1979, are worth quoting at length.

> The tremendous demonstrations in support of Pope John Paul II in Poland were not of a religious character, although the Church hier-

archy in Poland would have liked it to be so. There is no doubt that very many Poles did demonstrate their attachment to the head of the Roman Church and their purely religious emotions. But the majority manifested feelings, hopes, and desires of a different kind. They were concerned with civic rather than with religious matters. They were showing their attachment to the Polish tradition, to Polish history, to the Western world, to Latin civilization, to their thousand-year-old ties with Western culture and to democratic principles. For centuries this Latin world shaped the Polish mentality, and the Pope is its symbol. Westerners today fail to understand how Byzantine, how Russian contemporary communism is. Westerners do not understand that the regime which has ruled in Poland for the last 35 years is not only economically inefficient, but above all is contrary to the thousand-year-old national tradition, to the spiritual roots of Latin Europe, to the whole intellectual achievement of Western thought which provided a model for Poland for a millennium. And this is not just a question of spiritual links with the Roman Catholic Church, but a wider, multi-faceted problem. It touches upon all instincts, all thoughts, and all patterns of behaviour of individuals in Poland.

When dense crowds sang a traditional Polish song wishing the Pope a "Hundred Years" of life, they were not just demonstrating their loyalty to an extraordinary man and their reverence for the Bishop of Rome, but also their attachment to the authentic traditions of Poland which have been gagged and falsified for 35 years.[56]

Someone used to the light and dark places in Polish history might find little new in this, and an echo of the posturing of an interwar Poland affirming its Western culture while it subjected the Byelorussians and Ukrainians of its eastern third to harsh and discriminatory treatment scarcely justifiable by any traditional Western regard for the integrity and value of the individual. World War II, the genocide of European Jewry, and the postwar border shift changed all this, creating the smaller postwar Poland as a state ethnically near homogeneous. But today, the Western identification is probably less self-serving in a narrow sense than in the past, more creative as a path to understanding both the external and internal roots of the crisis which came to a head at the end of the 1970s. The Polish Independence Compact (PPN), an anonymous group more traditional in its outlook, appears analytic rather than chauvinistic in its words on Poland's "European" character.

There is in Poland a whole body of widespread, though not always well defined, views concerning Poland's membership of Europe. It is expressed in such slogans as: the Rampart, the Eastern Bastion, the Latin as opposed to the Byzantine tradition, etc. Opinions expressing the "Western" and "European" character of Poland refer primarily to the roots of Polish culture and civilization and to the fact that Christianity and, later, most of the components of our culture came from what is today called Western Europe and not from the Eastern and Byzantine source....Does Poland really belong to a Europe, so defined? From the point of view of the political system, no. Of tradition, yes; of social relations, only partially; of the aspirations of the majority, to a much greater extent; of its institutions (apart from the Church and some associations of creative artists), very little; of the thought processes of its scholars, artists, writers and clergy, very much so.[57]

Similar is the PPN's treatment of the strands in Polish history, less pronounced, that have emphasized elements of *separateness* from the West, which

> often resulted from the fear of an indiscriminate, automatic acceptance of Western models and ideals; sometimes from resentment of the indifference of Europe to our subjugation and suffering; seldom though from the hope that the inclusion of Poland in the Byzantine-Russian-Eastern circuit would provide real power.
>
> It is worth pointing out, however, that the calls for "separateness," insularity, "the Polish way," were usually tinged by a more-or-less wished or declared anti-democratic tendency. Of course the liberal vision of society is only one of many existing in the Western world, but it is only within its framework that the above mentioned values can be implemented.[58]

The words of Adam Michnik, quoted at length below, are striking in that first, the word "West" or "Western" is never used, and that second, they might almost echo the impression Western visitors familiar with life throughout the Soviet bloc have taken away, in both "good" and "bad" times for Poland.

> The reality of our country differs considerably from the reality of those countries which are our neighbours. We are less receptive to the process of Sovietization. Why?
>
> There are various factors which make us different; historical tradition, the Catholic Church, and the brave though so very realistic line taken by the Episcopate, the countryside which has defended itself in the face of collectivization; finally, unremitting social pres-

sure. This has manifested itself sometimes in violent explosions (Poznan 1956, March 1968, December 1970, Radom 1976), but generally in quiet, daily, dogged resistance. A resistance which is, as it were, incompatible with denunciation. The mental atmosphere of a part of the intellectual environment, lectures and seminars in institutions of higher learning, the carrying out of doctoral research and the publication of learned communication, novels, slim volumes of poetry, essays, meetings of the Union of Writers or the P.E.N. Club, films and theatrical presentations, museums, concerts and vernissages. And this comes largely from the work of people who sign no protest and perform no spectacular deeds of opposition. Yet it is equally due to them that we now breathe a different air in Poland. A spiritual air. And this daily creation of an invisible but fundamental strand in the culture and consciousness of the nation is not simply the result of reading *Zapis* or the *Biuletyn Informacyjny* or the publications of the Independent Publishing House. It is a result of the totality of Polish achievements.

This totality is becoming an object of envy to visitors who are citizens of other nations of the "camp." They do not envy us just for KOR, SAC and uncensored publications, but also for journals which are published officially. And not only for *Tygodnik Powszechny* or *Wiez* but also for *Tworczosc, Pamietnik Literacki* and even for *Polityka*. They envy us our full churches and our fully operational catechetical centres, the theatrical productions of Diemek and the films of Wajda, the appearance of our streets and our attractively dressed girls. Thanks then to all this we are preserving our identity and a capacity to keep up a resistance to the Sovietization process.[59]

In turning to the nation's Western tradition and national identity, dissidents also began to firm up relations with the population as a whole (which never, in the 1960s, showed much interest in the disputes of Gomulka's *apparat* and their revisionist challengers). Michnik contrasts the clear health and survival of language, religion, and national culture in Poland to the situation of her "Eastern neighbors"—the Lithuanians, Byelorussians, and Ukrainians *within* the USSR[60]—and then discusses the different situation of dissidents in the USSR, weak and with little mass contact or support, and of those in Poland.

Although the political police make life difficult for us, we feel that we are strong, since we have the support—moral and material—of broad sections of our society. We have the support of people who are not by temperament either politicians or heroes, who do not want to have to give up their comparatively stabilized family life, who certainly rarely decide to sign a protest letter, and who—I must say—actually take for granted the success of the campaign in defence of the workers of Radom and Ursus.[61]

One could not say—nor would they claim—that the Hungarian dissidents who articulate complex and general ideas and critiques enjoy support from "broad sections" of society. Their problem is different from that of the Poles or the Soviet dissidents: the co-optation of a society scarred and chastened in 1956, which has later received a "better deal," and better leadership in an economic and social sense than the most optimistic could ever have predicted on New Year's 1957. The "Western" theme is more muted there (although the Russophobia off which it can be "played" goes as deep, or nearly so, as in Poland), detectable more in the logic of dissident critique than in explicit formulation. It is, perhaps, most pronounced in an area of peculiar Hungarian concern: the fate of the large Hungarian minority in neighboring Romania, and more broadly in the contrast between Hungary's decompressed internal life and the repression and poverty across the border under Ceausescu. The matter of the minority is a concern the dissidents share with Kadar (whose relations with Ceausescu could hardly be called "fraternal" even in the much-stretched Eastern meaning of the word), but one they are not encouraged to express.

Beyond this, it is to Hungary's Western cultural heritage, as much as to Kadar's policies and style, that the continuing difference is seemingly attributed: dissidents know they would be worse off in Romania, but just as surely see this as insufficient to make peace with their home-ground version of the "system." Kalman Garzo, in a *samizdat* piece in 1982, makes all these points. "However much" Western praise of Kadar may offend, "We who are critical of that regime cannot remain blind: the difference between Romania and Hungary is greater than the difference between Hungary and Austria or Finland."[62] (One might take issue here: Hungary's "distance" from Romania is rooted in Kadar's policies and practice, in the NEM as well, but *not* in firm institutional change at the political core. Austria and Finland are parliamentary democracies, neither Hungary nor Romania is, although the first three are Western in their culture.) But Garzo is not satisfied by this comparison with Hungary's advantage:

> How disquieting it would be if Hungary's guarantee of stability lay in a simple comparison between ourselves and other Communist countries. This would be the first step towards ourselves resembling

Romania. "Look how badly the neighbours are doing"—this often heard, conceited and unpleasant phrase is not better than the envious phrases of our neighbours.[63]

Garzo is a critic from the *left*: he worries that Hungarian self-satisfaction over external comparisons could tip the current center of gravity over "towards the right—in the wrong direction."[64] But his critique has less of the search for the "correct" Marxist recipe, more of the general concern with freedom and autonomy, than one would have found among dissidents of the past.

"Leftism" of course *is* Western; critiques emanating from dissidents who so identify themselves need no less partake of the Western "affirmation." Critical, rather, has been the understanding that the *Soviet* model is, in the conventional terms of a democratic left, neither left nor right, but something *different*. Polish, Czech, and Hungarian dissidents turned in the early 1970s (though the last less so) to West European Eurocommunist and Socialist parties and media to publicize their messages, demands, and travails. Many of them were likely more "comfortable" seeking these channels; most, no doubt, overestimated the ultimate Euro-communist *impact* on Western politics and opinion (as did many Western analysts). Whatever one's assessment of the sincerity of Eurocommunist declarations of intent, it seems fair to say that for the East Europeans who sought their support and help, they were attractive because of the "Euro": because they were perceived as authentic examples of a Western left tradition, critical *in depth* of the Soviet Union and the non-Western political system it has fastened on the peoples of Eastern Europe. In all this, the East European dissidents, especially those who had grown up under socialism, the successor generation, reunited themselves unequivocally with critical elements of their Western heritage.

ECONOMY AND AUTONOMY

Protest over economic conditions is not a new theme in dissent. From the beginning, the tendency of centrally planned systems to gorge themselves on investment and armaments, to broaden and further broaden the heavy industrial base, has meant restrictions on consumption: housing, durables, services, other elements of the standard of living as the citizen-as-consumer experiences it. East Berlin, Plzen, Poznan, were bench-marks of protest over economics in the 1950s. These, however, were *worker* outbreaks in action: short, intense, typically limiting their demands and diagnosis to placards and terse statements of protest. While dissident intellectuals may have sympathized with the protests and deplored the conditions that gave rise to them, the economic structure that underlay these distortions was not a major object of examination. The point seemed to be to make "socialism" in the economy work better, yield the results it ostensibly promised—putting "right" a recipe that already assumed a rather bureaucratized economy, a status of wage/salary employee for the vast majority of the labor force, a marginal role for market forces, and state ownership of the overwhelming share of the means of production. Socialism was not, then, at issue. Critical intellectuals favored it, in this seemingly at one with the state/party *apparat*; the working class was not opposed; the old capitalist class, such as it was, removed through annihilation, expropriation, and pro-scription, was not politically "present" to resist.

This too has changed. Both the economic performance of socialist regimes and a change in the way dissidents think about economics and its link with political control have had an effect. As to the first, the record is distressingly clear. As the 1970s turned into the 1980s, the Polish macroeconomic crisis peaked: Gierek's overheated, overbor-rowed, import-dependent, and overcentralized economy hung on a pre-cipice. In Czechoslovakia, the costs of centralization, the mounting inefficiencies of an archaic industrial plant, acute dependency on energy imports, and the legacy of reforms aborted in 1968–69 brought price rises long deferred and minimal growth. Hungary's NEM, "brought to heel" in the early 1970s, was reexamined and, as a matter of policy at least, reintensified as the 1970s showed a darkening economic horizon. This forced Kadar and his economic public relations team to go to the country with warnings that, at best, it could expect a no-growth re-trenchment for the next few years.

Thus, the element of social contract which underlays, in a limited way, regime-society relations (the state's promise of growth providing modest but continual improvements in the living standard, in exchange for the society's acquiescence in the monopoly rule of the party) began to come apart, since the state could no longer "deliver," but was un-willing to "renegotiate" toward greater public participation in allocation decisions now grown more critical with economic stagnation. This, I would argue, recast the economic thinking of dissidents toward a deeper examination of the dynamics of socialist economics, toward a consid-eration of the long-term costs of the lost autonomy of individuals and groups in the economy.[65]

Most explicitly, and not surprisingly, these critical currents emerged in Poland. It would be going too far to detect the emergence of a conservative (neo- or otherwise) line of economic criticism, but the points made by many dissidents logically went to the core of long-accepted rationales for socialist economics.

The unification of political and economic control was a prime target. Stefan Kisielewski traced Polish socialism to the destruction and expropriation of large-scale private enterprise in the German occupation and the massacre of the Jews, leaving no one to *return* enterprises to. Then followed "levelling and liquidation" to obliterate all traces of the previous way of life, as Communist power arrived. "Instead of the proletariat creating the revolution, it was rather the revolution, imposed from above in a classless, propertyless void, which proceeded to create an industrial proletariat."[66] This "reverse pedigree" generated the sorts of distortions critics were later to attack. Kisielewski contrasted a capitalism wherein the owners' life-styles, however elevated, "form no more than a tiny fraction of this profit" versus the plowback in investments and interest, with the bureaucracies of administration, enforcement, and record keeping, which under socialism "devour a huge part of the national revenue" and occupy millions in useless work.[67] The 1977 Declaration of the "Democratic Movement" saw the government as usurper in its role of sole employer.[68] A PPN document warned, citing a possible positive example in Yugoslavia, that there are "those who consider that the consolidation of political and economic control in the same hands is a mistake."[69]

In Czechoslovakia, where in some ways both the Novotny and Husak regimes relied more heavily than elsewhere on the "welfare state," security-net aspects of state socialism, a Charter 77 document looked at the absence of unemployment and found that it had "been achieved at a price which was not necessary . . . it has produced a decline in economic efficiency and created widespread hidden unemployment" in superfluous jobs, etc.[70] Beyond this, it demanded that the individual "should be able to sell his labour power under the most favourable conditions," for a decent wage, with the right to organize freely.[71]

No one argued for a return to private ownership of heavy industry, natural resources, etc.: whatever the effects of this sort of nationalization, they are part of East European history, and no constituency seems prone to disturb them. But nor were these economic demands limited to adjustment and tinkering. They went well beyond that, in economics and in the political/administrative implications of rendering so many planning/counting/checking and reporting bureaucrats redundant. It is very much a *market* socialism the critics aim toward; one which, for some, would be quite close to democratic countries of "mixed" economy where the state's role is felt mainly in (a) nationalization of basic industry and resources and (b) social welfare policy. Since the interwar economies of East-Central Europe were already heavily statist in the first sense, what is being sought would not be historically so new. In its statement on "Poland and Europe," the PPN, looking forward to a "reentry" of Poland into Europe, sees as important a preparation of the Polish mentality via the study of "the extent and role of planning in a free market economy."[72]

Such reentry may be far away indeed, in the sense the authors intend. Still, the predominant sort of "unofficial" economic thinking, whether from the oppositional sources cited here or even from the independent, broad-spectrum group or consultative assembly "Experience and the Future," extends the base of economic criticism and combines it, especially in Poland, with a sensitivity to the sorts of *inequality* to which democrats of the left have always been sensitive. As the "Experience and the Future" report puts it, "A program must be worked out to halt the growing antiegalitarian tendencies in our society."[73] It may be that the health of East European economies will require *more* inequality: practicality and moral commitments can run against one another. But the Polish critics of corruption and enrichment under Gierek aimed at inequalities and injustice generated in an economic milieu whose accumulating *sicknesses* were evident for all to see. This, from an analytic perspective, is quite a different matter, and gives the lie to those who would denounce them in the conventionalized regime jargon as "rightists," "reactionaries," those who would like to "destroy the gains the working class has made."

Hungary's dissidents felt less reason to offer critique and counterprescriptions about economic design. Hungary came fairly far, fairly consistently, under the NEM, compared with other states. The economic problems are large, but Hungary's resource poverty, Poland's scale and potential for wealth, are facts which rational economics in the former, catastrophic policies in the latter, managed to reverse. The relative (if now imperiled) success of Hungary made it harder for dissidents to develop, then, any "programs" of broad appeal.[74] But in turning to a narrower potential audience—the intelligentsia—Konrad and Szelenyi, Bence and Kis, and others have attempted to clarify the *interests* of that intelligentsia, to suggest that the economic interests of the intelligentsia and the working class are *not* the same; that, in a sense, the intelligentsia is self-serving in conceiving of itself as the articulator and defender of working-class and broader societal interests.

Their arguments are complex, but the central point is clear. As Konrad and Szelenyi argue, until the intelligentsia understand the distinctness of their "class" interests vis-à-vis both the working class and ruling political elite, they cannot reach the point where any kind of political *alliance* with the working class can be constructed on a workable basis.[75]

Similarly, Bence and Kis posed the question of *whose* interest, beyond its own, the dissident intelligentsia articulated. Their answer was interesting. "Whose ideologues are the writers, journalists and philosophers in the underground? ... the answer is that among the important social groups there is not one whose interests find their representation in these people's activities."[76]

The sort of decentralizing, "marketizing" changes for which dissidents (and reform economists) call, are rational, are, on the evidence, a necessary if not sufficient element in changing misdesigned, misdirected economies. But in focusing on the element of self-interest intertwined with their advocacy—the fact that the well-trained, educated, imaginative will reap the benefits first—the Hungarian writers, even as they have called their fellow dissidents to further action and other intellectuals to join them, have touched on a sensitive point, quite in keeping with the difficult but often rewarding content of their work. "Autonomy" in the economy, as in political life proper, is not something to be consumed wholly by the intelligentsia.

COUNTERPOINT: UTOPIANISM IN THE GDR

Most of what has been said about Poland, Czechoslovakia, and Hungary thus far cannot, as a generalization, be extended to the GDR at the end of the seventies. This is strikingly true with respect to the proper subject of this essay: the thoughts, the ideas, the motivating and sustaining *ideology* of the dissidents, as articulated in their writings. Here, the GDR and its dissidents seem a world apart. Where others are moving away from Marxism, they affirm its continuing relevance. Where others find one-party monopoly a critical flaw, they call for the "right kind" of party to take command. Where other dissidents of the secular left see a common struggle for many shared values with religious and traditionalist dissidents, they see at worst enemies, at best people of whom it is well to be wary—the ever-lurking right. Where others see in the nations (better, states) of the West bodies whose values they share in many ways, whose well wishes (if not active aid) are sincere and to be welcomed, GDR dissidents see a "capitalism" with evils as deeply rooted as those of Stalinism, and a siren song all too appealing to East Germans, a pottage for which they would readily settle rather than striving to move further on toward their Communist birthright.

To this last state, end point, future consummation, uniquely, East German dissidents like Havemann, Harich, and most recently Bahro still bear an allegiance very distinct among the thinkers and writers we deal with here. Why this should be the case is partially evident, partially not so. We cannot hope to explain the whole of the GDR's exceptionalism in dissident thought, but several elements are worth noting. There is, first, a "freestanding" German Marxist tradition, historically independent of, and antecedent to, Russian and other East European Marxisms: it exists as background, independent of whether the GDR's Marxist dissenters refer to it.

Second, as Karl Reyman writes, there is the element of *das Systemdenken*, a German tendency "toward an all-encompassing perfectionism and either-or propositions [which] has given East Germany's official ideology an aggressive self-righteousness unequalled elsewhere in Eastern Europe."[77]

Third, a self-selective process of several layers underlies this German state: Communist intellectuals of anti-West, anticapitalist leanings went to the GDR as it was created. Millions of people, including many who would have later been dissidents of diverse stripe, went west to the FRG before the Berlin Wall was built. This has not been the experience of the other socialist states.

Fourth, the multiple ruptures of Versailles, the failure of the Weimar Republic, the rise of Hitler, and the national collapse of Nazi Germany left relatively little specifically "good" in a national tradition for critics of the emergent GDR to fall back on save Marxism. Again as Reyman notes, the crushing of the spontaneous East Berlin workers' revolt in June 1953 removed even the "ornamental" aspect of the Weimar spirit as part of the GDR's heritage, and "broke a link of political continuity. It is one of the reasons why, unlike in the other East European countries, political dissent in the GDR today shows relatively less fallback on the more liberal national traditions."[78]

Fifth, one could suggest that the unique problem of the GDR's rulers, passed from Ulbricht to Honecker—the existence of a free, prosperous *West* German state accessible via radio and television to the vast majority of their subjects, and thus a constant irritant—has an impact on their dissident opponents as well. Marxist critics of the FRG's affluence, "militarism," environmental exploitation, "bourgeois" civilization, and general culture abound in the FRG; the GDR's Marxists can see and read much of this. Committed as they are to their own viewpoint, it would be strange if they were not affected, not inclined to denigrate the example and reality of the Western "version" of Germany as an alternative, and thus fall back again on their own Marxist resources, rather than move toward the parliamentary-democratic, "centrist" example of the FRG's political system since the 1950s.

One could add more, but to little avail. The point is that the thinking of the Havemanns, Harichs, and Bahros is different. (We leave out, here, evidence of strikes and worker discontent, and of spontaneous, religion-based peace movements in the last few years, since these have not given rise to overall analyses and critiques of East German reality, and for the same reason the phenomena of literary politics and nonconformist creative writers.)[79]

Wolfgang Harich, who finally left the GDR in 1979, stands alone. Arrested in 1956 for overreaction to the Soviet Twentieth Party Congress and its condemnation of Stalin (Harich's line was strongly revisionist, critical of Soviet hegemony over the GDR, and in favor of socialist reunification of the Germanies), released in 1964, he has moved to advocate[80] something variously described as "a puritan society submissive to ecological (planning) authority";[81] "a rigid distributory state system";[82] "an iron dictatorship in a centrally planned economy."[83] This is his solution to problems of natural resource depletion, environmental pollution, and a set of other geophysical/demographic issues he sees as a world crisis. Antigrowth, anticonsumption, Harich sees the establishment of tight state control as critical, and the suppression of consumption in the socialist states as a step on the way: these are examples to whose emulation the *West* must be forced. In a sense, Harich is a "crank."[84] He is a dissident because neither the GDR nor the other socialist states appreciate a recitation of political repression and economic short-rationing as *accomplishments*, when they deny that these are the reality. Nor do they welcome criticism that they have not gone far enough in a direction they deny.

We may leave Harich, for his dissent fails to contact at any point of importance the dissident agenda elsewhere in Eastern Europe. Not so with Havemann, long a dissenter (who died in April 1982 in his seventy-third year), and Bahro, industrial manager who emerged to notoriety and arrest simultaneously with the West German publication of *Die Alternative* in August 1977,[85] and was amnestied from prison into the FRG in 1979.

We leave Bahro for last, since he alone, among dissidents in East Germany or elsewhere, has elaborated a lengthy critique of "real existing socialism" in the GDR *and* a full-scale map of the socialism he prefers. Havemann is more modest, but still much at odds, in his view of what is wrong and right with one-party polity, planned economy, and other attributes of East European systems, with the dissident thought expressed elsewhere.

For Havemann, the basic criticism is similar in gross outline to that of the earlier Budapest school: societies have grown socialist in character; the political superstructure has failed to develop and is now a "brake." It must be altered, but its supersession requires, still, "the party," a Communist party, and its continued presidence over a planned, socialist economy. Socialism remains progressive, "despite all," because it has abolished capitalism and prevented a return to fascism.

Havemann is not a Harich; his commitment is to a democracy, as he understands it. "Socialism without democracy, without democratic control ... without a democratic decision process ... is unthinkable."[86] But his commitment to a specifically *socialist* end renders issues critical to some other dissidents less salient for him. Stalinism was tragedy, in human lives taken and in the distorted economy on which the "superstructure" grew—but he seems to see it as essentially *reactive* to external threats stretching from the revolution to 1950.[87] One can question—surely Poles and Czechs would—his view of the roots of contemporary Soviet problems and potential. "All the handicaps and anachronistic contradictions with which the revolution had to contend following its victory, and also all the external threats, are now a matter of the past. An indigenous emergence of Stalinism in the USSR would be no longer possible under the present economic conditions."[88] It follows, then, that reaching "democratic socialism in a modern highly industrialized state such as the USSR today means simply an adjustment of the superstructure to the base."[89]

Havemann is an East German, not a Soviet dissident, but surely his GDR is in his view a modern and highly industrialized state. The problems of *its* superstructure he attributes not only to reaction to Western threats, but to the dictatorship of the party apparatus which, "accountable to no democratic control, survives to this day."[90] Still, in the march of history, the GDR did get off on the right foot; it is "much further advanced on the road to the future, to socialism, than are the German Federal Republic and the other West European industrial states."[91] It needs to be pulled back to the right path.

We have only to take the long-overdue second step: the step towards democratisation through abolition of the party apparatus's uncontrolled power. For some time to come we will certainly need the Party and state apparatuses with all their inescapable weaknesses and contradictions. For the withering away of the state is a protracted process. But it can take place only if every form of arbitrary power is bridled and nipped in the bud by a broad democratic control. Under present conditions the state is not withering away.[92]

Then, *how* protracted a process? With what prospects of a withering, and what sort of structures economic, political, social, to follow? To the last, as a thinker, Havemann clung to a utopian end abandoned by many others, a utopia hardly likely to be explicable, much less attractive, to East Germans concerned with the here and now. Like many secular-left dissidents in other states in the 1960s, Havemann saw "socialist/Marxist" struggles against Western capitalism as a *part* of the struggle; unlike them, he retained this view, unmuted, till the end. In 1977, he welcomed the recent "mighty surge of revolutionary force" in the FRG, connecting it with Berkeley student protests, and the "great revolutionary strike movement in France in May, 1968, during which students and workers joined together in the fight and gave a deadly scare to the French bourgeoisie."[93] In style, aura, and substance, he was increasingly distant from the ideology of dissent emerging elsewhere in Eastern Europe.

Bahro dates his dissidence from the Soviet invasion of Czechoslovakia, from his realization that a party once a necessity is now a block to the further development of socialism. The years of clandestine study and writing which followed after 1968 produced *Die Alternative*, occasioning a great deal of enthusiastic reaction from left circles in the West.[94] Bahro's critique is similar to Havemann's; his "alternative" is laid out at length and in detail, involving a new party to replace the old, the discovery of the "real content of social progress" to allow the move to socialism,[95] an economy reorganized and integrated by "free associations of producers." Bahro introduced new terminology, with his "subalternity" characterizing the segmented, subordinate state of the individual in the system, his "surplus consciousness," which might otherwise turn to raising political questions channeled by the regime into the safer material path of "compensatory consumption."

Bahro stands against the vertical division of labor, for universal higher education—or a functional equivalent—and, *inter alia*, for less repressive sexual upbringing.[96] His strong Marxism and avowed anticapitalism, shared by Havemann, are not unique in the GDR context. His *strong* defense of a one-party system, and his repeated admissions of the attractiveness of the Western "model" to the GDR masses, without drawing any conclusions on his own views from this, are rather more unusual. In an interview just after arriving in the FRG, he stated:

> Really only class differences justify separate parties. What is reflected in a whole spectrum of political parties—these conflicts of interest which are of a less fundamental nature than class conflicts, and which naturally do exist in societies as complex as the East European— should find pluralistic expression within the one communist Party. ... The needs of social organisation necessitate a convergent ideological and information process which has to be pluralistic, but must also come to decisions ... this process has to be guided.[97]

The "alternative" is Bahro's—not that of any public. Willing to go to prison for his ideas, he shows little sympathy for the "bourgeois" strivings of his fellow citizens: "All that's not 'intelligentsia' in the old sense tends—as far as the mood of the masses is concerned—hopelessly toward the image of the Federal Republic."[98]

This rather dim view of the proclivities of the man in the street finds repetition as he reflects on the effects of the GDR's attempts to depoliticize its own citizens. "The result is that they quite *irrelevantly* consider the well-being offered by the other system [FRG] as the ultimate goal of the individual development of essential human powers," (emphasis added).[99] These Westward, bourgeois longings make Bahro cautious; destabilization of the GDR is dangerous, and rather than mass action he appears to favor a somewhat elitist kind of debate with the regime over confrontation. "We must not—and this is the gist of my argument—jeopardise the stability of the GDR as a state. There is a great risk that the GDR would collapse if we risked a political confrontation, since the spontaneous desires of the masses are for the bourgeois way of life."[100] Instead, he favors pursuing "ideological hegemony" in the *whole* camp—"the case has to be won in Moscow," as he concludes from the Czech experience.[101] The question, perhaps, is how to win that case, if his program is so far from the "spontaneous" desires of the masses, whose pressure, after all, has been the engine behind the sorts of compromises Solidarity extracted, at least for a time, in Poland.

Thus, a program of opposition, if it leans away from the left, is flawed for Bahro. While expressing sympathy and solidarity, he also makes a point of his reservations about the "rightward" trend elsewhere in East European dissent. In Charter 77, "the ideological counter-potential has shifted to the right."[102] This, because there are "fewer people now who believe in the possibility of a socialist renewal. That was the chief counter-revolutionary effect of the intervention."[103] (One might wonder, since he evidently endorsed the Czech experiment, whether he means this—for was not the major counterrevolutionary effect on the democraticized conditions of people's *existence*, rather than on their beliefs?)

Bahro, of course, has not been without critics. An anonymous "SED functionary" attacked his clinging "to the utopian elements of Marx's image of communism," his defense "quite incomprehensibly from a humanistic standpoint [of] the boundless sufferings and victims which Stalinism has inflicted upon the most tested communists and millions of non-Party members," and his forgetting that not historical necessity but "the undemocratic and subjectivist rule of the Bolshevik system has brought such a fate on those people."[104]

Even more telling is the critique of Jiri Pelikan, socialist émigré and veteran of the Prague Spring.

> The principal demands of the majority of the working people are concerned with the democratization and not communism. . . . He thinks, however, that the demand for democratization and civil rights is some sort of a detour, whereas at this stage the broad masses see just this demand as the most immediate and important in all of Eastern Europe.[105]

There is little, then, in GDR dissent of the thematics increasingly common in Poland, Czechoslovakia, and Hungary: of a critique of the *concept* of a singly ruling party, of an "opening to the right" to broaden the base of dissent, of a rediscovery of a Western *cultural* identity counterposed to the Soviet model, or of a move away from a belief in the adequacy of Marxism. Bahro is evidently right that "in the GDR Marxism is more deeply rooted. I don't think there is another country in the socialist camp where Marxism is so widespread."[106] If this is the case, the cost seems to be a brand of self-confident dogmatism, indeed even a linguistic barrier, that renders critique irrelevant to the mass and its concerns, and programs that promise little but a new brand of utopia in which the people, generally resistant to such notions, are unlikely to connive.

Bahro strikes a note not dissimilar to Michnik's when he argues that "we must accustom the apparatus to looking an open opposition in the face."[107] But it is unlikely many would join the staring contest in defense of Bahro's program as it stands, or that the brand of *Systemdenken* which still sees only a Marxist solution to the problems of the GDR, which would preempt others yet to be heard from in designing altogether different alternatives, which continues so to fear "spontaneity," will convince people to choose *this* ground on which to make their stand.

CONCLUSION

Drawing on what the data and discussion in chapter 10 suggested about the moderate, "centrist" political convictions of East European publics, the burden of the present chapter would suggest in turn that dissident intellectuals in Poland, Hungary, and Czechoslovakia had, by the dawn of the 1980s, come closer to those publics as they broadened the ideological/moral base of their systemic critiques.

It would be cheering, then, to record—from the vantage point of 1987—that the result was effective pressure in one or more of these states leading to a transformation of state-society relations, a pressure linking mass publics and dissenting intellectuals in thought and action. Such, of course, has not been the case. Czechoslovakia and Hungary continued along their disparate but well-worn paths, sharing mainly the growing economic distemper from which no part of Eastern Europe has escaped. In Poland, the rise of *Solidarnosc* in 1980–81 confounded many of the pessimists among analysts of East European affairs—who could have predicted it?[108] The heady experience of a workers' movement, exhibiting tremendous organizational ability, entering into a "consultative" relationship with intellectuals, and forcing the state to yield ground, even as it became the articulator of *national* hopes, was difficult to foresee, difficult to forget.[109] That Soviet pressure and the internal dynamic of an embattled Polish leadership led to the repression of martial law in December 1981 is not, in retrospect, surprising.[110] It simply reminds one that the state's autonomy—the opening theme of this book—is critical, that guns are an asset whose value is magnified in the absence of legitimacy.

The early mid-1980s have been a grim time in Eastern Europe. Economic problems everywhere, from the precarious relative affluence of the GDR and Hungary, through Czech stagnation, to Poland's depression and the disasters brought upon Romanian life by foreign debt and Ceausescu's policies, have necessarily occupied both leaders and masses. Yet the political issues and popular aspirations detailed here have not been totally displaced by economic hardship, nor will they necessarily disappear if economic problems are solved. Post-martial-law Poland surely presents the picture of a threadbare economy, a society grown "tired" under many pressures, but *not* a beaten society. If state-society "stalemate" is an appropriate designation, it is stalemate at a new level, where the complexity and multiplicity of independent information and communication channels has made it impossible for the regime confidently to assert the absurd or untrue. This is no small thing.

The spectacle of a *Soviet* leader pressing various reforms at home, and pressing them on the reluctant and long-serving leaderships in Eastern Europe, would also have been hard to anticipate. Yet as such does Gorbachev present himself, as such is he evidently perceived by many—but not all—elements of East European publics. His calls for *glasnost'* and democratization are one thing; economic policies which move toward a tighter tying of their economies to the USSR while speaking of "reform" are another. His fate and that of Eastern Europe may well be intertwined. Should the management of East-West relations, or his domestic program in the USSR, become pretexts for leadership politicking *against* him, it is hard to see that a Gorbachev successor would try to bring *perestroika* to Eastern Europe. Should he successfully set in train a process of organized, benign change in leadership and policy in Eastern Europe, he will find many allies—or at least pragmatic supporters—among publics and intelligentsia there. But he will also run the risk that the *limits* of the change he is ready to foster and tolerate will not be enough for long-deprived East Europeans, whose appetites may grow with the eating. Unrest on a large scale in Eastern Europe, should it come, would again probably spell Gorbachev's political end. The times seem hopeful, but also risky, as the 1980s near an end.

NOTES

1. State, Society, and the Soviet Model

1. Theda Skocpol, *States and Social Revolutions* (Cambridge: Cambridge University Press, 1979), p. 29.

2. *Ibid.*, p. 31.

3. Samuel Huntington, *Political Order in Changing Societies* (New Haven and London: Yale University Press, 1968), p. 335.

4. *Ibid.*, p. 336.

5. *Ibid.*, p. 337.

6. *Ibid.*, p. 338.

7. See, e.g., Roger E. Kanet, ed., *The Behavioral Revolution and Communist Studies: Applications of Behaviorally Oriented Political Research on the Soviet Union and Eastern Europe* (New York: Free Press, 1971); Frederic J. Fleron, Jr., ed., *Communist Studies and the Social Sciences: Essays on Methodology and Empirical Theory* (Chicago: Rand McNally, 1969).

8. Huntington, *Political Order*, p. 1.

9. Frank Parkin, *Marxism and Class Theory: A Bourgeois Critique* (New York: Columbia University Press, 1979), pp. 125ff.

10. Skocpol, *States and Social Revolutions*, p. 25.

11. Parkin, *Marxism and Class Theory*, pp. 126ff.

12. Andrew C. Janos, "The One-Party State and Social Mobilization: East Europe Between the Wars," in Samuel P. Huntington and Clement H. Moore, eds., *Authoritarian Politics in Modern Society* (New York: Basic Books, 1970), p. 205.

13. Carl J. Friedrich and Zbigniew K. Brzezinski, *Totalitarian Dictatorship and Autocracy* (Cambridge: Harvard University Press, 1956), pp. 9–10.

14. Seweryn Bialer, *Stalin's Successors: Leadership, Stability, and Change in the Soviet Union* (Cambridge: Cambridge University Press, 1980), pp. 14, 26.

15. Moshe Lewin, "The Social Background of Stalinism," in Robert C. Tucker, ed., *Stalinism: Essays in Historical Interpretation* (New York: Norton, 1977), pp. 134–135.

16. Skocpol, *States and Social Revolutions*, p. 232.

17. Raymond Aron, *Eighteen Lectures on Industrial Society* (London: Weidenfeld and Nicholson, 1967), p. 95.

18. T. H. Rigby, "Stalinism and the Mono-Organizational Society," in Tucker, ed., *Stalinism*, p. 64.

19. *Ibid.*, p. 75.

20. Stephen F. Cohen, "Bolshevism and Stalinism," in Tucker, ed., *Stalinism*, p. 13.

21. Tucker, "Stalinism as Revolution from Above," in Tucker, ed., *Stalinism*, pp. 90–92.

22. A. Inkeles and R. A. Bauer, *The Soviet Citizen: Daily Life in a Totalitarian Society* (Cambridge: Harvard University Press, 1961).

23. Examples of social history rich in detail include the works of Moshe Lewin, especially *Russian Peasants and Soviet Power* (Evanston, Ill.: Northwestern University Press, 1968), and *The Making of the Soviet System: Essays in the Social History of Interwar Russia* (New York: Pantheon Books, 1985), as well as those of Sheila Fitzpatrick. See her *Education and Social Mobility in the Soviet Union, 1921–1934* (Cambridge: Cambridge University Press, 1979); and, in her editorship, *Cultural Revolution in Russia, 1928–1931* (Bloomington: Indiana University Press, 1978). Other, and more controversial, works on the social and political history of Stalinism are noted in the "Discussion" cited in the following note.

24. An illuminating recent presentation of many of the issues is the "Discussion" led off by Sheila Fitzpatrick's "New Perspectives on Stalinism," with contributions by Stephen F. Cohen, Geoff Eley, Peter Kenez, and Alfred G. Meyer, all in *The Russian Review* (October 1986), 45(4):357–413.

25. See the contributions of Zbigniew K. Brzezinski, ed., *Dilemmas of Change in Soviet Politics* (New York: Columbia University Press, 1969).

26. Alexander Dallin, "The Domestic Sources of Soviet Foreign Policy," in Seweryn Bialer, ed., *The Domestic Context of Soviet Foreign Policy* (Boulder, Co.: Westview Press, 1981), p. 343.

27. George Konrad and Ivan Szelenyi, *The Intellectuals on the Road to Class Power* (New York: Harcourt Brace Jovanovich, 1979), p. 74.

28. *Ibid.*, p. 141.

29. Milovan Djilas, *The New Class: An Analysis of the Communist System* (New York: Praeger, 1957).

30. Konrad and Szelenyi, *The Intellectuals, passim.*

31. Parkin, *Marxism and Class Theory*, p. 137.

32. Stanislaw Ossowski, *Class Structure in the Social Consciousness* (New York: Free Press, 1963).

33. Robert A. Feldmesser, "Social Classes and Political Structure," in Cyril E. Black, ed., *The Transformation of Russian Society: Aspects of Social Change Since 1861* (Cambridge: Harvard University Press, 1960), pp. 235–252.

34. *Ibid.*, pp. 238–245.

35. See *ibid.*, p. 248.

36. Lewin, "The Social Background of Stalinism," pp. 119, 120.

37. Reinhard Bendix, *Nation-Building and Citizenship* (Garden City, N.Y.: Doubleday Anchor Books, 1969), p. 175.

38. *Ibid.*, p. 177.

39. *Ibid.*

40. Melvin Croan, "Is Mexico the Future of Eastern Europe? Institutional Adaptability and Political Change in Comparative Perspective," in Huntington and Moore, eds., *Authoritarian Politics*, pp. 463–464.

41. Huntington, *Political Order*, p. 47.

42. Skocpol, *States and Social Revolutions*, p. 32.

43. Anthony Giddens, *The Class Structure of the Advanced Societies* (New York: Harper and Row, 1975), p. 98.

44. Ralf Dahrendorf, *Class and Class Conflict in Industrial Society* (Stanford: Stanford University Press, 1961), p. 186.

45. See chapter 5 in the present work. For a different emphasis, see Alex Pravda, "Is There a Soviet Working Class?" *Problems of Communism* (November-December 1982), 21(6):1–24.

46. See Roman Laba, "Worker Roots of Solidarity," *Problems of Communism* (July-August 1986), 35(4):47–67.

47. Alex Inkeles, "Models and Issues in the Analysis of Soviet Society," *Survey*, July 1966, pp. 3–17; also in Alex Inkeles, *Social Change in Soviet Russia* (Cambridge: Harvard University Press, 1968), pp. 419–433.

48. T. H. Rigby, "Traditional, Market, and Organizational Societies and the USSR," *World Politics* (July 1964), 16(4):559–557.

49. Wlodzimierz Brus, "Stalinism and the 'People's Democracies,' " in Tucker, ed., *Stalinism*, p. 239.

50. *Ibid.*

51. Tucker, "Stalinism as Revolution from Above," in Tucker, ed., *Stalinism*, p. 98.

1. State, Society, and the Soviet Model

52. Zbigniew Brzezinski, "Soviet Politics: From the Future to the Past?" in Paul Cocks, Robert V. Daniels, and Nancy Whittier Heer, eds., *The Dynamics of Soviet Politics* (Cambridge: Harvard University Press, 1976), p. 339.

53. *Ibid.*, p. 340.

2. Soviet Dissent and Social Complexity

1. Much depends, of course, on the definition of modernity. This chapter does not attempt to resolve the question in any general way, but the material which follows does touch upon one criterion for judging modernity—i.e., the degree of structural differentiation in a society. Some would say yes. Others, who find the differentiated parts lacking the *autonomy* that is regarded as characteristic of modern Western societies, would be less ready to agree that the contemporary USSR is modern. This, certainly, is not the only, or even necessarily the most important, criterion of modernity, but it is one to which several of the authors cited herein attach considerable imortance.

2. See S. N. Eisenstadt, *Modernization: Protest and Change* (Englewood Cliffs, N.J.: Prentice-Hall, 1966), p. 37.

3. On prerevolutionary development, see Theodore H. von Laue, *Sergei Witte and the Industrialization of Russia* (New York: Columbia University Press, 1963); also the essays by von Laue and Alexander Gerschenkron in Cyril E. Black, ed., *The Transformation of Russian Society* (Cambridge: Harvard University Press, 1960).

4. On Russian and Soviet political culture, see Frederick C. Barghoorn, "Soviet Russia: Orthodoxy and Adaptiveness," in Lucien W. Pye and Sidney Verba, eds., *Political Culture and Political Development* (Princeton: Princeton University Press, 1965), pp. 450–511. Concerning cultural influences on "development" in Tsarist and Soviet Russia, see Reinhard Bendix, *Nation-Building and Citizenship* (Garden City, N.Y.: Doubleday Anchor Books, 1969), pp. 183ff.

5. Z. Brzezinski, "The Soviet Past and Future," *Encounter* (London), March 1970, p. 6.

6. See Leonard Binder, "National Integration and Political Development," *American Political Science Review* (September 1964), 58(3):625.

7. For example, to what extent is Hollander correct in arguing that Soviet bureaucracy "has developed primarily as a device of control and only secondly as an instrument for the management of modernization?" Was the rapid increase, after 1928, of state "penetration" into every area of life an outgrowth of a conscious commitment, inspired by Stalin's pathological suspicion and distrust, to maximize totalitarian control almost as an end in itself, or was it an incremental process of ad hoc responses by the regime to resistance to "developmental" objectives (e.g., the resistance to forced collectivization)? See Paul Hollander, "Politicized Bureaucracy: The Soviet Case," *Newsletter on Comparative Studies of Communism*, May 1971, p. 14.

8. See Carl J. Friedrich and Zbigniew K. Brzezinski, *Totalitarian Dictatorship and Autocracy* (Cambridge: Harvard University Press, 1st ed., 1956; 2d ed., 1965). See also Carl J. Friedrich, ed., *Totalitarianism* (Cambridge: Harvard University Press, 1954).

9. T. H. Rigby, "Traditional, Market, and Organizational Societies and the USSR," in Frederick J. Fleron, Jr., ed., *Communist Studies and the Social Sciences* (Chicago: Rand McNally, 1969), pp. 170–187.

10. Mark G. Field, "Soviet Society and Communist Party Controls: A Case of 'Constricted' Development," in Donald W. Treadgold, ed., *Soviet and Chinese Communism: Similarities and Differences* (Seattle: University of Washington Press, 1967), pp. 189–190 (emphasis added).

11. *Ibid.*, p. 190.

12. Frederick J. Fleron, Jr., "Toward a Reconceptualization of Political Change in the Soviet Union: The Political Leadership System," in Fleron, ed., *Communist Studies*, pp. 222–243.

13. *Ibid.*, p. 232.

14. B. Meissner, "Totalitarian Rule and Social Change," *Problems of Communism* (November-December 1966), 15(6):58. (See also note 17.)

15. The term is Bendix's: *Nation-Building and Citizenship*, p. 177. Eisenstadt makes a related point in discussing "mass-consensual" orientations as one of the characteristics of modern societies (*Modernization*, pp. 15–16): "This tendency to broad, mass consensuality does not, of course, find its fullest institutionalized expression in all different types of modern societies. In many regimes in the first stages of modernization it may be weak or intermittent, while totalitarian regimes of course tend to suppress its fullest expression. But even totalitarian regimes attempt to legitimize themselves in terms of such values, and it is impossible to understand their policies, their attempts to create symbols of mass consensus, without assuming the existence of such a consensual tendency among the major strata within them and its acknowledgement by the rulers."

16. Rigby, "Traditional, Market, and Organizational Societies," p. 179.

17. Brzezinski, "The Soviet Political System: Transformation or Degeneration?" *Problems of Communism* (January-February 1966), 15(1):1–15. This and the other contributions to the discussion, including Boris Meissner's article cited above (note 14), were subsequently published in book form as Zbigniew Brzezinski, ed., *Dilemmas of Change in Soviet Politics* (New York: Columbia University Press, 1969). Henceforth page references to Brzezinski's and other symposium articles cited will be to the book version.

18. Brzezinski, ed., *Dilemmas of Change*, pp. 13, 20.

19. *Ibid.*, p. 26.

20. R. Conquest, "Immobilism and Decay," in Brzezinski, ed., *Dilemmas of Change*, p. 72.

21. F. Barghoorn, "Changes in Russia: The Need for Perspectives," in Brzezinski, ed., *Dilemmas of Change*, p. 41.

22. Meyer makes this point eloquently in his essay "Political Change Through Civil Disobedience in the USSR and Eastern Europe," in J. Roland Pennock and John W. Chapman, eds., *Political and Legal Obligation: Nomos XII* (New York: Atherton Press, 1970), p. 423.

23. For a discussion, see Eisenstadt, *Modernization*, pp. 40, 149–150.

24. Conquest, "Immobilism and Decay," pp. 70–71.

25. Meissner, "Totalitarian Rule and Social Change," in Brzezinski, ed., *Dilemmas of Change*, p. 83.

26. This pamphlet is discussed and quoted in D. Pospielovsky, "Programs of the Democratic Opposition," *Radio Liberty Research Paper No. 38*, 1970. The quotation given here appears on p. 6 of this research paper.

27. *Ibid.*, p. 7–9.

28. Meissner, "Totalitarian Rule," pp. 77–78.

29. Brzezinski, ed., *Dilemmas of Change*, p. 10.

30. Barghoorn, "Soviet Russia: Orthodoxy and Adaptiveness," p. 465.

31. On the concept of "accessibility," see William Kornhauser, *The Politics of Mass Society* (New York: Free Press, 1959), p. 53.

32. E. Shils, "Further Observations on Mrs. Huxley," *Encounter*, October 1961, p. 45.

33. F. Castles, "Interest Articulation: A Totalitarian Paradox," *Survey* (London), Autumn 1969, p. 127.

34. The phrase is Field's (see note 10), p. 190.

35. Kornhauser's remarks (*Politics*, p. 136) are suggestive of problems the Soviet system, in a time of large-scale crisis, might face because of this small number of "mechanisms" (in most instances, recognized groups) through which interests can be articulated. "Multiple independent social groups support authority by sharing in it," he writes, "that is, by themselves acting as intermediate authorities capable of ordering limited spheres of social life. In the absence of effectively self-governing groups, the state not only lacks restraint; it also lacks support."

36. Pospielovsky, "Programs of the Democratic Opposition," p. 13.

37. *Ibid.*

38. English translation published in the *New York Times*, July 22, 1968.

39. Amalrik, *Will the USSR Survive Until 1984?* (New York: Harper and Row, 1970).

40. For commentary on *Veche* and "A Nation Speaks," see D. Pospielovsky, "The Samizdat Journal Veche: Russian Patriotic Thought Today," *Radio Liberty Research Paper No. 45*, 1971.

41. See Michael Scammell, "Soviet Intellectuals Soldier On," *Survey*, Winter 1971, p. 100.

42. See Jonathan Harris, "The Dilemma of Dissidence," *Survey*, Winter 1971, p. 121.

43. For an eloquent argument supporting the prospective stability and staying power of the Soviet polity and institutional structure, see Tibor Szamuely's

contribution to the symposium entitled "The USSR Since Khrushchev" in *Survey*, Summer 1969, pp. 51–69.

44. Jerry Hough's stimulating essay "The Soviet System: Petrification or Pluralism?" *Problems of Communism* (March-April 1972), 21(2):25–45, makes an eloquent case for the staying power of the system, but his conclusions are rooted in evidence of strong adaptive capacities within the system and currents of change that are *increasing* such capacities. While his essay raises more issues and treats more topics than can be dealt with here, it is well to note at least his remark that "on all but the most central questions, party policy is less and less incorporated into clear-cut, undebatable ideology, with a consequent widening of the areas open to public discussion." This is scarcely a characterization of an "immobile" system. Moreover, as Hough rightly notes, "immobilism" and "irrelevance," applied to the polity, are general and somewhat vague terms, resting on unprovable assumptions about what a society "requires" at a particular time. However, the regime's position on the "most central questions" (presumably political) is one of relative immobility, and it is just this category of questions that the dissidents address. The regime may indeed be adaptive in many areas, but it may thereby strengthen its ability to sustain immobility on those issues it considers most critical to its survival—the very issues on which the Sakharovs and Amalriks challenge it.

45. See Pospielovsky, "Programs of the Democratic Opposition," pp. 15–17.

46. See Robert A. Dahl, *Polyarchy: Participation and Opposition* (New Haven and London: Yale University Press, 1971), pp. 76–80.

47. Andrei Amalrik, "Will the USSR Survive Until 1984?" *Survey*, Autumn 1969, pp. 76–78.

48. Harris, "The Dilemmas of Dissidence," pp. 118–119.

49. See note 44.

50. Hollander, "Politicized Bureaucracy," p. 18.

3. Generations and Politics in the USSR

1. For a perceptive recent discussion of these factors and other aspects of the succession, see Grey Hodnett, "Succession Contingencies in the Soviet Union," *Problems of Communism* (March-April 1975), 24(2):1–21.

2. A characteristic Western (or American) response to such problems (and one that provides evidence of a significant difference between the Western and Soviet political cultures) is to organize a widely publicized conference, such as the one in Princeton, New Jersey, in December 1968, which produced *The Endless Crisis: A Confrontation on America in the Seventies*, edited by François Duchene (New York: Simon and Schuster, 1970).

3. "Generation" is, of course, an exceedingly slippery and imprecise term. People are born all the time, not at intervals convenient for grouping under such

terms. It is used here in a very loose sense, bearing in mind its deficiencies as well as its familiarity.

4. Lucien W. Pye, introduction, in Lucien W. Pye and Sidney Verba, eds., *Political Culture and Political Development* (Princeton: Princeton University Press, 1965), p. 8.

5. Robert Conquest, "A New Russia? A New World?" *Foreign Affairs*, April 1975, p. 483.

6. Roy Medvedev, in the revised English-language version of his treatise on socialist democracy, which came to hand after the bulk of this chapter was written, makes somewhat similar points about apoliticality ("The majority of the people and a large part of the intelligentsia are politically passive—indifference, or even a conscious rejection of politics, has become an ingrained habit, a form of self-protection"); about the purposes of political socialization as conceived by the "dogmatists" ("to assure us that the general development of the country is proceeding correctly, that basically it was always moving in the right direction"); and finally about the popular view of the government ("an assumption by the common people ... that those in charge are pursuing a correct policy, that the leadership is composed of people best qualified to interpret Marxism"). (Regarding this last, however, I would scarcely agree that the common people's assumptions about their leaders' adequacy in interpreting Marxism are a major component in the legitimacy the leadership is accorded.) See Roy A. Medvedev, *On Socialist Democracy* (New York: Knopf, 1975), pp. 172, 197, 298, respectively.

7. See Anthony Downs, *An Economic Theory of Democracy* (New York: Harper, 1957).

8. Solzhenitsyn, from "The Smatterers," in Alexander Solzhenitsyn et al., *From Under the Rubble* (Boston: Little, Brown, 1975), p. 272.

9. J. Mieroszewski, "The Political Thought of *Kultura*," in Leopold Tyrmand, ed., *Kultura Essays* (New York: Free Press, 1970), p. 309.

10. V. Chalidze, *To Defend These Rights: Human Rights in the Soviet Union*, Guy Daniels, tr. (New York: Random House, 1974), p. 149.

11. See Andrei Amalrik's remarks on this in "Will the USSR Survive Until 1984?" in *Survey*, Autumn 1969, pp. 54–55.

12. G. Almond and S. Verba, *The Civic Culture* (Princeton: Princeton University Press, 1963), p. 20.

13. It was evidently in the "participant" sense that the Czech writer Ludvik Vaculik understood the word "citizen" when he said (at the Czechoslovak Fourth Writers' Congress in June 1967): "I believe that there are no citizens in our country any more." Yet a year later the "reserves" of the Czechoslovak democratic tradition had reasserted themselves in the Prague Spring. There were citizens; they had emerged from hiding. However, the vastly different traditions and history of Soviet Russia would make the "responsiveness" of the masses there to democratic-participatory stimuli from a liberalizing regime a matter of some doubt. For a summary of Vaculik's address, see Barbara Wolfe Jancar,

Czechoslovakia and the Absolute Monopoly of Power (New York: Praeger, 1971), pp. 73–75.

14. Many Soviet dissidents have characterized the mass political "mind" in their country in terms suggesting that democratic procedures, if allowed, could not flourish. Nadezhda Mandelstam sees much of the population as "mentally ill" and observes that no one could be "normal" after fifty years of Soviet history: *Hope Abandoned* (New York: Atheneum, 1974), p. 479. Solzhenitsyn, in his *Letter to the Soviet Leaders* (New York: Harper and Row, 1974), p. 52, argues that over the last fifty years "Russia's preparedness for democracy, for a multiparty parliamentary system, could only have diminished."

15. Almond and Verba, *The Civic Culture*, p. 25. Frederick Barghoorn has characterized the Soviet political culture as "subject-participant" culture; see his *Politics in the USSR*, 2d ed. (Boston: Little, Brown, 1972), pp. 20ff, and his essay "Soviet Russia: Orthodoxy and Adaptiveness," in Pye and Verba, eds., *Political Culture*, pp. 450–511.

16. See Alex Inkeles and Raymond A. Bauer, *The Soviet Citizen* (Cambridge: Harvard University Press, 1961).

17. Chalidze, *To Defend These Rights*, p. 19.

18. Paul Hollander deals perceptively with the moderation of mass expectations in *Soviet and American Society: A Comparison* (New York: Oxford University Press, 1973), pp. 388ff.

19. Amalrik, "Will the USSR Survive Until 1984?" p. 61.

20. For a discussion of such "secularization" in a related context, see my "From 'Utopia' to the 'Pragmatic' Society: Social Consequences of Economic Reform in Eastern Europe," *Revue d'Etudes Comparatives Est-Ouest*, March 1975, pp. 107–41 (paper originally presented at the International Slavic Conference in Banff, Canada, September 1974).

21. See Rudolf L. Tökes, "Dissent: The Politics for Change in the USSR," in Henry W. Morton and Rudolf L. Tökes, eds., *Soviet Politics and Society in the 1970s* (New York: Free Press, 1974), p. 8.

22. These are Tökes' terms; *ibid.*

23. Barghoorn (*Politics in the USSR*, pp. 60–61) sees such potential dissident elite-mass linkage as a matter of concern, albeit remote, for the regime. And indeed, such unorthodox tactics as stuffing Moscow mailboxes with *samizdat* appeals to "workers" to consider their distinctly underprivileged economic situation may be conducive to Politburo nightmares. But as Chalidze (*To Defend These Rights*, p. 170) indicates, people have learned their lesson well and are as likely as not to turn over such unauthorized material to the KGB.

24. Despite the "tightening of the screws" on dissidents over the past two years, the outflow of *samizdat* has apparently not abated, nor has the earlier suppression of the "Chronicle of Current Events" proved permanent. See Albert Boiter, "Samizdat Review: Summer 1974," *Radio Liberty Dispatch* 342/74, October 25, 1974; and "Samizdat Review for Autumn 1974," 44/75, January 30, 1975.

25. This was the general thrust of many of the pieces on the Soviet future published in this journal from 1966 through 1968 and collected in Zbigniew Brzezinski, ed., *Dilemmas of Change in Soviet Politics* (New York: Columbia University Press, 1969).

26. The writings of Jerry Hough, especially, point up the adaptiveness and stability of the system. See "The Soviet System: Petrification or Pluralism?" *Problems of Communism* (March-April 1972), 21(2):24–25; and *The Soviet Prefects: The Local Party Organs in Industrial Decision-Making* (Cambridge: Harvard University Press, 1969).

27. See Terry McNeill, "Some Reflections on the Soviet Political Leadership," *Radio Liberty Dispatch* 299/74, September 20, 1974, p. 17.

4. Workers, Politics, and Class Consciousness

1. Even one used to plumbing the depths of Soviet writings for the occasional nugget of information on "unofficial" attitudes and convictions will find a search through Soviet social science literature barren in results when the quest is for anything about working-class political perceptions. There are, surely, promising titles: M. T. Iovchuk and L. N. Kogan, *Dukhovnyi mir sovetskogo rabochego: opyt konkretno-sotsiologicheskogo issledovaniia* (Moscow: "Mysl'," 1972); R. A. Safarov, *Obshchestvennoe mnenie i gosudarstvennoe upravlenie* (Moscow: Iuridicheskaia Literatura, 1975); L. A. Gordon and E. V. Klopov, *Chelovek posle raboty* (Moscow: "Nauka," 1972). However, they deliver little of interest, as do most of the works of "public opinion research" from the mid- and late 1960s, some of which are discussed and summarized in W. D. Connor and Z. Gitelman, *Public Opinion in European Socialist Systems* (New York: Praeger, 1977), pp. 104–131.

2. See an interesting report which indicates the problems of investigators in defining social strata: I. I. Kravchenko and E. T. Fadeev, "Problemy izmeneniia sotsial'noi struktury sovetskogo obshchestva," *Voprosy filosofii* (1972), no. 6, pp. 137–147.

3. See R. Feldmesser, "Social Classes and Political Structure," in C. E. Black, ed., *The Transformation of Russian Society* (Cambridge: Harvard University Press, 1960), p. 239.

4. J. G. Gliksman, "The Russian Urban Worker: From Serf to Proletarian," in Black, ed., *The Transformation of Russian Society*, p. 313.

5. *Ibid.*, pp. 314–315; Gliksman notes that ca. 1900, "between one-third and two-thirds" of industrial workers were hereditary proletarians—an estimate which gives some notion of the limits on knowledge of the growth of the early working class.

6. As Z. Bauman wrote of Poland at a later date, in a work as applicable to the Soviet 1930s, "A relatively meagre group of pre-war industrial workers . . . were dissolved in a vast mass of peasant migrants, to whom the living standards

they met meant a genuine improvement in the standards they had known."
"Social Dissent in the East European Political System," *European Journal of
Sociology* (1971), 12(1):38.

7. V. Andrle, *Managerial Power in the Soviet Union* (Lexington, Mass.:
Saxon House/Lexington Books, 1976), p. 118.

8. Feldmesser, "Social Classes," p. 248.

9. The Harvard Project sample of emigres, reflecting the experience of the
1920s and 1930s, focuses, as the researchers involved acknowledge, on the ex-
ceptionally successful group whose mobility was atypically high. A. Inkeles and
R. A. Bauer, *The Soviet Citizen: Daily Life in a Totalitarian Soviety* (Cambridge:
Harvard University Press, 1961), p. 82.

10. R. A. Feldmesser, "Aspects of Social Mobility in the Soviet Union," Ph.D.
dissertation, Harvard University, 1955.

11. S. Ossowski, *Class Structure in the Social Consciousness* (New York:
Free Press, 1963), pp. 110–118.

12. Inkeles and Bauer, *The Soviet Citizen*, p. 242.

13. *Ibid.*, p. 254.

14. This argument is drawn from the whole of ch. 10, *ibid.*, pp. 233–254.

15. *Ibid.*, p. 234, table 57.

16. *Ibid.*, p. 245.

17. *Sotsialisticheskaia industriia*, October 16, 1971, p. 2, as cited in Andrle,
Managerial Power, p. 79.

18. *Ekonomicheskaia gazeta* (1968), no. 20, pp. 38–39, and *Sotsialisticheskaia industriia*, July 20, 1972, p. 3, as cited in Andrle, *Managerial Power*, p. 79.

19. Andrle, *Managerial Power*, p. 77, and sources cited therein.

20. Perceptions of the possibility of such negative mass reactions, readily
exploitable by the Soviet regime, have prompted some to point to dangers in a
U.S. policy toward the USSR which stresses human rights and might give the
appearance that a potentially "liberalizing" successor regime to Brezhnev and
Kosygin was submitting to foreign pressure.

21. Inkeles and Bauer, *The Soviet Citizen*.

22. R. Tökes makes roughly this argument in "Dissent: The Politics for
Change in the USSR," in H. W. Morton and R. L. Tökes, eds., *Soviet Politics
and Society in the 1970s* (New York: Free Press, 1974), p. 8.

23. H. Smith, *The Russians* (New York: Quadrangle Books/NYT, 1976),
pp. 241–272; also R. G. Kaiser, *Russia: The People and the Power* (New York:
Atheneum, 1976).

24. See Dicks' "Observations on Contemporary Russian Behavior," *Human
Relations* (1952), 5:111–176, reprinted in condensed form as "Some Notes on
the Russian National Character," in Black, ed., *The Transformation of Russian
Society*, pp. 636–652.

25. Although such research is still in rather preliminary stages, some early
results are striking, both in manifesting continuities between attitudes of the
Harvard Project "generation" and those of the post-1970 wave and in showing

the difficulties of adjustment to the unfamiliar and "anarchic" aspects of Western life. Such attitudes are observable among émigrés of Jewish origin who were already alienated from much of Soviet life, and whose education, generally at least complete secondary, and job status, predominantly white collar, are above the Soviet average. A fortiori, it seems plausible to argue that Soviet workers who remain in the USSR should manifest these attitudes in greater intensity. See Z. Gitelman, "Soviet Political Culture: Insights from Jewish Emigrés," Soviet Studies (October 1977), 29(4):543–564.

26. In The Russians, Smith calls it a "nostalgia for a strong boss."

27. Trotsky, viewing the social trends of the USSR 1930s, made somewhat similar points with respect to "conservatism." See The Revolution Betrayed (New York: Merit, 1965), especially pp. 144–185.

28. J. Revel, Without Marx or Jesus: The New American Revolution Has Begun (Garden City, N.Y.: Doubleday, 1971).

29. W. D. Connor, "Generations and Politics in the USSR," Problems of Communism (September-October 1975), 24(5):20–31.

30. What the dissident "subcultures" share is a politicization, which, of whatever nature, distinguishes them from the mass political culture. One finds a wide variation, from the liberal democracy espoused by Sakharov and some others, to the "reformist Leninism" of Medvedev, to various forms of Russian "nationalist-centralist" orientation—as well as some advocates of Stalinism itself. Whatever the differing potential of different currents of dissident ideology for attracting "mass" support, today the masses, including the workers, know little of and care little about either Sakharov-style liberals or Stalinist dissidents such as the former "Fetisov group."

31. A. Amalrik, Will the USSR Survive Until 1984? (New York: Harper and Row, 1970).

32. See M. Matthews, Class and Society in Soviet Russia (New York: Walker, 1972), p. 282, for some general comments along this line.

33. See W. Wesolowski, "Social Stratification in Socialist Society (Some Theoretical Problems)," Polish Sociological Bulletin (1967), no. 1.

34. See, e.g., P. Wiles, "Recent Data on Soviet Income Distribution," Survey (London) (Summer 1975), 21(2):28–41.

35. See, e.g., M. N. Rutkevich and F. R. Filippov, Sotsial'nye peremeshcheniia (Moscow: "Mysl'," 1970), p. 144.

36. Smith, The Russians, pp. 260–264; "An Observer" (George Feifer), Message from Moscow (New York: Knopf, 1969), p. 109.

37. See W. D. Connor, Socialism, Politics, and Equality (New York: Columbia University Press, 1979), especially ch. 8.

38. L. A. Andreeva and G. A. Levitskii, "Obstoiatel'stva, sposobstvuiushchie khishcheniiam (Opyt vyiavleniia obshchestvennogo mneniia)," Sovetskoe gosudarstvo i pravo (1969), no. 11, p. 105.

39. E. O. Smigel, "Public Attitudes Toward Stealing as Related to the Size

of the Victim Organization," *American Sociological Review* (June 1956), 21(3):320–327.

40. O. Ulc, *Judge in a Communist State* (Athens: Ohio University Press, 1972).

41. D. Matza, *Delinquency and Drift* (New York: Wiley, 1964), especially pp. 69–151; and G. Sykes and D. Matza, "Techniques of Neutralization: A Theory of Delinquency," *American Sociological Review* (December 1957), 22(6):664–670.

42. A. Etzioni, *The Active Society* (New York: Free Press, 1968), pp. 328–329.

43. *Ibid.*

44. V. Chalidze notes one 1966 example. See his *To Defend These Rights: Human Rights in the Soviet Union* (New York: Random House, 1974), p. 170.

45. The research of A. McAuley demonstrates this. See his *Economic Welfare in the Soviet Union* (Madison: University of Wisconsin Press, 1979).

46. G. Grossman, "An Economy at Middle Age," *Problems of Communism* (March-April 1976), 25(2):18–33; also M. Feshbach and S. Rapawy, "Soviet Population and Manpower Trends and Policies," in Joint Economic Committee, U.S. Congress, *Soviet Economy in a New Perspective* (Washington, D.C.: GPO, 1976), pp. 113–154.

47. P. Hollander, *Soviet and American Society: A Comparison* (New York: Oxford University Press, 1973), p. 388. Much of Hollander's analysis of Soviet mass aspirations and political consciousness (pp. 388–399) is similar to mine.

48. C. Jencks et al., *Inequality: A Reassessment of the Effect of Family and Schooling in America* (New York: Basic Books, 1972), pp. 232, 264–265.

5. Changing Times and the Soviet Worker

1. G. Bliakhman, "Sotsial'nyi portret sovremennogo molodogo rabochego," *Sotsialisticheskii trud* (1979), no. 10, pp. 62–69.

2. *Ibid.*, p. 63.

3. See J. D. Barber, "The Composition of the Soviet Working Class, 1928–1941," University of Birmingham, Soviet Industrialization Project Series (1978), no. 16 (mimeo).

4. AN SSSR, IMRD, *Sotsial'noe razvitie rabochego klassa SSSR* (Moscow: "Nauka," 1977), pp. 22–23.

5. E.g., the Mari ASSR. See S. P. Zakharova, "Ob osnovnykh istochnikakh i formakh popolneniia rabochikh kadrov promyshlennosti Mariiskoi ASSR v gody chetvertoi i piatoi piatiletok," in Ivanovskii Gosudarstvennyi Pedagogicheskii Institut (*Uchenye zapiski*, vol. 71), *Iz istorii rabochego klassa SSSR* (Ivanovo, 1970), pp. 125–130.

6. See AN SSSR, Institut filosofii, *Rabochii klass SSSR i ego vedushchaia rol' v stroitel'stve kommunizma* (Moscow: "Nauka," 1975), pp. 101–102.

7. T. A. Babushkina, V. S. Dunin, and E. A. Zenkevich, "Sotsial'nye problemy formirovaniia novykh popolnenii rabochego klassa," *Rabochii klass i sovremennyi mir* (1981), no. 3, p. 44.

8. *Ibid.* Indeed, for our own purposes, it is worth noting that rising levels of rural education over these years meant that an (eighth- or tenth-grade) school "leaver," rather than one with less education, became more typical of the countryside, and that the peasantry has always provided a larger number/share of armed service personnel, whose discharge has been the occasion for them to go to the city and join the workers in industry or, often, in construction. Thus, the earlier figures on "rural/farm" contribution might be construed as reflecting a heavy *intra*generational mobility of persons already working in agriculture, the latter reflecting more the *inter*generational movement of younger people.

9. M. P. Kim, "O nekotorykh osobennostiakh sovremennogo razvitiia rabochego klassa SSSR," in AON pri TsK KPSS, *Sovetskii rabochii klass na sovremennon etape* (Moscow: "Mysl'," 1964), pp. 6–7.

10. M. N. Rutkevich and F. R. Filippov, *Sotsial'nye peremeshcheniia* (Moscow: "Mysl'," 1970), p. 79.

11. F. R. Filippov, "Sotsial'nye peremeshcheniia v sovetskom obshchestve," *Sotsiologicheskie issledovaniia* (1975), no. 4, p. 16.

12. A. A. Khaliulina, "Istochniki i formy popolneniia rabochikh kadrov v tiazheloi promyshlennosti kuzbassa," in AN SSSR, Sibirskoe otdelenie, *Chislennost' i sostav rabochikh Sibirii v usloviiakh razvitogo sotsializma 1959–1975* (Novosibirsk: "Nauka," 1977), p. 113.

13. L. A. Gordon and E. V. Klopov, *Sotsial'noe razvitie rabochego klassa* (Moscow: "Nauka," 1974), p. 12.

14. AN SSSR, IMRD, *Sotsial'noe razvitie rabochego klassa SSSR* (Moscow: "Nauka," 1977), pp. 26–27.

15. N. A. Aitov, *Sovetskii rabochii* (Moscow: Izdatel'stvo politicheskoi literatury, 1981), p. 25.

16. O. I. Shkaratan et al., "Peremeny v sotsial'nom oblike rabochikh v epokhu razvitogo sotsializma," *Voprosy istorii* (1978), no. 5, pp. 11ff.

17. Alex Inkeles and Raymond A. Bauer, *The Soviet Citizen: Daily Life in a Totalitarian Society* (Cambridge: Harvard University Press, 1961).

18. Barber, "The Composition of the Soviet Working Class."

19. *Ibid.*, p. 15.

20. N. B. Lebedeva and R. Ia. Khabibulina, *Sovetskii rabochii klass: Traditsii i preemstvennost' pokolenii* (Moscow: "Mysl'," 1972), p. 74.

21. E. V. Somova, "Ob istochnikakh popolneniia rabochego klassa i inzhenernotekhnicheskoi intelligentsii," in *Protsessy izmeneniia sotsial'not struktury v sovetskom obshchestve* (Sverdlovsk, 1967), p. 112.

22. There is, of course, a large literature on class-based inequalities in access to higher education in the USSR, which contains much evidence of the processes

which, *inter alia,* contribute to the "retention" of working-class youth *in* that class. See especially Richard B. Dobson, "Education and Opportunity," in Jerry G. Pankhurst and Michael Paul Sacks, eds., *Contemporary Soviet Society* (New York: Praeger, 1980), pp. 115–137, and sources cited therein.

23. N. Panteleev, "Razvitie ekonomiki i podgotovka molodezhi k trudu," *Sotsialisticheskii trud,* no. 9, p. 31.

24. Babushkina, Dunin, and Zenkevich, "Sotsial'nye problemy," p. 46.

25. E. V. Foteeva, *Kachestvennye kharakteristiki naseleniia SSSR* (Moscow: "Finansy i statistika," 1984), pp. 93–94.

26. G. P. Kozlova and Z. I. Fainburg, "Rabochii klass i obrazovanie," *Rabochii klass i sovremennyi mir* (1982), no. 4, p. 29.

27. T. V. Riabushkin, "Pokazateli sotsial'nogo razvitiia rabochego klassa," *Sotsiologicheskie issledovaniia* (1980), no. 4, p. 21.

28. N. A. Aitov and S. F. Eliseev, "NTR i izmeneniia v sotsial'noi strukture rabochego klassa v razvitom sotsialisticheskom obshchestve," *Rabochii klass i sovremennyi mir* (1985), no. 1, p. 136.

29. A. I. Rybakov and A. I. Siniuk, "Vozrastnye razlichiia v tekuchesti rabochikh kadrov," *Sotsiologicheskie issledovaniia* (1983), no. 4, pp. 106–107.

30. Iu. P. Sosin, "Faktory ukrepleniia trudovoi distsipliny," *EKO* (1975), no. 5, translated in *Current Digest of the Soviet Press* (hereafter *CDSP*), February 18, 1976, pp. 8–9.

31. Riabuskhin, "Pokazateli," p. 23.

32. L. Ponomarev, "Shkola—trudovoe vospitanie—vysokaia effektivnost' proizvodstva," *Sotsialisticheskii trud* (1978), no. 1, pp. 30–31.

33. Babushkina, Dunin, and Zenkevich, "Sotsial'nye problemy," p. 47.

34. *Ibid.,* p. 44.

35. Foteeva, *Kachestvennye,* p. 94.

36. *Pravda,* June 28, 1983; *CDSP,* July 27, 1983, p. 25.

37. A. E. Kotliar and M. I. Talalai, "Kak zakrepit' molodye kadry," *EKO* (1977), no. 4, pp. 26–43; *CDSP,* September 21, 1977, pp. 1–3.

38. *Izvestiia,* January 29, 1977, p. 5; *CDSP,* February 23, 1977, p. 31.

39. Iu. Averichev, "Proforientatsiia molodezhi i prestizh rabochei professii," *Sotsialisticheskii trud* (1977), no. 6, pp. 130–132.

40. E. V. Belkin, "Professional'no-tekhnicheskoe obrazovanie v zhizhennykh planakh molodezhi," *Sotsiologicheskie issledovaniia* (1981), no. 2, p. 106; see also L. Kostin, "Upravlenie trudovymi resursami strany," *Planovoe khoziaistvo* (1978), no. 12, pp. 16–27.

41. I. E. Zaslavskii, V. A. Kuz'min, and R. T. Ostrovskaia, "Sotsial'nye i professional'nye ustanovki moskovskikh shkol'nikov," *Sotsiologicheskie issledovaniia* (1983), no. 3, p. 132.

42. *Sovetskaia Rossiia,* September 21, 1983, p. 3; *CDSP,* November 2, 1983, pp. 1–4.

43. *O reforme obshcheobrazovatel'noi i professional'noi shkoly, sbornik dokumentov i materialov* (Moscow: Politizdat, 1984), p. 42.

44. Felicity O'Dell, "Vocational Education in the USSR," in J. J. Tomiak, ed., *Soviet Education in the 1980s* (London and New York: Croom Helm/St. Martin's Press, 1983), pp. 127–128.

45. George Avis, "Access to Higher Education in the Soviet Union," in Tomiak, ed., *Soviet Education*, p. 203.

46. See O'Dell, "Vocational Education in the USSR."

47. Avis, "Access to Higher Education," p. 207.

48. *Literaturnaia gazeta*, March 7, 1984, p. 10; *CDSP*, May 2, 1984, pp. 13–15.

49. *EKO* (1977), no. 3, pp. 85–95; *CDSP*, August 3, 1977, pp. 8–9.

50. *Izvestiia*, January 27, 1984, p. 3; *CDSP*, February 15, 1984, p. 8.

51. N. Novoselov, "Schools for a Totalitarian-Technocratic Utopia," *Radio Liberty Research* (hereafter *RL*) 115/84, March 13, 1984, p. 2.

52. *Ibid.*, p. 2, n. 2; and see sources cited therein.

53. V. N. Turchenko, "Vazhneishaia sostavliaiushchaia prozvoditel'nykh sil," *EKO* (1983), no. 12, p. 80.

54. I. Bolotin and V. Chizhov, "Trudovye resursy i sistema narodnogo obrazovaniia," *Planovoe khoziaistvo* (1982), no. 8, pp. 103–104.

55. *Pravda* and *Izvestiia*, January 4, 1984; *CDSP*, February 1, 1984, pp. 1–9.

56. V. D. Voinova and V. S. Korobeinikov, "Obshchestvennoe mnenie o reforme shkoly—edinstvo i mnogoobrazie," *Sotsiologicheskie issledovaniia* (1984), no. 4, p. 99.

57. See O'Dell, "Vocational Education in the USSR," and Avis, "Access to Higher Education."

58. *Izvestiia*, January 7, 1984, p. 2; *CDSP*, February 15, 1984, p. 7.

59. *Izvestiia*, January 27, 1984, p. 3; *CDSP*, February 15, 1984, p. 7.

60. Voinova and Korobeinikov, "Obshchestvennoe," p. 100.

61. D. I. Ziuzin, "Orientatsiia shkolnikov na razlichnye formy srednego obrazovaniia," *Sotsiologicheskie issledovaniia* (1977), no. 1, p. 87.

62. *Ibid.*, p. 99.

63. Basic figures for academic school ninth grade, SPTU, and PTU adapted from O'Dell, "Vocational Education in the USSR"; the shares of entrants from eighth and tenth grades were derived from a combination of F. R. Filippov, *Sotsiologiia obrazovaniia* (Moscow: "Nauka," 1980), translated in *Soviet Education* (October 1984), 26(12):5, 50–62, and I. Bolotin and V. Chizhov, "Trudovye resursy," pp. 101–104.

64. B. A. Efimov, "Obrazovanie i sotsial'no-professional'noe podvizhenie molodykh rabochikh," *Sotsiologicheskie issledovannia* (1977), no. 3, p. 50.

65. V. G. Aseev, L. A. Gorchakov, and N. E. Kogan, "Kakim ty pridesh v rabochii klass?" in E. K. Vasil'eva et al., *Sovetskaia molodezh: Demograficheskii aspekt* (Moscow: "Finansy i statistika," 1981), pp. 62–63.

66. E. V. Foteeva, *Kachestvennye*, p. 148.

67. *Ibid.*, p. 145, citing B. E. Levanov, "Semeinoe vospitanie: sostoianie i problemy," *Sotsiologicheskie issledovaniia* (1979), no. 1, p. 118.

68. See the interview with A. P. Dumachev, chairman of the USSR State Committee on Vocational-Technical Education in *Pravda,* September 22, 1987, p. 3, and earlier comments by his Russian Republic counterpart, V. Kaznacheev, *Pravda,* September 12, 1987, p. 2.

69. Seymour Martin Lipset, "Whatever Happened to the Proletariat? An Historic Mission Unfulfilled," *Encounter,* June 1981, pp. 18–34.

70. Werner Sombart, *Why Is There No Socialism in the United States?* (New York: Pantheon, 1979).

71. This does not overlook the skill or economic diversity within the working class, but simply makes the point that in terms of (often overlooked) *origin,* it is more of a class than in the past. For a view of diversity, see Alex Pravda, "Is There a Soviet Working Class?" *Problems of Communism* (November-December 1982), 31(6):1–24.

72. On the possibility of *"khozraschet* medicine" and its implications, see David Dyker, "The Complex Program for Consumer Goods Production," *RL* 351/85, October 25, 1985, pp. 4–5.

73. This, it seems to me, remains true as well under a quite different "reading" of the relevant attributes of the contemporary working class, suggested to me by several colleagues: that the main trend, rather than a hardening into a conscious "class," is toward a *lumpenization* of the workers, a process marked by alcohol abuse, health problems, increasing corruption, indiscipline, etc. From this viewpoint the "new" working class, while lacking *political* potential, represents a large population segment capable, under pressure, of creating massive economic and social problems in an *un*organized reaction to unaccustomed pressure from above.

6. Social Policy in the Gorbachev Era

1. *Pravda* and *Izvestiia,* October 9, 1985, translated in *Current Digest of the Soviet Press* (hereafter *CDSP*), November 6, 1985, pp. 13–30.

2. *Ibid.*

3. See, e.g., Gorbachev's speech to a June 11, 1985, Central Committee meeting on accelerating scientific and technological progress, reported in *Pravda,* June 12, 1985, p. 1.

4. See the discussion of Keith Bush, "Ryzhkov's Speech to the Twenty-seventh Party Congress: A Tone of Sobriety," *Radio Liberty Research* (hereafter *RL*) 109/86, March 3, 1986, p. 2.

5. See Keith Bush, "Gorbachev's Speech at the Plenum: The Economic Backdrop," *RL* 39/87, January 28, 1987, p. 2.

6. See Philip Hanson, "The Plan Fulfillment Report for 1986: A Sideways Look at the Statistics," *RL* 76/87, February 26, 1987.

7. For a summary, see Vladimir Kusin, "A Note on Soviet Economic Performance in 1986," *RL* 127/87, March 27, 1987.

8. *Ekonomicheskaia gazeta* (May 1987), no. 22, pp. 2–5.

9. See *Pravda*, July 2, 1986, pp. 1–2.

10. See, e.g., Gorbachev's remarks in *Pravda*, November 16, 1986, p. 1.

11. *Sotsialisticheskaia industriia*, March 10, 1987, p. 1.

12. TASS English Service, March 5, 1987, 1712 GMT, in *Foreign Broadcast Information Service—Soviet Union* (hereafter *FBIS*), March 13, 1987, p. S-1.

13. *RL* 168/87, May 1, 1987, p. 13, citing Reuters, April 30, 1987.

14. *Trud*, June 9, 1987, pp. 1–2.

15. As Prime Minister Ryzhkov noted in his speech at the Twenty-seventh Party Congress in 1982 (the second year of the eleventh Five-Year Plan), "The increase in the population's real income virtually stopped." *Pravda* and *Izvestiia*, March 1, 1986, p. 2; *CDSP*, April 23, 1986, pp. 2–3.

16. See U.N. Economic and Social Council Economic Commission for Europe, "Perspectives on the ECE Regions: Centrally Planned Economies in the Period up to the Year 2000," November 19, 1985 (for presentation at the February 17–21, 1986, meeting of Senior Economic Advisers to ECE Governments), mimeo, p. 26.

17. See note 15.

18. Bogomolov, "Perspectives . . . ," p. 15 (emphasis added).

19. For a recent discussion, see David E. Powell, "The Soviet Alcohol Problem and Gorbachev's 'Solution,'" *Washington Quarterly*, Fall 1985, pp. 5–15.

20. *Pravda* and *Izvestiia*, April 5, 1985, p. 1.

21. *Pravda* and *Izvestiia*, May 17, 1985, p. 1.

22. *Pravda*, January 26, 1985.

23. See the discussion of the 1985 performance in Keith Bush, "Soviet Plan Fulfillment in 1985," *RL* 47/86, January 27, 1986.

24. For an assessment, see Vladimir Treml, "Gorbachev's Antidrinking Campaign: A Noble Experiment or a Costly Exercise in Futility?" *RL* supplement, 2/87, March 18, 1987, especially pp. 13–20.

25. The best recent treatment of this discussion is found in Murray Yanowitch, *Work in the Soviet Union: Attitudes and Issues* (Armonk, N.Y.: M.E. Sharpe, 1985).

26. *Pravda* and *Izvestiia*, November 23, 1985, pp. 1–2.

27. As reported by the chairman of the new State Agro-Industrial Committee, Vsevolod Murakhovskii, in *Literaturnaia gazeta*, January 22, 1986. However, the same source reported that as of late February (about three months after the redundancies were announced), "virtually all" of the 3,200 released had new jobs. See *Sel'skaia zhizn'*, February 21, 1986.

28. In *Sovetskaia kul'tura*, January 4, 1986; *CDSP*, February 19, 1986, pp. 1–4.

29. *Ibid.*

30. *TASS* interview, January 16, 1986; *RL* 35/86, January 17, 1986, p. 11.

31. *Sovetskaia kul'tura,* February 1, 1986, p. 3; *CDSP,* February 19, 1986, pp. 4–5, 23.

32. See Peter Hauslohner, "Gorbachev's Social Contract," *Soviet Economy* (1987), 3(1):67.

33. In *Neue AZ* (Vienna), June 6, pp. 4–5; *FBIS,* June 15, 1987, pp. S-54–56.

34. *New York Times,* July 4, 1987, pp. 1–2.

35. Whether such a pattern will be reversed is another question. The inertial drive away from the peak inequalities of the Stalin era is, after all, a matter of nearly three decades of policy and "drift"—a long time. At the Congress, Ryzhkov even noted that "elements of wage-levelling...have intensified recently." *Pravda* and *Izvestiia,* March 4, 1986; *CDSP,* April 23, 1986.

36. Bogomolov, "Perspectives," p. 83.

37. Hauslohner, "Gorbachev's Social Contract," p. 83.

38. *Ibid.,* p. 71.

39. *Nepszabadsag,* January 24, 1987, p. 5; *FBIS,* February 6, 1987, pp. S1–S6.

40. *Izvestiia,* November 1, 1986, p. 1.

41. TASS Russian Service, November 26, 1986, 1230 GMT; *FBIS,* November 28, 1986, p. R-8.

42. *Pravda,* February 17, 1987, pp. 3, 6.

43. *Ibid.*

44. Gorbachev told workers that management's pay would be put on this basis; see Moscow Television, July 26, 1986, 1430 GMT; *FBIS,* July 28, 1986, pp. R-1–10.

45. *Izvestiia,* April 26, 1985, p. 2.

46. TASS English Service, March 4, 1987, 1210 GMT; *FBIS,* March 11, 1987, pp. 5, 13.

47. Uncharacteristically, reported in the Soviet press (*Izvestiia,* December 4, 1986). For a commentary, see Elizabeth Teague, " 'Stormy Protests' at Soviet Truck Plant," *RL* 461/86, December 4, 1986.

48. *Trud,* June 9, 1987, pp. 1–2.

49. See note 44.

50. *Izvestiia,* April 18, 1986, p. 2.

51. See *RL* 295/86, August 4, 1986, citing *Ekonomika sel'skogo khoziaistva* (1986), no. 3, pp. 59–64.

52. *Sovetskaia kul'tura,* March 20, 1986, p. 3.

53. On meat, see *Trud,* August 22, 1986, cited in *RL* 231/86, August 22, 1986, p. 6.

54. See Hauslohner, "Gorbachev's Social Contract," p. 66.

55. *Komsomol'skaia pravda,* June 2, 1987, p. 2; *FBIS,* June 15, 1987, pp. S1–S4.

56. *Pravda,* March 28, 1986, p. 1.

57. *Pravda*, May 28, 1986, pp. 1–2.

58. E.g., Aganbegian in *Trud*, December 12, 1982, p. 2.

59. *Izvestiia*, June 2, 1986, p. 3.

60. See Connor, "Social Policy Under Gorbachev," *Problems of Communism* (July-August 1986), 35(4):42–43.

61. *Pravda*, November 21, 1986, pp. 1, 3.

62. See *Ekonomicheskaia gazeta* (October 1986), no. 43, pp. 15–16.

63. See, e.g., the interesting account of a cooperative café in Moscow in *Izvestiia*, May 1, 1987, p. 3; abstracted in *CDSP*, June 3, 1987, pp. 9, 19.

64. *Izvestiia*, June 2, 1986, p. e.

65. *Ibid.*

66. Radio Moscow, July 6, 1986; *FBIS*, July 10, 1986, p. R-13.

67. *Trud*, August 3, 1986, p. 2.

68. *Izvestiia*, August 20–21, 1986, p. 3.

69. *Izvestiia*, May 16, 1987, p. 2.

70. *Pravda*, December 20, 1986, p. 3.

71. *Izvestiia*, April 30, 1987, p. 6.

72. Interview with Deputy Prokurator-General Naidenov, Moscow Radio, November 23, 1986; *FBIS*, November 26, 1986, pp. S1–S8.

73. Victor Zaslavsky, *The Neo-Stalinist State* (Armonk, N.Y.: M.E. Sharpe, 1982), p. 159.

74. James R. Millar and Elizabeth Clayton, "Quality of Life: Subjective Measures of Relative Satisfaction," *Soviet Interview Project (SIP) Working Paper No. 9*, Urbana-Champaign, Ill., February 1986, mimeo, p. 10.

75. Donna Bahry, "Politics, Generations, and Change in the USSR," *SIP Working Paper No. 20*, April 1986, pp. 34–36.

76. *La Repubblica*, October 5–6, 1986; p. 12; *FBIS*, October 7, 1986, pp. 3–5.

77. Paul R. Gregory, "Productivity, Slack, and Time Theft in the Soviet Economy: Evidence from the Soviet Interview Project," *SIP Working Paper No. 15*, February 1986, p. 23.

78. Miller and Clayton, "Quality of Life," Figures 12A–12D.

79. Here I share, by and large, the interpretation adopted by Hauslohner.

80. *Sotsialisticheskaia industriia*, November 23, 1986, p. 3.

81. *Pravda*, April 27, 1987, p. 3.

82. *Ekonomicheskaia gazeta* (October 1986), no. 42, pp. 1, 4.

83. *Izvestiia*, April 18, 1986, p. 2.

84. An informative review of the debate appears in Aaron Trehub, " 'Social Justice' and Economic Progress," *RL* 382/86, October 7, 1986.

85. *Izvestiia*, July 7, 1985, cited *ibid.*, p. 4.

86. *Literaturnaia gazeta*, February 19, 1986, cited in Trehub, " 'Social Justice,' " p. 8.

87. V. Z. Rogovin, "Sotsial'naia spravedlivost' i sotsialisticheskoe raspre-

delenie zhiznennykh blag," *Voprosy filosofii* (1986), no. 9, p. 12, cited in Trehub, " 'Social Justice,' " p. 4.

88. Rogovin, "Sotsial'naia," p. 19, in Trehub, " 'Social Justice,' " p. 9.

7. Social Change and Stability in Eastern Europe

1. In general, coercion in its most extreme forms—like mass terror of the Stalinist 1930s in the USSR—was less pronounced in Eastern Europe. The reasons for this involve situational, temporal, cultural, and accidental factors beyond the scope of our discussion here. It will not do to *minimize* the amount of violence visited on East European populations in the later Stalin years, but, given the factors discussed below, it would be a mistake to see coercion as the sole "cement" holding these societies together during the early years of socialism.

2. "Functionalism" here is meant in the sense in which the American sociologists Kingsley Davis and Wilbert E. Moore used it in their elaboration and explanation of the persistence of inequalities in rewards and esteem. In essence, "jobs" are seen as having differential importance for society in the contribution they make. Those jobs both critical in importance and demanding talent and lengthy training are well rewarded, in order to motivate the talented to compete for them and discharge the responsibilities of the job effectively. See Kingsley Davis and Wilbert E. Moore, "Some Principles of Stratification," *American Sociological Review* (April 1945), 10(2):242–249, and since reprinted in numerous readers and collections.

3. Of course, workers were assured of more steady employment in a socialist economy. Unemployment, which had threatened much, but not all, of the prerevolutionary working class, no longer presented a major problem. For some, this new benefit weighed heavily in the new regime's favor; for others, whose skills had kept them steadily employed in the late 1930s, it was necessarily less relevant.

4. In some of the more war-ravaged states, socialism's early and generally short-lived "reconstruction" phase resulted in some improvements in living standards above the low of 1944–45. But the pace of improvement did not continue, and there is evidence that the public perception of rapid gains quickly diminished as early as 1947–48—before anything approaching prewar standards could have been reached, and as construction of the "foundations of a socialist economy" was just beginning. See, e.g., the interesting Budapest data reported by Robert Blumstock in Walter D. Connor and Zvi Y. Gitelman, et al., *Public Opinion in European Socialist Systems* (New York: Praeger, 1977), ch. 5. For a review of some changes in the Czechoslovak living standard between 1937 and 1957 (by which time life in many aspects had improved since the early 1950s),

see Edward Taborsky, *Communism in Czechoslovakia, 1948–1960* (Princeton: Princeton University Press, 1961), pp. 425–443.

5. See, e.g., Seymour Martin Lipset, *Political Man: The Social Bases of Politics* (Garden City, N.Y.: Doubleday, 1963), pp. 267–269; also Lipset and Reinhard Bendix, *Social Mobility in Industrial Society* (Berkeley and Los Angeles: University of California Press, 1963), pp. 76–83.

6. Lipset and Bendix, *Social Mobility,* pp. 11–75, have documented strong gross similarities in total manual-to-nonmanual mobility in the United States and West European countries, while also noting some differences in particular aspects, such as the predominant social origin of *elite* members.

7. See the interesting and informative work by two major Hungarian economic historians, Ivan T. Berend and Gyorgy Ranki, *Economic Development in East-Central Europe in the Nineteenth and Twentieth Centuries* (New York: Columbia University Press, 1974), especially pp. 242–264 and 315–318.

8. An effective and evocative treatment of a young peasant's efforts to make his way in Budapest is provided in Laszlo Nemeth's novel *Guilt* (London: Peter Owen, 1966).

9. Interwar mobility data are indeed hard to come by, and for the most part, we are confined to making judgments on the basis of the slow rates of economic change that necessarily would have restricted such mobility. Yet some Hungarian data, collected at different times using different methods, do indicate lower rates in the interwar period than those derived from socialist period data. For these data and a detailed discussion, see Walter D. Connor, *Socialism, Politics, and Equality* (New York: Columbia University Press, 1979), ch. 4, tables 4.16 and 4.18.

10. Interesting Polish studies at the subnational level include: a study of the occupational destinations of peasant sons, Michal Pohoski, *Migracje ze wsi do miast* (Warsaw: Panstwowe Wydawnictwo Ekonomiczne, 1963), and, by the same author, "Interrelations Between Social Mobility of Individuals and Groups in the Process of Economic Growth in Poland," *Polish Sociological Bulletin* (1964), no. 2, pp. 17–33; an early (1959) urban study in Lodz, Josef Kadzielski, "Miedzypokoleniowa ruchliwosc spoleczna mieszkancow Lodzi," *Przeglad socjologiczny* (Warsaw) (1963), 17(2):114–128; and a 1961 study of urban males from all over Poland, Stefan Nowak, "Psychologiczne aspekty przemian struktury spolecznej i ruchliwosc spolecznej," *Studia socjologiczne* (Warsaw) (1966), no. 2, pp. 75–105. Finally, research during 1964–67 in Lodz, Szczecin, and Koszalin resulted in two reports on the mobility of male respondents: Antonina Pilinow-Ostrowska, "Ruchliwosc zawodowa i jej konsekwencje," in Wlodzimierz Wesolowski, ed., *Zroznicowanie spoleczne* (Social Differentiation) (Wroclaw, Warsaw, and Krakow: Wydawnictwo Polskiej Akademii Nauk, 1970), pp. 339–373; and Krystyna Janicka, "Ruchliwosc miedzypokoleniowa," in K. M. Slomczynski and W. Wesolowski, eds., *Struktura i ruchliwosc spoleczna* (Wroclaw, Warsaw, and Krakow: Wydawnictwo Polskiej Akademii Nauk, 1973), pp. 61–101.

Yugoslav researchers also have undertaken quite complex and sophisticated analyses of mobility, although they lean less toward nationally representative samples and more toward those which try to capture the complexity of differential economic development by focusing on the extremes—usually "Westernized" and modern Slovenia on the one hand, and the quintessentially "Balkan" Macedonia on the other. For example, see Stane Saksida et al., "Social Stratification and Mobility in Yugoslav Society," in *Some Yugoslav Papers Presented to the Eighth World Congress of Sociology, Toronto, 1974* (Ljubljana: 1974), pp. 213–274.

11. Table 7.1 reflects some adjustments in the original data, e.g., the elimination of "other" and "no answer" responses to both origin and destination questions. The data also suffer some other problems of specificity and comparability. For example, the effects of economic development would be clearer if we had age-cohort data—our sources, like most mobility studies, include a mix of respondents of many ages. Moreover, some national samples consist of males only, while others include men and women, thus complicating cross-national comparisons. Given the generality of the arguments advanced here, however, these data problems are not so serious as they might be were our focus different. For more detailed discussion of the data problems, see my *Socialism, Politics, and Equality*, ch. 4.

12. Adam Wazyk, "A Poem for Adults," *Kultura*, August 21, 1955, translated in Edmund Stillman, ed., *Bitter Harvest: The Intellectual Revolt Behind the Iron Curtain* (New York: Praeger, 1959), pp. 121–132.

13. The countries are Australia, Denmark, France, Great Britain, Italy, Japan, the Netherlands, Norway, Sweden, the United States, and West Germany. Figures are adapted from S. M. Miller, "Comparative Social Mobility," *Current Sociology* (1960), vol. 9, no. 1; Lawrence E. Hazelrigg, "Occupational Inheritance: A Cross-National Analysis," in J. Lopreato and L. L. Lewis, eds., *Readings in Social Stratification* (New York: Harper and Row, 1974), pp. 469–473; and several other sources. See my *Socialism, Politics, and Equality*, ch. 4.

14. The countries include Australia, France, Italy, Norway, Sweden, the United States, and West Germany. Data are derived and adapted as reported in note 13. Since the data for several of the East European countries are based on mixed-sex samples, these figures may understate the real difference between Eastern Europe and the West concerning farm-to-factory mobility. Women, in both East and West, have traditionally been less inclined than men to leave their rural origins. However, the mobility studies from which our Western figures have been derived are based—as usual—on all-male samples. Were all the East European data derived from male samples, the calculated average mobility rates for the East European socialist countries probably would be greater.

15. Historical data on mobility are sparse indeed. The magnitude of the changes we are talking about, however, may be at least partially illuminated by

Hungarian census data. Thus, in 1930 only 3.8 percent of the sons of workers and peasants had moved into nonmanual occupations, while in 1949 (just as the consequences of revolution began to be felt), 7.0 percent had done so. See note 9. But compare these figures with the 1973 figure for manual-to-nonmanual mobility as presented in table 7.1.

16. On the relevance to legitimacy of effectiveness, in the economic sphere and elsewhere, see Lipset's *Political Man*, p. 64, and his *The First New Nation: The United States in Historical and Comparative Perspective* (Garden City, N.Y.: Doubleday, 1967), p. 68.

17. Stanislaw Ossowski, "Social Mobility Brought About by Social Revolution," working paper (in English), Fourth Working Conference on Social Stratification and Social Mobility, International Sociological Association, Geneva, 1957, as quoted in Lipset and Bendix, *Social Mobility*, p. 282 (emphasis in original).

18. Stanislaw Ossowski, *Z zagadnien struktury spolecznej* (Warsaw: Panstwowe Wydawnictwo Naukowe, 1968), p. 282.

19. The statistical technique used in the construction of table 7.1 is discussed in W. Edward Deming, *Statistical Adjustment of Data* (New York: Wiley, 1943), pp. 96–127. Under "random" movement, we mean to subsume all mobility that is not induced by structural change. Of course, nonrandom factors—among them the implementation of implicit or explicit social policies—do affect social mobility. Even a "no-growth" socialist economy, through "politicized" educational and promotional practices, doubtless would have encouraged at the margins more of certain kinds of mobility than a stagnant economy and presocialist regime did. In the larger context of broad national change, however, it is clear that economic development, and the changes it effects in the occupational structure, are far and away the most important factors at work. In this sense, comparisons between tables 7.1 and 7.2 are by no means unfair to the socialist regimes.

20. The dimensions of change may be more clearly understood when we examine the mobility "inflow" figures—the percentage of nonmanuals recorded in the national surveys of table 7.1 who were *children* of manuals (workers or peasants). The percentages are: Bulgaria, 77.8; Czechoslovakia, 76.3; Hungary, 77.4; Poland, 76.8; Romania (estimate), 63.1; Yugoslavia, 70.0. Since many of these studies were conducted in the late 1960s or early 1970s, such a renewal of the East European intelligentsia would not have had such quantitative impact by the mid-to-late 1950s. But the process would have been under way, with the effects mentioned.

21. Zygmunt Bauman, "Social Dissent in the East European Political System," *European Journal of Sociology* (1971), 12(1):38.

22. Here, following the procedure in note 20, we give the percentages at the time of the study of workers who were of peasant origin: Bulgaria, 61.5; Czechoslovakia, 37.5 (a testimony to its *earlier* development of a large working class and its relatively small peasant "recruiting pool"); Hungary, 54.0; Poland, 43.6;

Romania, 65.4; and Yugoslavia, 57.3. The data thus show a heavy "peasanti-zation" of the industrial work force.

23. Economists, no doubt, will find this characterization of living standards oversimple, ignoring various types of transfer payments, welfare allocations, etc. But many social benefits, although available *in principle*, were difficult to dis-tribute in practice in the early socialist period because of poverty and commit-ment to heavy investment. Housing, a critical "welfare" item, remained low in cost, but was overcrowded and was in many cases deteriorating rapidly in these years—thus "compensating" people for the low rents paid. Free education was, indeed, a benefit—but one whose payoffs were prospective and, therefore, part of the mobility process and its ultimate gains.

24. While it is true that, in general, the socialist states now exhibit a some-what more "modern" profile in their occupational structures, this does not mean that they have reached a "takeoff" point for increased mobility across the man-ual-nonmanual line. The pronounced growth of the "service sector," so char-acteristic of the postwar economies of many Western nations and projective of future economies in which nonmanuals constitute an absolute majority of all those employed, has not been matched in the socialist countries. And it can be argued that the "logic" and predominant tendencies of the socialist economies make such an outcome unlikely, at least in the near-to-medium term. See Gur Ofer, *The Service Sector in Soviet Economic Growth: A Comparative Study* (Cambridge: Harvard University Press, 1973), *passim*.

25. Indeed, apropos of the argument here, research in two Polish cities in the mid-1960s depicted "hereditary" intelligentsia (those whose parents had been part of this stratum) as less satisfied with their income levels and general material situation than upwardly mobile, first-generation intelligentsia—even though the former enjoyed higher actual income than the latter. See Antonina Pilinow-Ostrowska, "Ruchliwosc," pp. 367–369.

26. See, e.g., comments by the economist Ota Sik and the sociologist Pavel Machonin, as cited in Walter D. Connor, "Socialism, Work, and Equality," in Irving Louis Horowitz, ed., *Equity, Income, and Policy: Comparative Studies in Three Worlds of Development* (New York: Praeger, 1977), pp. 167–168. As one observer has noted, these "white-collar specialists" would most likely gain from policies stressing greater reward differentiation. See Frank Parkin, *Class Inequality and Political Order* (New York: Praeger, 1971), p. 177.

27. Svetozar Stojanovic, *Between Ideals and Reality: A Critique of Socialism and Its Future* (New York: Oxford University Press, 1973), p. 220.

28. This is not to say that *most* are critical—or that most need be in order to cause some problems for the East European regimes. Passive disaffection, cynicism, a retreat into "private" life, and a concern with material gains at the expense of political principle probably characterize most East European youth today, although this is not necessarily limited to Eastern Europe. See Paul Neu-berg, *The Hero's Children: The Post-War Generation in Eastern Europe* (New York: Morrow, 1973).

29. Various studies indicate high educational and career aspirations of working-class youth and parental desires to see offspring advance as well. For relevant data, see Mihailo Popovic, "Social Conditions and the Possibilities of Education of the Young People in Yugoslavia," in a special English issue of *Sociologija*, 1970, p. 251; and *Social Stratification in Hungary* (Budapest: Central Statistical Office, 1967), p. 89.

30. Thus arises the well-known proportional "underrepresentation" of worker and peasant offspring in universities. Many working-class families lack specific attitudes and practices which are "useful" to their children. Unskilled workers, in their "way of thinking," are still, according to two Polish authors, reminiscent of "the prewar proletariat." See Dariusz Fikus and Jerzy Urban, *Spoleczenstwo w podrozy* (Lodz: Wydawnictwo Lodzkie, 1968), p. 29. For a Hungarian article rich in material on these working-class problems, see Julia Juhasz, "Secondary Education of Working Class Children," *New Hungarian Quarterly*, Autumn 1970, especially pp. 132–134.

31. See, e.g., Wieslaw Wisniewski, "The Academic Progress of Students of Different Social Origin," *Polish Sociological Bulletin* (Warsaw) (1970), no. 1, p. 136; and M. Boiarskaia, "Problema vybora professii sel'skoi molodezh'iu," in G. V. Osipov and J. Szczepanski, eds., *Sotsial'nye problemy truda i proizvodstva* (Moscow: "Mysl'," 1969).

32. Srdan Vrcan, "Some Comments on Social Inequality," *Praxis* (International Edition) (1973), no. 2–3, p. 237.

33. In Czechoslovakia, workers in state agriculture, whose total "take" is frequently less than that of cooperative farmers, earned 85.5 percent of the average industrial worker wage in 1965, and 98.1 percent in 1973. See *Statisticka-rocenka CSSR 1974* (Prague: State Statistical Administration, 1975), pp. 135, 253. In Hungary, state agricultural manual workers earned 88.1 percent of the worker's wage in 1965, equaled that level in 1970, and then "fell back" to 94.1 percent in 1973. *Hungarian Statistical Yearbook 1973* (Budapest: Central Statistical Office, 1974), pp. 151, 242–243.

34. As a well-placed Pole told me, the prelude to the attempted 1976 price increases was very different from Gomulka's debacle of 1970, when little if any prior exploration of public reaction was undertaken. In 1976, however, government-sponsored opinion polling (its product, for the most part, "for internal use only") indicated the likelihood of quite adverse public reactions. On the other hand, economists' calculations stressed, as they have for some time, the pressing need for price reform. Gierek and his colleagues found themselves in the position of many officials in both East and West: forced to make a choice, anxious to base it on accurate data and perceptions of the situation, but faced with strong empirical arguments for entirely different choices. While the readiness to gather and use more information in decision making may be another hallmark of "mature" or "developed" socialism, this does not mean that those decisions will be any easier to make or more certain to produce favorable outcomes.

8. Workers and Intellectuals: A Dissident Coalition?

1. Richard Lowenthal, *World Communism: The Disintegration of a Secular Faith* (New York: Oxford University Press, 1964), p. 109.

2. What follows summarizes some points made in my *Socialism, Politics, and Equality* (New York: Columbia University Press, 1979).

3. Andras Hegedus, "The Main Characteristics of the Social Structure of East European Societies, and the Alternatives of Democratic Development of Their Power Structure," paper presented to the 1978 Annual Meeting of the National Association for Soviet and East European Studies, Cambridge University, Cambridge, mimeo, p. 8.

4. Hegedus, *Socialism and Bureaucracy* (New York: St. Martin's Press, 1976), pp. 116–117.

5. Ernest Mandel, "The Social Forces Behind Détente," in Ken Coates, ed., *Détente and Socialist Democracy* (New York: Monad Press, 1976), pp. 45–46.

6. For some comments on the nature of workers' demands, see David Lane, *The Socialist Industrial State* (London: Allen and Unwin, 1976), pp. 97–101.

7. See Jaime Reynolds, "Communists, Socialists, and Workers: Poland, 1944–1948," *Soviet Studies*, October 1978, pp. 516–539.

8. Ivan Svitak, *The Czechoslovak Experiment 1968–1969* (New York: Columbia University Press, 1971), p. 52.

9. Vladimir V. Kusin, *Political Grouping in the Czechoslovak Reform Movement* (New York: Columbia University Press, 1972), p. 36. For more on the committees on press freedom, see pp. 34–37; and Svitak, *The Czechoslovak Experiment*, pp. 74–75, 96–97.

10. H. Gordon Skilling, *Czechoslovakia's Interrupted Revolution* (Princeton: Princeton University Press, 1976), p. 132.

11. Galia Golan, *The Czechoslovak Reform Movement: Communism in Crisis, 1962–1968* (Cambridge: Cambridge University Press, 1971), p. 29.

12. See Alex Pravda, "Some Aspects of the Czechoslovak Economic Reform and the Working Class in 1968," *Soviet Studies*, July 1973, pp. 104ff.

13. Skilling, *Czechoslovakia's Interrupted Revolution*, p. 580.

14. Alexander Matejko, *Social Change and Stratification in Eastern Europe* (New York: Praeger, 1974), p. 114.

15. See the study of the Ikarus factory work force summarized in Radio Free Europe, *Hungarian Situation Report* (hereafter *HSR*) (May 17, 1978), no. 2, pp. 7–10.

16. On this in the 1968 Czechoslovak context, see Pravda, "Some Aspects of the Czechoslovak Economic Reform," pp. 121ff.

17. Matejko, *Social Change*, p. 219.

18. For documents protesting the proposed constitutional changes, see *Dissent in Poland, 1976–77* (London: Association of Polish Students and Graduates in Exile, 1977), pp. 11–24.

19. *Ibid.*, p. 71.

20. *Ibid.*, pp. 72–75.

21. Adam Michnik, "The New Evolutionism," *Survey*, Summer-Autumn 1976, p. 274.

22. See *Dissent in Poland*, pp. 112ff., for the texts of workers' letters from Radom and Ursus.

23. Quoted in *La Repubblica*, November 16, 1976, and cited in Radio Free Europe, *Polish Situation Report* (hereafter *PSR*) (November 29, 1976), no. 40, p. 11.

24. See *PSR* (February 18, 1977), no. 5, p. 10.

25. *Dissent in Poland*, pp. 180–186; and *PSR* (June 15, 1977), no. 16, pp. 1–2.

26. On this and what follows, see *PSR* (October 13, 1977), no. 25, pp. 5–9.

27. See H. Hajek and L. Niznansky, "Czechoslovak Dissent: Sources and Aims," Radio Free Europe, *RAD Background Report* (hereafter *RAD* (June 29, 1978), no. 143, p. 7.

28. See Radio Free Europe, *Czechoslovak Situation Report* (October 24, 1979), no. 33, pp. 1–6.

29. See *ibid.* (August 23, 1978), no. 28, pp. 1–2.

30. See Radio Free Europe, *Romanian Situation Report* (hereafter *RSR*) (February 18, 1977), no. 6, pp. 12–15.

31. *Ibid.* (December 6, 1977), no. 35, pp. 7–10.

32. On the Jiu Valley events, see *RSR* (August 12, October 12, and October 26, 1977), nos. 26, 31, and 32.

33. There are reports that some Jiu Valley miners expressed knowledge and support of Goma's letter. See *Liberation*, November 25, 1977, as cited in *RSR* (December 6, 1977), no. 35, p. 8.

34. See *RSR* (October 26 and November 22, 1977), nos. 32 and 34.

35. I find overstated the conclusion of Radio Free Europe analyst Patrick Moore, that the strikers had been able to "organize and advance demands in the manner of workers in developed countries—and not like villagers recently transferred to industrial sites." See "Dissent in Romania: An Overview," *RAD* (June 5, 1978), no. 112, p. 2.

36. *RSR* (December 6, 1977), no. 35, p. 8, citing United Press International and Agence France Presse dispatches of November 24, 1977.

37. Patrick Moore, "Romania: A Crisis of Leadership," *RAD* (September 27, 1978), no. 212, p. 2.

38. See Peter Moravets, "Criticism and Dissent in Hungary," *RAD* (August 23, 1978), no. 185. On the protest to the October Czech trials, see *HSR* (November 19, 1979), no. 21, pp. 13–15.

39. An exception was a letter of support from thirty-four intellectuals to the Charter 77 group in Czechoslovakia, an event largely ignored by Hungarian authorities. See *HSR* (January 25, 1977), no. 3, pp. 2–4.

40. On this, see Moravets, "Criticism and Dissent in Hungary."

41. See *HSR* (February 14, 1978), no. 4, pp. 2–4.

42. *Dissent in Poland*, p. 13.

43. Hegedus, *Socialism and Bureaucracy*, pp. 89–92. Hegedus sees a persistent lack of worker interest in participation in economic management in Hungary, which he attributes to "the alienation which developed under capitalism" and the continuing division of labor necessitated by realities of technological development (p. 45).

44. Jiri Pelikan, "The Socialist Opposition in Eastern Europe and the Western European Left," in Coates, ed., *Détente and Socialist Democracy*, p. 109.

45. *Ibid.*, p. 112.

46. Translated as *RAD* (October 13, 1978), no. 236, p. 8.

47. See *AFL-CIO Free Trade Union News*, May 1979, pp. 1–5; and *RSR* (March 19, 1979), no. 4, pp. 18–22, and (May 4, 1979), no. 8, pp. 3–5.

48. See *PSR* (December 2, 1978), no. 28, pp. 14–15.

49. *Ibid.* (March 3, 1978), no. 6, pp. 8–9; (May 30, 1978), no. 12, p. 8.

50. *Ibid.* (October 30, 1979), no. 23, pp. 3–5.

51. *Ibid.* (August 6, 1978), no. 19, pp. 7–10.

52. *Ibid.* (September 25, 1978), no. 22, p. 12.

53. *Ibid.*

54. I am grateful to Professor George Kolankiewicz of the University of Essex for drawing my attention to this phenomenon. As he has observed, such peasant-workers are especially sensitive to the possibilities of double taxing for pensions—an example of the unexpected structural problems created for the regime by social change.

55. See "Review of Uncensored Polish Publications December 1977–April 1978," *RAD* (July 6, 1978), no. 152, pp. 13, 17.

56. For a recent review of the spectrum of Polish dissent, see Adam Bromke, "The Opposition in Poland," *Problems of Communism* (September-December 1978), 27(5):37–51.

57. KSS-KOR, "Notes on Poland's Economic System: An Inside View," translated in *RAD* (August 9, 1978), no. 177, p. 17.

58. Zygmunt Bauman, "Officialdom and Class: Bases of Inequality in Socialist Society," in Frank Parkin, ed., *The Social Analysis of Class Structure* (London: Tavistock, 1974), pp. 129–148.

59. Marc Rakovski, *Towards an East European Marxism* (New York: St. Martin's Press, 1978), p. 33.

60. George Konrad and Ivan Szelenyi, *The Intellectuals on the Road to Class Power* (New York: Harcourt Brace Jovanovich, 1979).

61. This distinction between two types of protest and their sources is sug-

8. Workers and Intellectuals: A Dissident Coalition?

gested by Alex Pravda in his "Industrial Workers: Patterns of Opposition, Dissent and Accommodation," in Rudolf L. Tökes, ed., *Opposition in Eastern Europe* (London: Macmillan, 1979), pp. 209–262.

62. See Jacques Rupnik, "Dissent in Poland, 1968–1978: The End of Revisionism and the Rebirth of Civil Society," in Tökes, *Opposition in Eastern Europe*, pp. 60–112; and Abraham Brumberg, "The Open Political Struggle in Poland," *New York Review of Books*, February 8, 1979, pp. 29–34.

63. Rakovski, *Towards an East European Marxism*, pp. 67–68.

9. Workers and Power

1. Jadwiga Staniszkis, "On Some Contradictions of Socialist Society: The Case of Poland," *Soviet Studies* (1979), 31(2):167–187.

2. George Konrad and Ivan Szelenyi, *The Intellectuals on the Road to Class Power* (New York: Harcourt Brace Jovanovich, 1979).

3. Staniszkis, "On Some Contradictions of Socialist Society," p. 168.

4. Marc Rakovski, *Towards an East European Marxism* (New York: St. Martin's Press, 1978), p. 47.

5. Bogdan Mieczkowski, "The Relationship Between Changes in Consumption and Politics in Poland," *Soviet Studies* (1978), 30(2):262–269.

6. Janusz G. Zielinski, *Economic Reforms in Polish Industry* (London: Oxford University Press, 1973), pp. 40, 43.

7. Miklos Haraszti, *A Worker in a Worker's State* (New York: Universe, 1978).

8. Zygmunt Bauman, "Officialdom and Class: Bases of Inequality in Socialist Society," in Frank Parkin, ed., *The Social Analysis of Class Structure* (London: Tavistock, 1974), pp. 129–148.

10. The Successor Generation

1. See F. Stephen Larrabee, "Education in Eastern Europe: Progress, Problems, and Prospects," *Radio Free Europe Research*, March 9, 1973.

2. See Walter D. Connor, *Socialism, Politics, and Equality* (New York: Columbia University Press, 1979), pp. 117–214; also Paul Neuburg, *The Hero's Children: The Post-War Generation in Eastern Europe* (New York: Morrow, 1973).

3. Marc Rakovski, *Towards an East European Marxism* (New York: St. Martin's Press, 1978), pp. 65–66.

4. George Konrad and Ivan Szelenyi, *The Intellectuals on the Road to Class Power* (New York: Harcourt Brace Jovanovich, 1979).

5. Stefan Nowak, "Values and Attitudes of the Polish People," *Scientific American* (July 1981), 245(1):45–53.

6. Neuburg, *The Hero's Children*, p. 292.

7. A number of West European public opinion research organizations have carried out the Radio Free Europe Audience and Opinion Research (hereafter RFEAOR) studies cited and used here. The considerable traffic of East Europeans into Western Europe has provided numerous Poles, Hungarians, Czechs, and Slovaks for interview purposes. Respondent anonymity is observed and Radio Free Europe is not identified as the sponsor of the survey, in an attempt to eliminate any response bias. Given that virtually all the respondents in the surveys used here are *visiting* the West and then returning home, the obvious problems of refugee/émigré surveys are to a large degree avoided. The numbers are large, the mix of travelers broad, with many blue-collar and farm workers included as well as professionals. To correct for whatever bias may arise, sample proportions (age, education, occupational category, etc.) are adjusted to the parent population's proportions by the appropriate weighting of the categories. All in all, these RFEAOR data are rich—and underutilized in much of the writing on contemporary Eastern Europe. This is especially unfortunate since in the infrequent circumstances where in-country empirical research has addressed similar questions, the RFEAOR data tend to find confirmation rather than rebuttal.

8. See RFEAOR, "The Polish Self-Image and the Polish Image of Americans, Russians, Chinese, Germans, and Czechs" (1969); RFEAOR, "The Czech and Slovak Self-Image and the Czech and Slovak Image of Americans, Germans, Russians, and Chinese" (1970); RFEAOR, "The Hungarian Self-Image and the Hungarian Image of Americans, Germans, Russians, and Chinese" (1970).

9. Graphic representations in the original RFEAOR documents indicate the small deviations by age category—in my judgment, deviations too small to warrant lengthy discussion here.

10. *Tribuna*, September 15, 1976, no. 38; *Tvorba*, January 15, 1975, no. 3.

11. *Magyar Hirlap*, September 21, 1976.

12. *Ifju Kommunista*, January 1974.

13. See George Schopflin, "Opposition and Para-Opposition: Critical Currents in Hungary, 1968–1978," in Rudolf L. Tökes, ed., *Opposition in Eastern Europe* (London: Macmillan, 1979), pp. 142–186.

14. Nowak, "Values and Attitudes."

15. RFEAOR, "Czechoslovak, Hungarian, and Polish Expectations About Domestic Political Trends in the 1970s" (1972).

16. A. Josefowicz, S. Nowak, and A. Pawelczynska, "Students: Their Views of Society and Aspirations," *Polish Perspectives* (1958), nos. 7–8, p. 33.

17. *Ifju Kommunista*, July 1979.

18. RFEAOR, "The 'Best Government' as Seen by East European Respondents" (1976).

19. RFEAOR, "The Political Self-Assessment of Czechoslovak, Hungarian, and Polish Respondents" (1979).

20. Stephen Spender, *The Year of the Young Rebels* (New York: Vintage Books, 1969), p. 65.

21. RFEAOR, "The Political Self-Assessment of Czechoslovak, Hungarian, and Polish Respondents," p. 8.

22. Bogdan Denitch, "Religion and Social Change in Yugoslavia," in B. R. Bociurkiw and J. W. Strong, eds., *Religion and Atheism in the USSR and Eastern Europe* (Toronto: University of Toronto Press, 1975), pp. 368–387.

23. T. Jaroszewski, "Dynamika praktik religijnych i postaw swiatopoglado-wych w Polsce w swietle badan socjologicznych," *Kultura i spoleczenstwo* (1966), no. 1, p. 135.

24. A. Pawelczynska, "Dynamika i funkcje postaw wobec religii," *Studia socjologiczne* (1961), no. 10, p. 91.

25. *Ibid.*, p. 72.

26. Jarozewski, "Dynamika praktik," p. 138.

27. RFEAOR, "East Europeans and Religion" (1971).

28. *Ibid.*

29. *Forras*, October 1979.

30. Adam Michnik, "The Church and the Left: A Dialogue," in F. Silnitsky, L. Silnitsky, and K. Reyman, eds., *Communism and Eastern Europe* (New York: Karz, 1979), pp. 51–95.

31. RFEAOR, "Polish Expectations, Hope, and Fears Concerning East-West Relations in the 1970s" (1971); and "Hungarian Views on East-West Relations in the 1970s" (1972).

11. From Utopia to Autonomy: Thought and Action in the East European Opposition

1. The language in which such controversies were conducted, an ideological one frequently alien to the thoughts and traditions of non-Marxists, was of course no help in revealing their essence to those outside the party.

2. Adam Michnik, "The Church and the Left: A Dialogue," in Frantisek Silnitsky, Larisa Silnitsky, and Karl Reyman, eds., *Communism and Eastern Europe* (New York: Karz, 1979), p. 52.

3. Adam Michnik, "The New Evolutionism," *Survey*, Summer-Autumn 1976, p. 268.

4. Jacek Kuron and Karol Modzelewski, "Open Letter," in *Revolutionary Marxist Students in Poland Speak Out (1964–1968)* (New York: Pathfinder Press, 1968), p. 77.

5. *Ibid.*

6. See Antoni Zambrowski, "Reply to the Control Commission of the Polish United Workers Party," in *Revolutionary Marxist Students*, pp. 92–93.

7. See Bill Lomax, "From Intellectual Theory to Samizdat Practice," *Labour Focus on Eastern Europe* (hereafter *LFEE*) (May-June 1979), 3(2):15.

8. Vaclav Havel, "On the Theme of Opposition," *Literarni Listy*, April 4, 1968, in Andrew Oxley, Alex Pravda, and Andrew Ritchie, eds., *Czechoslovakia: The Party and the People* (New York: St. Martin's Press, 1973), pp. 132–133, 135–136.

9. Petr Pithart, "Political Parties and Freedom of Speech," *Literarni Listy*, June 20, 1968, in Oxley, Pravda, and Ritchie, eds., *Czechoslovakia*, p. 142.

10. Petr Pithart, "What Matters Is the Right to Self-Management," *Literarni Listy*, August 1, 1968, in Oxley, Pravda, and Ritchie, eds., *Czechoslovakia*, p. 202.

11. Ludvik Vaculik, "Two Thousand Words to Workers, Farmers, Scientists, Artists, and Everyone," *Literarni Listy*, June 27, 1968, in Oxley, Pravda, and Ritchie, eds., *Czechoslovakia*, p. 263; see also, in same source, Antonin Liehm, "Seriously Now, Let's Be Specific," *Literarni Listy*, June 13, 1968, p. 254.

12. Alexander Dubcek, "Speech to the Central Committee of the Communist Party," *Rude Pravo*, June 4, 1968, in Oxley, Pravda, and Ritchie, eds., *Czechoslovakia*, pp. 146–148.

13. See H. Gordon Skilling, *Charter 77 and Human Rights in Czechoslovakia* (London: Allen and Unwin, 1981).

14. Vladimir V. Kusin, *From Dubcek to Charter 77* (Edinburgh: Q Press, 1978); and by the same author, "Challenge to Normalcy: Political Opposition in Czechoslovakia, 1968–1977," in Rudolf L. Tökes, ed., *Opposition in Eastern Europe* (London: Macmillan, 1979), pp. 26–59.

15. Kusin, *From Dubcek to Charter 77*, p. 157.

16. Kusin, "Challenge to Normalcy," p. 41.

17. *Ibid.*, p. 46.

18. "Exiled Leader on Charter 77," *LFEE* (July-August 1977), 1(3):11.

19. *Ibid.*

20. "Letter from Hejdanek to a Friend," *LFEE* (July-August 1978), 2(3):15.

21. "Independent Socialists Outline Their Views," *LFEE* (November-December 1978), 2(5):6.

22. The documentation of Polish dissent is extraordinarily rich. Some major sources are *Dissent in Poland, 1976–77* (London: Association of Polish Students and Graduates in Exile, 1977); Peter Raina, ed., *Political Opposition in Poland, 1954–1977* (London: Poets and Painters Press, 1978); Peter Raina, ed., *Independent Social Movements in Poland* (London: London School of Economics and Political Science/Orbis Books, 1981). Recent monographic material is too numerous to cite.

23. Andrzej Szczypiorski, "The Limits of Political Realism," *Survey*, Autumn 1979, p. 24.

24. *Ibid.,* p. 27.

25. Social Self-Defense Committee "KOR," "An Appeal to the Nation," *Survey,* Autumn 1979, p. 76.

26. Maciej Poleski, "Freedom in the Camp," *Survey,* Winter 1980, p. 143.

27. Adam Michnik, "The Church and the Left," pp. 52–53.

28. *Ibid.,* p. 76.

29. Kuron and Modzelewski, "Open Letter," p. 86.

30. *Ibid.,* p. 87.

31. Jacek Kuron, "Reflections on a Program of Action," *Polish Review* (1977), 22(3):52.

32. *Ibid.,* p. 62.

33. *Ibid.,* p. 53.

34. *Ibid.,* p. 58.

35. *Ibid.*

36. *Ibid.,* p. 54.

37. See Raina, ed., *Independent Social Movements,* p. 322.

38. On Hungary's peculiarities, see George Schopflin, "Opposition and Para-Opposition: Critical Currents in Hungary, 1968–1978," in Tökes, ed., *Opposition in Eastern Europe,* pp. 142–186; and by the same author, "Hungary: An Uneasy Stability," in Archie Brown and Jack Gray, eds., *Political Culture and Political Change in Communist States* (London: Macmillan, 1977), pp. 131–158.

39. Miklos Haraszti, "In the Wake of the Invasion of Czechoslovakia, the Myth of Kadarism," *LFEE* (September-October 1978), 2(4):15.

40. George Konrad and Ivan Szelenyi, *The Intellectuals on the Road to Class Power* (New York: Harcourt Brace Jovanovich, 1979); see also Ivan Szelenyi, "Socialist Opposition in Eastern Europe: Dilemmas and Prospects," in Tökes, ed., *Opposition in Eastern Europe,* pp. 187–208.

41. Marc Rakovski, *Towards an East European Marxism* (New York: St. Martin's Press, 1978).

42. Gyorgy Bence and Janos Kis, "After the Break," in Silnitsky, Silnitsky, and Reyman, eds., *Communism and Eastern Europe,* pp. 133–140.

43. *Ibid.,* pp. 138–139.

44. Wlodzimierz Brus, review of Rakovski, *Towards an East European Marxism, LFEE* (March-April 1979), 3(1):21.

45. Rakovski, *Towards an East European Marxism,* pp. 52–53.

46. See Konrad and Szelenyi, *The Intellectuals.*

47. Rakovski, *Towards an East European Marxism,* pp. 67–68, 71.

48. Miklos Haraszti, "What Is Marxism?" in Silnitsky, Silnitsky, and Reyman, eds., *Communism and Eastern Europe,* p. 148.

49. *Ibid.*

50. A. Hegedus, in "The New Mechanism: A Balance-Sheet," *LFEE* (February-March 1980), 3(6):19.

51. Ivan Svitak, "What Words Can Do," *Literarni Listy,* July 18, 1968, in Oxley, Pravda, and Ritchie, eds., *Czechoslovakia,* p. 279.

52. Alain Finkielkraut, "Milan Kundera Interview," in Ladislav Matejka and Benjamin Stolz, eds., *Cross Currents: A Yearbook of Central European Culture, 1982* (Ann Arbor: University of Michigan, 1982), p. 16.

53. *Ibid.*, p. 17.

54. Pithart, "Political Parties," p. 143.

55. See Czeslaw Milosz, *The Captive Mind* (New York: Vintage Books, 1953); also *Native Realm* (New York: Doubleday, 1981).

56. Szczypiorski, "The Limits of Political Realism," p. 30.

57. PPN, "Poland and Europe," *Survey*, Winter 1980, pp. 186–187.

58. *Ibid.*, p. 187.

59. Adam Michnik, "Ticks and Angels," *Survey*, Winter 1980, p. 182.

60. On the significance of regarding *these* peoples as Poland's neighbors, and not Russia as such, see "On National and Religious Affiliations," *Survey*, Winter 1980, pp. 202–203.

61. Michnik, "Ticks and Angels," p. 183.

62. Kalman Garzo, "An Unofficial Hungarian View of Romania" (from *Beszelo*, May 1982), *LFEE* (Winter 1982–83), 5(5–6):34.

63. *Ibid.*

64. *Ibid.*

65. Who is a "dissident"? Who a "reformer"? In the area of the socialist economy, these categories are not hermetically sealed, and there is a fair degree of border crossing. One might say that the path from advocacy of economic reform leads to dissent when all conviction that in-system reforms *can* be introduced by the political leadership ceases, and the conclusion emerges that the political structure represents a systemic block to reform.

66. Stefan Kisielewski, " 'Planning' Under Socialism," *Survey*, Winter 1980, p. 20.

67. *Ibid.*, p. 28.

68. In Lidia Ciolkosz, "The Uncensored Press," *Survey*, Autumn 1979, p. 66.

69. PPN, "The Opponents of the System," *Survey*, Autumn 1979, p. 81.

70. "Charter Document No. 7 on Social and Economic Rights," *LFEE* (May–June 1977), 1(2):11.

71. *Ibid.*

72. PPN, "Poland and Europe," p. 193.

73. "Experience and the Future," *Poland Today: The State of the Republic* (Armonk, N.Y.: M.E. Sharpe, 1981), p. 144. The original is available as "Doswiadszenie i Przyszlosc," *Raport o stanie rzeczpospolitej i o drogach do jej naprawy—wersjy wstepna, Jak z tegu wyjsc?* (Paris: Instytut Literacki, 1980).

74. Although on a limited basis, such as in the case of the voluntary society to aid the poor (SZETA), they have taken a major role in self-organized activity.

75. Konrad and Szelenyi, *The Intellectuals*, pp. 220–233, cover in detailed

argument the linkage, or lack thereof, between worker and intellectual interests, in both political and economic senses.

76. Rakovski, *Towards an East European Marxism*, pp. 52–53.

77. Karl Reyman, "The Special Case of East Germany," in Silnitsky, Silnitsky, and Reyman, eds., *Communism and Eastern Europe*, p. 161.

78. *Ibid.*

79. See Werner Volkmer, "East Germany: Dissenting Views During the Last Decade," in Tökes, ed., *Opposition in Eastern Europe*, pp. 113–141; also Silnitsky, Silnitsky, and Reyman, eds., *Communism and Eastern Europe*, pp. 159–242, for a range of material on dissent in the GDR.

80. See Wolfgang Harich, *Kommunismus ohne Wachstum* (Reinbek, W. Germ.: Rowohlt Verlag, 1975); also Reyman, "The Special Case of East Germany," pp. 165–167; and *LFEE* (July-August 1979), 3(3):15.

81. Reyman, "The Special Case of East Germany," pp. 166–167.

82. Volkmer, "East Germany," p. 128.

83. *LFEE,* July-August 1979, p. 15.

84. This is not to deny that other dissidents in the GDR are not concerned about the environment and ecological problems. See Peter Winsierski and Wolfgang Buscher, *Beton ist Beton: Zivilisationskritik aus der DDR* (Hattingen, W. Germ.: Scandia-Verlag, 1981), and the discussion in Ronald D. Asmus, " 'Alternative' Thinking in the GDR," *Radio Free Europe* RAD/BR/146, July 12, 1982.

85. Rudolph Bahro, *The Alternative in Eastern Europe* (New York: NLB/Schocken, 1979).

86. Quoted from a radio interview by Reyman, "The Special Case of East Germany," p. 163.

87. Robert Havemann, "The Socialism of Tomorrow," in Silnitsky, Silnitsky, and Reyman, eds., *Communism and Eastern Europe*, pp. 174–175; originally in Havemann, *Berliner Schriften* (Berlin: Verlag Europaische Ideen, 1977).

88. *Ibid.*, p. 181.

89. *Ibid.*.

90. See "Havemann Appeal on Eve of Thirtieth Anniversary of GDR," *LFEE* (September-October 1979), 3(4):13.

91. *Ibid.*, p. 14.

92. *Ibid.*

93. Havemann, "The Socialism of Tomorrow," p. 181.

94. See the collection edited by Ulf Wolter, *Rudolf Bahro: Critical Responses* (White Plains, N.Y.: M.E. Sharpe, 1980).

95. Interview with Bahro, *LFEE* (November-December 1977), 1(5):5.

96. For some further comment on Bahro's ideas, see Walter D. Connor, "Varieties of East European Dissent" (review essay), *Studies in Comparative Communism* (Winter 1982), 15(4):396–412.

97. "Rudolf Bahro's Views on Eastern Europe," *LFEE* (November 1979–January 1980), 3(5):14.

98. *Ibid.*, p. 13.
99. "An Interview with Rudolf Bahro," *LFEE* (September-October 1978), 2(4):17.
100. "Bahro's Views on Eastern Europe," p. 14.
101. *Ibid.*
102. *Ibid.*, p. 13.
103. *Ibid.*
104. "High SED Official on Bahro" (originally in *Der Spiegel*, September 19, 1977), *LFEE* (January-February 1978), 1(6):11.
105. Jiri Pelikan, "Bahro's Ideas on Changes in Eastern Europe," in Wolter, ed., *Rudolf Bahro*, p. 179.
106. "Bahro's Views on Eastern Europe," p. 13.
107. Rudolf Bahro, "Introductory Lecture to *The Alternative*," in Silnitsky, Silnitsky, and Reyman, eds., *Communism and Eastern Europe*, p. 231.
108. Not, certainly, me. From the rise of KOR in Poland in 1976, however, it did seem that however unlikely worker-intellectual "linkage" expressed in political action might be, *if* it came, it would be in Poland. This required no particular perspicacity, and it was this position I took in chapter 8, written in late 1979 and published in early 1980. Later, after the birth and apparent legalization of *Solidarnosc*, two Washington colleagues volunteered retrospective evaluations: one praised me for being "prophetic," the other chided me for having underestimated the potential of Polish workers. I scarcely merit the first; I can plead, in mitigation of the second, that I had plenty of company.
109. Two most informative accounts, differing in perspective, are Timothy Garton Ash, *The Polish Revolution: Solidarity* (New York: Vintage Books, 1985), and Jadwiga Staniszkis, *Poland's Self-Limiting Revolution* (Princeton: Princeton University Press, 1984).
110. An "insider" account of top-level Polish decision making leading up to martial law, including Soviet pressures and Jaruzelski's response, was provided in 1987 by the defector Col. Ryszard Kuklinski; see the interview with him, "Woina z narodem widziana od srodka," in the Paris journal *Kultura* (April 1987), no. 4, pp. 3–57.